THE NEXT AGENDA

THE NEXT
AGENDA

BLUEPRINT FOR A NEW PROGRESSIVE MOVEMENT

edited by

ROBERT L. BOROSAGE

ROGER HICKEY

Westview
PRESS

A Member of the Perseus Books Group

Copyright © 2001 by Westview Press, A Member of the Perseus Books Group

Published in 2001 in the United States of America by Westview Press, 5500 Central Avenue, Boulder, Colorado 80301-2877, and in the United Kingdom by Westview Press, 12 Hid's Copse Road, Cumnor Hill, Oxford OX2 9JJ

Find us on the World Wide Web at www.westviewpress.com

Library of Congress Cataloging-in-Publication Data
The next agenda : Blueprint for a new progressive movement / edited by Robert L. Borosage and Roger Hickey.
   p.   cm.
  Includes bibliographical references and index.
  ISBN 0-8133-9814-2
  1. United States—Social policy—1993– . 2. United States—Economic policy—1993– . 3. United States—Politics and government—1993– .
I. Borosage, Robert L. II. Hickey, Roger.

HN65 .N48 2000
361.6'1'0973—dc21

00-043986

The paper used in this publication meets the requirements of the American National Standard for Permanence of Paper for Printed Library Materials Z39.48–1984.

10   9   8   7   6   5   4   3   2   1

To our parents

Contents

SHAPING THE FUTURE

EMPOWERING PEOPLE IN POLITICS

Illustrations

Tables

Figures

Preface

The Next Agenda is the expression of an ongoing public dialogue among activists and policy experts working to challenge the current limits of American politics.

That dialogue is central to the activities of the Campaign for America's Future—and the Institute for America's Future—founded a few years ago by more than 100 prominent Americans who felt the public debate about our country's future had moved too far to the right.

A book like this has many parents. *The Next Agenda* ultimately is the product of twenty remarkable contributors who combine scholarly expertise with a commitment to social change and economic justice. They gave this project their time and ideas because they share the belief that we have a new opportunity for dramatic reform in our country. We thank them for their contributions and for their dedication to ideas and analysis that can help build a better country in a more just global community. We will continue to work with them to ensure that these ideas move to the center of our national debate.

The Next Agenda is also the product of the people who have helped to build America's Future as an organization. We thank the foundations, labor unions, and individuals who have supported its efforts and helped it grow. We pay special tribute to the extraordinary young activists who helped us build an organization from an idea, including Elizabeth Kramer, Felicia Lugo, Erik Cole, Thomas Matzzie, and Kimberly Ostrowski.

Deadlines always arrive sooner than expected. Dealing with twenty busy and creative authors and two harried editors is no walk on the beach. This book could not have been completed without Jessica Myers, who helped us organize and edit it. We thank her for her dedication and skill. We also thank Carrie Ferrence, who copyedited manuscripts and corrected countless endnotes and sources. They worked under great pressure to turn the authors' drafts into a manuscript meeting a publisher's expectations.

We also thank our editor at Westview, Leo Wiegman, who understood the political moment and the potential of this book of essays immediately. His support and encouragement were unstinting, and his intelligence and good humor made even contractual dealings easy.

Robert L. Borosage and Roger Hickey

THE NEXT AGENDA

INTRODUCTION:
THE PROGRESSIVE MAJORITY

Robert L. Borosage and Stanley B. Greenberg

The new century offers a new opportunity to progressives: A political movement that champions the concerns of American families as they struggle to make their way in a time of unsettling change can spark a new era of progressive reform. Americans are looking for leaders who will stand up for them and help their families and the nation deal with the challenges they face. They seek ways to make the country stronger, to enable it more effectively to control the disruptions that pressure their families, threaten their communities, and separate the rich from the rest. They are looking for ways to reform a political system that they see as broken, awash in special-interest money, and stalemated by partisan bickering.

Their views are neither unfounded nor transitory. They reflect the realities of working families in the new global economy—even in a time of prosperity. The dynamics created by globalization and technological change, the growing divide between rich and poor, and accelerating environmental threats ensure that the pressures on working families are likely to increase, not decrease. Similarly, their social concerns—about a culture of sensation, the fragility of families, and the safety of their children—are also likely to grow, not lessen. Most Americans, we would argue, are open to a bolder politics than they are currently being offered.

And the country is now in a better position to meet that demand than ever. The end of the Cold War lifted the blinders that limited possibilities during that long conflict. The long period of economic growth—and the soaring incomes of the affluent—have served to erase the federal budget deficits that for so long crippled social imagination. The growing domestic impact of the global economy makes social guarantees more difficult but also more necessary.

Yet for too long our political debate has failed to respond. Partisan jockeying and political impasse in Washington feed growing public disengagement. Both parties are stained by a tawdry politics that reeks of corruption. In the lead-up to the 2000 election, the political debaters seemed content to refight old battles instead of boldly addressing new opportunities and new challenges.

This political timidity is, in part, the legacy of the conservative era that dominated American politics over the past quarter century. Years of large fiscal deficits, attacks on government, and political stalemate have sapped social imagination. When "surpluses as far as the eye can see" began appearing, no agenda for collective action was waiting. Even progressive groups concerned about education, housing, child care, and health care had limited their vision and hemmed in their hopes.

This book is designed to fill the vacuum—to offer ideas and strategies for progressive reform, grounded in the concerns that working Americans express and the challenges that the country faces. The chapters present guideposts for reforms that are commensurate with these challenges. They are focused on measures that will help empower citizens in their workplaces and in their communities. Conservatives in both parties have long been unwilling to propose meaningful social reforms. The reform agenda for aiding working families and strengthening the country has become a progressive project.

The question, of course, is whether politics can be shaped to make these measures possible. One of the reasons that there has been so little bold thinking is that there has been so little hope. To many, a progressive political revival seems an implausible daydream at best. Yet we would argue that the realities faced by working families—and their reactions to them—provide the basis for building a progressive majority for change.

FAMILIES UNDER PRESSURE

America has recently enjoyed the longest period of economic growth in modern history. Unemployment has fallen; inflation has been calmed. The dot.com revolution has begun to transform how we work, shop, and communicate. The global economy offers new vistas and the promise of new markets. Even the pressures of global warming and environmental limits open the way to new jobs, new technologies, and new markets in the transition to sustainable growth. As this is written, the celebration of America's new economy is reaching new heights.

Yet the world of most of America's working, middle-class families is a far remove from the affluent lifestyle that dominates in advertising and in television dramas. Most working people—particularly the three-fourths of all Americans who lack college degrees—find themselves working longer, with less security. With the expanded opportunities of the new global economy comes greater instability. Workers and managers have less long-term job security. Companies respond to competitive pressures by cutting back on health care, pensions, and other benefits. Small businesses find it harder to sustain stable business relationships, and must continually compete with foreign companies that pay cheaper wages and are hampered by fewer regulations. The service economy, which is the source of most new jobs, features small, fragile businesses that operate close to the margin. Communities are disrupted by plant closings. The same middle-class families that benefit from the new economy as consumers can find themselves suffering from it as workers and small business owners.

Sustained high employment resulted in wage increases over the past couple of years. Increases in the minimum wage, expansion of the Earned Income Tax Credit (EITC), and a revival of union activism also have helped lift low-wage workers. Yet wages have not made up the ground lost in the previous quarter century. With the new economy comes a growing divide between rich and working-class American families. In these good years, families can keep up with the bills, yet their worries continue about whether they can afford to send their children to college, can withstand a serious illness, or can support their parents' or their own retirement.

Few can raise a family on one income; yet when both parents work, strains increase. Children get less attention. Marriages grow more brittle. Nearly half of all American children will live in a divided family at some point in their lives. And they grow up in a culture of increasing salaciousness, which markets sex and violence in increasingly intrusive ways. Single mothers—often limited to low-paying jobs that don't provide health care—face truly heroic challenges in balancing work and caring for children. Decent child care is hard to find and harder to afford. Not surprisingly, working parents are deeply concerned about the safety of their children's schools and neighborhoods. They want schools to work, to offer a safe, nurturing environment for their kids, with high standards that help to transmit decent values and prepare them for the future.

As families grow more fragile, the burdens on them seem to increase. To give children a better chance at success, parents try to support them through college. Aging parents live longer, a blessing but often also a burden, particularly as their health care costs soar. And hard-pressed couples must find ways to pay for more of their own health insurance costs and retirement savings, as employers push more and more of these costs onto their employees.

Struggling to make their way in a time of accelerating change and increasing instability, working American families are looking for help. They want leaders who understand the pressures that they face, and who reflect the values that they respect. They are deeply suspicious that money allows special interests to trump the common good. They are open to sensible ideas to provide greater security to their families, improve opportunities for their children, and reward individual responsibility. They want to ensure that the new economy does not erode wages, job security, food safety, or environmental standards. They worry about the willingness of large corporations to move jobs abroad, even as they respect the sacrifice and hard work of small businesses. They want more investment and greater reform in schools so that their children will be prepared to succeed in a rapidly changing, high-tech, competitive world. They want large private institutions—HMOs, insurance companies, tobacco companies, and pharmaceuticals—to be held accountable.

And after years of public scandal, declining moral standards in the media, and terrifying shootings at schools and in neighborhoods, Americans are worried about whether the next generation will be raised with decent values. They wonder about their own ability to transmit basic values to their own children, who are enticed by an increasingly scabrous teen culture. They are looking for leaders who will help restore and reinforce these proper lessons. They do not expect politicians to be preachers, and are wary about those who wear their religion on their sleeves. But their concerns about individual responsibility and basic morality are likely to find increasing political expression.

People are skeptical not of the purposes of government but of its performance. They are increasingly impatient for action, not more rhetoric. They are seeking ways to strengthen the nation—stronger schools, safe retirement, and affordable health care—and are willing to think beyond short-term, individual gratification. Repeatedly in recent years, when asked about their preference between tax cuts and investing the surplus in bolstering Social Security or in education, most Americans have said they prefer investing in ways that make the community stronger rather than pocketing the money in a tax cut. Yet at the same time, widespread pessimism mocks this choice, for many question whether government will spend the money wisely and whether they would ever see much of a tax cut. Their desire for government action is tempered by their doubt that government can act effectively.

SEEKING CHANGE

The elections of the past decade reflect the voters' search for leaders who will take up their case. In 1992, voters turned to the relatively unknown governor of Arkansas who was stained by scandal. They were attracted by his promise to "put people first" and invest in health care, education, transportation, and technology. Bill Clinton reassured voters that he shared their values and concerns about crime and punishment, welfare and individual responsibility, but his main focus was on "the economy, stupid." A remarkable number of voters also abandoned the Republican incumbent to vote instead for the iconoclastic businessman Ross Perot, whose emphasis on deficits and on political corruption attracted disaffected working- and middle-class voters.

In Clinton's first two years, their hopes were disappointed. Clinton's promise of "health care that can never be taken away" ended in an unwieldy proposal that was blocked by a concerted attack from the insurance industry and the political right, and by continued divisions among Democrats. The president's first major legislative victory was on a budget plan dedicated to deficit reduction. The president apologized for the progressive tax increases in the plan, aimed at the wealthiest Americans, which Republicans burlesqued as the biggest tax hike in history. Clinton's second major victory was the passage of NAFTA, a trade accord largely negotiated by his predecessor, opposed by many in his own party.

In 1994, many voters who previously had supported Democrats stayed home, and others turned to Republicans, who at least promised to give them some of their money back from a government that wasn't working for them. Led by Newt Gingrich, Republicans claimed to be the party of political reform and traditional values, the party of term limits and law and order. Republicans took over several state legislatures and gained control of the House of Representatives for the first time in forty years.

The militant new House speaker, Newt Gingrich, proclaimed an end to the New Deal, the Great Society, and the "liberal Democratic welfare state," calling for a new "opportunity society." On the defensive, President Clinton agreed to a plan to balance the budget, projecting deep reductions in domestic spending. Democrats drew the line, however, on the Republican plan to combine tax cuts largely for the wealthy with reductions in Medicare, Medicaid, education, and the environment. Republicans discovered that the voters were not prepared to shut down the federal government, when they turned against the Republican "revolution" in large numbers.

In 1996, voters rebuked conservatives. President Clinton was reelected, campaigning largely as the defender of Medicare, Medicaid, education, and the environment (the phrase became a mantra, dubbed M2E2 by Clinton's aides). Clinton essentially ran against the Gingrich threat, and offered only very slight, mostly symbolic proposals—school uniforms, support for curfews, and more police on the street. The defensive strategy worked, but offered no mandate for his second term. Fewer citizens turned up at the polls in 1996 than in any election since 1924, and the president did not succeed in capturing a majority of the votes cast, despite a continued economic recovery. The defensive cast of Democratic politics did not change. The president's budget figures continued to project deep cuts in domestic spending, even cuts in Medicare despite the mandate of the 1996 election. Then politics became mired in scandal, with the White House and Democrats again knocked on their heels.

Yet, in 1998, Democrats surprised most observers by gaining seats, narrowing the Republican margin, as voters clearly demonstrated that they wanted Washington to focus on their concerns—with education and health care at the fore—rather than on the politics of personal destruction. The election results of the past decade suggest that the supporters of each party are relatively equally divided, with a large swing vote grounded in the working and middle classes.

AMERICA'S UNSETTLED MAJORITY AND THE CLINTON PRESIDENCY

Over the course of the decade, the electoral landscape has changed, marked by the shifting perspectives of what has been called America's Forgotten Majority—working, middle-class voters—those without college degrees, with average incomes between $30,000 and $50,000 a year. These were the core Reagan Democrats, the working-class families that Reagan brought into his conservative majority coalition.

Reagan, of course, benefited from the stagflation of the late 1970s, from "America Held Hostage" in Iran, and from the sense that things were spinning out of control. Reagan's appeal was grounded on basic values—patriotism, law and order, and morality—contrasted to a Democratic Party that seemed out of touch. Under Carter, Mondale, and Dukakis, Democrats failed to offer a progressive-populist economic agenda that might speak to the reality of working people, even as they defended various liberal social causes, from affirmative action to choice to the environment. These made it possible to burlesque them as "limousine liberals" who were more concerned about welfare moms than workers, about the rights of criminals than about those of victims, and about minorities than majorities.

But by 1996, President Clinton was able to contest for the votes of married women and married mothers, even if white, nonunion men remained largely alienated. Clinton's defense of Social Security, Medicare, and education programs spoke to women's basic concerns. His more symbolic efforts—e.g., unpaid family leave—opened up a conversation about the pressures on working families. The Reagan coalition was unraveling.

Clinton's presidency might be viewed as a transition from the conservative era of the previous quarter century to a possible new era of reform. As a candidate, Clinton skillfully articulated progressive themes. He called for broad economic growth and better access to health care. He championed the need to reform schools and invest in education, to preserve Social Security and Medicare, and to alleviate the pressures on working parents. In office, despite his personal scandals, he helped rebuild the public's faith in the possibility of government action. The increase in taxes on the wealthy, passed in his first budget, came as higher incomes were soaring. These tax increases contributed to the surpluses that now present government with a new opportunity. His focus on "making work pay"—expanding the EITC, increasing the minimum wage, and reaping the wage gains of high employment—combined with welfare repeal to speak to the values of working Americans. His emphasis on crime—particularly the much-advertised 100,000 additional police—helped neuter Republican "law and order" wedge politics. His targeted tax cuts for college tuition offered some help to parents just as the proportion of high school graduates going to college was rising. With the economy strong, deficits erased, crime rates going down, and out-of-wedlock births declining under his watch, Clinton helped resuscitate the legitimacy and effectiveness of government, even as scandal subverted his personal reputation.

Yet while Clinton opened up the conversation, he failed to forge a new majority for change. His caution—reinforced by repeated scandal and a hostile Republican congressional majority—kept him from grasping the opportunity offered by the new realities.

CONSERVATIVE DEFEAT

During the Clinton years, conservative Republicans lost the argument, even as the administration co-opted some of their ideas. The conservative revolution was unable to answer the real-world challenges that most Americans face. Conservatives' embrace of rugged individualism and unfettered markets sent a message to working Americans that in a world of increasing instability and rapid change, "you are on your own." The Gingrich Congress launched a broad attack on the welfare state—calling for dismantling the Department of Education, rolling back environmental regulation, and slashing taxes by cutting spending on Medicare, school lunches, education loans, home heating subsidies, and other programs for the poor. Its intent was symbolized by the shutdown of the government in the budget fight of 1995.

But Republicans discovered that although Americans might hate the idea of big government, they don't hate what big government does. The vast majority support public programs that provide security and opportunity for working and poor families. By the end of 1996, the Gingrich revolutionaries were in full retreat, scrambling to raise the minimum wage, increase spending on education, and pass modest health care reforms before the election. By 1998, Republicans were bragging about spending more on education than the president had proposed.

The Republican coalition grew more fractured. Republicans found themselves paying an ever higher price for being the party of white sanctuary, increasingly perceived as southern-dominated, intolerant, anti-choice, anti-immigrant, and anti-gay. They sacrificed their edge on law-and-order issues by denouncing federal officials as "jackbooted thugs" and parading their association with the gun lobby. Their attack on regulations and the environment, in service to industries and corporations that contributed large sums to their party, generated increasing concern. Once in office, Republican leaders abandoned their pledges about political reform, term limits, and expanding democracy. With each passing year, the pork barrel politics of inside deals and special favors grew more visible. They paid a heavy price among young voters particularly. The young—more tolerant, more open, more interested in investing in education and the environment, and more concerned about America's future—found conservatives increasingly unappealing.

As the debate about the global economy grew, the free market certitudes of conservative economics were increasingly questioned. On the right, social conservatives such as Pat Buchanan railed against trade deficits, mass immigration, and a global commercial culture that undermined conservative values. On the left, progressive movements demanded that the rules of the global economy protect worker rights and the environment as well as property. Voters in both parties agreed.

Adrift ideologically, Republicans united behind Reagan's centerpiece—large, across-the-board tax cuts. Yet even with growing budget surpluses, the tax cuts did not excite the electorate. The benefits went primarily to the affluent. Republicans could make no coherent case that the tax cuts would benefit the economy or make the nation stronger. Most working Americans turned out to be more interested in using the surpluses to invest in the future, to bolster Social Security and Medicare, than they were in getting pizza money back in a tax cut.

Under Reagan and Gingrich, conservative Republicans presented themselves as the party of change, the party that stood for a strong America, for the working majority; the party that would get burdensome government off the backs of people and kick-start the economy. Now they seem a party of big business and special interests, of intolerance and dated vision. They have little to offer to help working families and to make America stronger.

CENTRIST DEFAULT

The conservative reversals did not usher in a new period of reform, however. The Clinton administration seemed unwilling or unable to summon up the energy to make that push. The administration still suffered a bitter hangover from the defeat of its health care plan that soured it on large-scale reform. With Republicans controlling Congress, Clinton turned to a patient, generally successful rear-guard action. He co-opted conservative themes—a balanced budget, tax relief, and law and order— and tried to turn them to more progressive purposes—targeted spending, targeted tax cuts for middle-income Americans, and gun control. Clin- ton sustained much of his program in negotiations with Republicans, but was forced to limit the scope of his vision and agenda.

This was most clearly revealed in the administration's discomfort with one of the blessings of economic growth—the cascading projections of rising budget surpluses. Fearful that surpluses would open the way for Republican tax cuts, the administration called for "saving Social Security first"—a tactical ploy suggesting that some of the surplus owing to Social Security should be used to pay down the national debt. This step, it ar- gued, would make it easier to fund the shortfalls that might accompany the future retirement of the baby boomer generation. (Whether such shortfalls actually arise depends on the health of the economy in the next several decades.) Republicans immediately embraced this conces- sion to conservatives, calling for a "lock box" on Social Security sur- pluses. The Republicans did still call for tax cuts, but to a smaller and smaller audience.

As continued prosperity generated greater potential surpluses, the administration called for eliminating the national debt, first by 2013 and later by 2010. It later proposed to lock away the Medicare sur- pluses and create a "reserve fund." These proposals successfully bol- stered the argument that the Republican agenda of tax cuts was unaf- fordable and risky. But at the same time, the administration was sacrificing the opportunity to make a case for bold initiatives and sub- stantial social investments to meet real challenges. It offered no major initiative for the millions of Americans who could not afford health in- surance; and even with signs of voter support for significant invest- ments in education, it offered only small measures there. Investments vital to the revival of metropolitan politics (see Chapter 7) went un- mentioned. Despite the increasing numbers of poor mothers working and more children without health care, poverty also remained unad- dressed in policy discussions.

In the Congress, a bipartisan, centrist coalition began to form around remarkably conservative measures. New Democrats of the Democratic Leadership Council and a "different kind of Republicans," such as George W. Bush, embraced core reforms that featured privatizing enti- tlements—carving private accounts out of Social Security and turning Medicare into a voucher program (see Chapters 3 and 4). The bubbly stock market of recent years gave privatization an allure, but the privatization agenda is more attractive to elites, Wall Street, and insurance companies than to working families. By definition, the reforms increase individual risk and decrease collective security at a time when Americans are looking for more investment in the country and more shared security.

Most Americans see Social Security and Medicare as building blocks upon which they can depend. They want the programs strengthened, not weakened. Privatizing them would only increase social inequities; make people less secure; require more, not less regulation; and waste more on administration and management. Privatization can be justified, as Stanley Greenberg and Theda Skocpol have argued elsewhere, only on the basis of a reflexive commitment to market solutions.

The new center joins in celebrating the new economy. It embraces the global marketplace, without insisting on rules that will ensure that its blessings are shared and that national regulations on the environment, food safety, and workplace conditions are not eroded. It touts the new prosperity, and focuses its attention on upscale suburbs and on the college-educated, who have reaped most of the benefits. But this leaves it with little more than symbols to offer the majority of working American families, who struggle with dislocations, stagnant wages, and rising insecurities.

THE SURPRISE ELECTION

The presidential election of 2000 was expected to be a listless replay of this centrist consensus. The media reported on the new "battle for the center" between Gore's "pragmatic idealism" and Bush's "compassionate conservatism." When the election ended with the popular vote split—as well as the Senate, the House, and the statehouses—pundits naturally described a nation divided. But beneath the divisions were trends that showed the progressive promise.

The contrasting strategies were clear. "Compassionate conservatism" would distinguish George W. Bush from the discredited Gingrich revolutionaries. He presented himself as a "reformer," offering largely symbolic initiatives on school reform, faith-based poverty programs, environmental preservation, and low-cost housing. He also made a point of reaching out to minority communities to show that he was not as intolerant as the conservatives in his party. Bush hoped that by blurring the differences with Clinton and Gore on these issues, he might turn the election to questions of character and benefit from the scandals of the past.

Trailing badly in the polls, Al Gore lifted his campaign with his convention speech in Los Angeles. He detailed an agenda for America's "working families" and pledged to fight for them, taking on the "powerful interests" that stood in the way. Bush responded by detailing a program for "middle class families," seeking again to blur the distinctions.

Bush packaged his reforms in "small government" wrapping. His agenda of privatizing Social Security, vouchers for Medicare, and the Republican staple—deep, across-the-board tax cuts—was presented as "trusting the people."

Gore embraced an active government that would fight for working families. He stood against the Bush tax cuts as skewed to the rich, while squandering the opportunity to invest in health care and education. He touted a prescription drug benefit as part of Medicare rather than private insurance. He pushed sporadically for a "revolution" in education, promising investments in universal preschool, smaller classes, more teachers, and help for college tuition. He ended campaigning against the privatization of Social Security.

Republican campaigns—from Bush down to the congressional races—reflected the changing tide of opinion in the country. Republican ads could have been cut by a Democratic agency, pledging to save Social Security, invest in education, and provide prescription drug benefits. Republicans donned Democratic garb to appeal to the public's fancy.

Exit polls and a poll by Greenberg Quinlan for the Institute for America's Future revealed that the voters weren't all that divided on issues. Solid majorities favored progressive policy positions. They preferred investment over tax cuts, prescription drugs through Medicare rather than HMOs, spending on schools over vouchers. Gore won the votes of those who thought issues were most important by 55% to 40%, according to exit polls.

Voters also strongly preferred Gore's core message over Bush's. The Gore pledge to lead an active government working to produce prosperity for all was supported by a large majority over the Bush agenda of shrinking government through privatization and tax cuts in the name of trusting the people.

The electorate was divided not on the issues, but on the candidates. Bush succeeded in blurring distinctions on issues, particularly education, the key concern of noncollege-educated, white voters. And he won an overwhelming margin of those voters who voted on "character" rather than on "issues." Gore suffered from the bitter aftertaste of the Clinton scandals and lost ground in the debates that he never made up.

Gore's populist message is what enabled him to win a majority of the popular vote. Democrats generally would have benefited from greater contrast with Republicans on issues, not less.

THE PROGRESSIVE OPPORTUNITY

Conservative defeat, centrist default, and a public looking for help; a new economic opportunity to address unmet social challenges; and accelerating economic and social transformations that make bold reform ever more imperative: In these developments, the turn of the century has witnessed a new opening for a progressive renewal in American politics.

For this renewal to have effect, progressives must learn to speak to the reality of most American families. They should not be distracted by the allure of upscale suburbs nor misled by the demands of money politics. They need to speak to the real worries people have, identify the sources of those worries, and offer bold, democratic answers. The progressive message should begin with the remarkable opportunities and the forbidding challenges posed by the transformation of the U.S. economy, the fabled shifts from the national to the global, from industrial to information age, from assembly lines to virtual companies, and from disposable to sustainable. This new economy offers the possibility—if its blessings are shared, its excesses curbed, and its progress shepherded—of a stronger America, in which everyone benefits. But if nothing is done, if families are left to fend for themselves, this same transformation will continue to generate greater inequality, increasing instability, heavier burdens on families, and more social discord.

America's families must not be left to make their own way in a time of tumultuous change. Economic growth can be channeled. Corporations can be held accountable to basic values—worker rights, environmental quality, and workplace safety. Workers and communities can be empowered to bargain fairly with powerful private corporations and industries.

The new global economy is already a reality. Now it is vital to ensure that it works for working people. In an era of accelerating change and transformation, American families need greater social support. On the job, Americans need greater employment security, better wages, and secure benefits. In communities, help must be provided for Americans struggling to raise children, to care for elderly parents, and to participate in the local community. Social Security and Medicare—the foundation stones of a decent retirement—must be strengthened and extended, not cut back and weakened. Progressives must revive the demand for health care that cannot be taken away, mapping the way to affordable, universal, comprehensive health care. The United States devotes more of its GDP to health care than any other country and yet leaves more than 40 million people with no health insurance, and far more with insurance inadequate to the care that they need. Reform is imperative.

Progressives must also call for dramatic new investment in, and extension and reform of, the education system. Public education should be provided from preschool through college. The demands of the echo generation (the children of baby boomers), combined with the aging of schools and the impending retirement of a generation of teachers, require a national commitment to rebuilding schools, raising the salaries and respect paid to teachers, and ensuring that America's public education system ranks among the best in the world. At the same time, progressives should be arguing for investments in prenatal care, Head Start, and affordable housing to ensure that everyone has an equal opportunity from the start. Even the best schools can't work if children are not ready to learn.

On the job, working parents need greater help. Progressives should be pushing to turn growth onto the high road, raising the minimum wage, making it easier for workers to gain a voice at work, extending paid family leave, and providing small businesses with aid in offering better pensions. A new conversation on the hours of the workweek and on flexible time is vital for hard-pressed parents.

Progressives should take seriously the commitment to make work pay. Reducing welfare rolls is not the same as reducing poverty. Low-paid workers—particularly single mothers—need real support. All working families should be able to get the training and education they need, guaranteed health care, and affordable, high-quality child care. Every working American should be able to lift his or her family from poverty. Progressives need to revive the call for the inclusive social vision that inspired the movement for civil rights. We need to make the case for ensuring opportunity for all working Americans, and providing social supports for families of every racial and ethnic group, challenging those who would use race to divide and weaken support for social investment.

Similarly, progressives must commit themselves to helping families weather the disruptions caused by economic change, new technologies, globalization, and environmental transitions. The threat posed by global warming can be a source of growth as the economy makes the transition to sustainable energy, housing, and industry.

Progressives also should put forth an aggressive new investment agenda for America's metropolitan areas. This is both morally right and economically sensible. Our economic prospects will depend in large part on rebuilding the prosperity and vibrancy of our cities and their suburbs. Investment in cities—in schools, housing, transportation, and clearing out brownfields—as part of a metropolitan political strategy that links suburbs and cities in common cause will be vital to consolidating the progressive project.

And progressives should be leading the fight against entrenched corporate lobbies when they stand in the way of the common good—against a drug industry making excessive profits from publicly funded research; against an insurance industry employing new techniques of genetic discrimination to insure only the healthy; and against employers using technology to erode the privacy of employees.

But the progressive agenda cannot be simply an itemized list of programs. One of the products of the stalemate of the 1990s is a growing concern over the values and direction of American society and culture. This concern has elicited a political pandering that leaves states spending more on prisons than on schools.

Progressives need to speak clearly about social values that Americans embrace—hard work, individual responsibility, equal opportunity, and mutual aid. They should put forward aggressive programs to ensure that our streets and schools are safe, that crime is punished, and that violence is curbed. An aggressive, affirmative stance in these areas will enable progressives to talk about what works—not the warehousing of nonviolent offenders but their treatment and community service; not racial profiling but responsive community policing. Progressives should be unabashed in criticizing a culture that peddles sex and violence, that substitutes sensation for reason and scandal for analysis.

None of this is possible without dramatic political reform. Progressives should champion the need to revitalize our democracy. This requires bold steps to limit the influence of money and entrenched private interests on politics. Clean money campaign finance reform (see Chapter 12) is the first step. Progressives should be championing an aggressive politics of disclosure, exposing inside deals to public scrutiny.

And at the same time, progressives must take the lead in reviving a politics of participation—working to empower workers, engage people in communities, and build a people-based politics from the bottom up that can use mobilization to counter big money. For the Democratic Party, the challenge and the opportunity are clear: It will either reinvent popular politics, or find itself unable to speak to the fundamental issues of the day.

The conservative call for unfettered markets and individuals on their own has been found wanting. The centrist default, with its emphasis on increasing individual risk and decreasing shared security, offers no answer. A bold progressive alternative—grounded in clear analysis, shared values, and a vision of a society that grows together—can provide the basis for a new era of American reform and vitality.

Americans, we would argue, are ready. They are looking for a party that shares their values and understands their challenges. They want leaders who can speak sensibly to the struggle of daily life. They are ready to support a bold agenda for action, significant new initiatives that deal with real needs. A progressive story that speaks to them can forge a mandate and a new majority that will change America's future.

This book is divided into four major sections. The first outlines the progressive argument on the political economy. Jeff Faux reviews the current assumptions, reveals their limits, and shows why progressive initiatives are now essential if the current prosperity is to be extended and shared. William Greider and Robert Borosage review the growing struggle over the global economy, and suggest the next stage in the reform agenda. Both chapters underline the inability of the conservative consensus to address the crucial challenges facing the country and its working families.

The second section focuses on the renewing and extension of America's social contract, the guarantees that we make one to another. Theda Skocpol argues for the advantages of universal programs like Social Security over targeted programs, and challenges the assumption that incremental steps are all that can be done. Jonathan Oberlander and Theodore Marmor lay out a course toward universal health care, central to any progressive reform agenda. Heidi Hartmann describes long-overdue reforms that respond to the reality that women in America work to support their families. Richard Rothstein challenges the limits of the debates on education, suggesting that although we must work to make schools better, perhaps we might have a greater impact on learning if we ensure that children have adequate food, housing, and health care.

Joel Rogers and Bruce Katz detail a metropolitan strategy for high-wage and high-road growth. They make a strong argument that cities, so long neglected in our political debate, should be the center of a progressive project of reform and revitalization. William Spriggs and Lynn Curtis argue that the new prosperity makes it morally impossible to continue to ignore those who are left behind and provides an opportunity to lift up the growing concentrations of urban poor.

The third section, on shaping the future, addresses one of the looming new challenges that the country faces in the coming decade: the transition to environmentally sustainable growth. Carl Pope and Bob Wages engage in a dialogue about a transition agenda that could generate a labor-environmentalist coalition embracing dramatic change. At a time when progressives need to be bold, willing to think "outside the box," Peter Barnes and Rafe Pomerance outline a visionary plan, one that could ensure that working families benefit directly from the transition to sustainable growth.

The final section, on empowerment, discusses central challenges to political renewal. David Moberg makes the case for empowering workers, arguing that this goal will require a broad, new civil rights campaign linking the rights of workers to a broader movement for economic justice. Ellen Miller and Micah Sifry detail a program for clean money campaign reform and discuss the lessons learned from initial victories at the state level. Lastly, Roger Hickey explores the potential of a new political movement rooted in local and national citizen organizing—a movement that is already gaining strength, unified by a larger vision of the opportunity for progressive change.

These chapters do not provide a comprehensive program; but they do offer an idea of the kinds of efforts that will be vital to reclaim America for all Americans. Progressives must recover the confidence to make a strong case for collective action, to take back the government and turn it, once again, into an instrument for the common good. If the agenda is sufficiently compelling, a new majority will coalesce around it.

Part 1

CHOOSING GROWTH
WITH JUSTICE

1

WHAT KIND OF AMERICA DO WE WANT?

Jeff Faux

Debate about the future has often been central to American politics. For a half century before Ronald Reagan's election to the presidency, the mainstream consensus held that democratic government was an instrument for planning ahead. This was the assumption made by presidents Franklin Delano Roosevelt, Harry S. Truman, John F. Kennedy, and Lyndon B. Johnson, as well as by the post–World War II Republicans who offered themselves as more conservative managers of the same task. President Dwight Eisenhower's housing, highway, and education programs expanded the proactive public sector envisioned and embodied in the New Deal; and President Richard Nixon's welfare programs extended, if grudgingly, the Great Society's vision of aid to the poor.

The American experience was part of the twentieth-century expansion of social democracy, which emerged from the industrial conflict at the century's beginning and from later battles with fascism and communism as the most appealing political framework within which to shape the future. When the people of eastern Europe cast off the yoke of the Soviet Union, few expressed a desire for raw, dog-eat-dog capitalism. Most wanted the mixed economy of private markets and public responsibilities they saw in the prosperous countries of western Europe.

But the ascendancy of Reagan in America, following on the heels of Margaret Thatcher's rise in Great Britain, had recently challenged the center-left's claim on the future. Reagan offered a "City on the Hill" run by merchants, with a threadbare civilian government and an over-equipped army: The goal was to expand the market economy into the market society.

Ten years later, the collapse of communism was quickly interpreted by the right as a victory for laissez-faire and was used to discredit the very system of social democracy that in effect had saved capitalism. The idea that the populace might cooperatively plan its own future was buried in the scrap heap of history. When the Democrats returned to power, they remained in Reagan's ideological shadow. Bill Clinton pronounced, in elegy, "The era of big government is over."

A protracted economic expansion driven by a strong private sector during Clinton's two terms reinforced the notion that government has little to do with economic success. The skyrocketing stock market, the sprouting of high-tech billionaires, and the profusion of jobs were said to reflect the "new" economy of the Information Age, powered by swashbuckling entrepreneurs who ask of government only that it get out of the way. The evolution of a global marketplace, hastened by new communications and transportation technologies, seemed to place multinational corporations—particularly those in the business of finance—beyond the reach of national governments. The message from the champions of the new economy was clear: Your government can no longer protect you from the risks of the market; you are on your own.

But, continued the message, not to worry: The Clinton boom represents our crossing over to a new economic paradigm that is so full of opportunity that with a little pluck, and perhaps a little luck, individuals can build a prosperous future entirely on their own.

The jury is still out on the question of how new this "new" economy really is. There is little doubt that computerized networks are making dramatic changes in the way we produce and consume. But as Joseph Schumpeter, one of the twentieth century's great economic thinkers, reminded us, capitalism is a dynamic process of creative destruction, continuously in a state of transition. Every business cycle since the mid-nineteenth century has been driven in part by new technologies that opened up opportunities for profitable exploitation—railroads, electricity, telephones, automobiles, jet engines, and television. The present set of cutting-edge technologies is the latest segment in the longer continuum of ever evolving, "new" economies.

However technologically "new" the currently evolving economy turns out to be, it will not render obsolete questions of social justice and ecological sustainability, which can be addressed only collectively. Markets are humankind's most powerful engines of economic growth. But engines need regulating mechanisms—gears, brakes, steering wheels—to make them useful. Similarly, markets need public institutions—central banks, labor protections, tax systems—to curb their tendencies toward excessive inequality and instability. As market engines change, the regulatory mechanisms must also change. History has shown that when these mechanisms do not work well, neither does the market.

Today, because globalization and the acceleration of technological change have made life less stable and secure—for individuals, for enterprises, and for society—there is an even greater need for government responsibility in economic management.

Individuals need a strong public sector because the economy is rapidly breaking up the assumed relationship between employee and employer. It has become a cliché that workers must adjust to being churned through many companies, none of which will provide a secure working life. For Americans with confidence, connections, and degrees from prestigious colleges, this is an exciting prospect. But for most, the new economy means being in constant anxiety about their economic condition, as companies under pressure from brutally competitive markets abandon responsibility for health care, pensions, and job security. The shifting of risk from employers to employees eventually will create political demands for new sources of social insurance and safety nets in the public sector.

Enterprises need a strong public sector because economic growth is cyclical. In a mass consumption economy, when private spending slows, government spending must rise to maintain enough purchasing power to keep recessions from becoming depressions. Moreover, even in the recent boom times, the Federal Reserve and the U.S. Treasury have frequently intervened in financial markets in order to save specific investors whose portfolios were so large that their failure might endanger the rest of the market. Few things are as certain in economics as the forecast that at the next crisis in the economic cycle the federal government, no matter which party is in charge, will intervene in order to brake a downturn.

Our society needs a strong public sector also because a greater degree of public responsibility will be necessary to sustain and manage the very improvements in technology that the new economy is generating. The latest inventions have the power to transform human life in ways that approach science fiction—computers so tiny that they can travel through the bloodstream, seeking and destroying the causes of disease, and biotechnologies that can manipulate the human genome. The potential for extending life expectancy, raising living standards, and resolving the conflict between economic growth and environmental sustainability is enormous. So are the attendant risks. Unregulated and developed outside accountable social guidance, the technologies of our dreams could become living nightmares. To bring technology into the service of humankind, science must be exploited within the framework of a democratic dialogue about the future.

In our two-party system, the role of the Democratic Party has been to champion the use of government to guide and manage the market economy. But today that party remains caught in the trap Reagan set for it when he made the federal fiscal deficit the single most important economic issue on the nation's agenda. Murray Weidenbaum, who chaired Reagan's Council of Economic Advisers, later recalled the president's views of possible increases in the deficit resulting from his initial tax cut: "One, they won't occur; two, they'll be temporary; three, when they stick, they serve a good purpose—they keep the liberals from new spending programs."

Reagan was right. Clinton, after an initial attempt at a modest expansion of public investment, made paying Reagan-era debts his number one economic priority.

There was, to be sure, a tactical reason for the Democrats' embrace of fiscal conservatism: a perceived need to shed their image as "tax-and-spend" politicians. In fact, the deficit Clinton inherited was not the result of taxing and spending but of *borrowing* and spending; Reagan was the most reckless borrower in presidential history. Still, the Republicans, helped by conservative New Democrats, had cleverly managed to blame the deficit on the traditional liberals. As a result, ridding the party of this label might well have been necessary in order to get back to the agenda of proactive government. Certainly that is what prominent progressive Democrats were assuring their constituencies in the mid-1990s: Once the deficit was under control, they would support spending again. But when the budget was balanced, the same Democrats argued that running a surplus to strengthen Social Security was the only way to block the Republican Congress from irresponsible tax cuts. And indeed, Clinton's debt reduction trumped Republican tax cuts in the budget battles of 1999 and 2000.

But as journalist Robert Kuttner observed, what started out as a tactic was soon transformed into a principle. In January 2000, budget officials were forecasting a ten-year on-budget surplus of more than $2 trillion, or more than $4 trillion including the Social Security surplus. Yet the Democrats had joined the Republicans in assuring the average American that the national debt (not just deficit spending) was the devil's work and that reducing it to zero was the only way to save Social Security. When the *Wall Street Journal* asked Vice President Al Gore how he, as president, would respond to a recession, Gore said that he would reduce government spending, "just as a corporation has to cut expenses when revenues fall off." Calvin Coolidge couldn't have said it better.

The Democrats' embrace of conservative principles may backfire, causing a deep split among their working-class constituency. When the next recession strikes, raising the debt through deficit spending will be essential to maintain purchasing power. But it will be difficult to get political support for needed deficits if those with jobs believe that spending on the unemployed will come at the expense of the employed's future Social Security checks.

By conceding to Republicans the *language* of politics, which is the foundation of the competing stories about how the world should work, the Democrats are in danger of digging themselves deeper into Reagan's trap. Already they have acquiesced to redefining the government's role from that of management of the economy to the management of the federal budget. The problem of poverty in America has been redefined as a problem of reducing the welfare rolls. The problem of inadequate health care has been redefined as a problem of Medicare solvency, and that of inadequate pension coverage as one of Social Security solvency.

As a result, there was a steady drop throughout the 1980s and 1990s in the resources devoted to domestic public sector services (other than Social Security and Medicare) and investments. This set off a declining spiral in which decreasing levels of support led to increasing deterioration in public services. Meanwhile, the upward redistribution of income and wealth allowed the rich to shift to private suppliers of services, and diminished their interest in improving government. The ensuing lower quality of service has become living proof to all of the inefficiency of the public sector. The result is rising support for privatization and voucher-type programs, despite the lack of evidence that they perform better than, or in many cases even as well as, programs managed by the public sector. As the populace's quality of life has declined, so has the Democratic Party's base among both clients and providers of public services shrunk.

The resultant trend has been a growing disconnection between citizens and government, reflected in such phenomena as low voter turnout and lack of outrage at the accelerated corruption of democracy by the rising cost of campaign financing.

It is not at all clear that the Democratic Party can unyoke itself from the Republican project of making the market the ultimate determinant of society's purpose. Despite the fact that rising surpluses have liberated them from the Reagan budget snare, the party leadership—increasingly mortgaged to business interests—acts as if it were still caged. Like a longtime prisoner suddenly released from jail, Democrats seem reluctant to walk out to freedom.

In this discussion of the future of the U.S. political economy, therefore, *Democratic Party* is a placeholder both for the political organization and for an independent political movement that might emerge to champion the need for policies to make the economy—however new it is—work for everyone.

In any event, whoever is to seize this opportunity will have to understand the economic lessons of the previous decade, to address the economic problems that remain unsolved, and to rebuild politics around the setting of national goals.

WHAT THE ECONOMY IN THE 1990S TAUGHT US

The Clinton presidency was accompanied by the longest economic expansion in modern history. It is ironic that the economy became the basis for the electoral success of a "New" Democrat president. At the time, that wing of the party believed that the "Old" Democrats had overemphasized bread-and-butter economic issues and populist themes and ignored the importance of social morality and national security. But in the elections of 1992 and 1996, the winning theme was "the economy, stupid." Had the unemployment rate been 5.4 percent in 1992 rather than 7.5 percent, President George Bush would have been reelected; and if it had been 7.5 percent in 1996, instead of 5.4 percent, President Clinton would not have been. In a similar vein, in late summer 2000, Gore's remarkable resurgence against George W. Bush was clearly associated with his shift to populist rhetoric and promises of expanded government programs.

But the recent, record-breaking economic expansion has as many claimants as a winning lottery ticket: Conservative Republicans assert that the Clinton boom was created by Reagan's tax cuts ten years earlier.

Since Reagan's tax cuts then turned into tax increases, and since the same Republicans predicted that Clinton's first budget was sure to throw the economy into recession, they cannot be taken seriously. At any rate, inasmuch as the Democrats under Jimmy Carter were blamed for the oil price inflation of the late 1970s, it is a matter of simple political justice that the Democrats under Bill Clinton should enjoy accolades for the economic performance of the past decade.

In the early 1990s, the conventional wisdom among center-right economists, from moderate liberals like Paul Krugman and Alan Blinder to conservatives like Martin Feldstein and Alan Greenspan, was that the unemployment rate could not fall below roughly 6 percent without triggering an accelerating rate of inflation. At that point, according to theory, the capacity of the economy to expand output would be constrained by the inadequate productivity of the unskilled who remained unemployed. Instead of generating greater supply, increased spending would result in wages hikes, which would be passed along to consumers in price increases, generating a self-reinforcing wage-price spiral that could be brought down only by a recession—that is, by raising interest rates high enough to reduce spending and bring prices down.

The few economists who pointed out that there was little empirical evidence to support this theory and that the economy could achieve noninflationary unemployment rates of 4 percent or even lower were derided by the profession, dismissed by the media, and ignored by policymakers.

Yet, in September 1994, the unemployment rate fell below 6 percent; in June 1997, below 5 percent; and in April 1998, below 4.5 percent. By April 2000, the unemployment rate was 3.9 percent; at the same time, the "core" inflation rate (excluding energy and food, the prices of which are not primarily driven by domestic economic growth) had risen a modest 2.2 percent for the year. The rate of capacity utilization was 82 percent—considerably below the peak reached during the previous recession. Growth in productivity was still outpacing the rise in employment costs. The U.S. economic performance looked even better when compared with the mediocre effort of western Europe and the dismal failure of Japan in the 1990s. Indeed, viewed globally, the question is not so much why the U.S. economy grew at a healthy rate as why the other two major advanced economies did not. In Japan's case, it was a prolonged hangover from the bursting of the huge speculative bubble in the financial and housing markets in the early 1990s. Europe's sluggish growth was largely a function of the tight monetary policies that accompanied

West Germany's absorption of East Germany and Europe's preparations to introduce a common currency.

What *was* different about the U.S. expansion was its acceleration after the first five years. The initial recovery was not particularly remarkable. After falling in 1991, GDP rose at an average rate of just over 3 percent through 1996. Unlike most recent recoveries, however, it then picked up steam, averaging an annual growth of more than 4 percent through 1999.

This "second wind" is attributable to four factors: (1) the absence of inflationary shocks from outside the economy; (2) the willingness of the Federal Reserve to continue to accommodate growth with relatively low interest rates; (3) the stock market bubble and the boom in consumer spending; and (4) the feedback effect of growth on innovation and technological change.

The Absence of Shocks

The most important factor in the long 1990s recovery was what did *not* happen—an upsurge in inflation that would have induced the Federal Reserve Board to raise interest rates in order to halt the expansion.

In effect, the expansion of the 1990s exposed the unrealistically low expectations that both conventional economics and politics had of the economy. The double-digit inflation of the 1970s, which destroyed the presidencies of Republican Gerald Ford and Democrat Jimmy Carter, so haunted Washington policy elites that it obscured the actual causes of price inflation in the American economy in the twentieth century—war and/or global energy prices. The most recent serious episode of inflation had been generated by a short spike in energy prices in 1990, just before the Gulf War was launched. Similarly, rising energy prices stemming from the formation of OPEC, the international oil cartel, sparked inflation three times in the 1970s. The next most recent bout of politically troublesome inflation, that in the late 1960s, was not caused by overheated domestic demand but by President Johnson's refusal to raise taxes to pay for the Vietnam War. The inflationary spell prior to that one was ignited by the Korean War; the one before that, by the lifting of price controls after World War II; and the one before that, by the impact of World War I.

In the entire twentieth century, at no time did the U.S. economy experience significant inflation because domestic demand outran production capacity. Therefore, in the absence of war or an energy crisis, the economy of the 1990s could have been expected to achieve low levels of unemployment.

The Greenspan-Clinton Pact

The absence of inflationary pressure in the 1990s would not have been enough to keep the recovery going, had the Federal Reserve Board aborted it with high interest rates. One reason the Fed did not was because Bill Clinton and Alan Greenspan made an implicit deal. There was no public acknowledgment, apparently no written document, and perhaps not even a handshake or wink. Nevertheless, there can be little doubt that in return for Clinton's commitment to reducing the deficit and ultimately generating a surplus, Alan Greenspan kept interest rates low for most of the decade.

This was more an ideological compromise than an economic strategy. Greenspan is a longtime opponent of domestic spending. The tight monetary policy that led to the recession of 1990–1991 and to the defeat of George Bush enhanced Greenspan's reputation on Wall Street and his credibility as someone who was not afraid to take down a president. From the beginning of the Clinton presidency, the White House was aware that if Greenspan had been willing to engineer the defeat of a fellow Republican, he was unlikely to flinch from ruining a Democrat.

In any event, both men got what they wanted: Clinton, a growing economy; Greenspan, a smaller government.

The Stock Market Bubble and Consumer Debt

The Greenspan-Clinton pact in turn was a major support for the stock market boom of the late 1990s. The expectation that Greenspan would keep rates low created confidence among stock buyers, and rising share prices gradually drew more and more money into stocks. Soon, as has occurred throughout history, a speculative psychology took over, and stock prices began to levitate, often with little connection to profit performance.

The rising market made many upper-middle-class consumers feel rich; even though their incomes might not have been rising very fast, the value of their stock assets was. This "wealth" effect was an inducement to buy beyond their incomes, with the result that the American household savings rate dropped to zero and consumer debt rose to historic heights.

Like that of the 1980s, the expansion of the 1990s was based on a massive increase in borrowing. The former took place under the watch of a *conservative* president, and was driven by *government* debt — Reagan's borrowing-and-spending binge, which increased the debt of the federal government from $1 trillion to $4 trillion by the end of George Bush's term. In contrast, the expansion of the 1990s, under a presumably *liberal* president, was driven by *private* debt.

Productivity and Technology

The absence of supply-side shocks, the lower interest rates, and the consumer-spending boom permitted the U.S. economy to operate closer to its capacity. It also created the conditions for a rising rate of productivity growth, which has expanded that capacity.

Sustained, high levels of demand motivated businesses to accelerate investment at a time when an array of computer technologies was ready to be commercially exploited. This happy coincidence led to an explosion of computer-based processes — e.g., e-commerce, desktop publishing, and computerized design — that in turn stimulated consumer and business demand.

By the mid-1990s, the demand for labor was such that the long-term decline in real wages was halted; and as labor markets began to tighten, wages actually began to rise. This in turn further motivated business to invest in labor-saving, computerized systems. As a result, growth in productivity rose from 1.3 percent in 1991–1995 to 2.6 percent in 1995–1999.

The statistics probably overstate the productivity growth. Given the way computer production is measured, the upgrading of a computer is automatically considered a productivity increase, no matter what its actual impact on production. Moreover, over the long term, technological innovation tends to come in waves, so that at some point we can expect a slowdown as the profitability of the most recent innovations becomes exhausted and the next wave has yet to break.

Still, it is reasonable to conclude that the U.S. economy, given sensible policies and the absence of destabilizing shocks, has the capacity to maintain a long-term rate of productivity growth of at least 2 percent, as opposed to the roughly 1 percent growth in productivity from the mid-1970s to the early 1990s.

THE NEXT STEP: A PROGRESSIVE ECONOMIC AGENDA

The accelerated economic growth of the 1990s brought dramatic relief from some problems that were thought to be close to insoluble when the decade began. The fiscal deficit is one example: A higher rate of economic growth has been a major factor in moving the national budget from deficit to surplus, removing the deficit as a major issue for American voters.

Growth also eased the threat of Social Security "bankruptcy." Increased payrolls led to increased payroll taxes, which have extended the projected life of the Social Security Trust Fund. Just as important, it revealed that the pay-as-you-go Social Security System can, with modest adjustments, remain intact so long as productivity continues to rise.

Growth also dispelled certain myths about the unemployed, such as the notion that they are out of work because they lack skills, good work habits, or the appropriate attitude. By the end of the decade, millions of Americans who had been dismissed as "unemployable" when the decade began had found jobs.

Thus, the 1990s delivered what most economists had thought impossible: the interim goals of the Humphrey-Hawkins Act—a 4 percent unemployment rate, and an inflation rate of less than 3 percent. In doing so, the decade proved that full employment solves myriad problems.

But it has not solved them all. There is a great deal of unfinished economic business, including:

- maintaining high employment;
- investment in sustained, long-term growth;
- refashioning the social safety net;
- building a balanced international economy; and
- democratic setting of economic goals.

Maintaining High Employment

Now that we have proven that full employment is possible, the task is to make sure that we reach it and maintain it. First of all, this requires a

Federal Reserve policy of accommodating growth. The Greenspan-Clinton pact helped get us here. But as demonstrated in the last year of Clinton's administration, it is too fragile a deal upon which to base a long-term commitment to full employment. As Clinton's term came to a close, in June 1999, Greenspan began backing away and raising interest rates. Having been newly reappointed for a full term and having achieved his objective of getting political consensus on eliminating the debt, Greenspan had no need to continue honoring his unwritten agreement with Clinton, who was now a lame-duck president.

The lesson is that so long as the central bank remains in the hands of people who see the preservation of capital as their number one priority, it will be necessary to put political pressure on them to accommodate growth. Congress must embrace the framework of the Humphrey-Hawkins Act and use it as a standard for judging the Fed's macroeconomic performance. Certainly, a belief in the goals of the Act, which place as much priority on employment growth as on price stability, should be a criterion for the selection of Fed board members and of Greenspan's successor.

My point is not that elected officials should manage monetary policy but that they should set the priorities of that policy. In 1999, when Greenspan was asked by members of Congress why, if he was concerned about the "irrational exuberance" of the stock market, he did not use his powers to restrict stock market credit rather than to slow down the entire economy. He replied that he did not want to discriminate against individuals who had to borrow money in order to play the stock market. Given that people who borrow to buy stock are typically wealthy by any reasonable standard, Greenspan's decision favored that small group of speculators over working people, who would pay the costs of slower growth. No chairperson of the Federal Reserve should have the leeway to make such political value judgments.

Second, the goal of eliminating the national debt should be abandoned. When the next recession strikes, it will be necessary at the very least to allow a deficit to grow in order to maintain purchasing power. It makes sense for the federal government to run surpluses at times of full employment; but to make surpluses the overriding goal would be to repeat the mistakes that plunged us into the Great Depression. Zero debt would also make it more difficult to conduct monetary policy, which influences the size of the money supply through the buying and selling of U.S. treasury bonds.

Third, we need to remember that a modest rise in wages does not necessarily signal imminent runaway inflation. There is a constant shift in the shares that wages and profits take of business revenues. When the profit share expands, the Fed does not feel it necessary to slow down the economy; nor should it do so when the wage share expands.

Fourth, global supply shocks in energy (and to a lesser extent, in food) remain by far the most potent inflation threat. The economy is less energy-dependent than it was during the oil price shocks of the 1970s, but it is more dependent on foreign supplies. This fact suggests that we should place greater emphasis on guaranteeing existing energy sources—such as the strategic petroleum reserve—as a protection against rapid price escalation. At the same time, the United States needs to begin a long-delayed effort to ensure progress toward greater energy efficiency, beginning with a national commitment to raise real energy prices by a small amount each year for the next two decades. When the market price is low, energy taxes would rise. If the market price rises too rapidly, taxes would be reduced so as to maintain a slow, steady, upward trajectory. Such a policy would enable consumers and businesses gradually to adjust to a certainty of higher oil prices.

Protection against supply shocks also ought to inform our approach to agriculture. The 1996 Omnibus Farm Bill (also known as the Freedom to Farm Act) was a misguided effort to end the policy of supply management and throw farmers onto the volatile free market, where prices then were high. As they have for centuries, farmers responded by overproducing. Greater supply led to lower prices. When farmers' incomes dropped, the federal government, led by self-styled conservatives from farm states, rushed in with subsidies. The net result was a greater cost to taxpayers. We should return to the principles of long-term supply management to dampen instability in this critical market.

Fifth, the trade deficit must be taken seriously. The most serious threat to the United States' capacity to maintain high employment is not the federal debt—most of which is owed to Americans—but the trade deficit, which is relentlessly adding to the nation's *foreign* debt. The latter now exceeds $1.5 trillion, about 20 percent of GDP. Sooner or later the outward flow of interest and dividend payments will cause the dollar to tumble. Foreigners will require higher interest rates to compensate for a riskier dollar, slowing income growth and forcing the United States to run a trade surplus. The falling dollar will then raise the price of imports. Because much of the U.S. manufacturing base will have migrated overseas, there will be fewer domestically produced substitutes, so U.S. families will have to swallow the higher costs—at a time when slower growth will be slowing their incomes. A smaller industrial base will make it even harder to export our way out of the hole. Thus, each month in which excessive imports are off-loaded on U.S. docks adds to the financial pain Americans will have to bear come the day of reckoning. The use of the U.S. dollar and debt as reserve currency for most of the world's countries has forestalled the arrival of that day, but it will surely come.

This fact has two important implications for policy. One is that U.S. trade relationships with other nations must be restructured to achieve overall trade balance. This will require reversing the direction of current trade expansion agreements—the North American Free Trade Agreement (NAFTA), the World Trade Organization (WTO), the recent trade pact with China, and various other bilateral agreements—that have encouraged multinationals headquartered in the United States to invest in low-wage countries in order to export back into the United States. For every 10 percent increase in direct investment flowing into China from the United States, U.S. imports from China rise about 7 percent and exports fall about 2 percent. The United States should use the considerable leverage of access to its consumers to deny U.S. markets to nations that close their markets to goods from the United States.

The second is that the dollar should be encouraged to fall, not to rise. A high dollar is to the advantage of American investors in foreign countries. A low dollar, which makes U.S. exports cheaper, is to the advantage of American workers. Given the large trade deficit, the high-dollar strategy promoted by former Treasury Secretary Robert Rubin should be scrapped.

Sustaining Long-term Growth

Public investment is the act of consciously shaping the future. Despite the celebration of capitalist risk and private entrepreneurship, the increase in productivity in the 1990s was largely built on two pillars, both of which were products of government investment. The first was technological innovation. The computer, for example, was born, nurtured, and subsidized to maturity by the U.S. Army, as were the silicon chip and the Internet. The biotech industry dreams of enormous future profits on the basis of decades of investments by the National Institutes of Health. This is nothing new. Early in the life of the Republic, American leaders understood that investment in large infrastructure projects would not be made by private business because the projects were too expensive and too risky and took too long to realize. Moreover, the potential benefits to society at large were greater than the potential benefits to any single private investor. So the government organized—usually with private sector participation—the building of canals, highways, railroads, and airports. Government subsidized the building of the first assembly line, as it did the development of vaccines, long-distance radio transmission, and jet planes—each of which generated its own vast private industry.

The second pillar was public investment in education. In an Information Age, knowledge and the ability to think in abstract symbols are the keys to the future for individuals and society as a whole. The United States pioneered public education, and today, 90 percent of grade-school children still attend public school. Despite the faddish interest in vouchers among policy elites, they will continue to do so. But the performance of today's public schools is uneven, particularly among the poor. To a large degree this is a function of unstable neighborhoods, overburdened families, and absent social services, which leave public schools facing problems they are not equipped to resolve. Leaving aside debates about teaching methods and theories and about public school bureaucracies, a number of obvious shortcomings must be addressed. Classrooms are too large; poor children do not enjoy the computer-age infrastructure available to others; the teaching profession is too underpaid to attract and retain the high-caliber talent needed; too many classrooms have too many children and too few books and basic supplies; and the United States has a completely inadequate preschool system for low- and moderate-income families. To alter these facts, we will have to invest more resources.

Public investments in transportation and technology are also critical to future economic growth, yet they have not been priorities. In the twenty years from 1978 to 1998, real spending in these areas dropped from 2.6 percent to 1.6 percent of GDP. Today there is an estimated gap of at least $70 billion between annual spending needs and actual spending levels in these areas. (This estimate does not include expenditures on public health, low-income housing, child care, or environmental protection, which also would support future growth.) The ongoing spending gap translates into the everyday realities of dilapidated and overcrowded schools, inadequate training programs, jammed transportation systems, and a reduction in civilian research and development.

Increased public investment also could provide powerful economic support for one of the great moral tasks of post–Cold War America: rebuilding impoverished urban neighborhoods and the lives of the people trapped inside them. An effective urban strategy needs a sustained infusion of public investment—in housing, education, and public safety—in order to attract private capital for commercial development. Such a commitment is essential for narrowing the interrelated race-class divisions in America.

Ironically, despite the conventional wisdom that government spending on social investments is not popular, recent polls have consistently shown a preference among American voters for spending on education, health, and other specific national needs over a tax cut. At the very least, therefore—given the growing gap between investment needs and investment performance—the top priority for use of the surplus should be to raise substantially the level of public investment spending. But this priority should not depend on the surplus. Social investments are essential for maintaining growth; and like private investments in the future, they are worth financing with borrowed funds.

Restoring Workplace Security

The deregulated economy by its very nature is undermining the sense of community in the American workplace. Even when jobs stay in America, the work of producing goods and services has been increasingly outsourced from large corporations—often unionized—to small and medium-sized nonunion firms under heavy competitive pressure and operating on small profit margins. To survive, the latter have turned many of their employees into "contingent" workers—part-time, temporary, individual contractors—to avoid the obligations to provide health care and pensions, and most importantly, to evade responsibility for their fate. The strategy has spread to the largest and most successful of firms, such as Microsoft, a massive employer of "perma-temps." Greenspan recently cited a survey showing that substantially more American workers were worried about losing their jobs in 1998, when the economy was close to full employment, than in 1992, when it was in the midst of a recession.

As firms show less loyalty to workers, the feeling is reciprocated: Predictably, surveys show that workers today feel less loyalty toward their employers than they did a decade ago. Fewer workers sense that their fate and the fate of their employer are bound together. A study of New York

City hi-tech temporary workers, for example, found that they spend half of their paid working hours in activities to further their own careers—looking for another job, or honing skills to make themselves more marketable to the next employer—rather than their companies' objectives. This is an understandable response to employers' message to workers that they are on their own.

Ironically, the new technologies with the capacity to make workers more productive and industry more competitive require a closer and longer-term relationship between workers and their employees. Computerization allows new, horizontal forms of management that make an enterprise more flexible and quicker to respond to changes in the global marketplace. But these new forms require greater employee involvement in what a few decades ago were management responsibilities. A larger employee role in management, in turn, requires employees who are loyal and better trained, and who identify their success with that of the company.

Public policy should weigh in on the side of strengthening the workplace community, which can be done in two ways: First, we should decrease the enormous and unproductive pressures on companies for short-term profits and results. One means of doing this is by imposing a securities transfer tax such as that proposed by economist James Tobin, which penalizes short-term market players and encourages long-term investment. Another proposal, by financier Warren Buffet, would tax short-term capital gains at 100 percent.

Second, we should promote more democratization in the workplace. Over the long term, unionized employees are more productive and have a greater sense of loyalty to the interest of the enterprise. Indeed, with the accelerated pace of mergers and acquisitions, often the union is the only source of stability and the only repository of an enterprise's institutional memory. Unfortunately, U.S. labor law makes it extremely difficult for workers to organize, and employers have become more expert in using the law against their employees. Given the fact that three times as many American workers say they want to be in a union than are in a union, a labor law reform giving them that right in practice as well as in theory is long overdue.

Reknitting the Social Safety Net

Nevertheless, insecurity will remain a large part of an individual's working life for as long into the future as we can see. In the global economy, firms are unable to offer the long-term, protective benefits they used to. And if productivity growth continues at a higher level, it will mean an accelerated "creative destruction" of existing firms and more dislocation of jobs.

As previous eras of unbridled capitalism demonstrated, workers are unwilling to tolerate high levels of risk to themselves and their families simply to maintain a particular theory of competitive markets. Eventually, the actions of a government that, say, organizes the rescue of the 99 multimillionaires with a controlling interest in the Long-term Capital Management Fund but that does not care about the fate of tens of thousands of workers thrown into the street because of the speculative activities of Wall Street, become intolerable.

The logic of a more competitive, flexible, deregulated economy therefore leads to more government, not less. Specifically, a progressive economic agenda would focus on three primary areas: in order of priority, health care, pension security, and tax relief for working families.

Health Care

Universal health care is the Democratic Party's most important piece of unfinished business. There are now some 45 million Americans without coverage and another 30 million or so with coverage that is seriously inadequate. Keeping health care in the hands of the subsidized private market is not working. Moreover, there is ample evidence that private employers are becoming less interested in providing health care coverage to their workers.

Despite the widespread failure of the Clinton health care plan in 1994, the claim that the American public does not support universal coverage is wrong. Two years after the 1994 debacle, a majority of Americans thought that the country would have been better off if the Clinton plan had passed. Polls show much larger and consistent majorities for universal coverage guaranteed by the government.

The notion that the country cannot afford a universal health care system is also wrong. Americans now pay a total of $1.2 trillion for health care insurance and services. The savings from a single-payer system— "Medicare for everyone"—would be enough to get us universal coverage for the same money. The real issue is how to reshuffle the cost burden to finance a new system. Fifty percent of the U.S. health bill is paid by the public sector, which could simply be made available to a new plan.

About 25 percent is now paid by employers as health care benefits, which would have to be redirected to a new public financing system by making it a payroll tax. Another 25 percent is currently paid by individual health care recipients. This last part could remain a part of a universal coverage plan or it could also be shifted to a tax, such as a surcharge on the income tax. In 1998, such a tax would have cost the average middle-income family $731, in exchange for which they would never have to pay anything for health care.

Pension Security

To create a pension safety net that will hold up even in an insecure economy, we must first preserve the Social Security system of guaranteed income. Second, we must establish a public system by which workers can pool their retirement savings in a government-administered investment fund.

The first objective of a progressive pension system should be a minimal level of old-age security. This requires total opposition to the diversion of Social Security funds to any form of individual investment system. The greatest political catastrophe imaginable with Social Security is not that taxes will have to be raised, or even that people will have to retire later. It is the possibility that billions of dollars could be diverted to private stock markets and lost—leaving generations of elderly people stranded and impoverished, and severing the last shred of confidence in democratic government.

The basic problem of the Social Security shortfall is that people are living longer. Therefore, they will spend more of their lives on Social Security. As a result, each generation will have to pay a little more toward the retirement of the previous one. If the entire shortfall were made up by increasing the payroll tax, it would mean a tax increase of less than 2 percent. But at the same time, each generation will be richer because of productivity growth. Thus, at a modest increase in productivity of 1.5 percent a year, a typical worker twenty-five years from now would be making 45 percent more than the same worker today. If Social Security taxes were increased to cover the whole cost of the shortfall, the future worker's income would still be 24 percent higher.

But we need not raise the payroll tax to cover the whole amount. As a share of average earnings, the Social Security tax has fallen from 92 percent of earnings in 1937 to about 87 percent in 1997. If the so-called "cap" on Social Security taxes were placed at 90 percent of workers' earnings, the shortfall would be reduced to 1.5 percent of payroll. If the cap were lifted, the shortfall would shrink to less than 0.5 percent—an amount easily affordable to a growing economy over a period of seventy-five years.

Private pensions now provide about 14 percent of retirement income, and less than half of all workers are earning retirement benefits on the job other than Social Security. Where private pensions are still offered, employers are cutting back on their contributions. In 1979, they contributed 88 cents per work hour to pension plans. By 1994, they had cut back to 70 cents. Moreover, most companies that provide pension support no longer do so under "defined benefit" plans, in which the long-term risk is the employer's, but under "defined contribution" plans, in which the employee absorbs the risk.

Clearly, the vast majority of American workers cannot by themselves organize a retirement system to supplement Social Security. Therefore, the Clinton-Gore proposal for a voluntary, government-subsidized retirement savings account program in addition to, not as a diversion of funds from, Social Security, makes sense. The proposed Universal Savings Accounts (USAs) would provide low- to moderate-income workers with an automatic government tax credit deposited into a 401(K) plan similar to that offered to federal government employees.

Tax Relief
A third stitch in the social safety net is tax relief for low- and middle-income working families. Despite the record-breaking boom of the 1990s and the rise in labor productivity growth, real wages for half of American workers are below what similar workers earned in 1979.

Inasmuch as these are trends in before-tax earnings, increased taxes are not the cause of the problem; rather, the cause is the lack of bargaining power among most American workers. Even if tight labor markets can be maintained and unions strengthened, it will take time to rectify this situation. But a shift in the burden of taxes away from working families in the meantime could help the majority of families living from paycheck to paycheck.

One approach would build on the highly successful Earned Income Tax Credit (EITC). Economists Max Sawicky and Robert Cherry have proposed that the EITC be integrated with the child-dependent deduction and child credit to create a Universal Unified Child Credit for all families with children that would phase out as incomes rise. The idea has many virtues, including refundability, so that the poorest families would receive cash payments; elimination of the unpopular "marriage penalty" built into the current system; mitigation of the regressive impact of Social Security and Medicare taxes; and simplification of the system of tax credits for children, making it easier for people to take advantage of such credits.

The tax rates can be adjusted to change the level of progressivity. Sawicky and Cherry suggest a pattern of relief that focuses benefits on families making between $13,000 and $65,000 per year, which would cost taxpayers $390 billion over ten years. In comparison, President Clinton's 2001 budget plan calls for spending $350 billion over ten years on a series of small tax credits, none of which has much impact, spread over a large number of constituencies. At the same time, George W. Bush was proposing a roughly $1.5 trillion tax cut over ten years with benefits heavily tilted toward upper-income families.

Building a Balanced Global Economy

One hundred years ago, changes in transportation and communication technologies transformed the United States from a series of regional economies to an integrated continental market. In order to keep the continental economy in balance, we had to create continental institutions—e.g., a central bank, financial regulation, crop insurance, labor and environmental protections, social insurance, and so on. We were able to do so because we had a national constitution.

Today, the U.S. economy is becoming integrated with the larger, global marketplace through the relentless growth of technology and business organization. But there is no global constitution. Therefore the global marketplace has no institutions to keep it balanced. The WTO and so-called free-trade agreements such as NAFTA are really protectionist systems for global investors, which leave workers, farmers, and small business people to the mercies of a rigged market.

Financial markets especially have burst the bonds of national regulation. They are increasingly disconnected from the surrounding real economies of production and consumption and driven by computerized models for making quick profits in turbulent markets, adding to the herd behavior that makes prices more volatile and markets riskier. The International Monetary Fund (IMF) is no match for this phenomenon. It is not a central bank charged with nurturing global growth and stability. It is rather a shallow-pocket lender, conditioning its loans to troubled nations on austerity policies aimed at giving debt repayment through exports priority over domestic growth. Like the U.S. Treasury, it has a tendency to rescue dictatorships, big banks, and prominent hedge fund investors who are "too big to fail."

It is upon this set of narrow, inadequate, biased institutions that the leaders of the advanced nations are trying to build a global order. In the words of the former head of the WTO, Renato Ruggiero: "We are no longer writing the rules of interaction among separate national economies. We are writing the constitution of a single global economy."

The stakes for working Americans are enormous. If the new world constitution does not include *global* protections for workers, citizens' rights, and the environment, it will inevitably lead to an erosion of hard-won *domestic* protections. The notion that a global economy can produce benefits for the majority of working people without strong and enforceable rules defies logic and history.

At the contentious 1999 WTO meeting in Seattle, President Clinton acknowledged the commonsense proposition that labor rights should be enforced with trade sanctions, just as investor rights are. Charlene Barshefsky, the U.S. Trade Representative, called the notion that labor rights should be disconnected from trade "intellectually indefensible." Yet, the next spring, when confronted with business demands to accept a China trade agreement without labor protections—much less enforceable protections—the Clinton administration and most members of Congress caved in.

Given that the China vote was held during extraordinarily good times, the narrowness of the administration's victory indicates widespread doubts about this new world order. Those doubts will grow, and we can expect increased domestic pressure for extending global protections to workers and the environment. Hostility toward the current global trade and investment regime is not limited to developed nations' NGOs and labor unions. It is often even greater in developing countries whose leaders have surrendered sovereignty to global financial markets.

Even so, the problem cannot be solved within the current framework of international institutions. The WTO, the World Bank, the IMF, and the United Nations cannot muster the political will to overcome the power of multinational corporations working through their political clients, among the leaders of both developed and developing countries.

Within a larger framework, one can imagine a "grand bargain" in which the developing nations agree to enforceable social standards in exchange for guaranteed commitments of long-term development aid and debt relief. However, no existing institution of global economic governance is broad enough to encompass this kind of negotiation. Jacques Delors, former head of the European Commission, has suggested the formation of a global economic security council. But without a new policy agenda, the world hardly needs another supranational bureaucracy.

At the same time, the destructive instability of global financial markets must be addressed. The technical and political problems of creating U.S.-style regulations for international capital flows are enormous. Even the threatened meltdown of national economies in the wake of the 1997 global financial crisis was not enough to motivate the world's governments in that direction. A simpler solution—which does not involve complex sovereignty questions—would be the creation of a "Tobin"-style tax on international currency and security transfers. Such a tax would be relatively simple to administer, would slow down the movement of short-term money, and could produce revenues for Third World development.

Only the United States has the capacity to organize a serious global discussion of these ideas. Instead, Washington has often been the chief obstacle to putting them on the world's agenda. Change in this area will therefore require a strengthening of the political movement for balanced global rules within the United States. A basis has already been built through the process of resistance to NAFTA, the renewal of fast-track authority, and the vote against permanent trade relations with China.

One way to move forward would be a campaign for a revised NAFTA that would reflect a North American version of the "grand bargain." The United States and Canada could provide aid to Mexico and relief from some of the most onerous conditions the original NAFTA imposed on Mexico in exchange for a continent-wide system of enforceable labor rights and environmental standards. A positive proposal that appealed to potential constituencies in both Canada and Mexico would put progressives in the posture of shaping the future rather than defending the past.

Setting Economic Goals

These proposals are all well within the framework of pre-Reagan Democratic thought. Indeed, from that perspective, if Truman, Kennedy, or Johnson were to return today, they would be shocked that America still lacks universal health care and adequate funding of preschools for children from low-income families, and that fewer and fewer workers are protected by pensions. Despite the mainstream character of these proposals and despite their popularity in the polls, their supporters remain unable to overcome the ideology that demands that we frame our public future solely in privatized, market-centered terms.

So long as that perspective dominates, the Democrats will continue to play a supporting role in the Republican script, and the country will be deprived of meaningful choice. Democrats will not write a new script through blurred discussions of family values, community, or a vague "third way" wherein the signposts change direction like weathervanes, according to the latest political breeze. Neither will they write a new script by aping the commercial boosterism of hi-tech products of the future. The central question is not how computers will clean our houses or splice our genes but whether our society will simply react to technological change or will guide it in the service of human priorities. In today's political economy the future has become something to guess at and bet on. The task is to make it something to shape.

A more promising path to a politics concerned with managing the future would involve raising large, important questions that directly impact the lives of working families and that can only be answered through public action. One such question might be how much of the benefits of our economic growth we want to take in income and how much in reduced work time. The "official" workweek went from 65 hours in the 1860s to 40 hours in the 1930s, and has not changed since. Actual work time has increased—by more than 175 hours a year for the average worker since 1973. The negative effects of longer hours on health, family, life, and community stability are well known.

The companion issue to a shorter workweek is more flexible hours. The constantly changing work environment and the conflict between being a worker and being a parent makes flexible hours essential for family stability. At the same time, American employers want more leeway to stretch and shrink the workweek according to their needs.

It is time for a national discussion that brings these various dimensions of work time issues together. A proposal to shorten the workweek gradually, accompanied by a grand bargain giving employers more flexibility and workers more control of their time could create a rich democratic debate over America's future.

We must also re-create an infrastructure for wide citizen participation in debates over the nation's direction. Democrats should champion a framework for discussion in which the question of what kind of America we want is answered by the question of what kind of local communities we want.

In the mid-1970s, around the time of the bicentennial celebration of the American revolution, citizens and officials in a large number of cities and states engaged in a public dialogue about their future through meetings and discussion groups. Many came up with specific plans—a vision of California, or Atlanta, or Maine in the year 2000. For some, the focus was on land-use planning and transportation systems. Others became engaged in the issue of sustainability and energy efficiencies. Others moved to more difficult questions of the relationships between races, genders, and classes. Some of these efforts were high-quality. Some were little more than boosterism. But most supported a civic dialogue that enriched the quality of local citizenship.

These activities stopped dead after the election of Ronald Reagan in 1980. They remained dormant even after his departure, suppressed by his ideological and fiscal legacies, which dramatically reduced citizens' expectations of the public sector and their own role in it.

But the tide is going out on the radical antigovernment ideology that has poisoned the political debate for the past two decades. The centrist shift of the GOP after the Republican Congress's politically disastrous closedown of the federal government in winter 1995 reflects this reality, as does the Democrats' cautious testing of populist themes in the campaign of 2000. The projections of large, sustainable budget surpluses make the return to a sensible balance between private and public sectors credible once again. The public is demanding not "less" government or "more" government, but government that is responsive to needs that are unmet by the private market—both individual needs and the common needs of the national community.

Unlike the governments of many other advanced nations, where a substantial role in the economy for the public sector is broadly accepted, the

U.S. government has been most successful when it has been mission-oriented—when it has bent its efforts toward specific, clear-cut goals, such as barge canals, transcontinental railroads, health care for the elderly, and a man on the moon. Often these programs have been subsets of a larger project—settling the west, industrialization, fighting poverty, and the Cold War—that created immense synergies between public and private sectors. In the post–Cold War era, we have the opportunity to embark on a new American project: the democratic redevelopment of the United States.

Today, however, our more educated, technologically sophisticated, and skeptical public has little enthusiasm for letting the future be formed by large, distant bureaucracies. Therefore, the question of what kind of America we want a decade or two from now should properly begin with the question of what kind of communities we want. The federal government could support the process of answering that question by providing, at a modest cost, matching resources to state and local governments to establish community planning programs aimed at producing periodically updated social and economic goals for the next ten years. With Internet technology, citizens in different communities could connect with each other, sharing ideas and visions that would aggregate into regional and national investment priorities.

One practical and specific way to begin is to focus a national discussion on the future of metropolitan areas—where most Americans live. Suburbanization has brought traffic jams, alienated children, and dysfunctional work lives. Welfare reform has created the need for jobs and child care. The spread of digital and Internet technologies is transforming work, education, and culture. The integration of such issues could provide the basis for a new set of local and regional discussions—"millennial" rather than bicentennial—that could be launched across America to give citizens the opportunity to think about their community's future and to decide how they want to live together in, say, 2020.

*   *   *

Today's economic policies will determine tomorrow's economy and should therefore be based on an explicit vision of what we want tomorrow's economy to look like. Thus, at the core of the economic policy debate is the question, What kind of future do we want to create for ourselves and those who will follow?

To those who believe in a market society, the question seems irrelevant: The future will be determined by the market. But if we believe in a market economy *within* a larger, democratic society, then the question, and the political implications of our responses to it, cannot be avoided.

2
_____

GLOBAL FAIRNESS: THE HISTORIC DEBATE

Robert L. Borosage and William Greider

In October 1999, the previously obscure meetings of the World Trade Organization sparked mass protests in the streets of Seattle; a few months later, the routine annual meetings of the World Bank and the International Monetary Fund were besieged in Washington, D.C. The secretive international negotiations in Paris for a Multilateral Agreement on Investment attracted such public opposition that they were canceled. At the level of national politics, the largest pitched battles in the recent history of the U.S. Congress were fought over the granting of fast-track authority to the president on matters of trade. Clearly, a fundamental debate about the global economy has begun—and it is one that will likely be a defining political struggle of coming decades.

This is not a debate about protectionism against internationalism, as it is so often burlesqued. The argument is not about whether we should be part of a global economy but about the rules that should govern that economy: What limits will be placed on markets, on government's role, and on global corporations? Will they serve values other than profit? And how broadly will the benefits brought by U.S. economic prosperity be shared?

THE CONSERVATIVE CONSENSUS

From the 1970s through the 1990s, a conservative, laissez-faire consensus dominated the commanding heights of the global economy. It grew out of a corporate offensive launched in reaction to rising inflation and declining profits, seeking to dismantle the regulations and social accords that limited corporate actions. The Bretton Woods system of regulated currencies was abandoned, and national controls over capital flows were dismantled. Unions were attacked and weakened. The "oil shocks" of the decade—which were largely a reaction to inflation generated during the Vietnam War—left developing nations deeply in debt and on the verge of default, and the United States with stagflation and 20 percent interest rates.

Conservatives—led by Thatcher in Britain, Reagan in the United States, and Kohl in Germany—took over leadership of the industrial nations. Their mantra was simple and clear: Markets work; governments do not. Privatize, deregulate, dismantle controls, free up trade, cut back social supports. They not only pushed these prescriptions in Europe and the United States but also force-fed them to developing nations through the International Monetary Fund (IMF), the World Bank, and the U.S. Treasury.[1]

This agenda became known as the "Washington consensus": fiscal austerity; currency devaluations to promote exports and attract foreign investment; privatization of industries and services; liberalization of banking; and a weakening of unions and social supports.

The Washington consensus asserted extreme laissez-faire certitudes about growth and development. Get prices right, stamp out inflation, open up markets, reduce domestic demand, and produce for export. Don't worry about governance, democracy, worker rights, poverty, social justice, or the environment. Open markets will produce growth, and growth over time will produce a middle class. The middle class will usher in law, rights, and greater justice.[2] This was the "golden straitjacket," hailed by its popularizers as the key to the future. "There is no alternative," pronounced Thatcher, as she and her allies worked to make certain that was so.

LOOK ON MY WORKS. . .

Two decades later, the results are in. A global economy has been created that is dominated by large corporations and buffeted by immense speculative capital flows totaling more than $1.5 trillion a day. The world is smaller and more connected, making economic disparities among countries more obvious: Some have enjoyed remarkable growth; others have endured unimaginable catastrophe. Fantastic fortunes have been accumulated by a few, even as the poverty in which many live has deepened. Millions have found new opportunities; millions, new miseries.

Not surprisingly, the new global economy is working well for the great corporations and banks that make the rules and cut the deals. Of the 100 largest economies in the world, 51 are corporations. Annual gross sales at General Motors exceed Thailand's gross national product; General Electric is larger than Poland; and Wal-Mart sells more in a year than Malaysia produces. The combined annual sales of 200 global corporations equal one-fourth of the world's gross domestic product.[3] And corporate wealth is growing: By 1998, the ten largest companies in telecommunications controlled 86 percent of a $262 billion market; the top ten in pesticides, 85 percent of the market; in the computer industry, 70 percent; in pharmaceuticals, 35 percent; and in commercial seed, 32 percent.

But this global economy does not work very well for most working people: In 1999, 200 million more were enduring abject poverty (on less than $1 a day) than had been the case a decade earlier. More than eighty countries have per capita incomes lower than they were a decade or more ago. Although forty countries have maintained 3 percent annual growth in GNP since 1990, fifty-five countries have seen a decline in GNP per capita. In the 1990s, more than 80 percent of all foreign direct investment in developing or transitional economies went to just twenty countries, with China outstripping all others. Environmental despoliation is worsening. The satanic mills—sweatshops where children, mostly girls, work twelve-, fourteen-, or sixteen-hour days—have returned, often on contract to modern multinationals in export processing zones.[4]

The celebration of globalization is beginning to be tempered by a greater understanding of its costs. Joseph Stiglitz, former chief economist of the World Bank, has summarized the results of the Washington consensus as

- slower growth both in developing and in developed countries;
- increasing instability ("a boom in busts," with financial crises becoming more frequent and more severe);
- growing indebtedness; and
- increasing poverty and inequality. (A world in which the three richest Microsoft billionaires have more assets than the combined GNP of the forty-three least developed countries with their 600 million people mocks any sense of decency.)

As this is written, globalization continues to be celebrated, but some of the fizz has gone out of the champagne. In Asia, Japan is slipping back into a decade-long recession. China struggles against slowing growth and spreading deflation. Even the most successful of the so-called newly industrialized countries — South Korea, Indonesia, and Thailand — have found that a generation of progress can be lost in a few months of speculation.

In Russia, forced-march privatization has led to unprecedented economic catastrophe, reducing much of that industrial nation to barter. Africa has largely been written off by the multinationals. Workers in Latin America are losing ground. In Europe, pressure on wages continues to build as widespread unemployment lingers. Even in the United States, which is celebrating the longest period of economic growth in modern history, wages have not recovered the ground they lost over the previous quarter century. More working families are without health insurance. Pensions are fewer and smaller; and people are working longer and with less security.

THE SHAKEN CONSENSUS

Free trade and the free flow of capital were the centerpiece of the Clinton administration's economic strategy. The Washington consensus found no more avid apostles than the "New Democrat" president and the "Third Way" social democrats who followed him into office in Europe — Tony Blair in Britain, and Gerhard Schroeder in Germany. In his first four years, President Clinton earned kudos (and fattened his campaign coffers with Wall Street and corporate donations) by winning passage, over the opposition of much of his own party, of trade accords that had largely been negotiated by his Republican predecessors — the North American Free Trade Agreement (NAFTA) and the agreement setting up the World Trade Organization (WTO).

But Clinton discovered that popular resistance to the corporate-defined global order was growing, particularly within his own party. A right-left coalition in the House of Representatives blocked renewal of presidential fast-track authority, not once but twice. Negotiations on the Multilateral Agreement on Investment, as mentioned earlier, also were blocked. High-flying Nike had its wings clipped by consumer groups protesting sweatshops, sending it and other companies scurrying for the protective cover of self-styled and self-policed codes of conduct. A coalition of religious, activist, and student groups forced debt forgiveness for the poorest nations onto the global agenda. In the face of the ensuing large-scale demonstrations, the WTO failed to launch a new global round of trade negotiations. With manufacturing jobs continuing to be lost even in the midst of economic growth, popular skepticism has been growing in the United States toward free-trade platitudes.

In elite circles, the global financial crisis that began in Thailand in 1997 shook confidence. The imminent bankruptcy of a single hedge fund—Long-term Capital Management—had the world's central bankers peering into the abyss of global financial collapse. Forty percent of the world's economy slid into recession. Russia went belly-up, defaulting on bonds. Brazil teetered on the edge. The success stories of the previous decade—Indonesia, Korea, and Thailand—suffered the worst devastation. And despite all the talk of "crony capitalism," it was clear that these countries were vulnerable not because they had not reformed but because they had liberalized their banking industries under pressure from the IMF.

After the debacle in Asia, dissenting voices could be found in high places. Stiglitz issued stinging critiques of the ideological blindness of the Washington consensus. Financier George Soros warned of the "capitalist threat" and called for controls on capital speculation. Prime Minister Blair called for a "new Bretton Woods," referring to the top-level meetings out of which the post–World War II system of controlled currencies emerged. Free-trade advocate Jagdish Bhagwati denounced the "Wall Street–Treasury complex" in the pages of *Foreign Affairs,* calling for controls on speculation. The Council on Foreign Relations issued a report that supported national controls on short-term capital flows. In sum, the IMF's packaged prescriptions were under attack from both left and right. Even U.S. Treasury Secretary Robert Rubin started talking about the need for a "new financial architecture."[5]

Perhaps the strongest indication of elite concern was that President Clinton, ever a sensitive weathervane of acceptable opinion, moved rapidly to embrace the language of reform. In a series of speeches, he laid out the need for a progressive alternative to the conservative regime that he previously had embraced. At the University of Chicago, in June 1999, he called for trade agreements to "lift everybody up, not pull everybody down" and to "protect the environment and the rights of workers." He told attendees at the WTO meetings that more must be done to ensure that economic competition "never becomes a race to the bottom—

in environmental protections, consumer protections, or labor standards."
He called on the WTO to open up its deliberations, develop more democratic consultative groups, and work to incorporate core labor rights
and environmental protections into its trading rules. He told the governors of the IMF and World Bank that a "new financial architecture" was
essential to "tame the cycles of booms and busts." In a speech before the
International Labor Organization (ILO), he urged that core labor rights
be viewed as the "charter for a truly modern economy" and be made an
"everyday reality all across the world." As the WTO prepared to convene
in Seattle, Clinton said he stood with the demonstrators and believed
that labor rights and environmental protections should be enforced with
trade sanctions if necessary.[6]

AFTER THE STORM

But the worst financial crisis since the Great Depression wasn't felt much
in the United States. The U.S. economy kept growing and the stock market continued to rise. Although millions found themselves thrust into
poverty across the globe, the system didn't collapse. Even as the president
was hoisting the flag of rebellion rhetorically, his treasury secretary, Rubin, was standing at the gate, fending off the infidels. Rubin limited the
U.S. response to calls for debt relief, squiring through a reform agenda
that focused on "transparency" for banking institutions. Describing the
Clinton project, the *Wall Street Journal* commented that it looked a lot
more like patching the plumbing than like "new architecture."

The president quietly returned to the fold. He joined the Business
Roundtable and Republican leaders to force through Congress measures
granting China permanent most-favored-nation trade status, and expanding African and Caribbean concessions, without any provision for labor
rights or environmental protections in these countries. And he resumed
his vocal celebration of free trade, hailing global corporations as the
troubadours of freedom.

But the complacency demonstrated by Clinton and other U.S. leaders
belies continuing global economic instability. In the wake of the Asian
crisis, the United States became the buyer of last resort, providing the
market demand enabling Mexico and the Asian countries to recover,
and giving China its annual trade surplus. According to the IMF, the
United States has accounted for about 50 percent of world market demand in recent years.[7]

But the United States is now running a billion-dollar-a-day trade deficit, heading toward an unimaginable $400 billion total for 2000 alone. The cumulative foreign debt presently amounts to a staggering 20 percent of GDP (up from 13 percent in 1997). Twenty years ago, the United States had no foreign debt. The trade deficit and mounting U.S. indebtedness, as conservative Federal Reserve Chair Alan Greenspan has warned, cannot be sustained. Americans are headed for a day of reckoning with incalculable consequences.[8]

THE EMERGING ALTERNATIVE

The Clinton administration fended off initial efforts at reform. Calls for limiting currency and capital speculation were muted. Resistance to incorporating labor rights and environmental protections in trade accords continued. Even conservative ideas for curbing the IMF and World Bank went nowhere. In the 2000 U.S. presidential campaign, both Al Gore and George W. Bush supported the trade deal with China; both candidates ran as free traders (although in a concession to prevailing opinion among Democrats, Gore claimed to favor the enforcement of labor rights and environmental protections in future trade agreements). Many free-trade advocates call for greater assistance to workers displaced by trade, hoping to placate growing public resistance to free-trade agreements; but even in a time of burgeoning budget surpluses, neither the Democratic President Clinton nor the Republican Congress supported significant increases in funding for job-related education, retraining, or transitional support.

Is there no alternative? The global economy is not a creation of nature but the product of powerful interests. Its rules are not God-given but man-made. Coherent reform programs have been elaborated by many scholars and activists over the past decade.[9] Even more interesting, perhaps, is the reform agenda implicit in the large mass protests of recent years. Although protesters often have been scorned as Neanderthal protectionists or "know-nothing flat earthers," they have, in fact, put forth a coherent alternative to the Washington consensus. Elements of their agenda include:

(1) debt forgiveness, freeing impoverished countries from debts they will never be able to repay. Debt-relief advocacy organizations such as Jubilee 2000 and 50 Years Is Enough have forced industrial nations, however begrudgingly, to reassess the existing programs and offer greater

debt relief. Organizers have denounced the IMF's Structural Adjustment Programs (SAPs), which further perpetuate global inequities
and chains of dependence between the developed and developing
economies. They seek debt forgiveness that is not conditioned on increased privatization and trade liberalization but is instead focused on
sustainable and equitable growth. By allowing governments to refocus
their funding on basic needs, debt relief can aid the poor, open up opportunity for the next generation, and create an opportunity for countries
to define their own path to development.

The current debt-relief programs clearly are not working. In fact, research demonstrates that the longer countries follow SAPs, the higher
their debts become. Effective debt-relief and -forgiveness programs
could benefit industrialized nations as much as developing ones by increasing global efficiency, encouraging democratic government, jump-
starting stalled economies, and staving off future economic disruptions.

(2) radical reform of the IMF and the development banks, particularly an end to the harsh conditions they place on their loans to countries in crisis. Joseph Stiglitz, former chief economist of the World
Bank, wrote of the demonstrators gathered at the IMF and World Bank
meetings:

> They'll say the IMF is arrogant. They'll say the IMF doesn't really listen to
> the developing countries it is supposed to help. They'll say the IMF is se-
> cretive and insulated from democratic accountability. They'll say that
> IMF's economic "remedies" often make things worse—turning slowdowns
> into recessions and recessions into depressions. And they'll have a point.[10]

The demonstrators wanted the international financial institutions to
open up, to bring NGOs to the table, and to change substantively the
terms of their loans. They demanded that the bankers and speculators
who cause the crises be "bailed in," not bailed out—that they be made to
bear some of the costs of their bad loans. Many advocate an international
bankruptcy court that could force creditors to agree on repayment plans
for countries in crisis. They would require that the World Bank and the
IMF include labor and environmental impact assessments in their loan
agreements and stop insisting on measures that weaken worker rights or
environmental regulation. They want international financial institutions
to focus on the needs of the poor instead of cutting social supports in order to satisfy creditors and potential investors. An increasing number

think the World Bank and the IMF should be shut down and that new institutions, with new charters, should take their places.

(3) greater controls over capital and currency speculation. Perhaps the most interesting movement has been the campaign for a tax on short-term capital flows, called the Tobin Tax, after James Tobin, the Nobel Prize–winning economist who first proposed it. Amazingly, literally thousands have marched *for* this tax, leading the Canadian parliament and others to pass resolutions calling on the industrial nations to support the plan. The tax could slow the destabilizing flows of "hot money" as well as create a global public fund that could be used to finance long-term investment in developing nations. Such a fund would reduce the pressures on countries to depend on export-led growth and free up resources for more internal development.[11]

(4) the inclusion of core worker rights and environmental protections in the rules that govern trade. The WTO, according to its former director, aspires to create a "constitution for the global economy." What the protesters inside and outside the halls in Seattle were saying was that if there is to be a globally valid constitution, then surely its rules must reflect important values other than those of property rights and profit.

The WTO currently claims the authority to empower closed panels of trade experts to review national laws and regulations, overturning environmental and food regulations that conflict with global trade accords. Europeans have found that their opposition to genetically altered food runs afoul of the WTO's rules. The United States has been told that an attempt to limit the import of poorly refined gasoline also may not be allowed. Globalization has been used quite purposefully by corporations to escape and weaken national regulations and to undermine labor unions in negotiations.

So workers and consumers naturally want the global rules to reflect values other than the interests of corporations. Core worker rights, accepted by more than 100 ILO member nations, are basic human rights. They include prohibitions of child labor, forced labor, and discrimination, as well as protection of the right to organize. Today's global economy actively undermines these basic rights. The ILO report *Your Voice At Work* documents the deplorable effects of the current global economy on worker rights.[12] Workers' demands for decent compensation are countered by employers' threats to close or relocate their plants. Companies have evolved toward a strategy of "virtual production" in which a central management structure subcontracts a range of activities to small producers across the globe. This situation approaches the fantasy of General Electric CEO Jack Welch, who once said, "Ideally, you'd have every plant you own on a barge," ready to move if workers demanded raises or governments imposed new regulations. Companies routinely play countries against one another, forcing a "a race to the bottom," in which countries compete to offer the lowest wages, the longest hours, the most disciplined (i.e., compliant) workers, and the least regulation.

Ultimately, this low road undermines global economic growth. When a few small countries depend on export-led growth, as does Japan, the global economy is not threatened; but when dozens are forced to compete for the same external markets, suppressing demand at home and producing for export, the global economy is at risk. Excess capacity produces too many goods, and too few consumers have the money to buy those goods. Developing countries find themselves going up a down escalator; they have to run just to stay in place. If developing economies are to grow in strength, then the workers in those nations must be empowered to capture a fair share of the profits that they produce. This requires global protection of worker rights.

Ultimately, people will demand that their food be safe, their air clean, and their environment protected. Workers will organize to limit their exploitation. Sweatshops will offend basic values. Either the rules of the global economy will begin to enforce those values, or people will insist that their countries, their cities, and their communities enforce them.

Together these reform measures challenge the assumptions underlying the Washington consensus. The alternative agenda is based on providing countries with greater space to seek their own paths through the wrenching transitions of development, rather than forcing them to heel with a U.S. version of capitalism. Global engagement is assumed, but not via a forced march to export-led development. The aim is to increase long-term public support for basic needs while reducing the explosive, destabilizing force of short-term private capital flows—in other words, to put a leash on capital and to unshackle workers.

THE GROWING DEBATE

The alternative proposed in the streets is gaining ground even in the U.S. Congress. The Washington consensus isn't the consensus in Washington any longer. In the wake of the Asian crisis, even establishment economists have begun to reevaluate their assumptions. Markets generate creative destruction: They force people to abandon traditional ways of living, uproot old institutions, and transform societies. If this disruption is to lead to development, societies must find a way to withstand the market's brutal shocks; people must be led to embrace the new and to share in its benefits.

Markets must be embedded in laws that temper the human costs of change with social protections. Increasingly, democracy and worker rights are seen as essential. Russia's recent experience has proved the perils of the market without law. Indonesia has revealed the brittleness of even the most entrenched dictatorship. Democracy and worker rights are central to a robust civil society. Organized workers put a check on corporate corruption. They help force a wider sharing of wealth, greater public provision of education and health care. They are vital to help societies navigate through the storms of economic transition.

The evidence shows, as Harvard's Dani Rodrik wrote, that countries that empower workers enjoy faster and more sustainable growth, suffer fewer severe setbacks, and better withstand shocks. Such countries typically generate greater socioeconomic equality and greater internal demand, and therefore are less dependent on fickle export markets.[13]

And as Amartya Sen has pointed out, freedom is the means as well as the end of development.[14] Global rules that reinforce worker rights, environmental protections, and democracy are not a luxury affordable only to wealthy societies; they are a necessity for shaping the kinds of societies people want to live in.

THE NEXT BATTLE

The struggle over the rules of the global economy is being contested in many different arenas. With China admitted to membership in the WTO, that organization will find it more and more difficult to make worker rights and environmental protections part of its agenda. The WTO is likely to find itself enmeshed in an ever widening and more futile struggle to get China and other countries to enforce the rules they have agreed to. Given its lack of accountability and declining legitimacy, the WTO will face rising opposition as rulings by its closed panels of trade experts increasingly challenge national laws and regulations on the environment, food safety, taxes, and subsidies. An international citizens' campaign will continue to build momentum against the WTO; but the primary drive for reform is likely to turn elsewhere.

The next likely focus may well be the global corporations themselves, as foreshadowed by the remarkable Students Against Sweatshops movement. Students on campuses across the country have organized to protest the sweatshop conditions in which children their own age or younger labor to produce garments for U.S. markets. They are demanding that universities hold corporations accountable to a code of conduct—on core worker rights, environmental practices, and a living wage—as a condition of selling in the lucrative university logo market. Under pressure, a number of companies, led by Nike, scrambled to set up their own self-policed codes of conduct. In response, the students created the Worker Rights Consortium, calling on the companies to reveal their subcontractors, adhere to basic worker rights, and allow independent inspection and verification. Although the companies had pledged never to reveal their subcontractors, they have been forced to do so. Under public pressure, they also have undertaken social audits of their own factories, and some have increased the wage levels and improved the working conditions of their workers.

This student movement showed the power of the offensive, of telling a positive story about how the world might look if truly democratic values prevailed. The students combined muckraking—exposing the harsh facts of present realities—with concrete proposals for reform, making U.S. consumers more sensitive to the plight of impoverished workers abroad.

The transformation of the global economy can be accomplished only if citizens and their governments succeed in holding accountable the corporations that are the driving force behind global inequities. Concrete legislation should be proposed—laws that can be passed at the community or local level, or enacted by national legislatures. Americans have the sovereign power to impose rules on the behavior of U.S.-based multinational corporations. Congress in essence asserted this power in 1977, with the Foreign Corrupt Practices Act, which prohibits corporate bribery in overseas projects. That law was passed, in a more innocent age, in response to public outrage over repeated scandals showing that U.S. companies were buying off foreign governments. Modern-day human abuses in the global system are far graver than business bribes.

Americans also can move to define what companies their city, state, and federal governments will do business with, and which ones should be penalized or boycotted because of unacceptable practices. In a recent case, the Supreme Court overruled a Massachusetts law that penalized companies doing business in Burma, on the narrow grounds that a U.S. federal law had preempted the state law. State and local laws might also be challenged under the WTO agreement; but a series of successful WTO challenges would only serve to further discredit the current trade regime.

A first round of legislation might focus on empowering people on the other end of the global system—workers, civic activists, and communities in developing nations—by providing them with information that will help them speak and act in their own behalf: hard data on where and how global corporations conduct their operations. Laws could be passed in the United States mandating that U.S.-based multinationals report regularly on the names and locations of their contractors, including basic information about wages, hours, and conditions. European and Japanese unions, activists, and parliamentarians should be challenged to require similar disclosures from their global companies.

This information would reveal which multinational companies are actively subverting shared human values, and which nations are trying to improve conditions for their people or are participating in their exploitation. The regular reporting of such information would set the stage for subsequent legislation establishing minimum standards for corporate behavior on environmental protection, labor issues, and human rights.

The reforms should begin with simple, basic measures that are compelling to the American public. Such measures also would help reassure developing nations that the purpose of the reforms is not to stymie industrial development in low-wage economies or to impose American norms on their societies. (Poorer countries are naturally skeptical of American motives, since they've had extensive experience with the destructive effects of U.S. involvement in their affairs.)

A good place to begin is with safe working conditions. In 1993, the worst industrial fire in the history of capitalism occurred at a mammoth toy factory outside Bangkok, in which 188 workers were killed and 469 were seriously injured. All but a handful were women, some as young as 13 years. They were assembling toys for American children—Sesame Street muppets, Bart Simpson dolls, and other popular items marketed under brands such as Fisher-Price, Hasbro, Tyco, and Kenner, and sold by retailers such as Wal-Mart and Toys R Us. The casualties were high because fire exits were blocked or inadequate. Doors were locked to prevent pilfering. Flammable materials were stacked randomly on the shop floors. Not even the most rudimentary precautions had been taken against a possible fire. Desperate women jumped from upper-story windows by the score, their clothes already ablaze. The fire's toll surpassed the U.S. calamity—the famous Triangle Shirtwaist Factory fire of 1911—but resembled it in haunting detail. But this was simply one of the many similar tragedies that continually occur in industrializing Asia.

There is no mystery about how to build and operate a safe industrial factory. Here is where Congress and/or activist state legislatures could start. Congress could enact a law that prohibits entry for any goods made in a factory that is not independently certified as employing standard fire-prevention design and equipment, targeting large industrial plants.

Businesses will enlist pliant foreign governments to protest that the legislation is intrusive, a violation of sovereignty, and a national affront. But the reality is that the United States and other nations already demand the right to inspect foreign production and to track the content and origin of imported goods before trade is permitted. For example, the Federal Aviation Administration (FAA) routinely inspects production of foreign-made components for U.S. airplanes, and certifies work done offshore at overseas repair centers. Few managers of global corporations would knowingly fly in planes not certified by the FAA.

The reform sounds basic, but it challenges the heart of the corporate globalization project—the virtual corporation that operates a far-flung network of suppliers and subcontractors with no fixed accountability. The companies disavow any responsibility for their foreign-owned subcontractors; moreover, they drive a system that forces those same contractors to cut corners recklessly as they compete for the next contract. If Thailand enforces its own fire codes too rigorously, the virtual corporation finds subcontractors someplace else, where workers are cheaper and officials more compliant. It is vital that we help set a floor of basic human values that this competition cannot lower.

A similar reform in the environmental area could be to require companies to provide hard, precise data on the environmental impact of their activities. Right-to-know legislation in the United States, which requires companies to disclose what wastes they are discharging into the community, unleashed a wave of grassroots activity helping to strengthen and enforce environmental standards. Requiring companies to issue environmental impact statements and to disclose toxic releases at overseas production facilities would stimulate a similar process abroad. The practice would not intrude on any country's pollution standards, but it would equip citizens to act in their own behalf and would make it much more likely that countries will enforce their own standards. As Daniel Seligman, head of the Sierra Club's responsible-trade campaign, argues: "This has nothing to do with eco-imperialism. It simply holds our own firms accountable to our values. It's not dictating the levels of pollution, but it's giving communities, not just governments, the information they need to decide their own destiny."[15] Seligman would combine laws on disclosure with the legal recognition of foreign citizens' right to sue U.S. companies for damages in U.S. courts. This approach would ensure that corporate pressure on the foreign government would not foreclose a remedy for citizens whose lives were endangered or communities poisoned.

Parallel legislation could be used to reinforce core labor standards, the basic norms that virtually every country in the world has endorsed. The ILO has begun a campaign to get companies to post core worker rights provisions in every factory, in the local languages. Congress could require firms to disclose basic information—the names and addresses of contractors, the number of workers in each factory, what they make, labor costs as a percentage of value added, number of workers organized, compliance with host country's labor laws, compliance with the ILO's core labor standards, and certification that those standards are widely posted in the native language on the factory walls. Again, private citizens and nongovernmental organizations might be given legal standing to sue for damages if the companies falsify their reports to the U.S. government.

The next step—although far down the road—would be to require what the Students Against Sweatshops have lobbied for: that companies attest that their workers are paid a "living wage," an income sufficient to provide for basic subsistence in local terms. Companies would have to compare the cost of a basket of basic goods—food, housing, clothing, health, and education—with the wages paid to their workers.

With the U.S. Congress dominated by a bipartisan conservative majority, and with corporate money and influence more powerful than ever, it is hard to imagine even laws as rudimentary as these being passed soon. But that need not keep legislators from introducing such bills, organizing hearings on them, calling executives to explain themselves, and airing the conditions that the bills are designed to correct. As Nike and other clothing manufacturers have discovered, the American people will demand a response to corporate behavior that violates basic values.

Even if Congress is stymied, states and localities can take the lead. When conservatives in Congress were still branding Nelson Mandela a terrorist, states and cities were launching a boycott of companies investing in South Africa. The resulting disinvestment campaign not only forced companies to move out of South Africa but also led a skeptical Congress to pass its own boycott over Ronald Reagan's veto.

The principle that taxpayers can decide how they want their money spent, and can apply to such decisions values other than lower cost, carries considerable political weight. The recent Supreme Court decision overturning a Massachusetts state sanction against U.S. corporations operating in Burma may serve as a legal precedent for further challenges from corporate entities.[16] But if many states and localities begin passing laws that require corporations to certify that they are in compliance with core labor standards at home and abroad as a condition of doing business with the particular state or locality, such legislation is likely to survive legal challenge—or to provoke congressional action.

SUBSIDIZE VALUE

Americans think it deplorable that companies shut down plants in the United States and move jobs to low-wage countries. Even less popular are subsidies and tax breaks that encourage the process. Yet the U.S. tax code and government subsidies continue to do just that.

Central to a new focus on the global corporation should be a systematic reexamination of U.S. obligations to multinationals, starting with the largest "global corporations" that rely on the United States and its taxpayers as a home base. According to recent reports, for example, General Electric has been convening meetings with its jet-engine suppliers, informing them bluntly that they must move to low-wage Mexico or sacrifice their long-standing supply contracts with GE. Why, then, should U.S. taxpayers provide this company financing via the Export/Import Bank, OPIC insurance, and a range of other subsidies?

Similarly, a study by the New Economy Information Service shows that U.S. foreign direct investment is increasingly flowing not to developing democracies but to countries that trample basic democratic and human rights. With China capturing a far greater share of U.S. investment than any other developing country, this finding probably isn't surprising. But even with China out of the calculus, U.S. investment in countries rated "not free" or "partially free" is rising faster than in democracies. The U.S. presumably should be encouraging companies to invest in democratic countries that protect the rights of labor and adhere to international treaties on the environment. Yet the greatest percentage of U.S. Export/Import Bank financing goes to companies doing business in China.[17]

Congress has routinely passed legislation that mandates the consideration of labor rights and environmental protection standards in countries seeking bank loans, subsidies, or preferences under U.S. trade laws. But the legislation has been more often ignored than respected.

Now is the time for Congress to review this legislation and to strengthen the mandates in the law, particularly for subsidies. There is no good reason to subsidize large multinationals whose basic strategy is moving production and jobs abroad. Nor is there any reason to favor companies that invest in dictatorial regimes rather than in democracies. U.S. subsidies—whether in the form of loan guarantees, financing, or insurance—should be predicated on behavior that involves more than the maximization of returns for shareholders. Americans should be subsidizing firms that respect core worker rights, adhere to basic environmental protections, and follow new reporting requirements. Similarly, we should be encouraging investment in countries that are democratic; that protect the right to organize, and the freedoms of speech and of religion; and that are good environmental citizens. We should be subsidizing a move to the high road, not the low road. Reforms that impose national and community obligations on companies will not halt the processes of integration or trade but will change the choices for company managers in positive ways. As standards are imposed, multinational managers will be forced to make different judgments about where they invest their capital and how they operate their businesses.

THE RECKONING

These reforms are all feasible and can reasonably be expected to garner broad public support. But they seem almost fanciful in Washington, which is so dominated by corporate ideology and money. When President Clinton joined Republican leaders in Congress in pressing for a grant of permanent normal trading status to China, the bipartisan deference to corporate interests was apparent.

But the debate over globalization is changing rapidly, for two reasons. First, rising popular opposition has succeeded in frustrating the corporate trade agenda—blocking fast-track trade authority for the president, delaying negotiations on the Free Trade Area for the Americas, and helping to delay the launch of a new global round of negotiations under the WTO. The pitched battle over trade with China was instructive. In the end, the corporate position triumphed. Legislators who supported it in both parties chose to stand with their donors against the vast majority of voters, who opposed the deal. A broad majority of Americans continue to express opposition to the corporate trade agenda, despite the relative prosperity of the U.S. economy, the relative optimism of Americans about their own economic situation, multimillion-dollar corporate public relations campaigns, and overwhelming support from the mainstream media and from the academy.

Instead of gloating after the China victory, more thoughtful globalists returned to the question of what measures are needed to win back public support or at least to lessen public opposition. Their attention fixed largely on the traditional call for greater unemployment benefits, education and training support, and transition subsidies for displaced workers—an agenda that still generates more ritual rhetoric than real action.

But the need to discuss *some* agenda reflected a general awareness of the extent of opposition to the current course. If opposition is this strong when the economy is good, what will happen when the economy slows?

Stopping corporate trade measures does not stop the process of globalization. At this point, rules are needed more to curb corporations and capital than to empower them. With China's accession to the WTO, the corporate community has achieved much of what it hoped for. Now, multilayered efforts to hold corporations accountable are important in order to increase the incentive for reform.

The second major reason why the debate is changing is not political but economic. The brightest analysts understand that the system is becoming more unstable. The Asian financial crisis was the worst since the Great Depression. Yet no significant reforms of the financial system followed. The resulting imbalances in the real economy—with the United States running a $400 billion trade deficit, giving other countries a chance to recover—are inherently unsustainable. Yet apart from a few cautionary words by Greenspan, no steps have been taken to correct the imbalances. The Clinton administration preferred to treat the deficit as a sign of U.S. economic strength rather than a harbinger of economic peril.

These huge trade deficits feed rising opposition at home, as factories shut down and good manufacturing jobs are lost, even when the economy is strong. At some point in the near future, foreign investors will own enough dollars and will have sufficient U.S. bonds and stocks in their portfolios. They'll begin to question the strength of the dollar and to doubt the relative profitability of large, new investments in the United States. As European companies undertake sweeping reorganization and consolidation for the single market, the continent is likely to attract more and more investment. The euro, once it establishes a track record, is likely to become a competitive reserve currency to the dollar. When that begins to happen, the dollar will begin to lose value, and the United States will likely begin to import inflation as well as goods. The Federal Reserve will move to raise interest rates, bolster the dollar, and slow the economy.

An abrupt flight of foreign capital from the United States would be devastating—particularly for export-led countries whose economies are geared toward producing for the U.S. market. But even if the transformation takes place gradually and smoothly (and no bookie would take odds on that), it will change the content of political debate in the United States. Trade deficits will be directly connected to rising unemployment and slowing growth. Public skepticism about trade—already high—will soar, and might well give way to a xenophobic protectionism.

At that time, the alternative posed by the progressive movement against corporate-led globalization will become more imperative. Labor rights, corporate accountability, greater space for poorer countries to determine their own destiny—these and other reforms involve more than simply a call for fairness. They also provide essential remedies to the instabilities and contradictions of the present system. The pursuit of common decency—what people around the world would recognize as justice—is not in conflict with economic self-interest; on the contrary, it contributes to it.

If the United States loses its ability to provide a market of last resort, the core contradiction of the global economy—overcapacity and inadequate demand—will become far more visible. Multinational competition leads companies to expand their productive capacity for export and to suppress internal demand. The Washington consensus and its trade regime reinforce this tendency. Labor rights; public investment and spending; limits on short-term speculation; and a focus on basic needs are reliable means of bolstering market demand; but all are scorned under the current rules.

Reforming the global economy will not be easy. Even the Asian crisis failed to usher in any notable reform. Yet the global mobilization that is challenging the current order continues to build. It has already begun to expose the WTO, IMF, and World Bank. It has forced developing countries to rethink their austerity regimes. It has created a more sober discussion about the speculative casino economy and its destabilizing effects.

What is needed now, as AFL-CIO President John Sweeney has said, is a "new internationalism" that puts rules around the global economy to ensure that its blessings are shared, its excesses are curbed, and its imperious dictates are limited. That will require new ideas, new institutions, and new politics. One thing is clear: The grand debate has begun. And its course will do much to determine the possibility for a more progressive politics in the coming decades.

NOTES

This chapter is drawn from various published articles by William Greider ("Global Agenda," *Nation* [January 21, 2000]; "Shopping Till We Drop," *Nation* [April 10, 2000]; and "Time to Rein in Global Finance" [April 24, 2000]) and by Robert Borosage ("On the Fast Track to Nowhere," *Washington Post* [September 21, 1997]; "For a New Progressive IMF," *Foreign Service Journal* [April 1998]; and "The Global Turning," *Nation* [July 16, 1999]).

1. For a good overview of this period, see Daniel Yergin and Joseph Stanislaw, *The Commanding Heights: The Battle Between Government and the Marketplace That Is Remaking the Modern World* (New York: Simon and Schuster, 1998).

2. Joseph E. Stiglitz, "Fairness and the Washington Consensus," Council on Foreign Relations lunch presentation (March 6, 2000).

3. John Cavanagh and Sarah Anderson, *Field Guide to the Global Economy* (New York: New Press, 1999): 68.

4. These figures come from the United Nations Development Program, *Human Development Report 1999* (New York: Oxford University Press, 1999).

5. For a review of this debate, see Robert Borosage, "The Global Turning," *Nation* (July 16, 1999).

6. Ibid.

7. William Greider, "Shopping Till We Drop," *Nation* (April 10, 2000).

8. Alan Greenspan, "The American Economy in a World Context," address (May 6, 1999).

9. See, for example, International Forum on Globalization, "An Emerging North-South Labor-Citizens Agenda of Global Finance"; and "Alternatives for the Ameri-

cas: Building A People's Hemispheric Agreement," excerpted in Cavanagh and Anderson, *Field Guide to the Global Economy*.

10. Joseph Stiglitz, "The Insider," *New Republic* (April 6, 2000).

11. For assessments of the tax proposal, see Mahbub ul Haq, Inge Kaul, and Isabelle Grunberg, eds., *The Tobin Tax: Coping with Financial Volatility* (New York: Oxford University Press, 1996).

12. International Labor Organization, *Global Report: Your Voice At Work* (Geneva: ILO, 2000).

13. Dani Rodrik, *The New Global Economy and Developing Countries: Making Openness Work* (Washington, D.C.: Overseas Development Council, 1999).

14. Amartya Sen, *Development as Freedom* (New York: Knopf, 1999).

15. Quoted in William Greider, "Global Agenda," *Nation* (January 21, 2000).

16. Supreme Court, *Crosby v. National Foreign Trade Council*, Slip Opinion (June 19, 2000).

17. David Jessup, *Dollars and Democracy: The Post–Cold War Decline in Developing Democracies' Share of Trade and Investment Markets* (Washington, D.C.: New Economy Information Service, 1999).

Part 2

RENEWING THE
SOCIAL CONTRACT

3

WORKING FAMILIES: THE CENTERPIECE FOR REFORM

Theda Skocpol

During the summers, my family lives in Maine, where my son attends a day camp with other children from a broad cross-section of the community. At events for the kids, parents naturally fall to talking. I vividly remember one conversation I had with another mother there during the summer of 1994. It was August, and yearlong national and Congressional debates over comprehensive health care reform were coming to a climax. On the nightly news, President Clinton and Congressional Democratic leaders were still talking as if something major might pass before Congress recessed in September. As the children enjoyed ice cream and games, I sat on a picnic table and chatted with Annemarie McAndrew, the mother of Jeffrey, a friend of my son Michael.[1] This was the first time I had met Annemarie. She usually couldn't come to Jeffrey's day camp, because—as she now explained—she worked a long shift as a health aide at a nursing home in a neighboring town. As we talked, Annemarie told me about a recent emergency when they had had to rush Jeffrey in an ambulance to the hospital. She was still trying to pay that off. She didn't have health insurance at her job, and Maine's bare-bones public coverage for the kids would not cover an ambulance or any other "extras."

Wishing to say something positive and encouraging, I mentioned the Clinton administration's plan to guarantee "health care that's always there" for all Americans. "Maybe something will soon happen in Washington to help out with the health care," I offered, explaining just a bit about Clinton's Health Security proposal and the maneuvering around it. Annemarie listened politely and responded in a kindly tone, yet unmistakably looked at me as if I had just arrived from the moon. "Nothing they do there"—meaning Washington, D.C.—"ever makes any difference for people like me," she replied, putting a firm end to that phase of our conversation.

Annemarie was right, of course. Within weeks, the great 1993–1994 debate over universal health care had fizzled, succumbing to congressional inertia. Afterward, its sponsor, President Clinton, kept silent about the enormous loss that he—and the Annemaries of America—had suffered due to this congressional inaction. And Clinton never again took up the fight for universal health coverage. When Congress finally got around to enacting piecemeal reforms during 1995 and 1997—tiny steps, presented as huge breakthroughs—it did not extend health insurance to low-income workers like Annemarie. Other, more recent changes might help her children, but probably only partially and only if Annemarie is prepared to handle a lot of bureaucratic maneuvering and paperwork. Congressionally enacted "health reforms" applicable to adults have been regulations helpful to people who can afford to pay private insurance premiums or are covered by employer-provided insurance. Meanwhile, the ranks of the uninsured, crowded with Americans who work for modest wages, and their children, continue to grow inexorably by about a million each year.[2]

In the new century, Americans of goodwill need to transform civic life and politics so that people like Annemarie McAndrew and her children are at the center of the nation's systems of social support, not on the margins. It does no good to extend health care and a smattering of other benefits to some of the children of adults who work for modest wages, leaving the parents themselves out in the cold. Adapting to politics-as-usual, which is increasingly inhospitable to major new initiatives, many liberals have concluded that helping children is the best we can do. But ignoring working adults—above all, working parents—is ethically obtuse and politically dumb. This approach will not build the moral and political foundations to make the changes America really needs.

How can American politics be recentered to reach working families of modest means? It won't happen simply because policy intellectuals outline technically detailed proposals. And it won't happen through marginal bipartisan adjustments among dominant stakeholders in Washington—not given the realities of contemporary electoral politics and top-down advocacy politics. In electoral politics and beyond, there must be a new popular mobilization by and for ordinary American families. Working parents should be at the center of this mobilization, although they cannot be—and should not be—the only ones involved. The entire country has a stake in better support for working parents.

BUILDING A FAMILY-FRIENDLY AMERICA

Experts and civically active groups have already suggested many ways to sustain and improve America's existing social insurance programs while enhancing supports for working families. Too often, though, policy proposals are discussed as technical plans in isolation from one another. If promising ideas are to become more than rhetorical gestures in election-year speeches, they must be connected to an overarching agenda and strategy. Americans will be much more likely to support specific steps if they understand how each measure contributes to a society where all working men and women can support their families, contribute to the nation, and enhance opportunities for their children.

The Best Defense Is a Good Offense

Conservatives are campaigning to cut back and break up America's largest inherited social insurance programs, Social Security and Medicare. Throughout the 1980s and 1990s, antigovernment Republicans and market-oriented advocacy groups have taken advantage of new demographic and fiscal circumstances to provoke public anxiety about the expense and long-term viability of both of these federal programs. The generational imbalances that became so apparent in U.S. social provision after the 1960s allowed critics to argue that payroll taxes and "entitlement spending" for the elderly were "unfair" to the young. In the face of rising health care costs and an expanding elderly population, cuts in Medicare spending were used in 1995 and 1996 to help balance the federal budget. Now many Republicans and conservative Democrats advocate the elimination of Medicare's guaranteed benefits to the elderly on terms that would allow private insurers to lure the healthiest and wealthiest retirees away from broad insurance pools.[3] Meanwhile, critics of social insurance use the booming stock market to argue for individualistic alternatives to Social Security, suggesting that younger Americans can do better by investing (all or a portion of) payroll taxes in personal accounts managed by Wall Street brokers.

Preoccupied with battles about welfare, universal health insurance, and aid to poor children, progressive supporters of public social provision in the United States were slow to realize that Social Security and Medicare were in political danger. Finally, at the eleventh hour, as some Clinton administration planners showed signs of embracing the partial diversion of Social Security payroll taxes into individual investment accounts, progressives woke up and began to argue and mobilize on behalf of shared Social Security. Supported by liberal think tanks and advocacy groups, the feisty AFL-CIO led the way during 1998, pressuring elected officials and waging a broad campaign of popular education to remind union members—and many other Americans as well—why Social Security is both morally legitimate and vital to the material well-being of most retirees. This argument fell on fertile ground because privatization schemes are potentially very costly to taxpayers and beneficiaries, and the vast majority of Americans have a strong stake in Social Security's dignified, guaranteed, and slightly redistributive promised benefits.

Pushed by the newly aroused defenders of Social Security, President Clinton decided to endorse shared approaches to reform in his January 1999 State of the Union message. Supporters of social insurance breathed a nationally audible sigh of relief when the president called for "saving Social Security and Medicare" and advocated devoting most projected future federal surpluses to shoring up the finances of these programs.

But supporters of broad and inclusive social provision cannot afford to relax, because conservatives will continue their efforts to dismantle Medicare and privatize Social Security. The best defense of the core principles and shared revenue pools of Social Security and Medicare may require a good offense, not just an attempt to preserve the status quo. Because there really are marked generational imbalances in U.S. social provision, many needs of working-age Americans and their children remain unmet. As conservatives press to dismantle shared insurance for the elderly, the best response may be to increase the stake of people of all ages—and generations—in national social programs. The art of politics lies in designing proposals in such a way as to build broad political alliances.

One way to turn Social Security into a "generational alliance," as economist Barry Bluestone has put it, involves using current surpluses to finance improved education and training for American workers, including parents who seek to improve skills while caring for children.[4] Although the Social Security Trust Fund—the accounting of accumulated payroll taxes—will eventually have more charges against it than credits, it will remain in surplus for a couple more decades. In the meantime, the Trust Fund could finance GI Bill–style loans to post–high school students and working adults who need retraining to keep up with today's fast-shifting labor-market opportunities. The possibility of combining training with part-time parenting could be included in the loan program. As Bluestone has outlined in detail, training loans could boost the career prospects and incomes of many younger Americans, who could then repay the loans from their future earnings. Calibrated to each individual's wages over several decades following the use of the loan, the debts to the Social Security Trust Fund could be collected through automatic payroll deductions—just as Social Security taxes are—thus minimizing defaults. To create a win-win situation both for working-age adults and the nation's Social Security system, rates of repayment could be set to slightly more than replenish the funds (with interest) originally borrowed from the Social Security Trust Fund.

All generations would gain under such a system. Younger adults would enhance their earning power. The nation would benefit at once from better-trained workers and parents in a stronger position to provide for children. And over time, the Social Security Trust Fund would grow, as loans are repaid and the national economy grows faster. The social and political logic of this way of reforming Social Security for the future makes even better sense than using projected federal tax surpluses to reduce the national debt and issue IOUs to the Social Security Trust Fund. The United States does not really need to reduce its national debt to zero; it can readily afford to run modest deficits in the future. If funds eventually needed for Social Security are used to boost the skills and earning power of younger families, this raises new revenues for the future and allows current payroll taxes to do "double duty," increasing the stake all Americans have in the shared system of social insurance.

Another possibility for building a cross-generational alliance involves extending social insurance to single parents who work. When the Social Security system was first conceived during the New Deal, it was meant to address the chief "risks" of severe income loss that families might face over the course of a lifetime. Half a century later, however, important new risks are not addressed through social supports. Single-parent families, we have learned, are both more prevalent than ever before and highly pressured for time and money. These days many mothers (and quite a few fathers) end up combining family breadwinning with the nurture of children. Yet the U.S. legal system and social policies still treat single parenthood as if it were a freak occurrence. The burden is placed on the custodial parent, usually the mother. Especially if a woman with less than a college education is a single, working parent, she may not be able to earn a market income much above the poverty line, even if she works full-time. Furthermore, even middle-class single mothers often cannot work full-time while adequately caring for young children or managing the after-school activities of older offspring. Not just for economic reasons, but also because all of us want an orderly and participatory society—one where all single parents can supervise children and make it to soccer games—the nation as a whole has a very strong stake in improving the conditions faced by single-parent families.

Some years ago, policy experts proposed a cogent extension of Social Security to make a big difference for single, working parents at all income levels. The United States could institute a national system of Child Support Assurance.[5] Under this plan, either the Internal Revenue Service or the Social Security system would automatically deduct a set percentage of the wages of an absent parent (a percentage calibrated to the number of children requiring support) and deliver most of the money on a predictable and dignified monthly basis to the custodial parent. Because this would be an automatic step, care-giving parents would not be forced to go again and again to court or to a private collection agency to update awards and actually collect them. And noncustodial parents would face a more predictable and equitable system. Under a system of Child Support Assurance, America would be saying to all parents: You must contribute to the support of your children, and both care-giving and wage earning count. In return for contributing time, energy, and love on a daily basis, the custodial parent would receive some extra income beyond what she (or he) earns in the marketplace.

In an effective Child Support Assurance system, the burden of collection must be on the national government, which can use the payroll tax system and readily track absent parents across state lines using their Social Security numbers. What is more, the ideal Child Support Assurance system should include a fixed minimum benefit, set at about the level of a half-time, minimum-wage job. Funded out of general federal revenues as well as with small payroll deductions collected from noncustodial parents, minimum payments would go to custodial parents in cases where the noncustodial parents cannot be found or earn insufficient income (for example, unemployed or imprisoned men). No care-giving parent could actually live on this minimum assured benefit; it would not be "welfare." But he or she could use the minimum benefit to enhance income from a job—or else to cut back a bit on working hours, in order to be at home with children at important times of the day, such as after school.

Child Support Assurance would make life more secure and dignified for millions of American families, and thus for all of us indirectly. Both middle-class and low-income single mothers would be huge winners, giving millions more nonelderly Americans a stronger stake in social insurance. Yet this addition to Social Security could be created with little additional cost to the public fisc. True, a fraction of federal revenues would be committed to fund the minimum benefit at a reasonable level. But most of the revenues for child-support payments would come from automatic payroll deductions collected from noncustodial parents. The nation would gain a great deal for many vulnerable families, at very little new cost.

There are, in short, a number of obvious ways to make Social Security, broadly conceived, do more than it has in the past. Extensions of the national systems of social security to fund training and help solo working parents would make economic and fiscal as well as social sense. Beyond the ideas discussed here, there may be other ways to extend Social Security as it is reformed. The policy specifics are less important than the principles: to look for ways to build cross-generational and cross-class alliances through shared, rather than fragmented, systems of social support for all working families; to provide new protections to citizens who are serving the nation as workers and parents; and to find ways to generate additional revenues through economic growth and returns on investments, even as new protections are extended to younger Americans.

The Real Health Care Crisis

So far, I have focused on Social Security and related ways to enhance transfers through the payroll tax system; but the situation is more complicated with regard to Medicare and Medicaid. Strains on the U.S. system of health insurance for the retired elderly coexist with the continuing inadequacy of the national system to cover health care costs for working-age parents and their children. Adults who work in low-wage or part-time jobs or those who are self-employed often go without any health insurance. And this situation is likely to get worse, not better, as employers switch to part-time jobs and cut back the coverage they are willing to offer current employees and their family members. Another vulnerable group is employees in their late fifties and early sixties who retire or lose jobs before they have Medicare eligibility. Many employers will not cover early retirees; surviving spouses also can be left uncovered; and older workers who lose jobs often cannot find new ones with full health insurance coverage. And Medicare recipients themselves often struggle with expenses for prescription drugs or long-term care that are not covered by existing benefits.

Progressives should press for improvements in Medicare benefits and should look for ways to allow more and more categories of Americans— or their employers—to participate in the system. Suggestions for extending rather than dismantling Medicare may sound unrealistic in a climate of expert opinion that seems to be calling for abandonment of Medicare's guarantees in favor of subsidies to privately funded, managed care schemes. But the American citizenry may not buy the pundits' proposals. Americans of all ages are worried about the steady march of managed care plans, and they may not take readily to the idea of subjecting the elderly to travails about care and insurance coverage that the young already know all too well.

Employers have shifted most covered employees into managed care systems, aspiring to save money on health care; yet managed care plans often cannot cut costs much, unless they restrict options for doctors and patients. Such steps are bound to be controversial in a society with an aging population and high expectations about health care. We already see cascading demands to regulate managed care systems, to enhance choices for patients and the clinical freedom of doctors. As new regulations are put in place, managed care plans will have trouble saving money; and many will abandon sick or vulnerable patient populations, as they already are doing. Over time, a reformed and expanded system of Medicare for all citizens may look better and better to a majority of Americans—and not just for the elderly.

Support for All Working Families

Saving Social Security and Medicare, no matter how creatively, will not suffice to fill the glaring gaps in American social policy. Now is a propitious moment to move on to new frontiers. Not only has the budgetary future brightened; for better as well as for worse, "welfare" as we knew it prior to 1996 has been transformed. Major policy wars of the last generation can be declared over. With old battles behind us, we Americans can replace welfare assistance targeted on just a fraction of the very poor with enhanced social supports for all working families. Many new supports must be devised at the level of local communities, above all in conjunction with schools, churches, and community centers where parents and children routinely congregate. Beyond these, however, there must be new national initiatives, because only the federal government can enforce new rules for the market economy.

One of the greatest social scandals in late-twentieth-century America is the fate of men and women, including millions of fathers and mothers, who work daily and weekly at poorly paid full- and part-time jobs but get such paltry wages that they find it virtually impossible to sustain their families. The same workers often do not enjoy other benefits vital for families as well as individual workers—such as health insurance, employer contributions to pensions, and the right to take paid time off from work during family emergencies.

Despite the 1996 increase successfully championed by Democrats, America's minimum wage has lost much of its real value in recent decades. Americans concerned with social equity and family well-being should push for repeated increases; and next time, it might be possible to pass a minimum-wage increase that includes employer contributions to health insurance as well as a hike in take-home pay. Public support for raising the minimum wage, and general public support for the idea of asking all employers to contribute to health care, could be mobilized to move forward on two vital fronts for American working families. Although employer-financed health insurance is not the best option for the United States in the long run, the sooner all employers are required to pitch in, the easier it will become to move to a more unified system.

Enhanced social benefits available to middle- and low-income workers are also crucial for building a family-friendly America. Along with health insurance coverage, two other priorities are universal access to paid family leaves and affordable child care for working parents. The moral argument for these steps is clear-cut: Working mothers and fathers contribute to national well-being, not only as wage earners and taxpayers but also by bringing up children. They and their offspring deserve material support from the broader community to help meet today's challenges of combining work and family duties. Health care for all family members, time for family needs, and good child care choices are all acutely needed by working families. Good policies can be designed to express broadly shared American values and promote solidarity across income levels and between single-parent and two-parent working families.

To help all American employees spend time with newborns and respond to emergencies in the care of young and old dependents, the 1993 Family and Medical Leave Act offers a starting place. But the "right" to take time off without losing one's job needs to be made a practicable option for all workers and extended to all employees no matter what the size of the firm. Rights that apply disproportionately to privileged employees are not sufficient—certainly not the place to stop on the road to a family-friendly America. Realistically, making family leave a true right for American workers requires money. A combination of employer contributions and general tax revenues should be marshaled to cover the cost of paid family leaves. This could be done on a sliding scale for employers and employees alike: Smaller employers could receive more generous tax subsidies to cover family leaves; and the replacement of employee wages could be calibrated to give more to workers who earn modest wages, and less (but still some) to the highest-salaried employees who go on leave.

Family-friendly reforms should place a priority on ensuring supports for part-time as well as full-time (or overtime) workers. If part-time jobs had to include partial contributions to health insurance and pension benefits, employers would have less incentive to divide their workforces between full-time workers pressed to put in overtime and part-timers who go without benefits. That would help to ensure enough full-time jobs for all Americans who want to work. But at the same time, part-time jobs with pro-rated social benefits would help many working parents who try to sustain themselves and their children through a combination of various part-time jobs.

As more mothers engage in paid employment, long-term access to child care is a necessity for many solo-parent and two-worker-parent households. The need for solutions outside of family homes will become greater as women participate more and more fully in the labor force and stay-at-home grandmothers fade from the scene. Yet, today, quality child care options are often not available; and families who take home low or modest wages find the cost of even mediocre child care prohibitive. As economist Barbara Bergmann has spelled out in detail, a national system of subsidized child care for all working parents who need it would be a very effective antipoverty measure, although a costly one.[6] Such a system would also be a good investment in family well-being and early childhood education, with obvious payoffs for economic growth in the future.

Regulations and social benefits along the lines I have just covered will, of course, provoke strong opposition from conservatives—who claim that any "interference" with "free markets" is bad for economic growth. But a strong case can be made that exactly the opposite is true: Capitalism works best when wise regulations and public expenditures buffer its rough edges. This is especially the case when it comes to providing for family well-being. No economy, capitalist or otherwise, can long flourish if families cannot do their job of caring for the vulnerable and raising the young. The growing market economy in the United States is the underpinning of a decent life for most individuals and families, and we can be happy and proud that the economy has done so well in the 1990s. But it is a myth that vibrant market capitalism and adequate social supports for working families cannot go hand in hand. They can. In fact, America's economy will likely flourish in the new century only if we find optimal ways to spread the wealth and allow all families to raise healthy, well-educated, and well-supervised children; for those children are tomorrow's workers, consumers, and citizens.

American enterprises have done much to boost productivity and adjust to more competitive international markets. But competitive markets and agile enterprises do not automatically take account of the needs of families and communities. Public regulations are always needed to channel market forces in socially beneficial ways.[7] Yet America's economic regulations are outdated as well as incomplete. Indeed, they are so outdated that they often undermine market efficiency as such. Today we no longer have an economy centered around the father-breadwinner who goes off to work at a full-time, well-paid, lifetime job, leaving behind a mother to care for the home and family. Instead, single-parent or two-worker families are prevalent. Part-time jobs, or combinations of them, are often the jobs available to working parents. Employees may need to change jobs, or at least skills, several times during their work careers. Employers want flexible and adaptable skilled employees. Computers make work at home possible for many.

Some enterprises are already adapting to these changes; but the public rules of the game for the economy do not usually ensure that adaptations will be fair to less-privileged employees or will take adequate account of social and family needs. Better public policies—including health care and child care available to all citizens, and rules that part-time jobs should carry at least pro-rated benefits—would actually make the economy more efficient for employers as well as more equitable for employees at all wage levels. Working parents, above all, have a stake in such reforms because they do not have the flexibility that other adults may have to switch jobs or scrimp on services such as health care.

Adjusting the employment system to new family realities should be America's top social priority, especially given welfare reforms that are pushing millions more single mothers into the low-wage labor force. In a period of national economic growth, and at a time when all adults and parents are asked to make their way through paid employment, we in America should be asking: What kinds of employment conditions and public supports are needed to make it possible for all working parents to do their dual job? We should take strong steps to make sure that not just the highest-paid employees but all workers can sustain their families.

A Nation of Contributors

Ultimately, progressives must pursue a robust ideal: Because parents need time as well as money, the United States should work toward the norm of a thirty-five-hour workweek—with pay and benefits remaining at least at the levels they were at before the reduction in hours. However, this goal should not become a priority until after incomes and benefits are bolstered for low-wage working families. Work must pay, and it must be feasible in combination with single or dual parenthood, before we can consider a reduced national workweek. Otherwise, workweek reductions might redound to the benefit of skilled, higher-wage employees, leaving low-wage workers and their families in more desperate straits than ever.

This conclusion follows from the norms that have underpinned successful social policy making throughout American history. Americans favor broad social programs that reward individuals for their "contributions" to the community. In the past, "contributions" have been variously defined to include military service and motherhood as well as wage work. But at the turn of the twenty-first century, participation in the wage-employment system is universally understood as desirable for all adults, men and women, mothers and fathers alike. We can do much to reinforce social understanding that parental work is also valuable for the community. But Americans cannot be convinced that parental work, apart from at least part-time, paid employment, is socially honorable. Americans should strengthen and buffer the nexus between wage work and family. In our time, revitalizing the long tradition of inclusive U.S. social policy means focusing on the contributions and well-being of working parents, who are also expected to be involved citizens.

Together, the undertakings I have suggested would amount to a revitalization and extension of broad, shared social supports. Instead of allowing conservatives to dismantle shared social protections for the elderly in the name of righting the balance for working-age adults and their children, America can extend social supports to include younger families—especially the families of modest means who are currently left beyond the reach of many publicly funded or employment-linked benefits.

WILL AMERICANS SUPPORT IT?

The call to reconfigure social supports to build a family-friendly America amounts to a moral vision, not just a laundry list of legislative prescriptions. This runs against the grain of politics today, because our national conversations seem increasingly dominated by policy wonks and economists mired in technical details, or by media people focusing on short-term personal maneuvers and scandals. However, from the 1960s through the 1980s, conservatives in America showed that a politics of broad social mobilization around clearly articulated values, not just narrow policy prescriptions, could move the center of national debate and reshape the landscape of politics. Now it is time for Americans who believe government has a pivotal role to play in building a just society to undertake a similarly bold and visionary strategy. A family-oriented populism focused especially on working parents can revitalize the tradition of successful social policy making in American democracy—generating civic dividends in the process.

Pursuit of supports for working families can strengthen Americans' sense of community—not just in particular localities, but also across lines of class and race. To transcend the racial conflicts that have so divided and weakened the nation since the 1960s, supporters of social provision can combine continuing efforts to carve out new opportunities for African Americans with pursuit of social programs relevant to Americans of all ethnic and racial groups. A family-oriented strategy does both of these things. Supports for working families are especially vital for African

Americans, who often find themselves in a tighter economic and family squeeze than other Americans. Yet Americans of all ethnic and racial groups also need economic redress and social support. Shared programs will do the most for the severely disadvantaged as well as significantly help middle-class Americans.[8]

A family-oriented politics does not depend on everyone being a parent or on all families being alike. The issue is not sheer numbers of potential voters counted up as isolated individuals. Not every American adult is a parent; in fact, there are more U.S. adults living alone and proportionately fewer families with children than ever before. But sheer demography has never been destiny for social policy in the United States. Perceived contributions to the community matter more, as do possibilities for cross-class ties. Issues of parental responsibility and social support for parents can become a sympathetic focus for almost all citizens.

Consider retirees, for example. They may not be active parents right now; but most are grandparents who care about their children and grandchildren. Elders also understand the nation's and their own stake in productive workers. It is an odd feature of U.S. politics today that so many pundits are declaring "generational warfare" just as the country faces the prospect of more elders but fewer dependent children per adult worker. If work and family can be made to mesh more smoothly—helping adults to become optimally productive even as they are engaged and effective parents—then retirees, working-age adults, and children will all do well together. An aging society is not at all a zero-sum game.

Because support for families and working parents holds out the prospect of broad electoral appeal and alliance building, this strategy may hold the key to revitalizing and broadening a progressive Democratic Party. Women voters often favor politicians, mostly Democrats, who favor social supports for families. Yet such measures need not alienate most men, because they include steps to improve wage and benefit conditions vital to husbands and fathers. A vision built around the well-being of families is also likely to prove very appealing to Hispanic voters, who represent a vital new voting bloc for Democrats. This approach should help mobilize cross-racial support in the South as well.

A morally grounded appeal to shared concerns does better in American politics than any explicit call for class-based mobilization. The needs of less-privileged Americans must be made central to reconfigured social supports, but I disagree with the few on the left who are calling for an exclusively working-class-oriented populism. It is not just that there are too few unionized employees in late-twentieth-century America. There certainly are too few; and unions need to be supported and strengthened by everyone who professes concern for a vital civil society. But even if unions were to regain the economic and electoral leverage they enjoyed back in the 1950s—when more than a third of U.S. workers were unionized, as opposed to less than a seventh now—exclusively class-oriented politics would not suffice to remake American social provision. A popular politics featuring a vision of solidarity and security for all families can resonate with a revitalized labor movement and at the same time facilitate broader coalitions and ties between middle-class and downscale Americans. This kind of politics can also engage the energies of religious leaders and congregations, who can do more than any other force in American civic life to articulate why, as the U.S. Catholic Bishops so eloquently put it: "All economic life should be judged by moral principles. Economic choices and institutions must be judged by how they protect or undermine the life and dignity of the human person, support the family, and serve the common good."[9]

ORGANIZING FOR DEMOCRATIC CHANGE

American social politics will not change simply because people write essays. And it is equally clear that politics-as-usual is unlikely to allow working families much leverage in public policy making. Sure, political consultants may advise candidates to talk about "American families" during campaigns or in televised speeches. But when it comes to the legislative nitty-gritty, close attention is likely to be paid to what the best-organized and monied interests are saying, or to what the most prominent "experts" propose. Being realistic about getting legislation through Congress will, in the minds of many, dictate sacrificing the interests and values of ordinary working families—especially when budgets remain tight and it is taken for granted that taxes must be cut or left unchanged.

A new vision can help inspire the popular support to change this status quo, but people must also be organized—reconnected to ongoing civic and party activities as Margaret Weir and Marshall Ganz have explained in their brilliant essay "Reconnecting People and Politics."[10] At least two processes of popular mobilization and reorganization of politics need to proceed hand in hand, if American democracy is to reach for the missing middle. One process is frankly partisan, rebuilding the Democratic Party from the bottom up. The other should cross partisan lines, connecting centers of family activity across communities and states into a nationwide civic association of, by, and for the vast majority of America's families.

The Democratic Party for Real

At one time, for better and worse, the Democratic Party was grounded in a series of local and state political machines. There were disadvantages and social inequities in this situation. Party platforms and nominations tended to be brokered in those famous smoke-filled rooms, to which only loyal cadres were admitted. In most communities, African Americans and other minorities either had no place in the party bargains or else were expected to take minor rewards in return for faithfully turning out to vote. Women were expected to stuff envelopes and provide a symbolic presence, not to shape insider bargains.

But at least there was a "there" in the old-time Democratic Party. There were people and headquarters you could go to, to ask for something, to join in discussions, or to work on getting out the vote. There were activists who went out and contacted fellow citizens and asked them to vote or volunteer. Today the Democratic Party amounts to little more than a series of mass mailings and centers for collecting checks. Every month or so, I get a letter from some Democratic Party office: a long, canned statement, hopelessly bland, accompanied by a fake questionnaire, a tear-out wallet "membership card," and—of course, the real point—a return card and envelope for me to use when I send the big check. The party tells me, in the form letter, that it wants my opinions. But it really just wants my money so it can pay pollsters and consultants. In turn, party officials, or consultants hired by the party, tell individual candidates how to word their media messages and speeches to attract particular sets of swing voters, and after the election, how to phrase their messages explaining votes or "policy achievements." The consultants pretty much *are* the Democratic Party. In most communities and states, there are few opportunities for regular Democrats to talk with one another, or to talk back to the consultants and candidates. The people who talk to one another are the consultants.

There are organized groups surrounding the Democratic Party, and some, like the revitalized AFL-CIO under John Sweeney, have significant popular roots. So do groups in the environmental movement and the National Organization for Women, which includes local chapters. But most Democratic-leaning advocacy groups are little more than mass-mailing and check-collecting operations. Centered in New York or Washington, staff professionals decide what issues to raise with government and political candidates. In such advocacy groups, as in today's political parties, there is little opportunity for regular, two-way, face-to-face conversations with groups of citizens.

A new network of progressive Democratic groups needs to be knit together—a real counterweight to the Democratic Leadership Council—and not just centered in Washington, D.C. Progressive Democrats certainly need national centers of publication, communication, research, and advocacy. To a considerable degree these already exist: The *American Prospect* and *Washington Monthly* are Democratic-leaning magazines. The Economic Policy Institute, the Institute for Women's Policy Research, and the Center on Budget and Policy Priorities are Democratic-leaning research centers of the highest order. And the Campaign for America's Future is an energetic, populist, Democratic advocacy group. In addition to these central institutions, though, progressive Democrats should foster a self-conscious network of people who consider themselves Democrats or party sympathizers and who get together regularly for fun and discussion. Over time, such groups can help shape platforms, select and support candidates, and highlight issues in the larger community.

What is more—and this is the tricky part—any such network of progressive Democrats needs to be grounded in, and in regular touch with, ongoing social settings where individuals and families of modest means go about their daily activities. Otherwise, these groups could devolve into sets of issue activists. A way must be found to deepen activism within the Democratic Party—an activism that is in touch with cultural common sense and with the economic experiences of less-privileged Americans.

Families Associated

Progressive Democrats should mobilize and organize; but the middle cannot be revitalized through partisan activation alone. There must also be a renewal of associational activities centered on membership groups of actual working parents who get together regularly to deal with family issues. Throughout most of American history until the 1970s, huge, vital, voluntary associations linked membership lodges or clubs in thousands of local communities into federated organizations that had real presence, and recurrent meetings, in each state and at the national level.[11] The Patrons of Husbandry, or Grange, did this for millions of American farm families. Fraternal groups and veterans' associations and their ladies' auxiliaries did this for most working- and middle-class American men and their wives. Similar local and translocal ties developed among women involved in church-related associations: the Woman's Christian Temperance Union, the National Congress of Mothers (which became the National Congress of Parents and Teachers, or PTA, in 1924), and the General Federation of Women's Clubs. Some such popularly rooted voluntary associations still exist in the United States, but almost all have lost much of their membership and clout since the 1960s. Today's biggest association is the American Association of Retired Persons (AARP), which largely recruits and communicates with members through the mail.

Various people these days are thinking of trying to build a nationwide movement or association of parents. The National Parenting Association, for instance, is talking about establishing an "AARP for parents."[12] A new association may make sense, but the AARP may not be an ideal model. Parents are busy people, and none more so than working moms and dads in single-parent or two-worker families. So to engage them means to build from occasions, places, and networks in which they are already involved with one another—especially because of the need to do things with and for their children. Ways should be found to build—and extensively interconnect—actual groups of parents involved with day-care centers, church groups, after-school activities, sports activities, and support groups for parents of young children and caretakers of the elderly. A new family movement in America needs newsletters, meetings, a real identity—complete with symbols and logos—as well as discounts and information of the sort that the AARP provides; but it would be better to build from local communities outward, and to rely much more than does the AARP on membership participation and dues. A new family movement should build on existing connections and institutions, so that it will be rooted in actual relationships among ordinary citizens. Parent-members must actually control the movement.

Given the way in which civic organization now happens in America, it will be challenging to create a broad movement rather than many cause- or identity-specific organizations. We need a Movement for America's Families, not an organization of Hispanic families plus an organization of elder caregivers, plus an organization of parents of difficult teenagers, and so on. Around a central association there can and should be more specific efforts; but the sum must be bigger and more central than the parts.

Americans who care about recentering civic and political life must, in short, pursue strategies that look further ahead than the usual Washington time-horizon of the day after tomorrow. Supporters of a more equitable society and stronger social supports for families must frankly proclaim their moral vision, linking it to specific proposals. They must organize inside and outside the electoral system, pushing politicians and other institutional leaders toward a bolder stand on behalf of all working parents and their children, even as broad segments of the American public are brought together for action and discussion about the needs of communities and families.

NOTES

This chapter is adapted from chapter 5 of Theda Skocpol, *The Missing Middle: Working Families and the Future of American Social Policy*, a Century Foundation Book (New York: W. W. Norton, 2000).

1. I have changed the names of my son's friend and his mother.

2. Robert Pear, "Government Lags in Steps to Widen Health Coverage," *New York Times* (August 9, 1998): 1, 22.

3. This is carefully explained in Kip Sullivan, "Bad Prescription: Why Privatizing Medicare May Be Hazardous to Your Health," *Washington Monthly* 31(3) (March 1999): 27–32.

4. The original version of this plan is spelled out in Barry Bluestone, Alan Clayton-Matthews, John Havens, and Howard Young, "Generational Alliance: Social Security as a Bank for Education and Training," *American Prospect* 2 (summer 1990): 15–29.

5. Irwin Garfinkel, *Assuring Child Support: An Extension of Social Security* (New York: Russell Sage Foundation, 1992).

6. Barbara R. Bergmann, "Child Care: The Key to Ending Child Poverty," pp. 112–135 in *Social Policies for Children*, eds. Irwin Garfinkel, Jennifer L. Hochschild, and Sara S. McLanahan (Washington, D.C.: Brookings Institution Press, 1996).

7. Richard B. Freeman, ed., *Working Under Different Rules* (New York: Russell Sage Foundation, 1994).

8. On this point, see William Julius Wilson, *The Bridge Over the Racial Divide: Rising Inequality and Coalition Politics* (Berkeley and Los Angeles: University of California Press, 1999).

9. *Tenth Anniversary Edition of Economic Justice for All: Pastoral Letter on Catholic Social Teaching and the U.S. Economy* (Washington, D.C.: United States Catholic Conference, 1997): 1.

10. Margaret Weir and Marshall Ganz, "Reconnecting People and Politics," pp. 149–171 in *The New Majority: Toward a Popular Progressive Politics*, eds. Stanley B. Greenberg and Theda Skocpol (New Haven: Yale University Press, 1997).

11. For a full discussion, see Theda Skocpol, "How Americans Became Civic," in *Civic Engagement in American Democracy*, eds. Theda Skocpol and Morris Fiorina (Washington, D.C.: Brookings Institution Press; and New York: Russell Sage Foundation, 1999). Changes in U.S. civic life since the 1960s are discussed in Theda Skocpol, "Advocates Without Members," another chapter in the same book.

12. Sylvia Hewlett and Cornel West, *The War Against Parents* (Boston: Houghton Mifflin, 1998), pt. 4.

4

THE PATH TO
UNIVERSAL HEALTH CARE

Jonathan Oberlander and Theodore R. Marmor

Health care reform returned to the American political agenda in 1999, when the media once again were filled with stories documenting the numerous ills of American medicine: the growing ranks of the uninsured, the rising costs of treatment, and the deep-seated dissatisfaction of many physicians and patients with the quality of medical care and the health insurance constraints under which it is available.

Such stories have become familiar; similar indictments of American medicine dominated the media also during the first half of the 1990s. The enactment of national health insurance seemed, if only for a fleeting moment, imminent when Bill Clinton won the presidency in 1992. For the first time since Harry Truman, a president came to the White House having campaigned on a platform including national health insurance as a domestic priority. And President Clinton's chances of succeeding seemed far better than Truman's. Certainly, the strength of the "negative consensus"[1] in American public opinion—that system-wide, comprehensive reform was necessary—was both deeper and broader in the 1990s than in the 1950s. In addition, the American Medical Association (AMA), which earlier had been a primary obstacle to national health insurance, had lost much of its political influence by the 1990s and had softened its strident opposition to a government presence in health care.[2]

Nevertheless, the Clinton health plan met the same fate as four previous attempts at comprehensive reform of American medical care: legislative failure. By late 1994, the optimism generated by the election of 1992 had completely evaporated. In the end, the Clinton administration's carefully constructed plan could not even muster enough support to get beyond the committee level. Not only did the Clinton plan fail, but no health reform plan at all emerged from the Congress in 1993–1994.[3]

The important point historically is that opportunities for health care reform are few and far between. It was no surprise that in the aftermath of the Clinton debacle the issue of major health reform was pronounced dead for the foreseeable future. Controversial changes in the financing and organization of medicine soon replaced governmental reform on the public's agenda. A number of health care analysts touted the potential of the private sector, through what came to be called "managed care" and "health insurance competition," to control medical spending, reduce waste, and even expand coverage of the uninsured.[4] According to many commentators, the legacy of the Clinton debacle was policy caution. Health reform, it became conventional to claim, would not reappear anytime soon on the national political agenda. Politicians were unwilling to consider any proposals for system-wide reform, and the public was no longer interested in the plight of the uninsured.[5]

The resurrection of health reform in late 1999 as a national issue confirmed once again that futurology is, at best, a dubious enterprise. Most analysts of American politics and medical care had missed the mark badly. The issue returned far more quickly than virtually any observer had predicted in 1994 (whether it stays on the agenda remains to be seen). Indeed, how best to reform American medicine became a centerpiece of the contest between Bill Bradley and Al Gore for the Democratic presidential nomination. A number of stakeholder groups also professed renewed interest in addressing the problem of the uninsured, and a widely publicized conference took place, cosponsored by the consumer community and the insurance industry in January 2000. The debate over health reform was reborn, albeit with less fanfare than in the early 1990s. And the issue, in one form or another, is likely to be on the agenda when the new Congress convenes in 2001.

Now that the debate over health reform has reopened, the question is, What can and should be done? This chapter evaluates the prospects for reform; analyzes the current debates over different options; and elaborates a set of principles, goals, and strategies. At the time its writing, in June 2000, we could only guess at the probable electoral and economic conditions in 2001. Consequently, we conclude the chapter by examining the feasibility of health reform under various combinations of political and economic circumstances.

THE RETURN OF HEALTH REFORM

That health reform returned to the political agenda far sooner than most policy analysts anticipated should come as no surprise to veteran observers of American politics. The only consistent feature of policy analysts' predictions about health reform is how consistently wrong they have been. In the late 1980s, comprehensive health care reform was viewed as implausible in light of the ideological and fiscal constraints of the Reagan years. By 1992, its enactment was (incorrectly, as it turned out) seen as inevitable. In the aftermath of the Clinton plan's defeat in 1994, market-led reform and managed care were supposed to revolutionize American medicine without having to surmount any of the political obstacles that had killed the Clinton plan.[6] By 1997, however, a full-scale public and political backlash against managed care was well under way.[7] In 1998, an apparent consensus emerged that Medicare's financial problems required immediate and radical reform.[8] By the beginning of 2000, the new consensus was that adoption of a Medicare prescription drug benefit was imminent.[9] If economics is the dismal science, then health policy forecasting is more often than not science fiction. The lesson for reformers is that although it is certainly advisable to craft strategies matching short-term constraints, it is foolhardy to develop a single, long-term vision based on those constraints.

The reemergence of health care as a national issue reflects troubling trends in American medical care as well as changing political dynamics. Once again, the public spotlight has focused on the plight of the uninsured. In October 1999, the Census Bureau released a report showing that the number of Americans without any health insurance in 1998 had grown to 44.3 million, or 16.3 percent of the population—an increase of 1 million over the 1997 level.[10] The report, which received substantial media attention, underlined a disturbing fact: Despite record low unemployment and sustained economic growth as well as relatively restrained inflation in medical costs between 1993 and 1997, the numbers of uninsured in the United States had continued to swell. State and federal policy initiatives, including enactment of the Children's Health Insurance Program (CHIP) and Medicaid expansions for children and pregnant women, designed specifically to reduce the number of uninsured, had little effect. And if the number of uninsured was growing during the best of times, what would happen under less favorable conditions? Economic recession, higher rates of unemployment, and steeper increases in the costs of medical care tend to worsen gaps in health insurance coverage. Such conditions also unleash the full impact of recent policy changes— such as welfare reform, and the decoupling of cash assistance from Medicaid eligibility—on many Americans whose current insurance status is precarious. By one estimate, if the United States experiences an economic downturn, 20 percent of Americans under age 65 could be uninsured by 2009.[11]

Moreover, there is mounting evidence that the already torn safety net of providers serving the uninsured—public hospitals, neighborhood clinics, and others—is unraveling further. Safety-net providers are suffering financially, pressured by cutbacks in revenues both from private and from public sources. As more and more managed care firms have secured contracts to serve Medicaid patients, safety-net insurers have not only lost patients and thus crucial Medicaid funds to help cover their costs of treating the uninsured but they also have been left with the sickest and costliest clientele.[12] Access to the traditional institution of last resort for the uninsured—the hospital emergency room—is also fast diminishing. In the past decade, 400 of the nation's 5,000 emergency rooms closed, as for-profit hospitals sought to avoid the costs of uncompensated care.[13]

More recently, rising inflation in medical costs has increased the urgency of health reform. As previously noted, the United States enjoyed a period of relatively stable expenditures on medical care from 1993 to 1997. A slew of analysts interpreted the slowdown in American spending as evidence that managed care had solved the problem of medical inflation. Health maintenance organizations (HMOs) and other managed care plans, they argued, had transformed American medicine into an efficient model of market competition that was inherently superior to traditional fee-for-services medicine.[14] However, the triumph of managed care over health care inflation proved short-lived. In 1998, when health costs again began to rise sharply, it became apparent that the 1993–1997 decline in medical inflation was not primarily due to the efficiencies of managed care. The decline was instead a temporary development attributable to a combination of marketing strategies and short-term market conditions as well as to the aggressive use of market power to obtain price discounts.

As insurance firms sought to attract more patients and lock up market share for the long term, they cut premiums and offered more generous benefit packages. Managed care plans were unable to maintain their own initially attractive packages, because their "savings" were predominantly business strategies, not permanent efficiencies. Insurance firms, too, have been unable to sustain such losses over time and are now raising premiums to recoup their money. HMOs, which a short time ago were viewed as the salvation of public health insurance, have pulled out of the Medicare and Medicaid programs en masse.[15] Health care inflation in the private sector in 1998 rose by 7 percent and was projected to rise by even higher rates in 1999 and 2000.[16] But despite their premium increases, HMOs continued to lose money: According to Interstudy, 60 percent of HMOs had negative profit margins in 1998, and more premium hikes were anticipated. Employers who once believed that managed care was the solution to rising health care costs are increasingly disillusioned and seeking alternative approaches.

Clearly, any luster that managed care once enjoyed has worn off, and not simply in terms of its purported ability to control costs. The final development that has brought health reform back to the agenda is the deepening backlash against managed care. The dissatisfaction of patients with restrictions on their medical care and the deepening disquiet of physicians with the constraints health plans impose on their treatment options as well as their incomes have triggered a wave of anti–managed care legislation. By 1998, over thirty states had passed comprehensive patient protection bills. The backlash against managed care has expanded beyond federal and state legislatures to the legal arena. Congress is currently debating legislation to establish a patient's right to sue HMOs. In addition, a landmark case on the legality of bonuses that encourage physicians to withhold medical services has reached the Supreme Court. The anti–managed care movement itself has not raised the issue of universal health insurance. Indeed, many recent insurance reforms, in keeping with the history of American health politics, have been directed at protecting middle-class workers who are already well insured. However, what has emerged out of the reform movement in the last half of the 1990s is the clear sense that managed care is not the solution to the problems besetting American medicine.

Such were the developments within American medical care that helped bring health reform back onto the agenda. The defeat of the Clinton plan did not erase the problems of American medicine; it only temporarily obscured them. The growing sense that the market is not capable of solving these problems, and that something must be done about the uninsured, was epitomized by a January 2000 conference cosponsored by the Robert Wood Johnson Foundation, Families USA, and the Health Insurance Association of America. The conference—Health Coverage 2000—was promoted as a landmark event because it brought together stakeholders and advocacy groups across the political spectrum to discuss specific plans for meeting the needs of the uninsured. Although the various groups offered different solutions, they agreed on the need for major health reform.

Even more crucial than these developments in American medicine for placing comprehensive health reform back on the agenda has been the political entrepreneurship of the individual. In 1991, the election of Harris Wofford as U.S. senator from Pennsylvania catalyzed the "negative consensus" about American medical care that eventually led to the drive for national health insurance under the Clinton administration.[17] In 1999, the presidential campaign of Bill Bradley brought back that drive.

Bradley's concentration on national health reform as a centerpiece of his primary contest against Gore broke a taboo. He was the first major politician since 1994 to make the uninsured a national priority. Bradley's health plan, unveiled in September 1999, attracted substantial media scrutiny. It also drew Gore's attention. Although not all of that attention was favorable (we take up the advantages and disadvantages of the Bradley plan later in this chapter), Bradley's political challenge forced Vice President Gore to change his rhetorical focus. In his public statements on national health care policy during the primaries, Gore had been proposing a relatively modest expansion of CHIP; now he began describing this expansion as a first step toward eventual universal coverage.

Health Reform on the Agenda: 1992 Versus 2000

There are, however, a number of crucial differences in character, circumstances, and political-economic context between the debate over reforming American medicine in 2000 and the debate that took place in 1992. First, a far greater political appetite for discussion of comprehensive reform plans existed in 1992 than in 2000, when incrementalism was a buzzword of contemporary health policy. Second, the health debate in 1999–2000 was largely a Democratic Party debate. With the infrequent exception of Republican endorsements of Medical Savings Accounts and references to managed care protections, health reform was invisible in the 1999–2000 Republican Party's primaries. In 1992, in contrast, the political momentum for health reform was such that President George Bush had felt compelled to offer his own reform plan. Third, the 1992 debate focused on the problem of medical inflation and on the options—ranging from regulated competition to government budgeting—for controlling medical spending. The more recent debate has been virtually devoid of such talk. Fourth, coming in the aftermath of a recession, the debate of 1992 highlighted the anxiety of middle-class Americans over losing their insurance. Despite the continued increases in the ranks of the uninsured, the middle class's anxieties this time around are much more concentrated on protecting their medical care—and physicians—from the excesses of privately managed care. A fifth and related point is that the debate over health reform in 2000 emerged during a period of fiscal and economic prosperity. In contrast, the economic context of 1992 was dismal: The constraints of federal deficits, and the argument that health reform was crucial to global competitiveness, marked the earlier debate. Lastly, the 1992 debate took place against the backdrop of a health system moving toward managed care, whereas health reform returned in 2000 against the backdrop of a health system where managed care was a fait accompli and private regulation—to the alarm both of patients and of physicians—had grown considerably.

Health reform thus emerged in 2000 as an issue different in several respects from that debated in 1992. But it is critical to recognize that the changes do not all flow in one direction, in terms of their potential effects on the success of a future reform. For example, clearly the well-insured are not as nervous about losing their health coverage today as they were a decade ago. One inference is that this key constituency is less likely to be supportive of fundamental reforms that affect their own medical arrangements. On the other hand, the politics of surplus and economic prosperity create opportunities for reform. The same population that feels less threatened by the personal loss of coverage may be more inclined to support reforms that help others who are less fortunate. Indeed, recent opinion polls showed an increase in the amount of taxes Americans claimed to be willing to pay in order to fund government coverage for the uninsured.[18]

Nevertheless, the inescapable conclusion is that the position of health reform on the agenda is precarious. The entrepreneur who reopened debate on the desirability of comprehensive reform—Bill Bradley—exited the Democratic primary contest only seven months later. As Bradley faded from the electoral spotlight, so might the issue; there are no assurances that health reform will be a top domestic priority for the next president. The most likely scenario, as we discuss later in this chapter, is a focus on expanding coverage for children. In sum, the health reform debate has reopened; but what alternatives may emerge on the policy agenda, and for how long, is unpredictable.

Barriers to National Health Insurance

Even if health care recaptures a central spot on the national agenda after the 2000 elections, that is no guarantee that the president and Congress will enact any reform legislation. The assumption that attaining a position on the policy agenda and having public majorities as well as presidential support behind reform will guarantee a political victory has misled reformers time and again. If those conditions were sufficient to enact national health insurance, such a law would have been passed five decades ago.

The U.S. political system creates a number of barriers to the passage of any legislation, let alone a reform as controversial, ideologically divisive, and threatening to powerful interest groups as national health insurance. The political institutions of American government deliberately fragment power. Unlike a parliamentary system such as that in Great Britain, the U.S. system provides no assurance that the president will represent the same party as the congressional majority. Indeed, divided government has become a regular feature of American politics. Moreover, even if the president's own party enjoys majority status in both houses of Congress, reform will not necessarily follow. Perhaps the most important lesson of American politics for health reform is that partisan majorities do not necessarily produce policy majorities. Compared to parties elsewhere in the world, American political parties are weak. Members of Congress run their own campaigns, raise their own funds, and run independently from—and sometimes in opposition to—their party's platform. Their first political allegiance is not to their party or president but to their congressional district. Consequently, presidential sponsorship of major legislation, even with a Congress controlled by the president's own party, does not ensure presidential victory on any given issue—a lesson Clinton learned the hard way.

The internal organization of Congress further complicates the road to reform. Legislation must, of course, clear both the House and Senate to reach the president's desk. But the labyrinth that must be navigated before that step is daunting. Congress is organized into a series of committees and subcommittees that govern various legislative areas. However, substantial overlap exists across committees' jurisdictions; a single bill is often considered by a multitude of committees. In addition, two key committees—Ways and Means in the House, and the Finance Committee in the Senate—have acted in the past as gatekeepers for health insurance legislation. Failure to get a bill through these committees dooms it to defeat, even if there are congressional majorities in favor of the legislation (as was the case with Medicare legislation in the early 1960s).[19]

The fragmented structure of Congress and the relative weakness of American political parties combine to create a roadblock to reform, making it difficult or impossible to achieve the necessary level of consensus on a single piece of legislation. The U.S. legislature, measured in terms of its independence, administrative capacity, and ability to pursue policies that diverge from those sponsored by the executive, is the most powerful lawmaking body in the world. Members of Congress who head committees and subcommittees have their own platforms from which to introduce health care reform bills that differ from the president's or their own parties'. As a consequence, any debate over health reform produces numerous bills sponsored by congressional policymakers seeking to be entrepreneurs. The lesson is a sobering one for reformers. Even if there is a congressional majority in favor of national health insurance, it does not mean there is a majority for any one plan. The inability of congressional majorities to coalesce behind one plan doomed national health legislation during its last two appearances on the national agenda, in 1970 to 1974 and in 1993 to 1994.[20]

A second critical barrier to the adoption of national health insurance is the structure of health politics in the United States. Fundamental reform poses a tremendous threat to institutions that are invested in maintaining the medical status quo. This includes a large proportion of American hospitals and physicians, as well as almost all American health insurers, pharmaceutical companies, and suppliers of medical equipment and technology. These groups—what political scientists call "concentrated interests"—have much at stake both financially and organizationally, and are likely to block any reform that threatens to erode their position.[21] They are generally well organized, well funded, and willing and able to take advantage of fragmented political institutions and of the media. On the other side are more than 40 million uninsured Americans with a stake in universal health insurance; but the uninsured are a group only in the abstract, figurative sense. They are diverse politically, geographically, and ethnically; apart from being uninsured, they have little in common. They have no organization, few financial resources, and little political clout. The textbook view of American democracy is that groups with a grievance will organize and voice their grievance to a responsive political system. The textbook view of American democracy, as the case of the uninsured illustrates all too well, is overly simple. The uninsured may be large in number, but they are a diffuse interest group with tremendous barriers to organization. It is no accident that the list of medical lobbying groups and trade associations is endless, whereas there is not a single, prominent, national group whose primary purpose is advocating for the uninsured. Pitted against the organization and influence of the medical industry, the uninsured are no match.

The resulting imbalance in the arena of health politics is, as the Clinton administration discovered, profound. Although the administration found support for its plan from unions and consumer advocacy groups, the 1993–1994 debate was dominated by the health insurance industry. The infamous "Harry and Louise" ad campaign sponsored by the Health Insurance Association of America (HIAA) helped deflate public support for the Clinton plan by smearing it as a threat to the public. And congressional Republicans, who at first had considered an alternative to the Clinton plan a political necessity, quickly changed their minds after business interests made clear their steadfast opposition to any national health care plan.

The third major barrier to health reform has been public opinion. To be sure, analysts and politicians alike have vastly exaggerated the role of mass opinion in defeating national health insurance. An overwhelming number of Americans have consistently supported the idea that health care should be a right in the United States; and for the past fifty years, a majority of Americans have favored the adoption of national health insurance. There has been, in short, a "permissive consensus" among the public for universal coverage that would have allowed for the enactment of national health insurance under the right political conditions. Yet the depth and stability of public support for health reform remain suspect. Although Americans favor the idea of a national health program in the abstract, the number of supporters drops when respondents are asked about any specific plan. Polls also reveal a long-standing reluctance to pay much more in taxes to fund universal coverage. And perhaps most crucially, public opinion has proven volatile and subject to the influence of campaigns designed to discredit national health insurance. In 1993 and 1994, the insurance industry managed to define the Clinton plan to the media in terms that clearly served the insurance industry's own financial interests. Absent any probing, independent analysis of the president's proposal by journalists, the insurance industry's portrayal of the Clinton plan as big government reached the public unfiltered. The result was a striking drop in public support that seriously damaged the chances for passage of any bill creating a national health care plan.[22]

Thus, contemporary reformers must confront the prevailing antigovernment ideology of American politics. At a time when even Democratic presidents declare that the era of big government is over, strong skepticism pervades about the ability of the federal government to solve social problems. The factual basis for the claim that "government just can't do anything right" is demonstrably wrong, and major public programs such as Social Security and Medicare remain immensely popular. But regardless of the veracity of claims of government ineptitude, they are politically influential. Widely held by segments of the public, such views will continue to obstruct the enactment of any program that substantially increases federal responsibility—both fiscal and administrative—for financing medical care.

The political contest in the United States for national health insurance has not and never will be waged on a level playing field. Given the same political conditions that existed in the United States in 1993—presidential endorsement, public support, and partisan majorities—there is no other industrialized democracy in the world that would not have enacted universal health coverage. That is the cautionary message of this review of American health politics. Some analysts claim the institutional barriers to comprehensive reform are so strong that it will be impossible to achieve universal health insurance without first enacting constitutional reforms that radically alter American government.[23] We reject this analysis. The formidable barriers to enacting national health insurance in the United States should not be taken to mean that reform efforts are predestined to fail. If American political institutions were an insurmountable barrier to major social reform, then the Social Security, Medicare, and Medicaid programs would not exist. And although interest groups representing the medical industry enjoy a considerable political advantage, that too can be overcome. The AMA was considered untouchable until Medicare was enacted over its strident opposition.

The permissive consensus that has traditionally characterized public attitudes about national health insurance provides reason to believe that antigovernment sentiment can be overcome by persuading the public that health care is different. In short, although enacting a system of universal health insurance is very difficult given the constraints in American politics, it is far from impossible. Given the right circumstances, strategies, and plans, serious reform can succeed.

ANALYZING THE OPTIONS: FROM BRADLEY TO BUSH

Do any of the plans in the current debate meet the above criteria? That is, is there a plan now on the table that is both substantively desirable and politically feasible, that will finally surmount the political barriers and provide a workable, effective system of universal health insurance? The answer, unfortunately, is no. As we argue throughout the remainder of this chapter, there is no silver bullet or obviously compelling solution to America's medical care problems in the current political environment. What is desirable may not be feasible, and what is now feasible may not be desirable. Our aim in this section is to analyze briefly the health plans put forward by the major candidates in the 2000 presidential election, with an eye both to their substance and to their political efficacy.

The Bradley Plan

The strongest and perhaps the only legacy of Bill Bradley's campaign for the presidency was his focus on the need for comprehensive health reform. Bradley was the sole candidate who claimed to offer a plan for universal coverage (actually, by his advisers' estimates, the plan would not have achieved universalism but would have covered 95 percent of the population). Bradley was also the only candidate to talk extensively about the plight of the uninsured. And finally, Bradley was alone in making the critical argument that in the context of vast federal surpluses and a prosperous economy, universal insurance is not only affordable but should be a national priority.

Bradley deserves credit for resurrecting universal health insurance as a national issue. His willingness to talk again about substantial reform, however, did not earn the former senator many political points, let alone gratitude from the reform community. In fact, Bradley took fire within the Democratic primary from both the left and the right. Conservatives, along with Gore, criticized the plan as repeating the mistakes made by the Clinton administration during 1993 and 1994. It was said to be too ambitious in scope, too expensive in costs, and too liberal in philosophy. From the left, groups such as Physicians for a National Health Program (PNHP) attacked the Bradley plan as not ambitious enough and too similar to the Clinton administration's reliance on managed competition, and for leaving the current arrangements of an increasingly profit-oriented health care system largely intact.[24] Bradley ironically learned in the Democratic primaries the same lesson that Clinton did in 1994: Attempts to build support for a new health reform plan that appeal to both the right and the left may leave you standing in the middle, with no support from either side.

The aim of the Bradley plan was straightforward: Leave the employer-based insurance system intact while expanding health insurance coverage for the uninsured by providing them with subsidized access to the Federal Employees Health Benefits Plan (FEHBP). The FEHBP is a federally managed pool of private insurance plans presently available only to federal employees and their families. If the FEHBP were opened to the uninsured, Bradley projected that an additional 30 million Americans would gain health coverage.

The plan had four core components. First, it required that all children be covered by health insurance, either through their parents' plans or private plans under the FEHBP. Premium costs would be subsidized according parental income, with children in low- and moderate-income families having their premiums fully subsidized. Second, adults were given two choices: They could continue to participate in their current insurance plan or join one of the private plans in the FEHBP. Again, premium subsidies would vary according to income. Third, Bradley sought to "mainstream" Medicaid by providing all current recipients with a subsidy to join one of the private plans under the FEHBP as well. Finally, Bradley proposed to expand Medicare insurance to cover outpatient prescription drugs, with no cap on total claims.

The increased public costs under the Bradley plan—estimated by his advisers to be between $55–$65 billion a year—were to be financed by the projected federal surplus. In addition, Bradley's advisers estimated an additional $30 billion in savings from the application of information technologies to medical payments and records, reductions in wasteful and inefficient care, and unspecified "other cost-containment measures." Presumably, these unspecified measures were a cloaked reference to the expected savings from enrolling the uninsured in the FEHBP and taking advantage of the program's reputed performance in controlling medical costs. What the Bradley campaign did not mention—and what journalists completely missed—was that the FEHBP was simply another variant of the same sort of managed competition long championed by conservative health economists. In this and several other respects, the Bradley plan was ironically similar to the plan proposed by the Clinton administration five years earlier. The Bradley plan assumed that in the long run health insurance for the uninsured as well as better coverage for Medicaid recipients could be expanded by enrolling these groups in private health insurance plans. It took for granted that competition among the plans would produce substantial savings.

The Bradley plan embodied a curious mixture of political strength and substantive weakness. Politically, relying on the FEHBP and proposing that uninsured Americans have the right to participate in the same insurance program as members of Congress is powerful rhetoric that adroitly links expanded government responsibility for the uninsured with anticongressional sentiment. Moreover, Bradley's reliance on private insurance for coverage and on the federal surplus for financing had obvious political advantages over raising taxes to pay for a public insurance program. And the plan's steadfast nonintervention in current arrangements in the employer-based market, with no new restrictions on private insurers and no changes for already well-insured Americans, were certainly lessons gleaned directly from the Clinton debacle.

These same purported political advantages, however, were also responsible for a number of glaring substantive shortcomings in the plan. A major flaw was the plan's reliance on the FEHBP, which at that time was turning in its worst financial performance in a decade, with spending far exceeding growth rates in Medicare.[25] There is therefore no basis for assuming that any savings as a result of the FEHBP's managed competition would be available to help finance coverage for the uninsured. Consequently, future costs for covering uninsured Americans likely would be substantially greater than the Bradley plan projected, and its premium subsidies would prove increasingly inadequate, eroding its potential to reach universal coverage (and to guarantee Medicaid recipients access to private insurance). Bradley, in this respect, fell victim to the same infatuation with managed competition, and the same exaggerated promises made on its behalf by some health economists, that President

Clinton did. Without an employer mandate or taxes, the long-term financing of the Bradley plan would have been shaky.

A second fundamental problem was that the plan Bradley proposed contained no measures to reliably control the costs of medical care. As already noted, the assumption of savings within the FEHBP had no basis in fact. And the plan did not impose any regulatory or budgetary controls on private health sector spending, simply leaving the current insurance market untouched. The only savings projected were to come from computerizing medical records and implementing more practice guidelines, neither of which represented a remotely serious source of revenue. Internationally, universal coverage is associated with cost control. But the Bradley plan did not draw on any of the lessons of other countries' experience—such as budgeting national health expenditures and restricting diffusion of expensive technologies—in successfully restraining medical inflation.[26]

A third shortcoming was that despite its label as universal insurance, the plan left at least 15 million Americans uninsured. Bradley advisers argued that many of those left uncovered would be young, healthy adults who would decide not to accept the new coverage. Generally speaking, the argument is plausible. But it is also the case that many Americans who need medical care but cannot afford to purchase private insurance even with the subsidy would be left out. A system that is truly universal in coverage would benefit from administrative and economic efficiencies and would avoid the problem of clients repeatedly going on and off of government insurance, depending on their health status.

In the final analysis, Bradley deserves credit for pressing health care back onto the agenda and for arguing that it is morally irresponsible to ignore the uninsured in a climate of prosperity. Although we agree with many of the substantive criticisms made by single-payer groups such as PNHP, we believe their rhetoric has been too harsh; it does the reform community little good to attack the national politician most willing to push the United States closer to universal coverage. What is most striking about the Bradley plan, though, is the extent to which it evaded the hard choices that any workable system of national health insurance in the United States must ultimately confront: How to control costs in the most expensive medical care system in the world; whether to mandate that all employers provide insurance to their employees, and to propose new taxes covering the uninsured; and perhaps most crucially, how to regulate the practices of for-profit insurers and the incentives of market-based medical care that have put the U.S. health care system in its current predicament. Without seriously addressing these questions, no plan can expect to offer universal coverage while controlling medical inflation. The substantial changes in the political landscape of health reform since 1992 were underscored by Bradley's omissions. The only plan for comprehensive reform in 2000 did not address any of these issues.

Bush and Gore: Incrementalism in Vogue

Whereas Bradley sidestepped many of the issues crucial to workable universal coverage, Gore and George W. Bush did not even raise the issue. Health care was not prominently featured in the early stages of Bush's candidacy. Bush endorsed the conservative, incremental reform package of expanding Medical Savings Accounts (MSAs), increasing tax deductions, and transforming Medicare into a premium-support (voucher) system modeled after the plan of the National Bipartisan Commission on Medicare. In terms of expanding coverage, Bush proposed giving states greater flexibility under the CHIP program to cover more people, and providing a "health credit" of up to $1,000 per individual and $2,000 per family to cover the costs of insurance. He also called for the creation of "Association Health Plans" by the Chamber of Commerce and NFIB that would market new coverage plans to small businesses.[27]

Bush's package of health care measures would hardly dent the problem of the uninsured. MSAs, most health analysts agree, would disproportionately attract the healthy and wealthy, unraveling already frayed insurance pools and raising costs for sicker and poorer enrollees. Early experiments with MSAs have attracted much smaller enrollments than advocates had hoped and expected. MSAs require high-deductible, catastrophic insurance, which brings with it a level of financial insecurity and exposure to medical bills that most Americans are not comfortable with. Consequently, not only would MSAs fail to enhance access to medical care, they also would do nothing to control the costs of medical care (which is one reason why the AMA has actively campaigned for their implementation). The $2,000 health credit might help a segment of the uninsured; but it is far too low to help the millions of uninsured whose premium costs would far exceed the subsidy. Bush's Medicare plan would similarly worsen access to care for program beneficiaries by shifting costs of medical inflation to the elderly and disabled, and by creating incentives for chronically ill beneficiaries to join HMOs that studies demonstrate are ill prepared to care for their medical needs.[28] Lastly, the Texas governor offered few details about how he would expand CHIP, other than to promote covering more children as a desirable goal. Bush's health proposals, then, did not treat the expansion of health insurance coverage as a serious policy goal.

In contrast, Gore proposed a path of liberal incrementalism. The centerpiece of the vice president's plan was an expansion of CHIP to include not only more children but also their parents. This approach is a variation of the "pincer strategy" described later in this chapter. Gore called for expanding CHIP to children in households with incomes within 250 percent of the federal poverty line, allowing children over that threshold to buy into CHIP or Medicaid, and opening up CHIP to the parents of children already enrolled in the program. He also reiterated the Clinton administration's proposal to allow Americans between the ages of 55 and 64 to buy into Medicare. To be sure, Gore emphasized health reform to a greater extent than did Bush. And his proposals could have reduced the numbers of uninsured. In particular, his effort to transform CHIP into a program for American families, not simply children, represented an important effort to broaden the reach of health reform, with the political advantage of attracting the "missing middle" of adults working in low-wage jobs who do not qualify for Medicaid and do not receive insurance from their employers.[29] Yet Gore's health reforms fell far short of universal coverage. His advisers estimated that if enacted, Gore's plan would raise the proportion of Americans covered by insurance to 88 percent—not a substantial leap from the 85 percent presently covered. In a time of economic and fiscal prosperity, Gore's proposals were hardly bold—a fact that made it difficult for his campaign staff (as well as for many voters) to differentiate them clearly from Governor Bush's. Both candidates offered incrementalism without the goal of universal coverage or substantial reform, leaving the current medical system largely intact.

There is a broader lesson here for the politics of national health insurance. As the Bradley plan demonstrated, it is relatively inexpensive to finance coverage for the uninsured. After all, 85 percent of Americans are insured, and Medicare and Medicaid have already covered the most expensive populations. Affordability is not, and never has been, the central barrier to universal coverage. Other issues have done more to fuel the controversy: proposed changes to the current system that threaten the interests of insurers and other stakeholders; and the transfer of administrative and budgetary responsibility for individual medical care from private hands to the federal government. All of the plans offered in 2000—by Bradley, Bush, and Gore—avoided addressing these issues; and consequently none of them offered a compelling vision for the future of American medical care.

ALTERNATIVE PLANS

The debate over health care reform should not be limited to plans discussed in the political arena, especially given the weaknesses in the various proposals outlined above. We therefore consider three additional options in this section, each of which raises different political and administrative issues: the federalist option; the pincer strategy; and the single-payer approach.

The Federalist Option

This approach, in contrast to previous reform strategies, does not seek to organize a single health plan for the whole nation. Instead, it permits states to choose how to organize their own medical care arrangements while encouraging them financially to provide universal coverage and broad benefits. Making state choice the core principle of national health care reform allows for the decentralized emergence of multiple models. Consequently, the federalist option offers an opportunity to unify advocates of reform who agree on the goal of universal coverage but disagree on which plan should be adopted to reach that goal. The federalist option also directly addresses the diversity of American medical care. States vary widely in their political culture, wealth, medical care delivery systems, and experiences of health reform. Instead of enacting a single system for the entire country, the federalist option would allow states to choose how to reform American medicine within the context of federal guidelines.[30] In recent years, the federalist option has gained political momentum, with the introduction of legislation by Senator Paul Wellstone and endorsements of the Universal Health Care Access Network (UHCAN)[31] and the Service Employees International Union (SEIU) of the AFL-CIO.[32]

The starting point for the federalist option is the historical record of stalemate in American health care reform. Efforts to enact national health insurance have been stymied five times in the past century, and each of these five episodes has borne a strikingly different character. What made the complete unraveling of the Clinton health plan so frustrating was precisely that there was, at least early in the process, a realizable majority in Congress for national health reform that was nevertheless not converted into a programmatic legislative majority for any reform bill. The same can be said of reform efforts in the early 1970s, when other congressional majorities favoring reform failed to produce a legislative breakthrough.

The lack of consensus over which model of national health insurance the United States should adopt and the accompanying failure to enact legislation have obscured the extent to which reformers of different stripes favor the same goals: universal coverage, cost containment, and reform of private health insurance practices. Although no single proposal for health reform has attracted a legislative majority, in both the early 1970s and 1990s public and congressional majorities supported these fundamental principles. National health reform has been deadlocked recently by disagreement over means more than over ends. As explained earlier, the conditions of American political life—particularly the fragmentation of Congress and weakness of political parties—reinforce the tendencies among health care reformers to form multiple camps advancing competing proposals.

The federalist option increases the chances of a legislative majority's coalescing from reformers who disagree on the appropriate model for reform. Under that option, national legislation would be passed that encourages the states to enact universal coverage, insurance reform, and cost control, but gives the states choice over what types of reform they wish to implement. Congress would enact legislation offering federal financial support to all states establishing health plans that meet federal standards for national health care reform. To receive federal money for health expenditures, states would be required to enact health reforms that guarantee universal coverage, comprehensive benefits, administrative accountability, fiscal viability (including cost control measures), and portability (recognition of other states' forms of coverage). States would choose how to finance their portion of the health plan budget (though the majority of expenditures would come from federal sources). States would also choose how to structure health care delivery. As long as they met federal standards, they could choose to implement any one of a variety of systems ranging from a single-payer system to a competition among privately administered HMOs.

The federalist option thus solves the puzzle of how to translate a majority favoring health reform into legislation when that majority cannot agree on the precise shape of reform. Substantively, it recognizes the variation in state health care systems and reform preferences. Politically, it taps into the rhetoric of devolution, states' rights, and choice. It also puts opponents of reform on the defensive, shifting the focus of debate from the details of a particular plan to the fundamental question of whether legislators support universal coverage. However, the federalist strategy is not problem-free. The first and largest barrier it has to surmount is that it represents a new alternative in the American health reform debate—and one that lacks the familiarity of, for example, single-payer insurance. As both Clinton and Bradley learned, it is politically difficult to build legislative and public constituencies around ideas that have no prior history of support from legislators or consumer groups active in health care policy.

The objection most likely to be raised is that the state-by-state variation permitted by a federalist health system would be inequitable. Such a system would be unfair, in critics' view, because citizens' access to medical care services would be a function of the health system chosen by the state in which they reside. Another objection might be that the federalist strategy would circumvent national gridlock only to allow reform to fall victim to political deadlock at the state level. Some legislatures might replicate congressional failure to enact reform; or some states might resist the imposition of a federal mandate for health reform that they do not welcome for ideological or financial reasons. In addition, even though the federalist plan mandates a state plan for cost control, in the absence of a national budget for health care the state's control over medical care spending could be even less certain than under the single-payer model.

The Pincer Strategy

Another possible alternative for health policy reform is what we term the "pincer strategy": extending Medicare eligibility downward to age 55, while expanding Medicaid, CHIP, and other insurance sources both for children and for working adults. The pincer strategy is more incremental than either the federalist or single-payer approaches. Instead of creating a new medical care system, it seeks to build on existing institutions, gradually moving toward universal coverage. Families USA has proposed an exemplar of the pincer strategy.[33] Their plan would extend the Medicaid program to cover everyone whose individual or family income is at or below 133 percent of the federal poverty line. It would also provide federal matching funds to cover both children and adults in families with incomes up to 200 percent of the federal poverty level. Coverage could be received through expanding Medicaid or CHIP, creating a new program, or through subsidizing private insurance premiums. Federal transfers to states would exceed current matches, with the goal of ensuring that a higher proportion of the uninsured eligible for public coverage enroll in these plans than is currently the case. In addition, the eligibility age for Medicare coverage could be lowered from 65 to 55.

This approach has appeal for three reasons. First, it could substantially reduce the number of uninsured. Over half of the 7.5 million children and 15.8 million adults who were uninsured in 2000 lived in families with household incomes below 200 percent of the poverty line.[34] If this approach were implemented, the proportion of uninsured nationwide could be cut to 8 percent; and over time, the income threshold could be raised (e.g., to 300 percent), so as to move closer to universal coverage. Second, the pincer strategy would incorporate the uninsured into existing programs, requiring no dramatic innovations to finance the medical care of newly covered groups. Building on the state-federal partnership embodied in CHIP is also likely to have political appeal to lawmakers as well as to the general public. Third, as noted earlier, the pincer strategy moves health insurance reform beyond the traditional categories of the aged and children to include working adults. The uninsured are concentrated in low-wage, working families, and any serious attempt to improve coverage must target this group. Politically, there may be untapped appeal in providing subsidies to workers and their families who "play by the rules" and yet are left behind in the insurance market—not poor enough to qualify for Medicaid and not wealthy enough to afford to purchase their own insurance. The extension of Medicare eligibility to a population whose coverage difficulties are increasing (particularly given the accelerating erosion of private coverage for early retirees) also would command attention. For those in the 55–65 age group, medical problems typically increase, and private health insurance is expensive; yet retirement in many cases brings an end to coverage provided by employers.

Each of these advantages, however, has its downside: The pincer strategy simplifies administrative concerns by building on existing programs; however, one might reasonably question the effectiveness of Medicaid and CHIP as building blocks toward universal coverage. Enrollment in CHIP so far has been disappointing, and millions who are eligible for Medicaid have never applied for coverage. To some extent, this is due to the daunting bureaucratic and administrative hurdles that must be cleared in order to enroll. In addition, some state governments have deliberately tried to keep enrollments down by limiting outreach campaigns. Remedies for the latter problem have been proposed, such as raising the level of federal matching funds allocated to states, or alternatively, imposing penalties on the laggards. But the key question is whether, even with the appropriate policy reforms, the addition of new populations to Medicaid would improve recipients' medical care experiences or merely exacerbate existing problems. In the case of Medicaid, these are well documented: administrative inefficiency, limitations of access, and perpetual underfunding.

Lastly, the pincer strategy, unfortunately, would do little to control costs.

The Single Payer

The final option we want to discuss is what are conventionally referred to as "single-payer" plans—the model of choice for many reformers since the early 1980s. In fact, Medicare itself is a single-payer plan in the sense that the insurance funds that pay for Medicare's benefits are in a single program. The trouble with the term, however, is that it inadequately describes what most people who call for a single-payer plan really want. The dominant model of a single-payer, comprehensive public health insurance program is Canada's Medicare. There, the governing legislation prescribes broad physician and hospital coverage ("comprehensive care"), accessible terms (that is, no deductibles or coinsurance payments), public administration (for accountability), and portability (that is, coverage that protects Canadians whether they are in their home province or not).[35] The appeal of such an approach is obvious. Universal health insurance has been for most Canadians the country's postwar public triumph. It has brought a decent level of medical care to the country's citizens and consumes 40 percent less of the annual national income than is consumed by medical care in the United States. The necessary consequence of Canada's methods of financing and cost-control—paying for medical care from each provincial budget, setting budgets for hospitals, and limiting what doctors and drug firms can charge—is ongoing controversy. There is continuous discussion about how much to spend, on what, for whom, and under what rules of fairness of access or financing. There is also a democratic accountability that is truly astonishing when compared to the enormously fragmented and hence less accountable decisionmaking process in the United States. A necessary corollary is constant media attention to Canada's "single-payer" program, featuring constant claims by Canada's doctors and other medical occupations that "crises" are imminent or in full bloom.

Canada's Medicare system is more cost-efficient and more easily understood than other alternatives, and it places far fewer constraints on professional autonomy and patient choice than is the case within the current U.S. system. Indeed, the United States has the most intrusive regulation of medical care practice of any OECD nation, although the bulk of that intrusiveness arises from private regulation rather than public legislation. Perhaps that is why Canada's model has held such appeal for American reformers during the past quarter century. At the same time, however, this model has awakened the intense opposition of groups whose incomes would be harmed by such a reform. It is no surprise that the HIAA, the AMA, the trade association of the drug industry, and the managed care trade association have treated the Canadian model as the problem rather than the solution. In spring 2000 a newly formed group disingenuously describing itself as "Citizens for a Better Medicare" launched a multimedia campaign "urging American seniors to reject the Canadian model of health insurance and coverage of prescription drugs." Forty groups sponsored this campaign, including such traditional opponents of government health insurance as the Chamber of Commerce, the National Association of Manufacturers, and the pharmaceutical trade association. In short, the problem with the Canadian model is not an absence of substantive merit, but the intensity of opposition to it by financially interested and ideologically opposed parties.[36] This opposition need not lead us to abandon the single-payer model out of hand; but it does demand that we consider what we stand to gain strategically by holding onto this model when other options are available.

In sum, none of the above plans offers an easy path to universal coverage. All contain different mixtures of strengths and weaknesses; and all provide legitimate alternatives that may be more or less feasible and desirable under varying conditions. The question is how to move the debate in a direction where substantial health reform can command serious attention. We turn now to the lessons and strategies that should guide health reformers after the 2000 election and beyond.

Lessons and Strategies for Health Care Reform

If You Lose, Lose the Right Way

As our overview of the politics of national health insurance makes clear, the obstacles to enactment of substantial reform are formidable. Reformers must confront the reality that political setbacks and legislative defeats are not only possible but probable. As important as it is to shape the terms of victory, it is equally critical to influence the terms on which one loses. In 1948, President Truman's national health insurance plan went down to defeat; yet Truman used that defeat as a key element in his presidential campaign against the infamous "do-nothing" Congress. In contrast, after the Clinton health plan politically imploded in 1994, even the administration abandoned its own plan. The administration had no end-game strategy when legislative support for health reform failed to materialize; therefore the blame for the failure of health reform lay as much on President Clinton as it did on his congressional opponents. The lesson for reformers is this: If legislation cannot pass, there still may be political benefit to extract if responsibility for blocking expanded health insurance coverage can be clearly pinned on the opposition. In that respect, even unsuccessful legislative efforts may keep health reform on the agenda and in some circumstances may help expand support for it.

Don't Forget the Long Term

A related lesson is that although it may be necessary to respond to short-term political and economic constraints, it would be foolish to focus on short-term strategies to the point of abandoning long-term aims. The debate over Medicare is instructive. From the time the idea was first conceived, it took fifteen years of political struggle before federal health insurance for the elderly was adopted. Medicare's political sponsors accepted incremental steps that they believed would not detract from their ultimate goal; but they never abandoned the campaign for Medicare. American politics, with its individualistic focus and shifting coalitions, tends to prompt short-term visions and encourage impatience. Yet one clear option for reformers is to reject these pressures by agreeing on a single programmatic model and legislative goal, and to begin a long-term political campaign to secure eventual enactment. As with Medicare, this will require patience, time to build and maintain a coalition, and the commitment to absorb defeat. In the short run this may be a painful route; over the long haul it may prove the most rewarding.

Don't Let the Perfect Be the Enemy of the Good
(Or Why Canadian Single-Payer Insurance Is Not the Only Answer)

Perhaps one of the most serious barriers to adopting a national health system is the widespread perception that Americans have only two possible choices in health care: to preserve the status quo—the system of for-profit private insurance, along with Medicare and Medicaid, leaving 44 million Americans uninsured and medical costs largely uncontrolled; or to embrace the Canadian model of single-payer national health insurance, replacing current arrangements with public insurance and eliminating the role of private insurers in American medical care (except for services not covered by the public system). This dichotomy in the American health debate does not serve reformers well. It leaves the mistaken impression that the Canadian program is the only available model of universal health coverage. It ignores the comparably successful experiences of universal health insurance in Western Europe, Japan, and Australia. Unfortunately, the reform community itself has contributed to this misperception by focusing single-mindedly on Canada, and in some cases, misconstruing its lessons. The exclusive focus is unfortunate, from a political perspective.

Internationally, the Canadian system is unusual in the extent to which it embraces a one-tier conception of public insurance that bans private coverage for services covered by the government. Single-payer "purists" have implied that it is necessary to copy the features of the Canadian system in order to achieve cost-effective, universal coverage in the United States. They are wrong. The real lessons of Canada's experience are that universal coverage is conducive to cost containment; that slowing the growth of medical expenditures requires the concentration of financial responsibility and budgeting; that enforcing a uniform set of rules for health insurance results in administrative as well as economic efficiencies; and that enforcing one set of rules for medical care payment and enrollment is critical to controlling medical inflation.[37]

These lessons, however, have also been learned by a number of other countries. And they have been embodied in systems that are structurally different from the Canadian model, with less centralization and a larger role for private insurers. For example, we know from the German experience that it is possible to have multiple payers and still control costs if all of the payers abide by the same set of rules. We also know from the experiences of Germany, Australia, and other countries that it is not actually essential to have everyone participate in a single, public insurance system, as Canada does. These nations have a safety valve of private insurance that offers wealthier citizens an alternative to public insurance. Yet neither the quality of care nor the capacity to control costs has been obviously compromised in these nations' public insurance systems. What matters is that most people are in the public system, ensuring that it has both a broad-based political coalition and strong economic influence over purchasing medical services. What is not necessary is for everyone to be in a single system.

The point is not that the Canadian system is unworthy of emulation. On the contrary, we have both written about its long record of success and about how it could be adapted to circumstances in the United States. The recent revival of stories in the American media suggesting that Canadian health care is in crisis and unraveling are misleading and simply untrue. Such stories unfortunately maintain a long-established trend of American distortion of the Canadian experience. Single-payer advocates also have played a crucial role in arguing for reform and that public insurance alternatives to the U.S. system are both available and desirable. But the Canadian model is not the only one available to American health reformers, and indeed, it carries a number of features that make it difficult to import to the United States. If universal coverage is to be politically viable in the United States, pragmatic universalism, rather than ideological purity, must be the cornerstone of any successful campaign. Pursuit of a "perfect" health system at the cost of ignoring very good alternatives that attain the same goals makes neither intellectual nor political sense. Nor does it do much good for 44 million uninsured Americans. The case must be made that a pure single-payer system is not the only option for universal coverage in the United States.

Look for New Allies
The events of the past decade have provided new opportunities to expand the coalition for health reform. The transformation of the medical system through various managed care practices has created deep discontent among physicians with current arrangements. Already, consumer groups and physicians' associations have subdued their traditional en-

mity and are working together to pass both state and federal laws regulating HMOs and other managed care plans.[38] That alliance could reasonably be taken a step further. Given doctors' unhappiness with their growing lack of clinical authority and with the corporatization of American medical care, it is not difficult to envision an alliance for national health insurance that incorporates large segments of the medical community. Physicians may be increasingly persuaded that they will fare better under a public system that could reinstate their clinical autonomy than under the corporate control of private health plans. Historically, physicians have been a strong obstacle to large-scale reform. In the future, they may prove a key catalyst to its enactment.

Controversy Is Inevitable

The failure of the Clinton plan has given rise to an industry of commentary on its lessons. One set of lessons proffered is that for reform to succeed, it must be bipartisan and encompass a coalition that includes health care reform's strongest opponents, the insurance industry. These lessons purport to provide a political rationale for the incremental reforms discussed earlier. As the previous section makes clear, we believe it is sensible for reformers to look for new allies, and that the medical profession offers an intriguing potential for alliance. And, as we have argued, there may be plans that preserve a greater role for private insurance while achieving universal coverage. But any campaign for health reform that has as its main objectives avoiding controversy and bipartisanship will produce one of two results: political failure or adoption of anemic reform. By its nature, health reform will inevitably be controversial in the United States. The ideological, economic, and political stakes, as well as its impact on powerful interests, makes avoiding controversy a fool's errand. Neither is reform likely to be bipartisan. As already noted, it took fifteen years of deep ideological and political struggle to enact sixty days of hospitalization insurance for elderly Social Security recipients. Bipartisan support for Medicare came only in the end, when passage was already assured. Pursuing reform far greater in scope than federal health insurance for the aged will hardly deaden partisan battles. The aim should be to build a majority coalition for health reform, not universal agreement or national consensus on a new system. Such a consensus, whether among the public or stakeholders, is not only impossible, but it is not a necessary condition for enacting significant health care reforms in the United States.

Time Is on Our Side

Throughout the past decade, opponents of reform have raised the specter of the coming retirement of the baby boomers as a demographic "tidal wave" that threatens the American economy, political system, and intergenerational relations. In health care, the fear mongering has been particularly acute. Images of a growing elderly population devouring scarce medical resources—most of which are incorrectly portrayed as useless expenditures on dying seniors—are juxtaposed with the growing ranks of the uninsured. The anticipated doubling of Medicare enrollment in the next four decades, a number of analysts contend, means that the program is in crisis and the only way out is through radical reforms that voucherize Medicare and shift costs or cut coverage for the elderly. Moreover, the argument goes, if the government cannot afford the growing population in Medicare, how can we possibly afford to guarantee insurance for the entire population? The argument that demographic trends and Medicare commitments preclude universal coverage appeared in 1991–1992, and they are once again surfacing in the current debate.

Claims of demographic apocalypse, such as those popularized by commentators such as Pete Peterson, are misleading and reflect little or no understanding of international trends in population aging. They are designed to scare the public sufficiently to catalyze passage of the conservative agenda of privatizing both Medicare and Social Security. Demography, as we have argued elsewhere, is not destiny.[39] The United States can afford the baby boomers, and their retirement does not threaten the national economy or health care system. The fact that Medicare's enrollment will grow as the population ages is not a crisis. We should be thankful that we have a government program as successful as Medicare to pay for the medical costs of an aging population. The real crisis would be if we did *not* have a public program that protected seniors and their families from the financial burden of medical costs.

Clearly, defending Medicare from attacks should be the first order of business for reformers. It is imperative to argue that demographic trends are an argument *against*, and not for, risky and untested schemes such as vouchers. However, reformers can go even further in turning the demographic argument on its head. Empirical studies have shown that there is no relationship between the age structure of a country and its spending on health care, measured both historically and in contemporary terms. Many of the industrialized democracies have populations far older than that of the United States, yet they spend far less on health care. What do these nations have that the United States does not? National health insurance. In the context of systems that provide public control over medical spending and universal coverage, it is easier for countries to manage the costs of aging populations and to make decisions on where—and on whom—health care resources should be used. Indeed, reformers should argue that the best way to moderate the medical care costs of the baby boom generation is to enact a national health insurance program that gives the United States the same tools that other nations have available to absorb aging populations into their medical care systems.

Conclusion: Health Reform in Political Context

Health reform, we have argued, is not and never will be a dispassionate matter of selecting policy instruments from some menu of idealized options. The stakes of the contending parties foreclose such possibilities, as the history of American health politics amply illustrates. This means that an enlightened, progressive strategy in health care must take into account the political context of reform. It must consider the different environments that are obvious possibilities for the next decade and beyond.

The first requirement is to imagine what those multiple futures might be. One can think of six possible futures by varying both the political composition of the national government and economic circumstances. Imagine, for example, either rapid economic growth of the kind experienced in the second half of the 1990s or, on the other hand, a recession of the sort experienced at the opening of the 1990s. Imagine, further, three political contexts: one involving unified government at the federal level, in which Democrats prevail; one where Republicans dominate both the Congress and the executive; and a situation of divided government. The various possible combinations of these political and economic circumstances produce six alternative future scenarios, each of which bears different implications for a reform strategy.

The next task is to sort out more clearly what these possible futures imply for the reform strategies discussed above. A moment's reflection suggests that only under circumstances of flush economic times and Democratic Party domination would the single-payer option be a live possibility. Even under those conditions, however, it would confront tremendous opposition. Incremental expansion would, of course, also attract support under such circumstances, including universal coverage of children and lowering the age for Medicare eligibility. The introduction of economic and fiscal austerity would suggest a more defensive posture—protection of Medicare rather than its substantial expansion. Were Republican rule dominant amid favorable economic circumstances, one could imagine incremental reform along the lines of the pincer strategy as one option. Were recession to be the context, Republican leaders would in all likelihood seek further restraints on Medicare outlays through vouchers and oppose any measures that would substantially expand coverage. Under that scenario, there still may be political value in pushing for an agenda that seeks to expand coverage.

There is, we have argued, no single, magic bullet that can ease America's path to universal coverage. However, the most attractive option for health reformers at this time, and for the next decade, might be to build support for the federalist option. The federalist strategy, referred to by others as a state-federal partnership,[40] offers the prospect of genuine health reform and the advantages of political flexibility. The federalist option can be altered according to the various political-economic scenarios outlined above. For example, a pincer strategy of narrowing the number of uninsured in the short run could serve as a prelude to the long-run campaign for adoption of federalist health legislation. Similarly, under circumstances less favorable to reform, advocates could propose more incremental forms of the federalist strategy, emphasizing federal funding of optional state programs. And finally, under a political-economic scenario favorable to reform, we believe the federalist strategy offers the best hope for building a legislative majority for comprehensive reform. We recognize that embracing the federalist option would mean altering the past emphasis of American reformers on enacting the Canadian single-payer model. That would by no means be an easy transformation or compromise to make. But ultimately, it is a bold move that would enhance the chances for achieving universal coverage in the United States.

At present, it seems likely that the future decade will be one of turbulence, hard-to-chart adjustments, and little short-term prospect of substantive health reform. Dramatic, transformative shifts are less likely than are marginal adjustments and incremental reforms. But there is no denying the possibility of situational factors—of leadership, context, and happenstance—that could end up causing large programmatic changes. The character, as well as desirability, of these changes will be shaped in no small part by the choices that reformers make about the goals and strategies that should guide U.S. health reform.

NOTES

1. Paul Starr, *The Logic of Health Care Reform* (New York: Penguin, 1992).
2. Theodore Marmor and Jonathan Oberlander, "A Citizen's Guide to Health-care Reform," *Yale Journal on Regulation* 11 (summer 1994): 495–506.
3. Theda Skocpol, *Boomerang: Clinton's Health Security Effort and the Turn against Government in U.S. Politics* (New York: W. W. Norton, 1996).
4. For a critique of the meaning of managed care and its contemporary uses, see Theodore Marmor and Jacob Hacker, "How Not to Think About Managed Care," *University of Michigan Journal of Law Reform* 32(4): 661–684.
5. This view of the legacy of the Clinton health plan failure was embodied in a series of issues published in 1995, in a special volume of *Health Affairs* (14[1]) on "Health Reform: Past and Future."
6. Alain C. Enthoven and Sara J. Singer, "Market Based Reform: What to Regulate and By Whom," *Health Affairs* 14(1): 105–119.
7. On the backlash against managed care, see the special issue of *Journal of Health Politics, Policy and Law* released in fall 2000. See also Donald W. Moran, "Federal Regulation of Managed Care," *Health Affairs* 16(6): 7–21.
8. The consensus on the need for Medicare reform was reflected in the creation of the National Bipartisan Commission on Medicare Reform, led by Senator John Breaux (D.–La.) and Representative Bill Thomas (R.–Calif.).
9. Robin Toner, "Bitter Partisan Fight on Creation of Medicare Drug Benefits," *New York Times* (April 5, 1999).
10. Jennifer A. Campbell, *Health Insurance Coverage 1998* (Washington, D.C.: U.S. Census Bureau, 1999).
11. Kenneth E. Thorpe, *The Rising Number of Uninsured Workers: An Approaching Crisis in Health Care Financing* (Washington, D.C.: National Coalition on Health Care, 1997).
12. David Brown, "Medical Safety Net Seen in Peril," *Washington Post* (March 31, 2000); and Peter Kilborn, "The Uninsured Find Fewer Doctors in the House," *New York Times* (August 30, 1998).
13. Miguel Bustillo, "Treating an Emergency Care Crisis," *Los Angeles Times* (February 15, 2000).
14. James C. Robinson, *The Corporate Practice of Medicine* (Berkeley: University of California Press, 1999); and Paul Ellwood, Alain Enthoven, and Lynn Etheredge, "The Jackson Hole Initiatives for a Twenty-First Century American Health Care System," *Health Economics* I (1992): 149–168; and Regina Herzlinger, *Market-Driven Health Care* (Cambridge: Harvard University Press, 1999).
15. Peter Kilborn, "HMOs are Cutting Back Coverage of the Poor and Elderly," *New York Times* (July 6, 1998).
16. Katherine Levit, et al., "Health Spending in 1998: Signals of Change," *Health Affairs* 19(1): 124–132.
17. Jacob Hacker, *The Road to Nowhere* (Princeton: Princeton University Press, 1997).

18. Kaiser Family Foundation, *National Survey on Health Care and the 2000 Elections* (Menlo Park, Calif., January 2000). The Kaiser survey found that 53 percent of Americans were willing to pay a substantial amount (at least $30 per month) in additional taxes to cover the uninsured. Although there is reason to wonder how deep and strong that sentiment is, it may reveal public preferences changing in a period of economic prosperity.

19. Theodore R. Marmor, *The Politics of Medicare* (Chicago: Aldine, 1973).

20. On the politics of national health insurance in the 1970s, see Paul Starr, *The Social Transformation of American Medicine* (New York: Basic 1982).

21. Theodore R. Marmor, *Political Analysis and American Medical Care* (Cambridge: Cambridge University Press, 1983).

22. Lawrence Jacobs and Robert Shapiro, "Don't Blame the Public for Failed Health Care Reform," *Journal of Health Politics, Policy, and Law* 20(2) (1995).

23. Sven Steinmo and Jon Watts, "It's the Institutions, Stupid: Why Comprehensive National Health Insurance Always Fails in America," *Journal of Health Politics, Policy, and Law* 20 (1995): 329–372.

24. David U. Himmelstein and Steffie Woodhandler, "Bradley Rehashes Stale Ideas," *USA Today* (September 30, 1999).

25. For a discussion of the FEHBP's recent problems, see Jonathan Oberlander, "Is Premium Support the Right Medicine for Medicare?" *Health Affairs* 19(5): 84–99.

26. Joseph White, *Competing Solutions* (Washington, D.C.: Brookings Institution Press, 1995).

27. Jonathan Cohn, "W.'s Health Plan Is Conservative All Right," *New Republic* (May 1, 2000).

28. Oberlander, "Is Premium Support the Right Medicine?"

29. *Missing middle* is a phrase coined by Theda Skocpol, referring to social policies that target working families. See T. Skocpol, *The Missing Middle: Working Families and the Future of American Social Policy*, a Century Foundation Book (New York: W.W. Norton, 2000).

30. For more about this approach, see Theodore Marmor, Jerry Mashaw, and Jon Oberlander, "National Health Reform: Where Do We Go From Here?," in *Health Policy, Federalism, and the American States*, eds. Robert Rich and William White (Washington, D.C.: Urban Institute Press, 1996): 277–291; and Jerry Mashaw and Theodore Marmor, "The Case for Federalism and Health Care Reform," *Connecticut Law Review* 28(1) (fall 1995): 115–126.

31. Ken Frisof and Ted Steege, *The Universal Health Partnership: A Proposal to Take the Final Step to Universal Coverage* (Cleveland: UHCAN, 1998).

32. SEIU, "Service Employees International Union's Proposal: American Health Security Plan," unpublished document.

33. Families USA, "The Building Blocks of Universal Coverage," paper presented at the Conference on Health Coverage 2000, Washington, D.C., January 2000.

34. Families USA, "The Building Blocks."

35. For a more elaborate analysis of Canadian medical care, see Theodore Marmor, *Understanding Health Reform* (New Haven: Yale University Press, 1994).

36. Theodore Marmor and Kip Sullivan, "Caricatures of the Frozen North: Fact and Fiction in American Understanding of Canada's Universal Health Insurance Program," *Washington Monthly* (July/August 2000).

37. White, *Competing Solutions.*

38. Jonathan Oberlander, "Shifting Strategies: American Physicians, Managed Care, and Professional Sovereignty," unpublished paper, University of North Carolina–Chapel Hill, Department of Social Medicine, 2000.

39. Theodore Marmor and Jonathan Oberlander, "Rethinking Medicare Reform," *Health Affairs* 17(1): 52–68.

40. Frisof and Steege, *The Universal Health Partnership.*

5
_____

ECONOMIC SECURITY FOR WOMEN AND CHILDREN: WHAT WILL IT TAKE?

Heidi Hartmann

American women's lives have changed enormously over the past several decades: The work life of the typical young woman today is likely to be longer than her married life.[1] As a result, the typical young woman will find work a more important source of economic security than marriage. Today, women are having fewer children, spaced more closely together; their child rearing years are reduced in number and are often spent outside of marriage, and their years spent working in the labor market are increased—yet they typically will earn less than men.

If marriage can no longer be counted on to sustain a woman economically (if it ever could), what sustains a woman when she cannot work, during childbirth, child rearing, illness, or old age? Until now, society has relied on parents—particularly on married parents—to bear most of the costs of childbirth and child rearing. It is husbands who have generally financed maternity leaves for their wives and supported stay-at-home moms. Women who spent most of their productive years on child rearing also often relied on their husbands' retirement benefits. Today, the typical married man has a working wife, and the typical child is just as likely to be living with a working mom (single or married) as a working dad.

This is the changed reality for American families today; but—most observers would agree—public and private institutions and workplaces in the United States have not changed to accommodate this new reality. Schools are generally still open only about six hours per day, whereas the average workday is eight hours, and overtime work is often required; reliable after-school and child care programs are often hard to find, leading parents to patch together makeshift solutions; and most parents have no access to paid time off for family reasons. A substantial minority of parents also have no health insurance for themselves or their children. And without long-term marriage to a higher-earning male, a woman's lower lifetime earnings doom her and her children to a relatively low standard of living, and quite possibly, to poverty either during her child rearing years or in her old age. Solutions to these problems have been implemented in many countries but not yet in the United States.

The supports provided to working parents in many other industrialized countries are not available here—publicly supported child care, child allowances (which increase family income beyond what parents are able to earn), paid family leave (often up to one year or more), housing allowances, universal health care, more generous universal pensions, and fewer work hours. These supports, generally available to all parents (and often to nonparents as well), are particularly helpful to single women who parent alone. These programs spell the difference between poverty and a decent standard of living. None of these countries has a poverty rate, either among single mothers and their children or among elderly women, as high as that in the United States, though some have similar or higher rates of nonmarriage.

Which policies should we be seeking to implement in the United States, and in what order of priority? Are the policies of other countries feasible here? In this chapter, I look at these questions particularly from the female vantage point, for up to now it has been women who have done the bulk of family care work. And it is women's economic security that is most at risk because of the family care responsibilities they take on. Women's economic equality with men is particularly hard to achieve if there are no societal supports for family care. As long as women have children, it will be difficult for women to achieve economic independence if there is no help for child rearing. In the United States, there appears to be a profound patriarchal drag of a particular form on workplace and community institutions and policies. By failing to develop collective supports for families, we doom women to economic dependence on individual men. We seem to have a strong, individualist patriarchy that matches our form of virulent, individualistic, free-market capitalism. Public policies are needed to ensure that women have full access to economic resources, that they be as capable of supporting themselves and their dependents as are men, and that they not be economically dependent on individual men.

Furthermore, for women to have full equality with men as citizens (which is the basic goal of feminism), their legal rights must be established and protected through a mechanism like the proposed Equal Rights Amendment to the U.S. Constitution. Their reproductive rights must also be as free and as unencumbered as are men's: both the right to have children and the right not to have them must be securely established legally and supported financially for those in need.

However, even if women had full reproductive rights and a complete menu of family care supports, without equal pay in the workforce, women's long-term economic security would still be compromised. Thus, all of the goals and remedies we associate with the modern women's movement—equal pay mandated by the Equal Pay Act of 1963; equal access to jobs, benefits, and promotion opportunities mandated by Title VII of the 1964 Civil Rights Act; and equal access to higher education mandated by Title IX of the Higher Education Act—are just as important as they have ever been, because women still lack basic equality in the labor market.

This chapter is organized in two parts. The first describes in detail some of the recent changes in women's lives and considers where women have made the most progress, where they remain most vulnerable, and what the future is likely to hold. The second outlines a policy agenda that, if pursued, could truly achieve economic security for women *and* their children.

CHANGES IN WOMEN'S LIVES

Women Are Increasing Their Labor Market Work Substantially

Women are entering the labor market in greater numbers and are remaining in it longer and for a greater proportion of their lives. They have been increasing their education and on-the-job skills. They are working more hours and for better pay. They have entered a wider range of jobs, including many traditionally closed to them. They have taken on more financial responsibility for themselves and their families. In a sense, as economic actors, women *are* becoming more like men; but without policy changes, their path to full equality is blocked.[2]

Figure 5.1 illustrates the historic growth in women's labor force participation—a growth that has occurred in three ways. First, each new cohort (age group) of women has worked more than the one before. Second, each cohort of women has generally worked more as they have aged (until nearing retirement age). And third, each cohort of women has worked more steadily during their child rearing years, spending less time out of the labor force when they have children. There is now no dip at all in average labor force participation rates for women in their twenties and thirties, when childbearing and rearing are most common. Women's labor force participation is increasing among women of all marital statuses: Married women work the equivalent of nearly twelve weeks more per year now than in 1979, for example.[3] Single mothers' labor force participation has increased dramatically with the economic boom, the recent increase in the Earned Income Tax Credit, or EITC (which provides cash supplements to low-income working parents), and the decrease in the welfare rolls. And as Figure 5.2 shows, men's labor force participation has been falling, just as women's has been increasing, at almost every age. Thus, again, we see that women's and men's employment behavior appears to be converging.

Today, women constitute 46 percent of the labor force overall; and we can expect that proportion to reach 50 percent or more, in proportion with their share of the population, over the next several decades. Women are voting with their feet—by moving into the labor force and staying there. Despite repeated pronouncements to the contrary (that women are returning home to have children, for example), the general trend toward women's greater commitment to paid work is likely to continue, particularly since women are making more investments in their own education and training.

Young women today are earning 55 percent of the bachelor's degrees, 56 percent of the master's degrees, and 40 percent of the doctorates (as of 1996). Women are increasingly pursuing courses of study and earning degrees in business, law, medicine, and computer science. Forty-four percent of medical students are women;[4] and women are approaching parity in numbers with men in law programs.[5] The proportion of female computer and information science majors at the bachelor's level increased from 14 percent in 1971 to 28 percent in 1996. During the same period, women's share of business and management majors increased

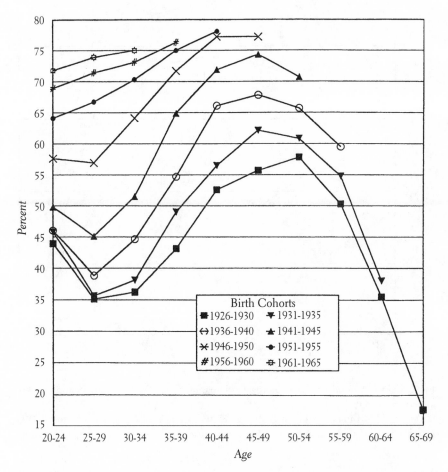

FIGURE 5.1   Trends in Labor Force Participation Rates for Women, 1950–1995, by Birth Cohort

SOURCE: M. Anne Hill and June E. O'Neill, "A Study of Intercohort Change in Women's Work Patterns and Earnings," Report to the U.S. Bureau of Labor Statistics, 1990, as cited in Marianne A. Ferber, "Women's Employment and the Social Security System," *Social Security Bulletin*, 56(3):33–55, 1993. U.S. Bureau of Labor Statistics, *Employment and Earnings*, January 1996, Table 3, U.S. Department of Labor, Washington, DC.

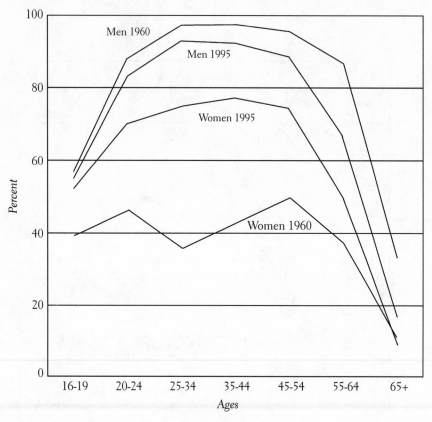

FIGURE 5.2   Trends in Labor Force Participation Rates for Men and Women, 1960 and 1995, by Age
SOURCES: U.S. Bureau of Labor Statistics, *Handbook of Labor Statistics*, August 1989, tables 3 and 4; U.S. Census Bureau, *Statistical Abstract of the United States*, 1999, table 650.

from 9 percent to 49 percent.[6] Despite greater similarity in women's and men's courses of study, however, there is still room for improvement in several areas. Only 12.5 percent of engineering Ph.D. recipients in 1996 were women; and psychology is the only science in which women receive the majority of doctorates earned.[7] Also, minority women still accounted for only 5 percent of Ph.D. degrees earned by U.S. citizens in 1992.[8]

TABLE 5.1   Growth in Women's Earnings by Educational Level, 1978–1998

Educational Attainment	Women's Mean Annual Earnings		Growth in Real Earnings, 1978 and 1998	
	1978[1]	1998	Dollars	Percent
Less than 12th grade	$10,993	$17,252	$6,259	57%
High school only	$15,480	$23,841	$8,361	54%
Some college	$16,103	$28,998	$12,895	80%
College	$21,020	$39,655	$18,635	89%
College plus	$29,008	$53,092	$24,084	83%

[1]1978 earnings are expressed in 1998 dollars using the CPI-U index.
SOURCES: Data for 1998 from *Money Income in the United States*, U.S. Census Bureau, 1998; data for 1978 from U.S. Census Bureau's Web site.

Despite women's recent catch-up in college graduation rates, a look at the stock (rather than the annual flow) of college graduates in the adult population reveals that women still lag behind men in college education. Women still have some distance to go before their educational attainment equals that of men. As the catch-up process continues both in education and in lifetime labor force participation, women should be able to expect that their wages will continue to catch up to men's as well. Given current labor market trends, however, that expectation may not be realized.

Table 5.1 shows women's earnings by educational level. Not only do women with higher levels of education earn substantially more than those with less; they also have experienced the greatest wage growth in percentage terms over the past two decades. Because additional education clearly pays off for women in the labor market, and because there is increased emphasis on the importance of education to equip everyone to compete in a global high-tech marketplace, we can expect women to continue to increase their educational attainment. This trend is, of course, favorable to women's increased wage growth.

As women's educational attainment has become more similar to men's, the jobs women hold have also become more similar, and this also has been favorable for their earnings growth. For example, women have been entering the professions and management jobs especially rapidly and are now slightly overrepresented in these occupational groups compared to their share of the labor force as a whole. In 1998, women held 49 percent of all professional and managerial jobs. The proportion of personnel and labor relations managers who were women increased from 44 percent in 1983 to 66 percent in 1998. Among financial managers, the proportion of women increased from 39 percent in 1983 to 53 percent in 1998. The health and medicine managerial occupations enjoyed an increase from 57 percent to 79 percent women in this same fifteen-year period.[9]

But women's and men's job patterns are not similar enough. Substantial sex segregation is still found in the labor market. In law, women made up only 29 percent of lawyers and judges in 1998. In that same year, women made up only 8.3 percent (a 0.2 percentage point increase from 1983) of the precision, craft, and repair occupations. And they experienced a decline in their representation as machine operators, assemblers, and inspectors (from 42 percent in 1983 to 37 percent in 1998).[10] Even more troubling, women's share of information technology jobs (electrical and electronic engineers, computer systems analysts and scientists, operation and systems researchers, computer programmers, and computer operators) fell from 40 percent to 29 percent between 1986 and 1999.[11]

And women are still overrepresented in traditional women's jobs, despite the general improvement in occupational broadening that has occurred. Women still hold more of the lower-paid jobs — minimum-wage jobs, temporary jobs, and part-time jobs. Women hold about 60 to 65 percent of these less desirable jobs, including all forms of contingent work.[12] The majority of women still work in female-dominated occupations — for example in clerical, retail, and service work — jobs that tend to be low paying. In fact, although the extent of sex segregation in the labor market has declined in the past several decades, as measured by the index of sex segregation, more than half of women (or men) would have to move to jobs dominated by the other sex for women and men to have equal distributions across all jobs in the economy. While the index of segregation had fallen to 53 by 1990, it was 67.7 in 1970. Some of the decline has been due to the relatively stronger growth of many jobs that were already integrated by gender, and some has been due to women's entry into jobs formerly dominated by men. Women's progress in entering a broader range of occupations is, however, unmistakable.[13]

Will the trend toward greater gender integration in high-paying occupations continue? Both "high-tech" and "high-touch" jobs are expected to grow more rapidly than total employment. Many of the jobs that are projected to grow the fastest through 2008 are high-touch jobs traditionally dominated by women: personal care and home health aides, physical therapy assistants and aides, occupational therapy assistants and aides, social and human service assistants, and dental assistants. Rapid job growth is also predicted in the following high-tech jobs, most of which are not typically held by women: systems analysts, computer engineers, medical records technicians, operations research analysts, data processing and equipment repairers, and sales workers in securities and financial services. In between high-tech and high-touch, combining some of the characteristics of both types of jobs, are several additional occupations that are expected to have high job growth: paralegals, medical assistants, surgical technologists, and dental hygienists. All of these occupations—high-tech and high-touch—are expected to grow by 40 percent or more by the year 2008; some of the computer-related occupations are expected to more than double in size. (For comparison purposes, the overall labor-force growth rate for the same period is estimated at 14 percent.)

The occupations that are expected to add the largest number of jobs, some of which are large occupations that are not particularly rapidly growing, also include several disproportionately held by women: cashiers, janitors and cleaners (including maids), retail sales workers, teachers' assistants, waitpersons, registered nurses, general office workers, and receptionists and information clerks. Each of these occupations is expected to grow by 300,000 to 600,000 jobs by 2008. Of the thirty occupations expected to add the most jobs, eleven (more than one-third) are ranked in the bottom quartile on average earnings.[14] Thus, low-wage jobs are overrepresented in these areas of substantial future job growth.

Many of the new jobs that will be available to women are those in which women already predominate and earn low wages (home health aide, personal care and home health aide, cashier, maid, retail sales workers, teachers' assistants, waitpersons). It will be difficult to reduce the concentration of women at the bottom of the labor market if the bottom experiences much of the job growth. And the 2 million women with limited skills who have entered or will enter the job market from the welfare rolls likely also will exert some downward wage pressure on already low-wage jobs. If the public sector continues to be cut back and employment growth in education, health, and management slows, many of the labor market sectors that provided excellent job growth at good wages to women in the past will shrink in relative importance. Barring a recession, there will be plenty of new opportunities for women, but many will not be especially well paying. These projections in job growth suggest that continued progress in narrowing the wage gap will become more difficult.

Women's Pay Still Lags Behind Men's

When women are asked, in survey after survey, what they want, most women respond: "pay equity" or "equal pay." In three polls of working women conducted in the past several years, large proportions reported problems with lack of pay equity and wanted a solution. In *Working Women Count*, a 1994 government report, 49 percent of women reported that not "getting paid what a job is worth" was a serious problem on the job. In a 1997 survey conducted by the Department of Working Women at the AFL-CIO, 94 percent of working women described equal pay as very important, and two in five cited pay (equal pay, discrimination, or low pay) as the "biggest" problem women face at work. In a follow-up survey in 2000, 87 percent of working women responded that stronger equal pay laws are important.[15] This response is common throughout the income spectrum: Women from the executive suite to the factory floor, from the office to the washroom feel they are undervalued, underpaid, and held back in their careers because of their gender. Among *Fortune* subscribers who were also managers, 77 percent of women (as well as 43 percent of men) reported in 1995 that they believed women need more experience or a higher degree level than men to qualify for the same job. A 1995 survey of female executives at Fortune 1,000 companies found more than half agreeing that "male stereotyping and preconceptions of women" had held back their careers.[16] The 1998 Catalyst census of women in top management in Fortune 500 firms found that only 16.2 percent of corporate officers were women and only 3.8 percent of those with the top titles were women. Yet among these high earners—all in similar jobs—women earned only 72 percent of what men earned. Women's dissatisfaction with their wages remains, despite the fact that the pay gap between women and men has narrowed significantly over the past few decades, in keeping with the general progress women have made in the labor market. Unfortunately, progress in closing the wage gap has recently come to a halt.

In the late 1960s and early 1970s, women earned 59 percent of what men earned (comparing the median annual earnings of men and women who worked full-time, year-around). In 1998, the latest year for which annual earnings data are available, women earned $25,862 at the median, compared with men's earnings of $35,345, or about 73 percent of what men earned. That *is* a significant, positive change, though many would argue it is too little, too late—or at least too little, too slow. Moreover, part of the reason for the closing of the gap is that men's earnings have fallen; so one should not attribute all of the narrowing of the gap to genuine progress made by women. As Figure 5.3 shows, men's real wages (in 1998 dollars) generally fell from the late 1970s through the mid-1990s; during this same period, women's wages rose fairly steadily in constant dollars, at least until about 1992. The experience in the economic growth of the mid-1990s has been different, more favorable for men, less for women. Men's real wages began to rise again; and if women were to have continued to narrow the wage gap with men, their real wages would have had to rise even faster.[17] However, that did not happen; in some recent years (1993, 1994, 1995), women's real earnings actually fell. As Figure 5.4 shows, the ratio of women's to men's wages has moved up and down in the 1990s, so that in 1998—the last full year for which annual earnings data are available—women earned only 73 percent of what men earned, below the peak of 74 percent in 1996 and 1997. As Figure 5.5 shows, the ratio of women's to men's median *weekly* earnings for full-time workers (a slightly different wage series) also ceased its climb in the 1990s—the trend line fitted to these data shows clearly that the pattern in the 1990s is one step forward, one step back. For the entire period, depending on which beginning and ending years are used, calculations show that one-half to three-fifths of the narrowing of the gap was due to the fall in men's real earnings.[18]

Despite the negligible growth in real wages for men between 1970 and 1998, they still outearn women (on average) at every age. In fact, the wage gap grows as women and men age, as Figure 5.6 shows. The gap is relatively small for young women and men, but thereafter men's wages increase sharply, whereas women's do not. The average woman in her working prime (that is, in her early forties) makes only about the same as a man in his late twenties. The Institute for Women's Policy Research recently calculated the cost of the wage gap to the average woman: Over her entire working life she would earn about $500,000 less than if she earned the same as the average man.[19]

Although the gap remains large today, and worsens for women as they age, in my judgment it is likely to continue gradually to narrow over time.[20] But just how much, and how fast, is the question. Certainly,

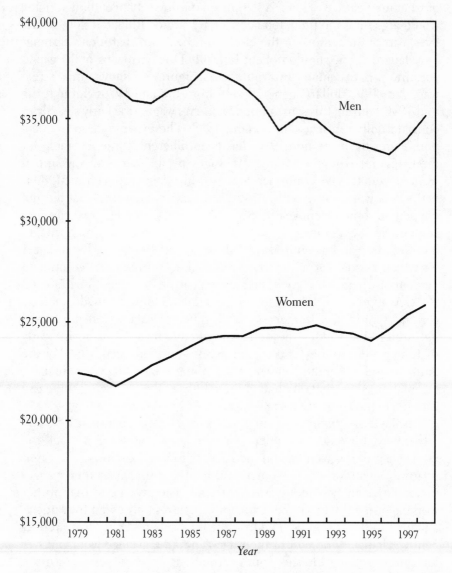

FIGURE 5.3   Median Annual Earnings of Full-Time, Year-Around Workers, 1979–1998 (in 1998 dollars)
SOURCE: IWPR analysis of March current population survey data, workers aged 15 and older.

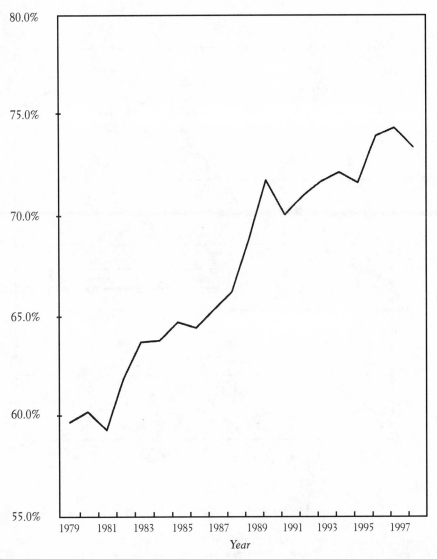

FIGURE 5.4   Women's Median Annual Earnings as a Percentage of Men's, 1979–1998
(full-time, year-around workers)
SOURCE: IWPR analysis of March current population survey data, workers aged 15 and
older.

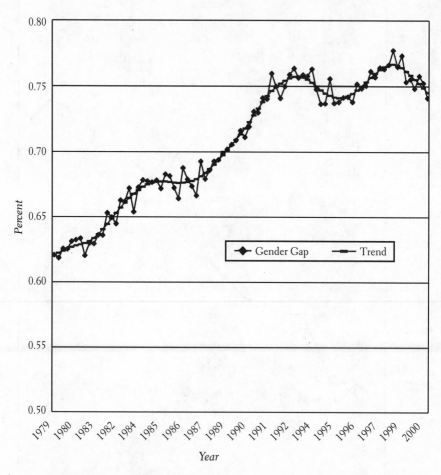

FIGURE 5.5 Women's Median Weekly Earnings As a Percentage of Men's 1979–2000 (full-time workers)

SOURCE: Economic Policy Institute analysis of Bureau of Labor Statistics median weekly earnings, full-time workers, ages 25–54. Stamp 6.0 used for trend extraction.

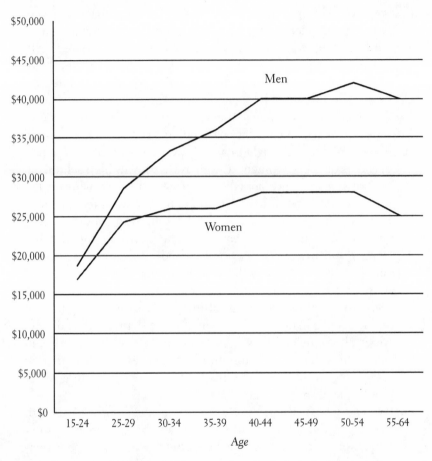

FIGURE 5.6   The Female–Male Wage Gap Over the Life-Cycle (1998 median annual earnings, by age, of full-time, year-around workers)
SOURCES: Institute for Women's Policy Research analysis of the Current Population Survey, 1999, March Demographic Supplement.

concerted action by government, business, and labor unions will be needed to make further progress.

The factors that will affect the rate of closure include

Resumed real wage growth for men. Men's real wages have begun to grow again, catching up with U.S. productivity growth, which has been on the rise for several years. Women's real wage growth has not kept pace. The gender-based segregation in the labor market makes continued differential wage growth rates for women and men likely.

Growing inequality. Women at the bottom have been doing less well in recent years: Their wages have fallen, relative to those earned by better-educated, higher-earning women. In most of the past decade, wages for women (as well as men) with high school educations or less have actually fallen in real terms, whereas the wages of college-educated women have continued to grow. Earnings for women of color still lag behind those of white women, and in recent years, the gap between the two has stopped closing and has even widened a bit, perhaps also because of lower wages to those at, and near, the bottom. Since more women than men are clustered at the bottom of the wage scale, the continuing growth of inequality between the bottom and the top is likely to affect women more than men, tending to widen the female/male wage gap rather than close it. The failure of the federally set minimum wage to keep up with inflation contributes to this growing inequality, as does the falling share of unionized workers in the labor force as a whole.

Further changes in women's education and experience. Although women in the past several decades have been increasing their educational attainment and their time spent in the labor market, both absolutely and relatively to men, the rate of change is likely to slow in the near future, since women are approaching parity with men (and in terms of numbers of new bachelor's and master's degrees, have even surpassed them). Eventually, when women have caught up to men in these areas, these factors will no longer tend to narrow the wage gap between women and men as they have done for the past several decades.

Uneven economic growth. The wage gap is affected by the job sectors in which growth occurs. Are the growing sectors ones in which women's earning opportunities are relatively good or relatively poor? In the past few decades, women have benefited from high growth in areas in which they were already working—for example, in health, education, and clerical work; but high rates of growth are not expected to continue uniformly in all these areas. Government cutbacks and slower growth of government are likely to affect women's employment disproportionately, especially in the professions and management, since a high proportion of women professionals and managers work in the public sector.

Government enforcement. The size of the gap will also depend on government action in enforcing equal employment opportunity and affirmative action, both so that women have a share of jobs in all sectors and so that they are not subject to discrimination in wages. Research done by the National Research Council/National Academy of Sciences as well as by the IWPR has shown that these programs when enforced do work to benefit both white women and women of color (as well as men of color).[21] Cutbacks in budgets for the government enforcement agencies that occurred in the 1980s have not yet been fully restored; and as the female labor force grows in size, more resources are needed just to maintain current levels of enforcement. In view of the expected labor market trends, more and more effective enforcement will be needed.

Women's earning power is undoubtedly the most significant component of their economic liberation. The stagnation of women's wage growth both in absolute and in relative terms in the 1990s is a grave cause for concern and warrants both the more systematic use of existing remedies and the development of new remedies for pay inequity in the labor market.

Women Increasingly Support Their Families Financially

Do women have the same relationship to families as men? Obviously not; but in several ways their relationship is becoming more similar, although important differences remain. Figure 5.7, which shows the proportion of working parents in families of different types for all families with minor children, indicates that women have been taking on more

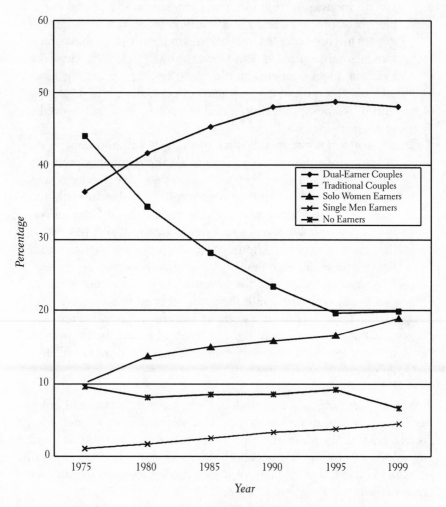

FIGURE 5.7   The Increasing Responsibility of Women Workers for Family Financial Needs (all families with children under 18)

SOURCES: IWPR calculations based on Howard Hayghe, "Family Members in the Workforce," *Monthly Labor Review*, vol. 118, no. 11, March 1990; and labor force activity data from the U.S. Bureau of Labor Statistics.

financial responsibility for families. Dual-earner couples, in which both parents work for wages, have grown from about one-third of families with children in 1975 to nearly half in 1999. The proportion of families with only working mothers in the family has nearly doubled, from about one-tenth to nearly one-fifth. Mothers are more likely to be breadwinners than ever before—they are now just about as likely as fathers (about seven out of ten) to be working to support children at home.

Women are not, however, equally likely to have a partner at home to take care of daily family life. About 20 percent of families with children are still of the "traditional" type: They have a father working outside the home and a mother at home (but this number is down from nearly half of all families in 1975). In contrast, only a very few of the 19 percent of families with working mothers (in single-earner families) include a husband at home. Most of the latter families are headed by mothers alone. And only about 4.5 percent of all families with children are headed by a non-married, working father, so that men are much less likely than women to experience the difficulties of being the custodial single parent.

Interestingly, Figure 5.7 shows a very small increase in the proportion of families of the traditional type between 1995 and 1999 (of 0.2 percentage points), in which the mothers do not work. It is likely that this is mainly due to a recent decrease in labor force participation among low-income married women, as wages have fallen in absolute terms for less skilled women. At the same time, the proportion of families in which mothers are the only earners increased sharply between 1995 and 1999, consistent with the increase in labor force participation of single mothers. (Although many of these single mothers also have limited skills, they have much less choice about whether or not to work, since welfare reform now mandates work. Also, the EITC rewards their work effort with a tax credit, whereas most married women—even those with low incomes—will have family incomes that are high enough to be beyond the range of eligibility for the credit.) Most of the small decline shown in the proportion of dual-earner couples between 1995 and 1999 (0.7 percentage points) is accounted for by the increase in working mother families.

Clearly, with the increase in dual-earner couples and working, single mother families, women are rapidly closing the "family provider" gap. However, given their lower earnings, they are not as successful as men at keeping their families out of poverty. Among working single mother families, 24.2 percent are poor, whereas only 4.5 percent of married couple families (most of which include a working father) are poor.[22] Moreover, there's another important way in which men's and women's support of families differs. Women spend a great deal more time taking care of families than do men. Thus, men need to close the "family care" gap.

Men are able to have both a family and a career simultaneously, whereas women are more likely to pursue a career, especially a high-level career, alone—presumably because the demands of work and family conflict too much for women but not for men. But even in the family realm some progress has been made; not only have men been increasing, slightly, the time they spend on housework, but women also have been spending less—for several reasons. First, when women work outside the home they simply spend less time working inside the home (teenage children are apparently doing more, and more families are using child care providers). Second, women have reduced family care time by having fewer children and having them closer together. Third, men are spending more time on a few domestic chores—especially child care, cooking, and shopping.

Between 1978 and 1988, employed married women decreased their hours of housework by 3.52 hours per week on average, whereas married men, with both employed and nonemployed wives, increased their housework hours by about 1.4 hours on average. Thus the relative burden of housework has shifted some within the family: Whereas in 1978 the ratio of men's to women's housework hours in married couple families with employed wives was 26 percent, by 1988 it had increased to 38 percent. As Francine Blau explains, this reallocation of a share of the housework to men within the family is a new development. Although it is consistent with women's increased employment and earnings in the 1980s, this development is surprising, since housework hours decreased in that ten-year period for every other demographic group studied, including single men.[23]

What does the future hold for the family gap? I expect to see the underlying demographic trends that pull us toward greater equality in financial support of the family to continue in the same direction. The birthrate is likely to continue its historic decline (although short-term increases will also likely occur from time to time); and the proportion of families headed by single parents is likely to continue to grow, as both nonmarital births and divorce rates remain high. Since women's labor force participation will continue to grow, more married couple families will have two incomes, and the proportion of so-called traditional families, distinctly in the minority now, will shrink further in the long run. I also expect to see some progress by men in closing the family care gap. The more hours women spend in work for pay outside the home, the more family responsibilities men necessarily take on.

Unfortunately, putting together what we know of women's earnings with their increased financial responsibility for themselves and their families, we must conclude that many families are losing family income because of the low earnings of wives and mothers, including both single and married mothers. According to a 1999 report published by the Institute for Women's Policy Research and the AFL-CIO, the average family with a working woman loses $4,229 each year due to the lower pay of women relative to men who are comparable in education and age. For all families relying on women's earnings (single mothers, married couples in which both work, and self-supporting single women), the annual loss due to unequal pay is $200.6 billion (in 1997 dollars).[24] If women were paid equally to comparable men, about half the poverty of families supported by working single mothers would be eliminated.

ARE WE CLOSING THE POLICY GAP?

The most serious public policy problem with regard to working families in the United States, it seems to me, is that policies continue to be based on the "traditional" model of a male worker with a wife at home. Federal income taxes, the Social Security system, and unemployment insurance benefits all do more for the family with a male breadwinner and an at-home wife than for the dual-earner couple, despite public opinion to the contrary. For example, the U.S. income tax system allows the splitting of family income between a working spouse (usually the husband) and a nonworking spouse (usually the wife), so that the couple receives a "marriage bonus" of lower taxes (compared with the taxes they would pay if not married). When a working wife earns about the same as a working husband, the tax penalty on marriage, known as the "marriage penalty," is fairly high (it can be several thousand dollars per year); in terms of taxes paid, the couple would be better off unmarried. There is no marriage penalty for the couple in which one spouse does not work.

Under Social Security, married women who have worked all their lives and contributed taxes to the system often receive no more in retirement benefits than wives who never worked outside the home. Some years ago, men whose working wives died had to sue in order to get the widower's benefit to which their minor children were entitled, whereas widowed women got them automatically. Families with working wives just did not fit the traditional norm, and as a result, they were under-served until the system was challenged.

With respect to unemployment insurance, benefits are more readily available to workers who are "fully committed" to the labor force—that is, those who work full-time. Recent IWPR research shows that many part-time workers (and workers with inconsistent labor force attachment or low earnings) tend to be excluded by earnings tests, which measure not only the level of earnings but also their accumulation over the course of a year. Family-related reasons for leaving work are generally not con-sidered valid, and eligibility is often denied in such cases. Thus, women workers are more likely to be excluded from receiving unemployment insurance benefits.[25] In sum, there remain far too many mismatches be-tween today's realities and policies developed yesterday but still in force.

A Five-Point Policy Agenda

1. Increase Women's Wages
Most of all, I would urge a focus on policies that increase women's wages. Being an economist by training, I believe that if women had earn-ing power more equal to men's, their power in other arenas—the house-hold and the body politic, to name just two—would also increase. Sev-eral types of policies are needed to raise women's wages.

Policies to End Discrimination   The Equal Pay Act of 1963 is good as far as it goes, but it addresses pay differences between men and women only when they occur in identical or nearly identical jobs, and as men-tioned earlier, most women do not work in the same categories of jobs as men. Moreover, the remedies under the Equal Pay Act are limited: The only restitution for women who are found to have been discrimi-nated against is back pay. Enforcement has declined together with the budget for enforcement agencies, at the same time as the female labor force has been growing. Title VII of the 1964 Civil Rights Act is broader, addressing discrimination in pay, benefits, hiring, promotion, and other spheres, but its enforcement mechanisms have also been cur-tailed through budget cuts. Affirmative action is often required of those employers found guilty under the Civil Rights Act or among those that have federal contracts. Women have benefited from affirmative action policies, and such policies must be strengthened, not weakened, if women's opportunities are to continue to expand.

Pay equity, or comparable worth, is a newer approach that is needed to ensure that equal-pay policies deal with the reality of job segregation and have the power to continue to close the gap between women's and men's wages. Women's concentration in certain occupations typically results in lower pay for both women and men working in those occupations. The proposed Fair Pay Act, introduced in Congress by Eleanor Holmes Norton and Tom Harkin, would require employers to make statistics on pay rates available to workers so that they could compare the pay rates of jobs held by men and women, minorities and Whites within the firm. If a worker formally complained to the Equal Employment Opportunity Commission (EEOC) that the pay rate of her or his job was unfair due to the gender or race/ethnicity of a disproportionate share of its workers, it would be up to the employer to show how the pay was determined without reference to the composition of the job's incumbents. If the worker's claim were upheld in court, the employer would have to adjust the pay rate of the underpaid job. In this way, firm by firm, job by job, workers could get redress for gender- or minority-based wage discrimination in jobs in which such groups predominate.

Pay equity policy is an essential component of raising women's wages. Equal pay and equal opportunity/affirmative action policies are not sufficient by themselves. An IWPR study of pay equity adjustments made in state civil services shows that pay can be raised in women's jobs without major disemployment effects and that the male-female pay gap is narrowed by such measures. Moreover, states that targeted adjustments at predominantly female jobs raised women's pay substantially with only a modest increase in spending (about 1.0 to 3.5 percent of the total wage bill), narrowing the gender pay gap by between five and eight percentage points.[26]

Solidarity Policies   Policies that raise wages at the bottom of the pay scale are particularly important for women. Raising the federal minimum wage and indexing it to inflation would help millions of women, many of whom support families on their own, particularly now that welfare assistance is time limited and more women whose earning potential is low are going to work. Living wage campaigns for local, state, and federal government contractors will help some low-paid workers achieve higher pay; these campaigns are also likely to help women and minority men disproportionately. Collective bargaining is an important strategy that helps all workers; but research shows that it tends to help women and minority male workers more than it does white men (many of whom would be better able to get high wages on their own).[27] Labor relations laws should be reformed to make it easier to organize unorganized workers, particularly in the service sector and where nontraditional employee-employer relationships are common, and to make the penalties more severe for employers who violate workers' rights. The labor movement's renewed emphasis on organizing workers is very welcome, particularly since the share of all workers protected by collective bargaining agreements has fallen. Women's representation among unionized workers has increased, and women are generally a majority of the new workers being organized as well.

2. Support Child Rearing

It is important that we support child rearing for all families at all income levels. Public schools are the main form of support provided for parents. Child care for younger children, along with before- and after-school care, when needed, and paid family leave should be available to all parents.

Child Care   The most important support families need is help with child care. A larger public role in the provision of child care is important for several reasons. First, parents need financial help most during the years when their children are young. Their earnings then are often lower than when the children are older and out of the house. For low-income single mothers who pay for it, care often consumes about 20 percent of their earnings. These mothers clearly need help with child care expenses. Second, high-quality child care is expensive. Families with moderate means find paying for high-quality care a financial burden that interferes with meeting other needs, and there is some evidence that they underspend on child care (i.e., spend less than is required to get the quality they would like to have). If good care for all children is an important social goal, then society may not be able to rely on parents to purchase it, because they either can't or won't pay as much as it costs. Third, child care is the kind of product that the consumer cannot effectively monitor—much like food preparation, health care, or airline travel. In these situations, a government role in controlling health and safety is critical.[28]

Currently, child care provision in the United States is a patchwork quilt. Higher-income families, and fully subsidized ones, tend to use child care centers most, because of their reliability and quality. Many other families use various informal arrangements, such as a family day care home run by a neighbor or relative; and most families need to use more than one child care arrangement every day. Support to rationalize this system and have the public schools provide more early childhood care is growing. In the District of Columbia, every elementary school has at least one prekindergarten class for four-year-olds; and like the kindergartens, the programs operate for the full school day. In Georgia, funds from the state lottery support universal prekindergarten programs for four-year-olds, also open at least 6.5 hours per day, about 180 days per year. Connecticut, New Jersey, and New York also have substantial public school programs for prekindergarteners. Many other states also have implemented prekindergarten programs and are considering more universal care. Of course, to meet the needs of working parents, such programs need to offer extended hours and summer care as well. In addition, care needs to move down the age range to include three-, two-, and one-year-olds, and even infants. The public provision of child care should be a priority.

Family and Medical Leave   The 1993 Family and Medical Leave Act provided, for the first time in U.S. federal law, a right to be absent from work to take care of one's family or to take care of one's own illness. It provides for up to twelve weeks of unpaid leave for workers who have worked at least 1,250 hours in the prior year at firms of fifty or more employees, after which time they can return to their former job or an equivalent one. It is important both to extend this protection to more workers, including those who work at smaller firms, and to provide paid leave, since few workers will be able to maintain their family's standard of living when subjected to a pay loss of several weeks. A number of states are exploring ways to provide paid family care leave through new or existing temporary disability insurance (TDI) plans mandated in the workplace (which provide partial wage replacement, much like unemployment insurance, to workers with non-work-related illnesses), as well as through state unemployment insurance plans. TDI, currently mandated by only five states, is itself an important income protection even if it does not include paid family leave, because it provides workers with income when they are sick or temporarily disabled. In the five states that require it

(California, Hawaii, New Jersey, New York, and Rhode Island), women workers are a disproportionate share (about 60 percent) of the beneficiaries, primarily because they are covered for childbirth.[29] Research has shown that many low-wage workers, especially single mothers leaving the welfare rolls, do not have paid sick leave for themselves.[30] Even a short illness might force them back on the welfare rolls. Required TDI plans would partially remedy this lack, since most provide partial wage replacement for periods of illness or disability of between twenty-six weeks and one year. The average woman claiming disability in connection with childbirth receives eight to ten weeks of partial pay. In many other industrialized countries, paid sick leaves as well as paid family care leaves (often for up to one year, at close to 100 percent of salary) are part of the social insurance system. Perhaps the absence of such a provision in the United States is another holdover from the era when many wives did not work: When the husband became ill or disabled, a stay-at-home wife could perhaps enter the labor market and attempt to replace his earnings, at least partially.

In an era when so many women and men work and children generally attend school, no one is available to enter the labor market to make up the lost earnings that result from illness or family care. It is absurd that the United States does not have a method to ensure that families have some type of replacement income when the adults cannot work. For poor women without husbands (or with unemployed husbands), welfare provided a minimal income that allowed women to care for their children. This source of support is much less available now because of the five-year lifetime limit on benefit receipt enacted in the 1996 welfare reform bill. Even poor mothers with limited job skills are now expected to work; but even those who usually work will need help in the event of childbirth, or the need to care for a child's, another family member's, or their own illness. These basic life-cycle events are not now provided for in the U.S. social insurance system. Only retirement and unemployment are taken care of through universal systems.

3. Make Work More Family-Friendly: Shorten the Workday
Besides paid and unpaid family leave, other policies can make work more family-friendly: Making overtime hours voluntary rather than required; offering flexible schedules; making part-time work or reduced hours available in career-track jobs (with wages and benefits comparable to full-time work, on a prorated basis); providing on-site child care (if

warranted by employee demand); or providing resource and referral services for child care, elder care, and other family care needs all would help workers accommodate their work and family needs.

My favorite in this category would be reducing the length of the working day. A shorter workday (e.g., six hours instead of eight) for everyone would contribute enormously to the quality of life, as it would relieve the time squeeze that occurs when all of the adults in the family are working. It would also contribute to gender equality in the home and workplace if both men and women worked a six-hour day. The standard workday has not been reduced since the 1938 Fair Labor Standards Act set the workweek at forty hours and the standard day at eight hours. This standard is based on a patriarchal division of labor in which, at least for middle-class and skilled-workers' families, a mother stayed at home to care for children and the home. It is difficult to sustain a forty-hour workweek when both adults are working outside the home. When both adults work forty hours or more, the work of taking care of family members either gets done less well than it should or adds to overload and stress. One way for workers to relieve this stress and share in future productivity growth, in addition to or in lieu of future wage increases, is to reduce working hours but not total pay. This option is now being seriously considered in other countries, and it deserves greater consideration here. Workers in the United States currently work more hours on average than workers in any other country.

4. Supplement Low Incomes

The foregoing policy initiatives are designed to be universal—available to all workers regardless of income level. They are likely to be especially helpful to those with low incomes. But even with these policies, those with low incomes will need additional help.

The wages that many women will be earning—especially those supporting families on their own—will not be enough to provide them and their children a decent living. The most important supplement to the earnings of low-income parents is currently the EITC. It has been very effective at encouraging single mothers to work and now provides a grant (or "tax refund") of about $4,000 per year to a parent with two children and a full-time, minimum-wage job. Married parents are also eligible; but if two single parents, both receiving the EITC separately, decide to marry, they will likely face a very high tax penalty to marriage, as their combined higher earnings likely will place them beyond the eligibility range for the EITC. Reducing marriage tax penalties among low earners should be a high priority for public policy makers. One way to accomplish such a reduction would be to grant larger tax credits to two-earner than to one-earner couples at the same income level.

Other income supplements that should be used more include child care subsidies (fewer than 15 percent of eligible children are receiving child care subsidies), housing subsidies (only about one in three low-income families get any form of housing assistance), and transportation subsidies.

An important protection for workers comes into play when they are between jobs through no fault of their own. Unemployment insurance (UI) is a combined federal and state program in which states set the eligibility standards and benefit levels and employers pay the premiums to cover the benefits in that state. The federal government provides administrative funding and administers a trust fund to provide extended benefits in severe recessions. Unfortunately, UI is a good example of another program that has not adapted to social changes over time. The share of unemployed workers collecting benefits has fallen from about one-half to less than one-third. New labor market entrants and those who leave work voluntarily have never been covered. Many high-wage workers are eligible to receive UI benefits when unemployed; but many part-time workers, temporary workers, and low-wage workers—all categories that have been growing—are not eligible for benefits, either as a matter of state law (which, for example, often excludes those looking for part-time work), or because they do not earn enough to meet their state's eligibility criteria. Domestic violence, changes in shifts that require making new child care arrangements, child care arrangements that fall through, having a sick child, or moving to follow a spouse to a job in a different area are all reasons for leaving work that affect women more than men and that often disqualify workers for unemployment benefits. UI policies need to be updated to accommodate the new realities of families' lives, in which mothers work in the labor market nearly as much as fathers, women nearly as much as men, and in which new work relations and low-wage jobs are proliferating. Minimum federal standards for eligibility would be useful for mandating basic coverage for low-wage and part-time workers in all the states.

The Clinton administration recently issued federal regulations allowing (not mandating) states to use their UI systems to provide paid parental leave for parents of newborns and newly adopted children, and several states may do so; but conservatives have vowed to challenge this new initiative in Congress. As a benefit provided under the UI umbrella, paid parental leave would be available to all workers; but because UI provides only partial wage replacement, these benefits are most likely to be used by lower-wage workers—those least likely to have employer-provided, fully paid sick leave or parental leave available.[31]

No matter how many work supports there are, there will always be people who cannot support themselves, and these people, too, need assistance. When the reauthorization of welfare reform is acted upon in 2002, more attention needs to be paid to the "hard to serve"—those with multiple work barriers who are likely to need longer-term assistance, beyond the five years currently authorized. In addition, it is important that poor women be supported while they complete their education. The federal law allows only one year of higher education or job training to count as a work activity (and the states are required to have rising proportions of their case loads in work activities), so many states are discouraging welfare recipients from completing two- and four-year college programs and intensive job training programs. Yet, as we have seen, women need education and training to earn wages high enough to support families. Supporting women for longer periods of "nonwork" in order to prepare them for higher-paying work in the future is a good long-run investment.

5. Strengthen Retirement Benefits for Women

Currently, the economic disadvantages women experience over a lifetime are summed up in their Social Security benefits when retired. Although Social Security keeps many older women from being poor (50 percent would have incomes at or below the poverty level without Social Security benefits), older women still experience more poverty than older men. Of older women who live alone, 18 to 22 percent are poor, compared with only about 7 percent of older men. Since the Social Security benefit is based on lifetime earnings, women's lower earnings result in their lower benefits in retirement. Currently, marriage to a higher-earning male helps compensate many wives and widows who draw benefits based on their husbands' work records rather than their own, but it does not compensate them fully. One way to boost women's own earnings records (besides pay equity, which also would help tremendously) would be to give women earnings credits for time spent out of the labor force, having children or taking care of them (or providing other types of care). These care-giving credits could boost the earnings records of those for whom it is especially important—single mothers who cannot rely on a husband's earnings record.

And because wives who work and pay into the system often do not receive more in benefits than wives who never worked, it would be useful to find a way to enable married women to benefit from the work they did and the taxes they paid in. One way to do that would be to increase benefits to widows (and widowers) by allowing them to keep 75 percent of the benefits the couple received together when both were still alive. This increases benefits for all widows, but more so for those who worked and have some earnings record of their own. Widows currently constitute the largest group of elderly poor women. However, divorced women and women who never married are as likely, if not more likely, to be poor in retirement; therefore, ways to increase benefits going to low earners and divorced women also need to be developed. The National Council of Women's Organizations' Task Force on Women and Social Security has recommended a number of ways to increase benefits to these groups.[32]

Lastly, the coverage of private retirement pensions needs to be expanded, and the implications of the shift from defined benefit plans to defined contribution plans need to be further explored for their potentially negative effects on women. Retired women workers are much less likely than men to have pensions from their employment; and those who do, have much smaller benefits. Only 30 percent of women currently receive pension benefits, compared with 48 percent of men. Clearly the low rate of pension receipt, even among men, suggests that the United States needs to develop some type of universal, fully portable pension system that will protect workers in old age. Increasingly, employers are shifting to defined contribution plans, to which usually both employees and employers contribute a set proportion of pay (although contributions from both are not required), and which tend to be more portable than defined benefit plans. Women, when given the chance to participate in an employer-sponsored plan, do so in proportions almost as high as men. However, protections for a wife's economic interest in her husband's pension are not as strong with defined contribution plans. Many wives who have had low earnings because of time spent caring for family members may find that their husbands have disposed of lump-sum pension payments without providing for them. With no private pensions, or inadequate ones, many workers and their wives must rely completely on Social Security, which, although it provides very valuable basic protection, was never designed to be retirees' only source of income.

A plan like the one outlined above would increase economic security for women and their families. These policies would help women at all income levels and in all stages of their life cycle—as children, students, mothers, workers, and retirees. Pay equity, public provision of child care and paid family care leave, a shorter workday, income supplements for those in need, and stronger retirement benefits would help close the policy gap and reorient U.S. public policies toward the needs of today's families—dual-earner couples, single mothers, and single fathers. If we took the typical woman's life cycle as a guide to public policy—a life cycle that includes child rearing and the care of others—public policies would be more family-friendly for all types of families. Public policies based on a hypothetical, traditional family structure must be replaced with policies that meet the needs of today's more diverse families. Each individual, male or female, should have the opportunity to develop her or his potential fully, to contribute to society, and to have a decent standard of living. Especially in the high-growth economy the United States is currently enjoying, Americans have a tremendous opportunity to lead, to point to the real problems, and to offer real solutions that take into account the needs of all adults as workers and nurturers, and of dependent family members as well.

NOTES

1. Author's calculations based on labor force participation data and data on marital and divorce histories.

2. And, as discussed below, perhaps we also want men to become more like women in some respects.

3. Lawrence Mishel, Jared Bernstein, and John Schmitt, *The State of Working America, 2000–2001* (Ithaca, N.Y.: Economic Policy Institute and Cornell University Press, 1999), table 1.17.

4. U.S. citizens only, excluding nonresident aliens. For medicine, the numbers exclude veterinary medicine, optometry, and pharmacology.

5. U.S. Department of Commerce and Bureau of the Census, *Statistical Abstract of the United States: 1999* (Washington, D.C.: U.S. Government Printing Office, 1999), table 332.

6. Ibid., table 331.

7. Ibid., table 332.

8. "Women, Minorities, and Persons With Disabilities in Science and Engineering: 1994," NSF 94–333 (Arlington, Va.: National Science Foundation, 1994).

9. U.S. Department of Commerce, Bureau of the Census, *Statistical Abstract of the United States: 1999*, table 675.

10. Ibid.

11. Council of Economic Advisers [CEA], *Opportunities and Gender Pay Equity in New Economy Occupations* (Washington, D.C.: CEA, 2000).

12. A study sponsored by the Institute for Women's Policy Research (IWPR) and conducted by Roberta Spalter-Roth and Heidi Hartmann using a new definition of contingent work, estimates that of all workers, about 1 out of 6 are contingent workers, 61 percent of whom are women ("Gauging the Consequences for Gender Relations, Pay Equity, and the Public Purse," in *Contingent Work: American Employment Relations in Transition,* eds. Kathleen Barker and Kathleen Christensen [Ithaca, N.Y.: ILR Press and Cornell University Press, 1998]; also available as a discussion paper from IWPR, Washington, D.C., 1998).

13. Francine D. Blau, "Trends in the Well-Being of American Women, 1970–1995," *Journal of Economic Literature* 36(1) (March 1998): 112–165.

14. George Silvestri, "Employment Outlook, 1998–2008: Occupational Employment Projections to 2008," *Monthly Labor Review* 122(11) (November 1999): 51–77.

15. U.S. Department of Labor, Women's Bureau, *Working Women Count! A Report to the Nation* (1994); AFL-CIO, *Ask a Working Woman* (1997); AFL-CIO, *Working Women Say . . .* (March 2000).

16. Cited in Francine D. Blau, Marianne A. Ferber, and Anne E. Winkler, *The Economics of Women, Men, and Work,* 3d ed. (Upper Saddle River, N.J.: Prentice Hall, 1998).

17. Recent research at the IWPR found that only in 9 of the 50 states and in the District of Columbia did the wage gap between women and men narrow between 1989 and 1997 because women's real wages rose faster than men's. In 23 states, the gap narrowed because men's real wages fell while women's increased; and in 12 additional states the wage gap narrowed because women's real wages fell less than men's. In several states the gender wage gap increased. See Amy B. Caiazza, ed., *The Status of Women in the States,* 3d ed. (Washington, D.C.: IWPR, 2000).

18. Heidi Hartmann and Julie Whittaker, "Stall in Women's Real Wage Growth Slows Progress in Closing the Wage Gap," briefing paper, IWPR (Washington, D.C., February 1998).

19. Heidi Hartmann and Julie Whittaker, "The Male-Female Wage Gap: Lifetime Earnings Losses," *Research-in-Brief,* IWPR (Washington, D.C., March 1998).

20. Karen Smith ("The Status of At-Risk Groups Now and in the Future," paper presented at the conference "Social Security and the Family," held at the Urban Institute, Washington, D.C., June 19, 2000) projects that women's and men's average earnings will further diverge in absolute terms between 2000 and 2040 but that the wage ratio of women's to men's average earnings will increase slightly, by about 2.8 percentage points for women and men between the ages of 25 and 62, including both part-time and full-time work (so that the gender gap in wages will narrow slightly in relative terms).

21. Barbara F. Reskin and Heidi I. Hartmann, eds., *Women's Work, Men's Work: Sex Segregation on the Job* (Washington, D.C.: National Academy Press, 1986); and M. V. Badgett and Heidi Hartmann, "The Effectiveness of Equal Opportunity Poli-

cies," in Margaret Simms, ed., *Economic Perspectives on Affirmative Action* (Washington, D.C.: Joint Center for Political and Economic Studies, 1995).

22. U.S. Department of Commerce and Bureau of the Census, *Poverty in the United States: 1998, Current Population Reports*, series P-60, no. 207 (Washington, D.C., September 1999), table 3.

23. Blau, "Trends in the Well-Being of American Women."

24. Heidi Hartmann, Katherine Allen, and Christine Owens, *Equal Pay for Working Families: National and State Data on the Pay Gap and Its Costs* (Washington, D.C.: AFL-CIO and IWPR, 1999).

25. Young-Hee Yoon, Roberta Spalter-Roth, and Marc Baldwin, *Unemployment Insurance: Barriers to Access for Women and Part-Time Workers* (Washington, D.C.: National Commission for Employment Policy, U.S. Department of Labor, 1995), available from the Institute for Women's Policy Research (IWPR), Washington, D.C.; and Annisah Um'rani and Vicky Lovell, *Unemployment Insurance Reform for the New Workforce* (Washington, D.C.: IWPR, 2000).

26. Institute for Women's Policy Research, "Pay Equity and the Wage Gap," *Research-in-Brief*, IWPR (Washington, D.C., January 1995); and Heidi Hartmann and Stephanie Aaronson, "Pay Equity and Women's Wage Increases: Success in the States, A Model for the Nation," *Duke Journal of Gender Law & Policy* 1 (1994): 69–87.

27. Roberta Spalter-Roth, Heidi Hartmann, and Nancy Collins, "What Do Unions Do for Women?" research report presented at the conference "Labor Law Reform: The Forecast for Working Women," sponsored by the Women's Bureau, U.S. Department of Labor, in Washington, D.C., October 14, 1993; available from IWPR, Washington, D.C.

28. Heidi Hartmann, "The Economic Realities of Child Care," testimony before the Subcommittee on Human Resources, Committee on Education and Labor, U.S. House of Representatives (Washington, D.C., April 21, 1988) and Supplementary Statement (May 5, 1988).

29. Stephanie Aaronson, "What Is Temporary Disability Insurance?" *Research-in-Brief*, IWPR (Washington, D.C., May 1993).

30. Jody Heyman and Alison Earle, "The Work-Family Balance: What Hurdles Are Parents Leaving Welfare Likely to Confront," *Journal of Policy Analysis and Management* 17(2) (spring 1998).

31. Annisah Um'rani and Vicky Lovell, *Unemployment Insurance Reform for the New Workforce* (Washington, D.C.: IWPR, March 2000).

32. Heidi Hartmann and Catherine Hill, with Lisa Witter, *Strengthening Social Security for Women: A Report from the Working Conference on Women and Social Security* (Washington, D.C.: IWPR and National Council of Women's Organizations, March 2000).

6

TO IMPROVE STUDENT LEARNING:
ASK THE RIGHT QUESTIONS

Richard Rothstein

Average academic achievement of poor children, especially African Americans and Hispanics, lags far behind that of white children. This achievement gap is a cause of continuing disadvantages for minority children in the college admissions process and in the labor market. There is a broad consensus in America today that if we could reduce the achievement gap, we could enhance the life chances of minority and poor children, contributing to a more equal society.

Most research designs and policy discussions about narrowing this gap focus on how schools can be improved to provide disadvantaged children with an education comparable to that received by white children. Policies most frequently advocated include smaller class sizes for disadvantaged children, particularly in the early grades; better-qualified and better-trained teachers, particularly for inner-city schools; after-school and summer tutoring or extra instructional programs; scripted instructional programs; and full-day kindergarten, and the extension of kindergarten to four-year-olds from disadvantaged families.

Policies like these will undoubtedly help to improve the academic achievement of disadvantaged children. But they are expensive and unlikely to be implemented fully. It would be wise for policymakers to consider whether other types of policies might also be effective or more effective in reducing the gap.

It is widely recognized that a child's academic achievement is the product not only of the quality of school the child attends but also of the education and educational preparation the child has received outside of school—in the family, in the community, and from peers. A predisposition to learn can be enhanced by environmental conditions—whether a child is well nourished, has appropriate health care, and has other physical necessities for learning (e.g., stable housing that provides a place to study).

When researchers attempt to separate the effects of schools from the effects of other influences on academic achievement, they generally conclude that *the nonschool factors are more important.* We would be more likely to produce high average academic achievement for all children if all children had advantageous social background characteristics and school quality remained the same than if all children had better schools and the children's current background characteristics were unchanged.

Although this is widely recognized, few policymakers attempt to improve the academic achievement of disadvantaged children by addressing deficiencies in the children's social background directly, because policymakers assume this is too difficult to do. Instead, they assume that school improvement, though less powerful than social and economic reform in generating high achievement, is a more practical route.

But this assumption is rarely examined. Indeed, there may be relatively easy-to-implement social and economic reforms that would have a powerful impact on student academic achievement. It is time to move beyond a misconception of schools as the only hope for lifting the achievement of disadvantaged children and to explore the feasibility and effectiveness of other reform approaches.

SCHOOLS ARE NOT THE ONLY EDUCATIONAL INSTITUTION

In educational research and policy, most educators, researchers, and policymakers assume that schools are the primary determinants of student achievement and that the influences of families, communities, peers, and broader social forces are only modifiers of, rather than independent influences on, educational outcomes. This approach is without theoretical basis. In fact, families, communities, and peers are educational institutions that contribute directly to student achievement. They can impart knowledge, inspire students to learn, reinforce the learning or motivation transmitted by others, or offset the educational influences of others. We don't really know which of these institutions is primarily responsible for academic outcomes; the likelihood is that different ones may be primary for different groups of children at different times and under different circumstances.

The late sociologist James S. Coleman[1] used the phrase *social capital* to describe aspects of education that result from these nonschool institutions. Some children reside in homes and/or communities where their attempts to create their own human capital are generously supported by the presence of social capital. For other children, the necessary social capital is not so readily available.

Coleman distinguished between two levels of social capital that played a role in the creation of human capital: the family and the community. *Family social capital* refers broadly not only to intrafamilial relationships but also to resources that contribute to children's academic growth through these relationships. Such resources include parents' educational background, which may affect expectations for student performance; material resources that support student learning; parenting styles and philosophies (for example, whether parents read to young children, or restrict how much television children can watch); and family cultural values (which may affect, for example, the assumptions parents make about occupational goals for their children).

Family capital may vary within the same family for different children because parenting styles may change as parents age, and because the intellectual stimulation received by a child may change as family size increases. For example, children with fewer siblings may benefit from more family capital than those with more siblings, either because the former benefit from more undivided adult attention or because older children develop mentoring skills in the process of caring for younger ones, and younger children have fewer opportunities for similar development.[2]

Community social capital refers to resources of communities in which families live as well as to the transmission mechanisms by which communities influence students' academic performance. Community social capital can include relationships between and among parents in the community, relationships between children and other adults, and the relationships parents have with institutions in the community. Even in families with high social capital, a lack of social capital in the community can have a negative influence on children's academic achievement and school attainment.

A child's social capital can also be enhanced or diminished by peer group relations and expectations. Although the nature and extent of peer group influence is complicated by the fact that parents may play an important role in choosing or in influencing a child's choice of peers (in which case family capital has a spillover effect on community capital), there is little doubt that peers can and do have an influence on children's academic achievement and motivation.[3]

Some have argued that African American children are dissuaded by their peers to do well in school, if such ambition is equated with "acting white."[4] Judith Rich claims that peers have greater influence on a child's personality (including academic motivation and ambition) than do parents.[5] Where family capital and other forms of community social capital are absent, peer groups can create their own social capital, which may be hostile to schools and their educational mission.

Broader social, economic, and cultural forces also may directly affect student achievement or be transmitted by temporary responses in the workings of family and social capital, or of peer influences. It is probable, for example, that the apparent decline in academic achievement of American students in the late 1960s and early 1970s was caused, in part, by adults' loss of authority during the Vietnam War and the civil rights movement.[6] Schools during this period might not have done anything differently, but academic achievement might have declined because youths paid teachers less heed. One cause of low academic achievement by some African American and Hispanic students may be the expectation that a discriminatory labor market will nullify their academic efforts.[7] A low unemployment rate could inspire adolescents to stay in school in order to qualify for better jobs that are evidently available; alternatively, it could depress student achievement if adolescents are seduced by part-time work opportunities[8] or if they drop out of school to take full-time jobs. A recent decline in the percentage of young males (but not females) enrolling full-time in college after secondary school may reflect the competition of employment opportunities in a strong economy[9] or the higher costs of college education. Whatever the explanation, it is likely that these trends are affected more by economic forces than by school effects.

In addition to family and community social capital and the broader social, economic, and cultural forces that affect achievement, each child's preexisting human capital (genetic endowment) interacts with each educational institution (families, communities, peer groups, the economy and culture, and schools) in a unique way. But human capital is not limited to what a child has at birth; it can also be enhanced or diminished by acquired health characteristics (such as adequate nutrition, or the lack thereof, exercise, or disease), each of which influences how an individual learns from the various educational institutions.

These various forms of capital can and often do congregate to tip the scales decisively toward certain groups of children and away from others. In his book, *The Truly Disadvantaged: The Innercity, the Underclass, and Public Policy*, William Julius Wilson[10] noted that in the 1960s and 1970s, stable African American families followed industry to the suburbs, and in consequence, community social capital unraveled in the-inner-city neighborhoods they left behind. As employment opportunities in these inner-city neighborhoods dwindled and strong adult role models disappeared, crime rates, drug use, and the presence of gangs escalated, diminishing all forms of social capital. Children who remained had fewer successful adult role models and fewer networks that extended into communities where economic opportunities flourished. The contributions of social capital to educational outcomes may not be linear: Neighborhoods with negative (or positive) characteristics may require these characteristics in a minimum quantity before a "tipping point" is reached and they influence student achievement.[11]

In short, families, communities, peer groups, culture, economic markets, and schools are all educational institutions. Changes in any of these can affect the academic performance of students. We know very little about the relative importance of each of these educational institutions. Most analyses today conclude that about 75 percent of the *variation* in student achievement is attributable to student social and economic characteristics. But this conclusion should not be confused with a claim that 75 percent of academic learning is acquired outside school. The massive, federally sponsored study completed in the 1960s by Coleman and his colleagues, titled *Equality of Educational Opportunity*,[12] concluded that *variation* in student achievement could best be explained by variation in family and social capital, not by variation in school practices; but it did not suggest that schools did not contribute to learning. Even if the most important influences on relative student achievement come from other educational institutions, schools, if properly focused, can also play an important role.

Despite the reality that academic outcomes can be affected by families, communities, peers, and broader social and economic forces, most policymakers today treat schools as the *only* determinant of student achievement. For example, all researchers understand that poverty tends to reduce the family capital upon which students can draw, and if concentrated, can also reduce the social capital upon which students can draw. But because education researchers treat these impacts as secondary, they conclude that the remedy for this situation is to increase the ability of schools to compensate for the weak positive influence of families on schools. The conventional way of doing this is to increase school resources, and a typical figure is 20 to 30 percent—schools are assumed to require 20 to 30 percent in additional resources for each pupil from a poor family—although some estimates are much higher.

If the positive influence of families on human capital is at a less-than-desirable level, it is true that we could attempt to offset this weakness by increasing the strength of the influence of schools on human capital. But there is an alternative, and possibly more effective intervention. If the positive impact of families on human capital is weak, we might consider whether strengthening the influence of families themselves might better contribute to students' human capital and thus to their achievement. Perhaps this is not practical, and the only alternative is to strengthen schools to compensate for weakness in families. But the practicality (i.e., the relative cost-effectiveness) of these alternatives is rarely considered.

We do consider, and sometimes adopt, many policies to strengthen families and communities. But these policies are rarely considered in terms of educational outcomes. If we want to improve the employment prospects of inner-city youth, for example, we consider whether improving their access to good housing might be a way of doing so. But if we want to improve the academic test scores of inner-city youth, we immediately consider which school compensatory programs would be most effective. We rarely consider whether improving students' access to good housing might *in itself* produce higher test scores as effectively as school compensatory programs, if not more effectively. My goal in this chapter is to promote that kind of consideration.

THE RELATIVE COST-EFFECTIVENESS OF INSTITUTIONAL INTERVENTIONS

There is ongoing interest among educators in the "production function"—that is, what quantity of resources, applied in what fashion, will produce a given gain in student academic achievement. Most contemporary literature focuses on one of two resource applications as having the greatest potential: smaller class sizes, particularly in the lower grades and particularly for low-income students; or better-qualified (and therefore better-paid) teachers. In a recently published article, Dominic Brewer and his colleagues[13] compare these treatments, and calculate that the $5 billion to $6 billion per year required to fund President Clinton's proposal to hire 100,000 new teachers to reduce first- through third-grade class sizes to eighteen pupils would be sufficient alternatively to raise average teacher salaries in those grades by $10,000 per year, thereby attracting high-quality teachers. Although the authors do not conclude that investment in teacher quality would be more effective than investment in the teacher-pupil ratio, they challenge policymakers to show that the achievement gains resulting from the latter treatment would be greater than those resulting from the former.

In another study,[14] researchers used a meta-analysis of education production function studies to calculate the consensus expectation of achievement gains from the application of a $500-per-pupil increase to a variety of school improvements. Assuming an average class size of twenty-five pupils and average teacher salary of $35,000, spending an additional $500 per pupil on lowering the pupil-teacher ratio should improve test scores by 0.04 standard deviation units (equal to about 1.3 percentile points); spending it on increasing teacher salaries should increase scores by 0.16 standard deviation units; spending it on increasing teacher experience would increase scores by 0.18 standard deviation units; and spending it on increasing teacher education would increase them by 0.22 standard deviation units.

An increase of $500 in per-pupil expenditure would translate into a national increase in school spending of about $23 billion. If spending on elementary and secondary education continues to grow at recent rates, we can expect to add this amount to school spending within the next five years or so. It is prudent to ask whether this increase should be spent on class size reduction, teacher education, or improving the social context of schooling. We should want to know not only the comparative academic impact of a $23 billion expenditure on a variety of school interventions, but also the comparative *academic* impact of spending those dollars on alternative institutional reforms. If an ongoing school expenditure of $23 billion can be expected to generate, at best, a gain in test scores of 0.2 standard deviation units (approximately equivalent to 7 percentile points), how does this payoff compare to the test score gain that would likely result from an investment of $23 billion each year in the nation's family or social capital, or in economic and social reforms that might improve student motivation?

This question suggests areas of investigation that are as important as the investigation of which school resource increases will likely be most productive. It is puzzling that educational research and policy have generally ignored this task, assuming that it is impossible. In the words of Erik Hanushek: "While family inputs to education are indeed extremely important, the differential impacts of schools and teachers receive more attention when viewed from a policy viewpoint. This reflects simply that the characteristics of schools are generally more easily manipulated than what goes on in the family."[15] In view, however, of how daunting it has proven to manipulate school resources to generate dramatically higher student achievement, and considering the magnitude of resource growth that schools have enjoyed and are likely to continue to enjoy, this assumption deserves rethinking: $23 billion is a lot of money, and it might provide significant levers to affect "what goes on in the family."

Terrel Bell, secretary of education during the Reagan administration, did much to persuade Americans of the urgency of school reforms in his 1983 report *A Nation at Risk*. Assessing his role in the school reform movement ten years later, Bell wrote: "[We] had placed too much confidence in school reforms that affected only six hours [a day] of a child's life and ignored the other eighteen hours each weekday plus the hours on weekends and holidays. . . . In the face of many negative influences on our children that come from outside the school. . . we have foolishly concluded that any problems with the levels of academic achievement have been caused by faulty schools."[16]

To sum up, we know that a great deal of the variance in achievement is related to factors beyond school, and therefore, that direct nonacademic intervention at the individual, family, and community levels (designed to increase the capital of each) can increase educational outcomes. It is time for researchers and policymakers to consider the cost-benefit implications of public expenditures (school-based versus non-school-based) to improve educational outcomes. The remainder of this chapter highlights growing evidence that investments beyond the school building can have a direct impact on educational outcomes, and suggests areas and methods for determining the cost-benefit implications of such investments.

FAMILY CAPITAL: INCOME

Higher family income is associated with higher student achievement, but little is known about how income affects achievement. Assuming that we can separate the impact of income on achievement from the impact of other family characteristics that generally accompany family income (e.g., better-educated parents), what is it that higher-income households purchase that affects student achievement? Does better nutrition, better health care, or better housing contribute to higher achievement? Perhaps it is not purchased goods and services that improve achievement but the feelings of self-confidence and self-worth that accompany longer-term higher incomes in a free market economy? The latter explanation conflicts with the American political tradition, which tends to deny the reality of "social class" distinct from what money can buy. One analysis found, however, that although a five-year average of higher family income had a systematic influence on achievement, there was little association between a single year's income and educational achievement.[17] This may reflect a social class effect, or it may simply reflect the fact that one year's higher income alone may not be sufficient to purchase the goods and services that produce higher achievement.

In the early 1970s, the federal government conducted an experiment to determine the effect of higher income on a variety of outcomes. Families were randomly selected to receive the benefit, which took the form of a negative income tax; families in the treatment group received as much as 50 percent more income than families in the control group. The effect on children's test scores was inconsistent and inconclusive; yet in several cases, dramatic test score improvements were observed.[18] The experiment did not continue long enough to make conclusions about the long-term effects of income transfers.

Policy debates about public education focus not only on the importance of improving mean student achievement but also on the importance of narrowing the gap between the achievement of socioeconomically disadvantaged and advantaged children, and particularly between the achievement of African American and white children. If income does have an impact on achievement in ways not presently understood, surely a matter for concern should be that the family incomes of poor (generally lower-scoring) children have declined relative to those of middle-class (generally higher-scoring) children. African American poor children are far more likely to be poor for extended periods, whereas white poor children are more likely to move in and out of poverty. Sustained poverty is more highly associated with low achievement than episodic poverty.[19] Thus, the growth of poverty is likely to put more pressure on the racial achievement gap than on the overall gap in test scores between poor and non-poor children.

The income ratio of families at the twentieth percentile of the nation's income distribution to families at the sixtieth percentile fell from 43 percent in 1973 to 39 percent in 1989 and 38 percent in 1997.[20] When family income is apportioned on a per capita basis, equally to all adults and children in each family, the apparent growth of inequality in income per child is greater: The ratio of average income per child in families in the bottom quartile of the family income distribution to that of families at the midpoint of the family income distribution, fell from 60 percent in 1970 to 57 percent in 1980 and to 51 percent in 1988.[21] This suggests that if income is related to achievement, reducing income inequality might be an effective means of reducing achievement gaps between poor and middle-class children.

There is some evidence that a long-term decline in wages of workers at the bottom of the wage distribution may have been stopped or even reversed since 1996, as a result of a continued strong economy with a low unemployment rate.[22] If these gains continue and are reflected in greater family income and income per child in poor families, and if this income growth is associated with higher student achievement, it suggests that educational policy makers and researchers should devote greater professional concern to the importance of a strong economy for education and to the policies that may contribute to it (not only wage and tax policies but also macroeconomic fiscal and monetary policies). Of course, for most national economic policies, comparison groups do not exist; it is impossible to determine what student achievement might have been in the absence of certain macroeconomic policies. However, an inability to calculate the precise impact of, for example, moderate interest rates from Federal Reserve policies on the academic outcomes of disadvantaged children is no reason to ignore the importance of this impact. If the impact is real, then the consideration of such factors in macroeconomic debates may be as important for improving achievement as are suggestions about class size, teacher qualifications, or other school reforms.

In an article published in *Child Development*,[23] researchers concluded that an increase over a four-year period in average family income from the poverty line to twice the poverty line was associated with a 3.6-

point increase in the IQ of five-year-olds. When children from persistently poor families were compared with those from families whose income never (during the five-year study period) fell below the poverty level, the IQ gap was 9 points. In both cases, other family characteristics were controlled, suggesting that monetary income itself, and not other highly correlated socioeconomic characteristics (e.g., mother's education, female head of household, etc.) was the important factor. Another study, published in the *Journal of Human Resources*,[24] concluded that an increase in a typical family's income of $10,000 per year in 1988 was associated with young (around five and a half years old) children's test score gains equivalent to 3.9 percentile points. The effect was nonlinear, being more pronounced at lower income levels.

Susan Mayer has estimated that doubling family incomes from $15,000 to $30,000 per year, in and of itself, would result in an increase in five- to seven-year-olds' test scores of only 1 or 2 percentile points, with greater increases posted by children whose family incomes are higher for five years than by children whose family incomes are higher in a single year. She found similar small effects also for other outcomes, such as educational attainment and teenage childbearing. She concluded, "The overall benefit to children from extra income could still be greater than the benefits of any other policy that costs the same." The effect on young children's test scores could be greater for children whose families are at lower income levels, and the cost of doubling family income for poor families would be much lower than the cost of doubling family income for everyone. Mayer did not distinguish among the effects of income gains from various sources. It is possible that the effects on test scores differ for different mechanisms: for example, when income is raised by increasing the Earned Income Tax Credit (EITC) for working families, or when it is raised by increasing welfare benefits.[25]

If a $23 billion national expenditure were directed at a permanent income increase for the lowest-income families, would the resultant achievement gains compare favorably with those expected from a similar expenditure on teacher education or class size reduction? Researchers have only begun to explore such issues, but the challenge beckons: In 1995, approximately 19 percent of all U.S. school-age children lived in families whose incomes were below the poverty line, and about 11 percent of all families had incomes below poverty level.[26] The average poor family in 1997 had income that was $6,602 below the poverty line; the total national poverty gap (i.e., the amount of money required to bring each poor family's income up to the poverty line) was about $48 billion. The total poverty gap for families with children would be somewhat less. Of all poor adults, 67 percent worked in 1996.[27] Thus, if an appropriate mechanism could be found, a significant impact on the poverty of families—especially those whose low incomes most negatively impact test scores—could be achieved for a $23 billion annual expenditure, the amount equal to a per-pupil expenditure increase of $500.

Family income is relatively amenable to policy intervention, certainly in comparison to school interventions. The real issue is whether we are as confident that income policies will have as much of an impact on student achievement as school policies. One program currently in existence to supplement the incomes of low-income workers is the EITC. In 1996, the Internal Revenue Service distributed $26 billion through the EITC program to 19 million low-income taxpayers, three-fourths of whom were families with children.[28] Thus, an expenditure of $23 billion, if directed to an expansion of the EITC, would virtually double the size of that program, would make a considerable dent in poverty in America, and might have a beneficial impact on the academic achievement of poor children. Education research should focus on estimating how great that impact might be.

Indirect expenditures to increase family income (and thus family capital) might have similar effects. Large increases in the minimum wage may produce job loss or feed inflation. But if the likely job loss is relatively small compared to the income growth of employed beneficiaries, we should not dismiss such a policy peremptorily. What magnitude of a permanent minimum-wage increase would be necessary to produce a gain of 7 percentile points in the test scores of children from working poor families? If the cost in higher inflation or lower economic growth is comparable to the $23 billion we may be prepared to spend on class size reduction or teacher education, the alternative of a minimum-wage increase may be reasonable.

FAMILY CAPITAL: NUTRITION

What if, instead of spending funds for undifferentiated income support to the poor, public policy instead targeted the expenditures to subsidize particular goods or services that poor families most need to purchase? What would the effect on achievement be in this case? Because we do not presently understand the mechanisms for translating family income into academic achievement, it is difficult to know how such funds should be spent; but we do have some clues.

In experimental studies, children given vitamin and mineral supplements "showed test score gains that significantly exceeded the controls."[29] Inasmuch as vitamin and mineral nutritional supplements are relatively inexpensive, this is a particularly productive area for investigation of relative costs and benefits.

One study found a significant association between achievement test scores of inner-city kindergarten children, and the deviation of these children's weight from the normal weight for children of that age and gender.[30] Most provocative in this study was that, at least for African American inner-city children, weight was more strongly correlated with tests of school achievement (the Stanford Achievement Test) than with measures of cognitive or visual-motor-perceptual ability. This finding suggests but does not prove that nutritional deficiencies in young children might cause more temporary than permanent damage, and thus that direct nutritional subsidies to poor families and their children might be alternative ways to spend funds effectively to improve achievement.

FAMILY CAPITAL: PRENATAL CARE

There is also an association between very low infant birth weight and poor academic performance. Education researchers should calculate the national investment in prenatal care that would be required to produce achievement gains equal to a given investment in classrooms or teachers. Perhaps a relatively inexpensive investment in the nutrition of low-income pregnant women would generate test score gains. In one experiment involving mothers believed to be at risk for delivering low birth weight babies, the babies born to mothers given liquid protein dietary supplements exhibited more behaviors associated with later test score gains than did babies born to mothers in a control group. But there has been no definitive long-term follow up of this experiment.[31]

One intervention almost certain to have an impact is reduction of smoking by pregnant women. Smoking by pregnant women has been found to cause an approximate mean decrease of four points in their children's IQs.[32] This is an enormous decrease and would have a big impact on later academic test scores. Although the harm to infants caused by maternal smoking during pregnancy receives wide attention in America today, with notices on every package of cigarettes, the potential payoff for further reductions is great enough that they should be a continued focus of policy, and where appropriate, expenditure of funds designed to improve academic achievement.

FAMILY CAPITAL: LEAD EXPOSURE

It is widely believed that lead poisoning has been eliminated as a danger to American children; but a nationwide health survey recently conducted by the Centers for Disease Control concluded that 4.4 percent of the nation's children between the ages of one and five years had harmful levels of lead in their blood.[33] The problem is particularly acute for low-income children: 8 percent of children in families enrolled in Medicaid and 12 percent of children in families receiving WIC supplementary food benefits had dangerously high levels of lead. These levels were high enough to "cause reductions in IQ and attention span, reading and learning disabilities, hyperactivity and behavioral problems." According to a 1993 study by the National Research Council of the National Academy of Sciences, further study may result in a lowering of the threshold for identifying dangerous exposure, leading to a conclusion that considerably more than 4.4 percent of the nation's children have a reduced learning capacity due to lead poisoning. Yet fewer than 20 percent of children in low-income families—that is, those most at risk of lead poisoning—have even been screened for dangerous levels of lead in blood.[34] Screening rates vary widely among states, in part because although federal guidelines permit Medicaid coverage of screening for lead poisoning, not all state Medicaid program guidelines take advantage of this regulation.

Children most at risk from lead in their blood come from the same family income groups whose children characteristically score below national norms on academic achievement tests and whose other achievement outcomes are low. These are also the children for whom class size reductions are most indicated. It would seem reasonable for education researchers to estimate whether funds spent on screening for lead poisoning and on subsequent remediation and treatment (primarily by identifying and removing sources of lead) might produce achievement gains comparable to those obtained by class size reduction or other school interventions for low-income children. Such a comparison might be particularly fruitful because once class sizes are reduced in the primary grades, the reductions will likely be permanent and will incur ongoing expenditures in excess of current rates. But if existing sources of environmental lead can be identified and removed, the extent of screening and removal could be reduced without a loss of the academic achievement gains that might have been realized by such a program.

FAMILY CAPITAL: HEALTH CARE

Poor children are more likely to be admitted to a hospital, and to have longer hospital stays once admitted, than children of families with higher incomes. According to data collected in the early 1980s, poor children lost 40 percent more days of school each year than non-poor children. Twice as many poor children had iron-deficiency anemia as non-poor children. Poor children were two to three times as likely to have severe vision impairment as non-poor children.[35] Even if these data improved somewhat in recent years (poor children, for example, lost 30 percent more days of school than non-poor children in 1991), the description is still broadly accurate.[36] Each of these conditions affects academic achievement.

Greater access to health care could ameliorate many of these problems and contribute to equalizing academic achievement for poor and non-poor children. Nearly 11 million American children—that is, 15 percent—are without health insurance; but the percentage of poor children without health insurance is considerably higher, as 32 percent of poor people of all ages are without health insurance.[37] If greater access to health care would produce greater health in poor children, academic outcomes could improve considerably. Uninsured children of all income groups have 25 percent more absences from school, and they are more likely than are insured children to have undiagnosed and easily remediable problems (e.g., vision and hearing impairments) that affect academic achievement.

In 1989, the federal government initiated a pilot project in Florida in which school districts were to purchase group health plans covering their enrolled students. Enrollment in group health plans began in 1992. In 1995, the federal government concluded its role in the project; the state of Florida has continued the program with its own local and state funds. The program cost the state and local school districts a total of $16.7 million in 1996–1997, for 37,000 enrolled children—that is, about 3.4 percent of Florida's school population in the sixteen counties participating in the program that year.[38] When these costs are averaged over the entire school population in these counties, the cost per pupil was about $15.18.

After 1997, the program was expanded, using new federal funds from Title XXI of the Social Security Act (the Children's Health Insurance Program, or CHIP) and funds from Florida's settlement with tobacco companies. By 1999, the program had expanded to cover 63,000 children in forty-one counties, and eligibility for subsidies was increased to include children from families with incomes up to twice the poverty line.[39] Even if the point is reached where all uninsured children in Florida are enrolled (about 245,000 children), the overall cost is unlikely to exceed $100 per pupil. The state estimates that its 1996–1997 subsidy of this program was fully recouped in reduced emergency room visits by children who now had primary care physicians and preventive care. (Some of this offset was realized by private charity hospitals rather than by the state.)

The most common illnesses diagnosed by participating physicians were asthma and attention deficit hyperactivity disorder (ADHD). These conditions, if left untreated, can cause serious academic problems—the former, because of significant rates of absence associated with the disease. Although there are good policy reasons to be concerned with children's access to health care beyond the school effects, it seems reasonable to ask how the average achievement gains that result from such a program compare with those that could be generated by other objects of per pupil spending increases.

Seven other states had begun planning similar programs before the adoption of Title XXI in 1997, and now all states can receive federal funds for such programs. As the programs must be implemented gradually, there are opportunities for research comparing the academic effects for children who are enrolled to those for children not (or not yet) enrolled.

Another approach, more common prior to the adoption of the federal CHIP program, has been to staff schools with nurses and clinics, especially in disadvantaged communities. The National Association of School Nurses recommends a nurse-to-student ratio of 1:750, with a ratio of 1:125 for severely, chronically ill or developmentally disabled populations.[40] Utilizing an overall ratio of 1:750, the cost of staffing schools with a nurse would be about $80 per pupil. If nurses were concentrated in schools with disadvantaged populations, it seems reasonable that achievement gains would be one of the outcomes. It should be possible to compare student achievement in schools that have nurses with student achievement in demographically similar schools that do not.

FAMILY CAPITAL: PARENTAL AGE

It is widely understood that children born to teenage mothers are at risk of academic failure. In the book *Student Achievement and the Changing American Family*, researchers concluded that the mother's age at childbirth is an important predictor of a child's future educational achievement.[41] If their analysis is correct, this aspect of family capital's impact on student outcomes presumably arises because more mature mothers make greater contributions to their children's academic achievement than do less mature mothers. In contrast, another analysis has concluded that among poor African American teenage mothers, lower age at a child's birth may be associated with higher academic achievement.[42] This counterintuitive finding may reflect the fact that in very poor black communities, children born to teen mothers are more likely to be raised by grandmothers or other members of an extended family, whereas children born to poor mothers in their twenties may be raised without as much extended family support. It may also reflect that for the very poor, health deteriorates as women age from the teen years to the twenties, so that children born to women in the latter group have less healthy mothers. A high priority for research, therefore, is to resolve this apparent conflict in conclusions about the impact of teen motherhood on achievement. If it turns out that teen motherhood has adverse consequences for children's academic achievement, then we should ask ourselves, What investment in adolescent sex education and mental health would be required to produce gains in academic achievement equal to the gains produced by equivalent investments in class size reduction or teacher training? If only a small part of $23 billion were invested in adolescent health clinics, it might go a long way toward producing student academic gains by raising mothers' average ages.

FAMILY AND SOCIAL CAPITAL: HOUSING

As noted above, there seems to be an association between abnormally low weight for age (as a result of nutritional deficiencies) and poor academic performance. One study found that children from families who received housing subsidies were less likely to have abnormally low weight for their age than were children from families who were on waiting lists for such subsidies but had not yet received them.[43] The authors note that families with housing subsidies spend a higher proportion of their incomes on food than do eligible families who are not receiving housing subsidies. Thus, the authors conclude, housing subsidies permit families to redirect income to nutrition, avoiding low-weight crises and their consequent depressing effects on academic achievement.

Housing subsidies may also increase family income in other ways that affect student achievement. For example, subsidized housing may permit low-income families to afford apartments with more adequate space in which children can study or do homework. Or housing subsidies may impact achievement by stabilizing living arrangements. If, as seems probable, low-income families move frequently, then housing subsidies may permit low-income families' children to remain in the same schools. High rates of student mobility are considered by educators to be an important cause of low student achievement in poor communities. A 1994 report of the United States General Accounting Office concluded that about one-sixth of all third-graders nationwide had attended three or more schools since the first grade, and these frequent movers were disproportionately found among low-income and minority students: 30 percent of children from families with incomes below $10,000 had attended at least three different schools by the third grade, whereas only 10 percent of children from families with incomes above $25,000 had done so.[44] Another analysis, of mobility in particular cities, found annual average transiency rates approaching 50 percent; and a disproportionate percentage of students in this high-mobility group were African American and Hispanic children from poor families.[45]

Mobile students lose continuity of instruction; lose the peer relationships with familiar friends that provide security for learning; and cannot take easy advantage of remedial programs for which diagnoses emerge over time, or of programs for which eligibility must be established. For example, mobile students are less likely to receive Title I reading services for which they would be eligible.[46] Not only are test scores depressed and dropout rates elevated for highly mobile students but achievement of all students in high-mobility schools suffers because teachers must devote instructional time to reviews for newcomers and to the organizational tasks of incorporating them into classrooms. Schools with high rates of mobility must frequently reconstitute their classrooms in order to avoid placing all newcomers in a single class. Even without reconstitution of classrooms, teaching strategies tend to deteriorate in schools with high mobility. For example, teachers are more likely to teach discrete units instead of integrating instruction across units and subjects, and they are more likely to spend time reviewing old material than introducing new units.[47] The movement for greater accountability in American education is also frustrated in schools with high mobility: Stable students may make achievement gains that are missed in school averages that include the test scores of recent arrivals.

Student mobility can have several causes, including parental job loss or transfer, school choice programs, and family breakup or reorganization. But an important cause of student mobility in low-income communities is almost certainly unstable and inadequate housing. There is a serious shortage of housing for low-income families in urban areas, and many families with children either double up with friends or relatives for intermittent periods or move when they cannot keep up with obligations to pay rent. In extreme cases, families move in and out of shelters or other nonstandard housing.

Of 1.7 million renter families with children in 1995 who were "working poor" (i.e., families whose income from work was equivalent to the minimum wage from a half-time, year-around job), 80 percent spent more than 30 percent of their incomes for rent and utilities, and 42 percent spent more than 50 percent of their incomes for rent and utilities. One-third of these families either lived in overcrowded housing or were doubled up with other families.[48] The spending of such a high proportion of limited income on housing not only indicates housing problems that contribute to low achievement but also signals that children may be suffering other hardships that contribute to low achievement (e.g., nutritional deficiencies).

If families acquire stable housing located in a less distressed neighborhood, a child's social capital may improve along with his or her family capital; or the family's social capital may improve, leading back in turn to a further improvement in family capital. For example, if stable housing is located in a safer neighborhood, parents may feel more secure about leaving children in the neighborhood when they leave for work. If this security improves the parents' work reliability and employability, family income could increase, resulting in further capital improvements that contribute to learning.

There is a long history of educational research on the effects of student mobility on achievement. Yet this research almost invariably leads policymakers to consider how schools can accommodate the special needs of mobile students—for example, by improving the speed with which student records follow student school transfers; providing busing so that students can avoid changing schools when their families move; or designing special remedial tutoring programs for mobile students.[49] Some researchers have considered whether mobility can be reduced by urging parents to consider the impact of moving on their children's achievement, and some school district policymakers have used this approach.[50] Educational research, however, rarely considers whether directing resources to reduce mobility directly—for example, by means of housing subsidies—may be a cost-effective approach to improving test scores, aside from its other beneficial results.

The availability of publicly funded housing subsidies reduces student mobility. A study of New York City families housed in homeless shelters found that families who received housing subsidies within five years were twenty-one times more likely to be stable (in the same apartment for at least twelve months) than families who did not receive such subsidies.[51] But nationwide, only one-fourth of working poor families with children received any kind of public housing assistance in 1995. There were 569,000 working poor families who received no housing assistance and who paid more than 50 percent of their incomes for rent and utilities; another 463,000 paid between 30 and 50 percent of their incomes for rent and utilities.[52] The Department of Housing and Urban Development estimated in 1997 that the average cost of housing subsidies was $5,499 per year, per unit.[53] Thus, an immediate expansion of the Section 8 program to cover all working families with children who presently spend more than 50 percent of their incomes for rent would cost only $3.1 billion annually. Expansion to cover all of the working families with children that presently spend more than 30 percent of their income for rent would cost a total of $5.7 billion annually. These amounts should be considered in the context of the heretofore described expected increase in elementary and secondary education spending of $23 billion, much of which will undoubtedly be directed at the most disadvantaged children, the very children whose families lack adequate housing. An annual housing expenditure of $5.7 billion is equivalent to a per-pupil spending increase of about $121, spread equally among all elementary and secondary school pupils. No research has yet been undertaken to determine the relative gains in student achievement from the expenditure of $5.7 billion on Section 8 housing vouchers, as opposed to class size reduction or recruitment of more qualified teachers; but the possible results are sufficiently provocative that such research should be a high priority.

In Albuquerque, public housing is dispersed throughout a large metropolitan area in order to avoid concentrating the poor in isolated ghettos. In their 1994 paper, David Rusk and Jeff Mosley[54] compared the academic outcomes, over a ten-year period (1983–1984 to 1992–1993), among public-housing children whose neighborhood schools were predominantly middle class to outcomes among similar children whose neighborhood schools were predominantly poor. They found that public-housing children attending schools where less than 20 percent of their classmates were poor or nearly poor (i.e., eligible for free lunch) had standardized test scores 13 percentile points higher than similar public-housing children attending schools where more than 80 percent of their classmates were poor or nearly poor.

The findings from these studies suggest three distinct sets of issues that are in need of further research: One is the disruption to education caused by moving from one neighborhood (or school) to another, especially when it happens with frequency, and whether housing programs are effective in reducing differences in ability and generating improved outcomes. An entirely separate issue is the identification of the negative influence on academic outcomes of a neighborhood without great social capital, regardless of how long a family remains there. A third issue is the quality of a family's housing, and the effect that poor resources (lack of space for study, or greater stress from overcrowding) have on learning, regardless of the neighborhood in which a residence is located.

SPECIAL EDUCATION

Up to this point, I have discussed possible expenditures to increase disadvantaged students' family and social capital as a means of improving their academic outcomes. I have suggested that the effects of these expenditures on academic outcomes should be considered in comparison to expenditures likely to take place in schools seeking improvements in academic outcomes (e.g., through reduced class sizes and increased teacher qualifications).

Possible expenditures to improve family capital may also have the effect of *reducing* some expenditures currently made by schools. The object of the greatest school expenditure increase in the past three decades has been special education: Of new funds given to elementary and secondary schools from 1967 to 1996, 40 percent went to special education; only 23 percent of the new money went to regular academic programs. Special education in recent years has accounted for 19 percent of all school spending.[55]

Only a small part of special education spending can be attributed to family capital deficiencies that are easily remediable by policy intervention, but this part still represents considerable spending; reducing it has the potential to offset the cost of some environmental interventions. The special education categories most preventable by relatively low-cost environmental intervention are "learning disability" and mild mental retardation (i.e., an IQ from 70 to 95).

In 1995–1996, 5.8 percent of all elementary and secondary students were classified as learning disabled — 51.3 percent of all special education students.[56] The proportion of *learning disabled* — a category that blends seamlessly into the category of *nondisabled slow learners* — "is one of the most sensitive barometers of the biomedical status of children and the psychosocial climate in which they live," in the words of D. P. Hallahan. Poverty, substance abuse by pregnant women, nutritional deficiencies, toxicity (e.g., lead poisoning), and social instability may all contribute to learning disability: "Based on physiological factors, a certain percentage of the population is at risk for developing a learning disability. Given enough social support and/or a nonstressful life-style, however, some of these individuals may function well and never be identified as having a learning disability."[57]

As noted earlier, smoking by pregnant women is associated with a four-point decrease in their children's IQ scores. But the impact of smoking by pregnant women may have its greatest consequences for education finance in its impact on extreme cases — children who are categorized as "mentally retarded." An astonishing 35 percent of mental retardation cases in children are apparently caused by smoking during pregnancy.[58] In 1995–1996, 1.3 percent of all elementary and secondary students, and 11.3 percent of all special education students, were classified as mentally retarded;[59] thus, approximately 0.5 percent of all U.S. schoolchildren suffer mental retardation from maternal smoking during pregnancy.

We do not yet know with certainty how much of the cost of special education is attributable to the accommodation of learning disabilities that could have been prevented by better nutrition, social support, and/or a nonstressful life-style, or which of these factors might be facilitated by, for example, more stable housing. But assume that one-third of the children presently identified as learning disabled could function normally if we made greater family and social capital investments, and assume that each of these children presently requires one to two hours a day of work with a resource specialist, perhaps in groups of six children with similar remedial needs. Similar resources are required for mildly mentally retarded children, one-third of whose cases, it was noted above, could have been prevented by an effective campaign to eliminate maternal smoking during pregnancy. Assume further that the typical special education resource specialist working with learning-disabled and mildly retarded children has a daily case load of twenty-four (four groups of six children each). If the salary and benefit cost of a typical resource teacher along with associated support, diagnostic, and administrative services is about $60,000 per year, then greater investment in family and social capital could be offset by savings of over $2 billion annually in special education costs.

CONCLUSION

Researchers have developed renewed interest in controlled experimentation, where possible, as a superior means of detecting the impact of specific resource treatments on achievement. Because specification of family, community, and economic variables is so imprecise given present knowledge, nonexperimental studies that attempt to parse the responsibility for achievement shared among schools, families, and communities are likely to continue to be inconclusive at best, or contradictory at worst. This is true as well of so-called natural experiments because of the imprecise standards required for identifying control groups. Two true educational experiments involving random assignment of children to treatment and control groups have therefore gained wide recognition—the Tennessee class size experiment and the Perry preschool experiment. In the former, students were randomly assigned to regular classes (the control group), reduced-size classes, or regular classes with a paraprofessional aide. Researchers found that a reduction in class size from about twenty-two to about fifteen produced test score gains, with greater gains for minority students than for whites.[60] In the latter, a pool of low-income African American three-year-olds were randomly assigned to receive preschool services (including teacher home visits) in the mid-1960s. Follow-up studies of the experimental and control groups over the next twenty-five years found higher academic achievement, better high school graduation rates, and higher marriage rates, along with lower welfare utilization and criminal activity for the experimental group that had received the preschool services.[61] The replication of these experiments and the design of others to examine social and economic treatments of families, communities, and schools should now be high priorities.

Levers to improve academic achievement may be found in family, income, and social policy as well as in schools. Education researchers have generally ignored these alternative levers, believing (without careful examination) that school improvement is more amenable to public policy than are improvements in family or community characteristics. This belief may not be warranted. Not only have school improvements that generate large achievement gains, especially for disadvantaged students, been difficult to identify and implement, but they are very expensive. Some relatively inexpensive interventions to improve family and social capital may have the potential to generate larger academic achievement gains. Policies to improve child and maternal prenatal nutrition, environmental conditions (lead contamination, for example), or the age of mothers at first-time birth come immediately to mind. Reduction of smoking by pregnant women could have dramatic payoffs in academic outcomes of children. Raising the income floor of the working poor through tax or minimum-wage policies could also have measurable consequences in improved student achievement. Policies to improve the access of low-income families to adequate housing may be the most productive intervention for raising academic achievement.

As a wealthy nation, of course, the United States can and should invest more in its schools and more on lifting poor children out of poverty. But there are always resource choices to be made. If there are dollars available from the budget surplus to improve the academic achievement of disadvantaged children, we have an obligation to spend those dollars where they will do the most good. If we can get more of an education benefit from, for example, an EITC expansion than from class size reduction, then we have an obligation to spend more on the former and less on the latter. This is not an argument in favor of reducing demonstrably effective investments in schools; it is an argument that in their assessments of cost-benefit implications of public expenditures to improve educational outcomes, researchers and policymakers should consider a wider range of alternatives.

NOTES

This chapter was adapted from *Making Educational Investments in Children* by Richard Rothstein (Washington, D.C.: Finance Project, 2000), by permission of the Finance Project. Preparation of this work was supported in part by the Peabody Center for Education Policy at Vanderbilt University, and by *20/20 Vision*, a report of the Consortium on Renewing Education (November 1998), which commissioned the background paper on which the chapter was based. The conclusions and opinions expressed in this document are those of the author alone, and do not necessarily reflect, in whole or in part, the conclusions or opinions of the Consortium on Renewing Education, the Peabody Center for Education Policy, Vanderbilt University, the Ball Foundation, or any of the officers or individuals associated with these groups.

1. James Coleman, "Social Capital, Human Capital, and Schools," *Independent School* (fall 1988): 9–16; and James Coleman, "Social Capital in the Creation of Human Capital," *American Journal of Sociology* 94 (Supplement) (1988): 95–120.

2. R. B. Zajonc, "Family Configuration and Intelligence," *Science* 192 (April 16, 1976): 227–236.

3. William Evans, Wallace Oates, and Robert Schwab, "Measuring Peer Group Effects: A Study of Teenage Behavior," *Journal of Political Economy* 100(5) (1992): 966–991.

4. Signithia Fordham and John U. Ogbu, "Black Students' School Success: Coping with the 'Burden of Acting White,'" *Urban Review* 3 (1986).

5. Malcolm Gladwell, "Do Parents Matter?" *New Yorker* (August 17, 1998).

6. Willard Wirtz et al., *On Further Examination: Report of the Advisory Panel on the Scholastic Aptitude Test Score Decline* (Princeton, N.J.: College Board Publications, 1977).

7. John Ogbu, *Minority Education and Caste: The American System in Cross-Cultural Perspective* (New York: Academic Press, 1978); and John Ogbu, "Racial Stratification and Education in the United States: Why Inequality Persists," *Teachers College Record* 96(2) (winter 1994): 264–298.

8. Laurence Steinberg, *Beyond the Classroom: Why School Reform Has Failed and What Parents Need to Do* (New York: Simon and Schuster, 1996).

9. Tamar Lewin, "American Colleges Begin to Ask, Where Have All the Men Gone?," *New York Times* (December 6, 1998).

10. William Julius Wilson, *The Truly Disadvantaged: The Innercity, the Underclass, and Public Policy* (Chicago: University of Chicago Press, 1987).

11. Jonathan Crane, "The Epidemic Theory of Ghettos and Neighborhood Effects on Dropping Out and Teenage Childbearing," *American Journal of Sociology* 96(5) (1991): 1226–1259; and Malcolm Gladwell, "The Tipping Point," *New Yorker* (June 3, 1996).

12. James S. Coleman, Ernest Q. Campbell, Carl F. Hobson, James McPartland, and Alexander M. Mood, *Equality of Educational Opportunity* (Washington, D.C.: U.S. Government Printing Office, 1966).

13. Dominic Brewer, Cathy Krop, Brian P. Gill, and Robert Reichardt, "Estimating the Cost of National Class Size Reductions Under Different Policy Alternatives," *Educational Evaluation and Policy Analysis* 21(2) (summer 1999).

14. Rob Greenwald, Larry Hedges, and Richard Laine, "The Effect of School Resources on Student Achievement," *Review of Educational Research* 66(3) (1996): 331–396.

15. Erik Hanushek, "The Trade-off Between Child Quantity and Quality," *Journal of Political Economy* 100(1) (February 1992): 84–117.

16. Terrel Bell, "Reflections One Decade After *A Nation at Risk*," *Phi Delta Kappan* (April 1993): 594–597.

17. Eric Hanushek, "The Trade-off."

18. Susan Mayer, *What Money Can't Buy: Family Income and Children's Life Chances* (Cambridge: Harvard University Press, 1997).

19. Greg J. Duncan, Jeanne Brooks-Gunn, and Pamela K. Klebanov, "Economic Deprivation and Early Childhood Development," *Child Development* 65(2) (1994): 296–318.

20. Lawrence Mishel, Jared Bernstein, and John Schmitt, *The State of Working America: 1998–1999* (Ithaca, N.Y.: ILR Press, 1999).

21. Victor R. Fuchs and Diane M. Reklis, "America's Children: Economic Perspectives and Policy Options," *Science* 255 (January 1992): 41–46, table 3.

22. CEA [Council of Economic Advisers], "The Annual Report of the Council of Economic Advisers," in the *Economic Report of the President* (Washington, D.C.: U.S. Government Printing Office, 1999), chart 3.3.

23. Greg Duncan et al., "Economic Deprivation and Early Childhood Development."

24. Anne M. Hill and June O'Neill, "Family Endowments and the Achievement of Young Children with Special Reference to the Underclass," *Journal of Human Resources* 29(4) (1994): 1064–1100.

25. Mayer, *What Money Can't Buy: Family Income and Children's Life Chances.*

26. NCES [National Council for Education Statistics], *Digest of Education Statistics* (Washington, D.C.: U.S. Department of Education, 1997): 98–115, tables 20, 21.

27. Mishel et al., *The State of Working America: 1998–1999*, tables 6.10, 6.19.

28. Tom Herman, "Tax Report: The Earned-Income Credit," *Wall Street Journal* (January 7, 1998); and GAO (U.S. General Accounting Office), *Earned Income Tax Credit: Claimants' Credit and Income Patterns, Tax Years 1990 Through 1997*, GAO/GGD 97–69 (Washington, D.C.: U.S. General Accounting Office, 1997).

29. Ulric Neisser, Gwyneth Boodoo, Thomas J. Bouchard Jr., A. Wade Boykin, Nathan Brody, Stephen J. Ceci, Diane F. Halpern, John C. Loehlin, Robert Perloff, Robert J. Sternberg, and Susan Urbina, "Intelligence: Knowns and Unknowns," *American Psychologist* 51 (1996): 77–101.

30. Robert Karp, Roy Martin, Trevor Sewell, John Manni, and Arthur Heller, "Growth and Academic Achievement in Inner-City Kindergarten Children," *Clinical Pediatrics* (Philadelphia) 31 (1992): 336–340.

31. Neisser et al., "Intelligence."

32. Carolyn D. Drews, Catherine C. Murphy, Marshalyn Yeargin-Allsopp, and Pierre Decoufle, "The Relationship Between Idiopathic Mental Retardation and Maternal Smoking During Pregnancy," *Pediatrics* 97(4) (April 1996).

33. GAO [General Accounting Office], *Lead Poisoning: Federal Health Care Programs Are Not Effectively Reaching At-Risk Children*, GAO/HEHS 99–18 (Washington, D.C.: U.S. General Accounting Office, 1999).

34. Ibid.

35. Barbara Starfield, "Child Health and Socioeconomic Status," *American Journal of Public Health* 72(6) (June 1982): 532–534.

36. Barbara Starfield, "Health Indicators for Preadolescent School-Age Children," in *Indicators of Children's Well-Being*, eds. Robert M. Hauser, Brett V. Brown, and William R. Prosser (New York: Russell Sage Foundation, 1997).

37. Robert Pear, "Americans Lacking Health Insurance Put at 16 Percent," *New York Times* (September 26, 1998).

38. Florida Healthy Kids Corporation, *Healthy Kids Annual Report, February 1997* (Tallahassee: Florida Healthy Kids Corporation, 1997), insert ("May Update" [May 7, 1997]).

39. Florida Healthy Kids Corporation, *Healthy Kids Annual Report, February 1999* (Tallahassee: Florida Healthy Kids Corporation, 1999).

40. Personal communication with Judy Robinson, executive director, National School Nurses Association, March 15, 1999.

41. David W. Grissmer, Sheila Nataraj Kirby, Mark Berends, and Stephanie Williamson, *Student Achievement and the Changing American Family* (Santa Monica, Calif.: RAND, 1994).

42. Arline Geronimus, "Teenage Childbearing and Personal Responsibility: An Alternative View," *Political Science Quarterly* 112(3) (fall 1997).

43. Alan Meyers, Deborah A. Frank, Nicole Roos, Karen E. Peterson, Virgina A. Casey, Adrienne Cupples, and Suzette M. Levenson, "Housing Subsidies and Pediatric Undernutrition," *Archives of Pediatric and Adolescent Medicine* 149 (October 1995): 1079–1084.

44. GAO, *Elementary School Children: Many Change Schools Frequently, Harming Their Education*, GAO/HEHS 94–45 (Washington, D.C.: General Accounting Office, 1994).

45. David Kerbow, "Patterns of Urban Student Mobility and Local School Reform," *Journal of Education for Students Placed at Risk* 1(2) (1996): 147–169; and James Bruno and Jo Ann Isken, "Inter- and Intraschool Site Student Transiency: Practical and Theoretical Implications for Instructional Continuity at Inner-City Schools," *Journal of Research and Development in Education* 29(4) (summer 1996): 239–252.

46. GAO, *Elementary School Children.*

47. Kerbow, "Patterns of Urban Student Mobility."

48. Jennifer Daskal, *In Search of Shelter: The Growing Shortage of Affordable Rental Housing* (Washington, D.C.: Center for Budget and Policy Priorities, June 15, 1998).

49. GAO, *Elementary School Children*; and Kerbow, "Patterns of Urban Student Mobility."

50. David B. Schuler, "Effects of Family Mobility on Student Achievement," *ERS Spectrum* 8(4) (fall 1990).

51. Marybeth Shinn, Beth C. Weitzman, Daniela Stojanovic, James R. Knickman, Lucila Jimenez, Lisa Ducon, Susan James, and David H. Kranz, "Predictors of Homelessness Among Families in New York City: From Shelter Request to Housing Stability," *American Journal of Public Health* 88(11) (November 1998): 1651–1657.

52. Daskal, *In Search of Shelter*, table 1.

53. GAO, *Section 8 Tenant-Based Housing Assistance: Opportunities to Improve HUD's Financial Management*, GAO/RCED 98–47 (Washington, D.C.: General Accounting Office, 1998), table 3.1.

54. David Rusk and Jeff Mosley, "The Academic Performance of Public Housing Children: Does Living in Middle-Class Neighborhoods and Attending Middle-Class Schools Make a Difference?," unpublished paper, the Urban Institute (May 27, 1994).

55. Richard Rothstein, *Where's the Money Going? Changes in the Level and Composition of Education Spending, 1991–1996* (Washington, D.C.: Economic Policy Institute, 1997).

56. USDOE [U.S. Department of Education], *To Assure the Free Appropriate Public Education of All Children with Disabilities: Nineteenth Annual Report to Congress on the Implementation of the Individuals with Disabilities Education Act* (Washington, D.C.: GAO, 1997).

57. D. P. Hallahan, "Some Thoughts on Why the Prevalence of Learning Disabilities Has Increased," *Journal of Learning Disabilities* 25(8) (1992): 523–528.

58. Drews et al., "The Relationship Between Idiopathic Mental Retardation and Maternal Smoking."

59. USDOE, *To Assure the Free Appropriate Public Education of All Children with Disabilities.*

60. Frederick Mosteller, *New York Times* (September 26, 1998).

61. Lynn A. Karoly, Peter W. Greenwood, Susan S. Everingham, Jill Hoube, M. Rebecca Kilburn, C. Peter Rydell, Matthew Sanders, and James Chiesa, *Investing in Our Children: What We Know and Don't Know About the Costs and Benefits of Early Childhood Interventions* (Santa Monica, Calif.: RAND, 1998).

7

METROPOLITAN POWER: THE NEXT URBAN AGENDA

Bruce Katz and Joel Rogers

Despite recent talk of urban revival, investors' discovery of "new markets" in the inner city, and the emergence of "new urbanism" and "smart growth," America's urban crisis continues. Although the long expansion of the 1990s has finally begun to draw urban residents into the labor market, the inner cores of our major metropolitan regions continue to be plagued by social problems—crime; unemployment; concentrated poverty; rotting infrastructure; and poor transportation, health, social services, and schools. The resulting fiscal and other strains long registered in central cities are now appearing in older suburbs, particularly "inner-ring" suburbs. In many respects, these suburbs—lacking a core commercial base—are even less prepared than cities to grapple with these myriad economic, fiscal, and social challenges.

Consider, from an urban perspective, the recent numbers on population, jobs, and income. Between 1980 and 1997, twenty-three of America's twenty-five largest cities either declined while their metropolitan areas grew or grew more slowly than did their surrounding suburbs. From 1994 to 1997, in a booming labor market, only one-fifth of our 100-odd largest cities posted job growth rates exceeding those in their suburbs, while most trailed miserably behind. Over that period, for example, the central business districts in Ohio's seven major cities experienced a net increase of only 636 jobs, even as their suburbs gained 186,410 new ones. From 1989 to 1996, cities posted a net loss of more than 4 million middle- and upper-income households, and the suburban median income advantage swelled from 58 to 67 percent.

Cities have a disproportionate share of households with income below the national median. Urban poverty rates are double suburban rates—18 percent versus 9 percent—and urban poverty is increasingly concentrated. Between 1970 and 1990, the total number of residents in high-poverty neighborhoods—defined as neighborhoods in which at least 40 percent of residents are poor (virtually all of which are in our central cities)—doubled, from 4 million to 8 million. In addition to being largely detached from the broader economy and exponentially more troubled than neighborhoods with more modest poverty rates, high-poverty neighborhoods are racially segregated from the white majority. In 1990, only one in twenty poor Whites lived in them, compared to one in three poor Blacks. Defining a ghetto as a high-poverty neighborhood in which two-thirds or more of the residents are black, we find an increase by more than 50 percent between 1970 and 1990 in the number of ghetto census tracts.[1]

The trends described above are not inevitable results of market and demographic forces. Rather, they are the result of decades of antiurban public policy—a bias that in some measure is distinctive to America. In contrast to most developed capitalist nations, the United States slights urban renters in favor of suburban homes, urban bus and subway riders in favor of suburban automobiles, and urban infrastructure in favor of exurban and rural development projects. We have spent trillions building nonmetropolitan roads, but nowhere near that on metropolitan ones or on mass transit, on which federal spending has never exceeded one-fifth of highway funding. The overwhelming share of federal and state economic development program support also goes to nonurban sites—more highways and other sprawl-supporting infrastructure, exurban tax credits, and low-interest loans for new development.

Nonmetropolitan regions are not required to pay the costs of maintaining the poor and dispossessed, the largely nonwhite populations left behind by such acts of favoritism. Burdened with concentrations of poverty, cities are forced to spend more on social services of all kinds: police, fire protection, health care, and even education. Every one-point increase in municipal poverty rates is associated with an increased cost to urban residents of more than 5 percent for police protection. And among larger cities, more than 40 percent of school budgets are currently devoted to costs associated with greater poverty.

In large part due to the increased urban concentration of poverty, real municipal costs for basic services increased some 15 percent in the 1980s, and likely did so again in the 1990s. But during the same period federal and state support for cities actually declined. The federal share of county government revenues declined by better than three-quarters (from 8.8 to 2.0 percent), and of city revenues by better than two-thirds (from 11.4 to 3.6 percent), from 1980 to 1992. State governments also joined in the general withdrawal of funding, often with devastating consequences for urban fiscal stability. Consider the largest population centers: Between 1975 and 1992, the combined federal and state share of local revenues dropped from 53 to 32 percent in New York City, from 24 to 6 percent in Los Angeles, and from 28 to 18 percent in Chicago.[2] Funding has not yet been restored to previous levels, at the same time as local government has taken on ever greater responsibilities.

The effect of these policies and of the resulting income and fiscal dynamics is straightforward. They lower the costs to individuals and firms of living and working outside or on the outer fringes of our metropolitan regions, and increase the costs of living and working in the core. They push investment out of high-tax, low-service urban areas and into low-tax, high-service, favored suburban quarters, concentrating poverty in the central city core and increasingly squeezing the working class suburbs in the middle.

Indeed—with a few notable exceptions, such as the Community Reinvestment Act—even most federal policies dedicated to "urban renewal" have created more problems than solutions. Until recently, federal public housing policy tended to encourage the concentration of poverty and the spatial isolation of the poor. More than half of all public housing residents still live in high-poverty neighborhoods. Targeted investments to spur economic development have had mixed results. A succession of variations on the "enterprise zone" idea—in which businesses get tax breaks and other regulatory relief in return for their investments in central cities—have been strikingly disappointing in results. Such plans have generally ignored important variations in local circumstances and ideal business strategies, and typically have produced only lower-end jobs. With some exceptions, brownfield reclamation efforts have been torturously slow. The problem with "place-based" strategies is that they are inattentive to the broader regional dynamics that determine the fate of individual places. As a strategy to relieve the distress of our central cities, this is the equivalent of pouring water on a hot skillet rather than turning down the flame.

Federal efforts to give the central-city poor greater access to educational and employment opportunities likewise have rarely had the desired effects. Despite the metropolitan nature of labor and residential markets, the federal government has delegated responsibility for workforce and housing voucher programs to thousands of local public housing authorities and workforce investment boards. The Detroit metropolitan area, for example, has more than thirty separate public housing authorities, which greatly limits the residential mobility of poor families. The hyperfragmentation of governance makes it difficult for low-income recipients to know about suburban housing vacancies or job openings, let alone to exercise choice in the metropolitan marketplace.

Could we do better? Yes, but only if we recognize, after better than a half century of sprawl, that "urban" means "metropolitan"—central cities, but also their surrounding, older suburbs, and even the larger economic regions delineated by the effective labor market. Thus broadly described, metro regions house about 80 percent of the U.S. population and produce virtually all of the national wealth. How these metropolitan regions are organized and governed will thus largely determine how most Americans do in life, and how the nation fares—but the nation appears not to recognize this fact. Cities also got to be cities in the first place because they had distinct advantages as places to work and live. Those advantages still exist, and in some ways are being further underscored by developments in the "new economy"—but this too is largely unrecognized, even sneered at, by a set of policies that continue to undermine urban centers.

One reason, of course, is politics. The U.S. political system is highly federated, and locally fragmented. The Chicago metro region alone includes 265 separate municipalities, 1,200 separate tax districts, and parts of six different megacounties—all with clear incentives not to cooperate with each other. If "all politics is local," the essence of local politics, of course, is to make sure that your ward or district does better than the one next door. That means reducing calls on revenues and securing as much taxable wealth as possible. From exclusionary zoning to tireless competition to lure prospective business to the local exurban site, the natural impulse is to beggar thy neighbor and put up walls—the very antithesis of regional cooperation in pursuit of shared prosperity.

What is newly hopeful in this picture, ironically, is that suburban sprawl has reached a point where this sort of politics is no longer viable for the majority of residents of metropolitan areas. Having "run against the city" for years, the residents of both older and newer working-class suburbs now have a material interest in joining with the city to insist on greater equity within their regions. In virtually all major U.S. metropolitan areas, for example, those who would benefit from regional tax base sharing—in the form of lower tax burdens and better services—now comprise about two-thirds of the voting population. And the generally white, working-class suburbanites are the decisive swing voters in virtually all elections. The numbers are there, in other words, for a new metro coalition, and the incentive is certainly there for one or another of the major parties to try to form it.

In addition to pitting jurisdictions against one another, urban politics in the United States has long featured an effective war among different communities of interest. Old urban politics, from which we have not yet escaped, pitted labor against community, and untamed development against environmentalists and those concerned about quality of life. It obscured relevant divisions within business and let the rich exurbs off too cheaply. But many of the mutual antagonists in this old politics are at least beginning to see an interest in alliance. Elected officials from cities and inner suburbs; downtown corporate, philanthropic, and civic interests; minority and low-income community representatives; environmentalists; slow-growth advocates in the new suburbs; unions; farmers and rural activists; and religious leaders all are realizing that uncoordinated suburban expansion brings needless costs.

As a public philosophy or style of administration and self-government, regionalism has a long and generally tattered political history in the United States. Of the 80 percent who live in metropolitan areas, only about 5 percent are subject to some democratic regional government. This situation will not change absent prior changes in our political culture—most pointedly, perhaps, around issues of race. Local governments will need to be shaken up as well. The points of resistance clearly are many, and a democratic metropolitan strategy will need to be fought for to be achieved. This time, though—if the facts cited above are any indication—the project would have political legs.

Lastly, even though many of the steps we recommend would actually save the government money, this moment of national fiscal health seems ready-made for new investment. No one can claim that the United

States cannot afford to save its cities. It is merely a matter of political leadership and will.

WHY SAVE CITIES?

Before outlining the components of that project, however, let's consider again why it is worth pursuing. Specifically, why do virtually all Americans, not just residents of our central cities, have a stake in metropolitan revival?

One reason is political morality: American democracy is supposed to be "for the people"—ideally, all of them, or at least the majority. With some 240 million people in our metropolitan areas, 140 million people in the central cities and older suburbs, and some 70 million (including 20 million children) in the declining central cities, antiurban policies don't qualify on either count. Whatever the enduring appeal of western movies filmed on desolate plains and in reimagined frontier towns, or the importance of the continuing crisis in family farming, American society is basically metropolitan. The country is composed of cities and a series of connected suburbs; its economy is made up of a series of regional labor markets and sites of production and exchange. With most of the public consisting of metropolitan residents, not to have a sensible metropolitan policy is not to have any sensible public policy, period.

American democracy is also supposed to be about equal opportunity to enjoy a decent life. Yet especially in our central cities, large portions of the population are exceptionally poor, poorly served by exceptionally bad public services, and subject to exceptional violence. No one disputes the results—in high infant mortality, poor health, stunted development, and shattered lives—or the fact that these results unmask any pretension to having given all citizens an equal shot at the American dream.

Lastly, American democracy is supposed to be about healing the scars of racism first scored 400 years ago, and claiming our ethnic and racial diversity as the strength that it obviously is. But even as we have made great progress is removing formal barriers to racial equality, our urban policies have had the effect of drastically limiting its substantive achievement. In combination, the antimajoritarian, discriminatory effects of urban decline compel our collective attention.

Other reasons why all Americans have a stake in the health of U.S. cities are related to public health, the environment, and the general quality and stress of everyday life. Our cities now have half the population density they had two generations ago. Some effects of this peculiarly American form of metropolis are all too visible: water and air pollution, the ongoing destruction of natural beauty, and the greater stress created by traffic congestion. Some implications remain hidden—for example, the rampant fiscal disparities that undermine the ability of older communities to support public goods of all kinds, from opportunities for safe recreation to quality public education.

A third reason, suggested above, is purely economic. Sprawl and central city degradation are wasteful. They waste land, water, and energy, and squander existing assets; as new houses, factories, and schools go up in the outer rings, perfectly good buildings, with established links to usable infrastructure, get boarded up farther in. Take the excess costs on new construction and natural resources and add in the untimely depreciation of old capital stock: The result is annual waste of staggering proportions. Then there are also the economic costs of human neglect. Abandoning our central cities means forsaking the productive potential of their inhabitants and paying heavily to contain their resentment, as ballooning budgets for new prisons and police make evident.

The opportunity costs of all that unrealized potential productivity are enormous. Forget about the exceptional talents that might be squandered—the potential future Nobel prize winners or great artists who are not learning how to read. Simply subtract the average lifetime earnings of those without decent health, education, or job access from those with these basic goods. Multiply by 70 million, or even 20. It's a big number—in the trillions—which translates into a lot of foregone tax revenue for the general population.

Then there is the cost linkage. Many suburbanites are prepared to pay the costs and forego the benefits just mentioned, as the price of their isolation. But that isolation is an illusion. Within regions, the economic fortunes of central cities and their suburbs, especially their inner-ring suburbs, are increasingly entwined. By the late 1980s, across a very wide range of metropolitan regions, every $1,000 gained or lost in per capita city income was associated with a $690 gain or loss in per capita suburban income. And indeed, recent evidence suggests the urban-suburban economic linkage is getting tighter over time.[3] Declining central cities mean a poorer suburban future.

The greatest economic cost, however, derives from the role that metro regions play in determining the pattern of national economic activity.

Put baldly, revived urban regions are key to reviving broad wage growth and reversing current trends toward increasing inequality.

Why? Because, despite all the talk about how American wages are now set in Beijing, adverse trends in American income and wealth distribution today result as much from domestic policy choices as from the downward pressures of international competition.[4] Specifically, we have made "low-road" strategies of response to new competitive pressures too easy and "high-road" strategies too hard. Low-road firms compete by keeping prices down, which means keeping costs down—beginning, typically, with wages. Applied across the economy, low-road strategies lead to sweated workers, economic insecurity, rising inequality, poisonous labor relations, and degraded natural environments. High-road firms focus on "value competition" (with higher wages supported by customer willingness to pay for higher quality, better design, and superior service) and require continual innovation in quality, and thus depend on more skilled and more cooperative workers. In general, high-road strategies are associated with higher productivity, higher pay and better labor relations, reduced environmental damage, and greater commitment by firms to the health and stability of surrounding human communities—all needed to attract and keep skilled workers and managers.

Firms can make money on either path, but social gains are vastly greater on the high road. The principal failure of the past two decades—and it is political as much as economic—is that we have not done what we must to move the economy onto the high road. Embarking on the high road is associated with various transition costs, and staying on it depends on a variety of social supports. Those supports include effective educational and training institutions; better functioning labor markets, with fuller information about requirements for job access and advancement; advanced infrastructure of all kinds; modernization services to diffuse the best manufacturing practices; and throughout, barriers to low-road defection (e.g., high and rising wage, safety, or environmental performance floors). Because such supports typically lie beyond the capacity of individual firms, they need to be provided socially. We have not provided them, and the results are clear in the sorry U.S. labor market and productivity data of the past two decades—stagnating or falling wages, rising inequality, and until very recently, anemic productivity growth.

Which is where cities come back in. Whatever their present difficulties, metropolitan economies are the natural base for a high-road economy. In fact, to the extent that we have any high-road production and service delivery in the United States, it is disproportionately concentrated in metropolitan regions. And this concentration is no accident. High-roading and metro density naturally go together—an affinity that is expressed in three ways.

First, density helps firms directly. Economists, geographers, and economic development analysts use the concept of "agglomeration" to describe the benefits in skills, productivity, and consumer access that result when activities are concentrated in particular places. In addition, firms in such regions don't just happen to be near each other and share a regional labor market. They do business with each other in a way that connects them as if, in some ways, they were complementary plants of a single enterprise. At the extreme, some of their capacity may even be thought of as shared. Precisely because they want to keep their machinery busy, each has strong incentives to make overflow work available to "competitors"; only by doing so will they earn the quid pro quo of being asked to do the same for those competitors. Agglomerations are in turn associated with "increasing returns" on any given investment. When a single firm in one of these agglomerations improves its cost and quality performance, it creates a competitive advantage for the customers and suppliers in its cluster. Simply put, firms learn more and faster from each other.

Second, density helps relieve the costs of providing the public goods—education and training; formal supports for cross-learning and upgrading among firms; integrated regional labor market services and worker credentialing systems; modern forms of transport, energy, water supply, and communication linkages on which such advanced production depends. It is much cheaper and easier to supply such goods with the human and material resources that density provides.

Lastly, density facilitates worker organization by providing the proximity and sheer numbers needed to support the infrastructure of member servicing and new organizing. Worker organization, in turn, directly helps close off the low road by obstructing the impulse toward wage reduction. And worker organization helps pave the high road too. Without the knowledge and cooperation of workers, firms will find high-roading all but impossible—and both are easier to secure if workers are organized and confident that they too will benefit from increased quality and productivity.

In sum, metro regions historically offered and still hold the promise of extending a virtuous cycle of earnings-led productivity growth. Agglomeration—especially when it includes a sectoral mix that favors highly skilled labor—is a clear predictor of higher employee earnings. Those higher earnings justify and call forth a higher level of capital investment per employee. Higher labor quality and this higher capital intensity beget higher productivity, which supports continued premium labor compensation. This in turn attracts skilled employees, and the virtuous cycle is repeated. The virtuous cycle is not only of historical interest; it persists today. According to a recent *Business Week* analysis, "Cities still seem best able to provide business with access to skilled workers, special-ized high-value services, and the kind of innovation and learning growth that is facilitated by close contact between diverse individuals."[5] Indeed, as Harvard economist Edward Glaeser has argued, the density of cities offers the perfect milieu for the driving forces of the new economy: idea fermentation and technological innovation.[6]

THE NEXT URBAN AGENDA

What would it take to harness the economic power of our metro regions, improve the quality and equity of life within them, and move the coun-try more generally onto the high road of shared prosperity? In general terms, the essential tasks are to use public powers to close off the low road and help pave the high road; to target infrastructure and other pub-lic investments with a specific eye to exploiting metro economic advan-tages; and throughout, to provide incentives for greater regional coopera-tion and leadership. The following ten steps would provide a good start to metro reconstruction.

Invest in the Working Poor

The first step is to invest in working families and their children. This is based on the simple premise that people who work and play by the rules should not be poor. They should have access to quality health care and affordable housing. They should be given the same incentives as middle-class families to save for retirement or important family purchases. Their children should receive lifelong benefits of early childhood education.

The federal government could achieve these goals through several means. It could expand direct supports for families, such as housing vouchers and the Earned Income Tax Credit (EITC). It could create new incentives, like the Clinton Administration's proposed Universal

Savings Accounts, to help working families accumulate wealth and link up with the financial mainstream. Whatever path is chosen, the unifying theme is to invest in people and through people, in the places where they live. These investments will not be cheap; but they are a necessary element of the post-welfare world, in which work is the organizing principle for social policy.

Promote a High-Road Economy

The second step is to remove the subsidies and incentives that the government now provides to low-road firms. Governments at all levels should announce that they will not award contracts or development grants to firms paying wages below a certain minimum (e.g., the poverty line), polluting above a certain level, or with a record of illegal resistance to worker organization. They should then move to mandate such standards generally and gradually to raise them. For example, phasing in a significantly increased minimum wage would do wonders for shutting down the low-road option and requiring firms to compete by improving quality. Or, more radically, we might revive discussion of a negative income tax or basic income grant, which would not directly threaten low-wage employment but would let workers, not owners, decide what should be done about it.

Reinvest in Older Communities

The third step is to reinvest in our older communities and spend public money where the people are. This would encourage local governments to increase density rather than avoid it and reward the natural agglomerations of people and firms by letting them recapture their individual tax dollars for collective self-improvement.

Federal transportation policy provides an appropriate starting point for a reinvestment agenda. With the completion of the interstate highway system, Federal transportation funds should now be used in metropolitan areas almost exclusively for the repair and maintenance of existing highways and for the expansion of alternative transportation strategies that relieve congestion, encourage energy-efficient mass transit, and promote more balanced growth patterns. Federal funds should be used to build new highways in metropolitan and adjoining areas only in exceptional circumstances and only when linked to the expansion of affordable housing. This makes economic sense on two grounds. First, it compels exurban retail and commercial and residential projects to stand on their own merits. Second, it puts infrastructure money where we know it will have the greatest bounce—in denser sites of economic activity that will leverage the performance of the surrounding region. Other infrastructure investment in our older areas is also recommended—in schools and public buildings, parks and public recreational facilities, and the like. Our urban infrastructure represents an enormous sunk cost, of enormous value. It should be reclaimed.

A reinvestment agenda also could promote the creation of geographically targeted regional investment funds, capitalized with individual or organized worker retirement savings. Under this idea, borrowed from Canada, funds would be invested in a demarcated region, and investments typically would be accompanied by criteria (e.g., environmentalist standards) aimed at advancing the quality of life or improving the infrastructure in that region. Investors in such funds would get a "double bounce" on their investment: a competitive risk-adjusted market rate of return, and an improvement in their own community. The organization of such funds on a multiregional basis would permit regional diversification against risk, yet would be consistent with respect for geographic solidarities. An investor in Los Angeles, New York, or Milwaukee could be assured that his or her dollar into the fund would result in a dollar of investment in his or her region; but actual investment flows could be cross-regional, with the Los Angeles investor actually partially underwriting investment in New York or Milwaukee, and vice versa. However they are structured, sources of alternative investment are an important tool for regional economic development. The U.S. federal government could encourage the development of investment pools like those in Canada by providing a tax credit for savings invested in such funds. If the Canadian experience is any guide, the credit pays for itself within just a few years, all the while building worker wealth.

Land-Use Planning and Growth Management

The fourth step is to put in place responsible land-use planning at the regional level. Unless we begin to manage the process of growth on the metro fringes, we will undermine any remedial efforts happening in the core. If 25 percent of a region continues to develop only expensive homes and jobs, neglecting worker housing, that 25 percent will rapidly draw off all the wealth and growth in the region. At the same time, it will commit the region to sprawling land use that is vastly disproportionate to population increases—worsening congestion, energy use, and pollution, and increasing social separation.

State governments are critical in rewriting the rules of development. The new rules should include setting outward limits for growth in the form of an urban growth boundary; siting new infrastructure (e.g., roads and sewers) and new housing together; developing at a density that will support some minimal form of public transportation; and assuring the provision in all subdivisions of a fair share of affordable housing. Oregon has already put these new rules in place. Minnesota also has adopted a structure that would encourage regions to develop along these lines, but the state has often failed to implement such statutes.

The federal government should also support the growing interest in land-use planning at the state and local level. First, it should provide resources for the preservation of open space in metropolitan areas and the reclamation of urban land for productive use. The Clinton administration's "Better America Bonds" proposal, modeled on a number of state programs passed in 1998, is an excellent start. The proposal would use tax expenditures to leverage $9.5 billion in state and local bonds for the preservation of open space and the cleanup of brownfields. The proposal could be improved by channeling additional resources toward states and jurisdictions that are practicing smart growth policies in transportation, housing, and economic development. Second, the federal government should enforce environmental laws such as the Clean Air Act and Endangered Species Act. The recent advances made in the Atlanta and Seattle metropolitan areas are in large part due to the federal government's judicious use of its regulatory powers in the environmental arena.

Seek Equity in the Provision of Local Public Services

The fifth step is to promote tax equity between local communities in metropolitan areas. Regional tax equity reduces fiscal disparities between local communities and competition among local communities for businesses that have already located in a given region, and by lessening the direct fiscal consequences for zoning decisions, makes regional land-use planning more possible. Many regions have either ameliorated or solved this problem through consolidation or annexation. Some parts of the nation have progressive school equity systems that eliminate much of the burden of funding local schools from the central cities and older suburbs. As with land-use planning, the responsibility for furthering regional tax equity will fall mostly on state governments. Minnesota has pioneered a system that preserves local autonomy at the same time as it creates greater regional equity in the provision of public services through the sharing of a portion of the local property tax base. Regional tax equity should be considered by all local governments. In addition to the potential socio-economic benefits, it carries a number of political benefits: It does not threaten local autonomy; it need not involve difficult discussions of race, class, and housing; and it creates a scenario in which the majority of citizens will immediately receive lower taxes and better services.

Extend Regional Governance

The sixth step (a natural corollary of the last three) is to promote and extend regional governance. Using all of the powers at its disposal, the federal government should encourage the development of democratic metropolitan development authorities, with broad responsibility for infrastructure and other regional investment. Metropolitan planning organizations (MPOs), already set up to develop regional transportation plans and to allocate enormous federal and state transportation resources, might be a natural forum for such oversight activities, but they first would need to be made more representative and accountable to the regions they serve. Presently, MPOs are often dominated by high-growth, suburban political interests and real estate developers and make region-shaping decisions without significant public input. Frankly, part of this is because older, core communities—particularly, areas of concentrated poverty—have never thought these decisions were relevant to their future. Ultimately, MPOs should evolve into directly elected structures and should assume growing responsibility for implementing the initiatives discussed above.

Assure Affordable Housing Regionally

The seventh step is to provide affordable housing throughout a region. Close to half of the total hours people spend commuting are due to their inability to find housing closer to their workplaces. Poor families are particularly affected by the lack of affordable housing in the suburbs, persistent discriminatory patterns in the rental market, and the paucity of transportation options. Providing affordable housing throughout a region could produce substantial benefits. It could reduce the concentration of poverty, reduce racial segregation, and stem the polarization occurring between the region's communities. It could get workers closer to new jobs and reduce congestion on roadways. And it could expand housing choices by allowing a variety of households (e.g., older people and newly single mothers and fathers) to remain in their communities even though their financial and physical conditions have changed.

States and localities have a clear role to play in the affordable housing arena, through land-use and zoning decisions. Yet the federal government remains a prime player through its spending programs (e.g., housing vouchers), tax expenditures (e.g., low-income housing tax credit), credit enhancement activities (e.g., FHA, Fannie Mae, Freddie Mac), and oversight responsibilities (e.g., the Fair Housing Act). The time is ripe for the federal government to reengage in the affordable housing business.

The most important step for the federal government is to close the gap between low-wage incomes and market-rate rents. Investing in the working poor by increasing the minimum wage, expanding the EITC, and increasing the number of new housing vouchers will help to meet this goal.

Yet the federal government also needs to expand the supply of affordable rental housing. Effective federal tax incentives—like the low-income housing tax credit—should be expanded. Because housing is a regional issue and not just a local one, the federal government should also use tax incentives to help create new regional housing trust funds. These trust funds would enable cities and suburbs to work together to expand the supply of affordable rental housing, particularly in areas where jobs are growing fast. A $1.5 billion federal investment could help create a $10 billion pool of housing trust funds, which could leverage tens of billions of dollars more in private sector investment. These funds could be allocated in a way that encourages local communities to carry their "fair share" of the low- and moderate-income housing needs of a region.

Federal tax incentives could also be expanded to boost home ownership in places where home ownership rates are exceedingly low. Incentives could include a tax credit that goes directly to first-time home buyers (as in Washington, D.C.) and a tax benefit that entices developers to construct or renovate affordable homes (e.g., the existing tax credit for rental housing). Such incentives would enhance the ability of working families to accumulate wealth and would contribute to the stability of neighborhoods by lowering the costs of home ownership.

Federal action, however, should not be limited to additional investments. The federal government should shift governance of the housing voucher program to the metropolitan level. As described above, the federal voucher program—now serving over 1.6 million families with rental subsidies—is administered by thousands of separate public housing bureaucracies operating in parochial jurisdictions. Competitions should be held in dozens of metropolitan areas to determine what kind of entity— public, for-profit, nonprofit, or a combination thereof—is best suited to administer the program locally.

Fix Labor Market Administration

The eighth step is to design and implement regional workforce strategies. In an ideal world, labor markets would be "transparent" to participants, and job requirements and opportunities would be universally understood. Career ladders, permitting advancement from entry-level jobs to more advanced ones (both within individual firms and across industry sectors or clusters), would be known too, and respected by employers. Those seeking employment or advancement would have opportunities to acquire the human capital needed to achieve their goals, with public supports in training and other monies directed toward preparing people for jobs that were known to exist or to be coming open. Employers intent on taking the high road would have confidence that they would be able to draw on a skilled workforce. This "ideal" world—very far from present urban realities—is in fact not that difficult to achieve. It simply requires the organization of employers, industry-wide, for the purpose of identifying and declaring their common skill and employment needs; the connection of such employer consortia to the public training system; and the broadcast of opportunities to the community at large. Experience in Milwaukee (with the Wisconsin Regional Training Partnership) and elsewhere indicates that this can be done. The Milwaukee effort enjoyed support from businesses (which experienced reduced search costs for qualified employees, and increased planning capacity), organized labor (which experienced higher wages and greater job security), and traditionally neglected central city communities (which finally found out precisely what job requirements were, in sufficient time to satisfy them). The recent efforts of the Department of Labor to encourage such "regional skills alliances" or "high-road regional partnerships," are welcome, but their role in labor market administration should be better integrated into the administration of the new Workforce Investment Act.

Regional workforce strategies also require regional transit systems that meet the real needs of firms and workers in economies that are rapidly decentralizing. In many metropolitan areas, city buses continue to stop literally at the border of the central city, greatly impeding the ability of urban workers to access suburban jobs. Express bus services from labor markets in central cities to job centers in suburbs are the exception. Here, too, federal intervention would go a long way. In the near term, federal incentives should be tailored toward transforming the small "job access" demonstrations in the Department of Transportation into initiatives that have more systemic effects on the commuting patterns of low-income workers. Ultimately, the federal government should require the integration of metropolitan transit systems as a condition for receiving federal funds.

Promote Mindful Devolution and Local Reform

The ninth step is to reinvent the partnership between the federal government and local and regional governments. It is clear from the preceding discussion that the federal government must play a very large role in reviving our metro areas; it is also obvious that local resources and know-how are key to solving local problems. It should be equally clear that devolution will not achieve its aims of more efficient and equitable government service if it is fiscally punitive and procrustean in mandate. The federal government must give local leaders greater opportunities for input in the design and implementation of federal programs and policies. Urban markets are highly diverse and call for distinctive solutions. Cities should get more federal resources, and should be allowed to tailor federal resources to their own market realities and local priorities.

The federal government might, for example, allow high-performing cities to dedicate some portion of their federal grants to priorities that are set by local leaders. In cities facing gentrification, emphasis might be placed on ensuring housing affordability for poor, working families. In cities facing a massive exodus of people and jobs, emphasis might be placed on restoring neighborhood markets or assembling land to attract business investment. But we emphasize that *the trade-off for more responsibility would be more accountability.* Cities would be allowed to exercise this option only after local leaders agree to be held to high standards and performance benchmarks. Only locales where close collaboration exists between cities and suburbs would enjoy maximum flexibility.

Not all cities, of course, are ready to be effective partners with the federal government. Philadelphia, for example, has fifteen different agencies with partial responsibility for the disposition of urban land; and the bureaucratic mess of most large urban school systems is well documented. In these places, federal investment is presently used to compensate for rather than to fix broken systems. Federal resources should be used to leverage reform and greater openness and accountability, not to conceal inefficiency. Troubled public housing authorities need to be taken over and broken up. Resources for land reclamation should be provided only to places that can show progress in streamlining the process for assembling and disposing of urban land. In many cases, greater diversity of urban service providers, and increased competition among them, should be considered as a tool in administration. This will sometimes mean taking things out of the hands of city personnel and putting them into the hands of community groups or other private providers. Unions, for example, might be encouraged to return to their historic role as sources of worker training. The goal in all cases is to make government and public service provision more transparent, efficient, and accountable — certainly a goal widely shared by the public. In part, that means transferring some authority from the municipality to the region; but it often will require changing the nature of service delivery as well.

Change Local Economic Development Practice

The final step is to overhaul local economic development policies and practices. Most city and county economic development authorities commit a series of self-defeating mistakes in the assignment of public supports to economic development. By and large, they promote job growth without attention to the quality of jobs being generated; this tends to increase fiscal stress even as it increases employment, as the occupants of the low-wage jobs that result draw down services without contributing to the tax base. Authorities tend to focus on attracting new employers to the region rather than on retaining and improving existing, leading employers; this misses the opportunity presented by existing agglomerate effects and distinctive regional strengths. Authorities also tend to lower standards for firms and to resist accountability requirements in extending public assistance to them; both actions encourage low-roading and harm (through increased competition) the high-road firms the region should want to encourage. Authorities tend to underinvest in the public goods (training, modernization, and so on) that high-road firms need, and they have few mechanisms for getting organized, representative input from employers, labor, and the community. The results are waste due to decisions based on bad information, or lack of public support for new development initiatives.

Reversing these practices is the aim of the part of the high-road metro agenda that is more narrowly focused on economic development. This aim also would be immensely facilitated by passage of the other elements, enumerated above, which would reduce the jurisdictional competition for employment that substantially drives present practices. But high-roading can also be supported directly. In all aspects of economic development spending, infrastructure support, pollution prevention, abatement programs, and the like, the federal government should reward regions or states that move toward high-road production. Comparative progress toward the high road can and should be measured, and special federal monies should be contingent on progress achieved. Independent of what the states do, the federal government itself should much more attentively target its resources toward encouraging high-roading. It should target aid to integrated regions, clusters within them, and firms within those clusters.

ARE WE DREAMING?

But is there really any reason to believe that any of these things will be done? Although we cannot know the future, we are encouraged by the broad economic and political trends noted at the beginning of this chapter, as well as by a number of other developments.

First, although any talk of a general revival of U.S. urban areas would be an overstatement, there are promising signs of life in cities today. Many older cities are experiencing the first sustained renewal they have seen in decades. Particularly in the past several years, an array of social indicators—violent crime, unemployment, poverty, and urban home ownership—have been moving in the right direction. Cities like Chicago, Atlanta, Cleveland, and Boston, which had been steadily losing large numbers of residents for decades, recently have recorded slight increases or only minor further declines in population. Cities also are rediscovering their competitive assets. They are home to many of the nation's leading universities and medical research centers. They offer the growing number of "empty nesters" an attractive lifestyle, with easy access to cultural amenities, health services, and other necessities of daily life. They remain, and increasingly exploit the fact that they are, the cultural and entertainment magnets of their regions.

Today's urban political leaders are also a different breed than their predecessors. Mayors in Chicago, Cleveland, Detroit, and elsewhere now control the school systems in their cities. Mayors in Boston and Oakland are spearheading new policing and community strategies to reduce crime. Mayors in Washington, D.C. and New Haven are exercising a creative blend of fiscal discipline and managerial reform. And mayors in Denver and Milwaukee are changing the physical landscape of their cities with ambitious efforts to expand parks, remake downtown areas, and reclaim vacant land for redevelopment. Moreover, the current generation of municipal leaders has a greater appreciation of the fact that cities cannot solve their problems on their own and must actively seek more regional cooperation.

The competitive and other advantages of cities, including their centrality to national economic health, are much more widely recognized now than they were twenty years ago. Indeed, the notion that cities generate positive externalities for the nation—from environmental improvement to a more secure infrastructure for high-wage production, not to mention new ideas and production techniques generated through the interaction of residents—has become central to mainstream economics. For the first time in years, analysts steeped in economic theory are generating arguments for the importance of cities and ideas for policies to resuscitate them. New policy initiatives in this area aim to do far more than just throw money at problems; and the leaders who have authored these policies can proceed with a very secure intellectual foundation for the claim that investment in urban areas makes good sense for business as well as for society.

Consensus is growing in the public policy community—not only on the importance and the economic strengths of metropolitan regions but also on the best ways to harness those strengths. Parts of our new urban agenda may be disputed in some quarters; but the larger portion of it is not new, and its desirability is not in dispute. Sprawl would be reduced, planning capacity would rise, wages would increase and inequalities decrease, neighborhoods would become less segregated and safer, public goods would be more abundant, and democracy would more evidently show its contribution to the economy. The strategy would be self-reinforcing. As subsidies to sprawl decrease, the attractions of metropolitan locations rise. As investment dollars return to metro cores, productivity within them increases, making higher wages more affordable. As organization of the natural high-road basis of the economy proceeds, standards for job entry and advancement can be formalized and publicized, which helps equalize wages. Better wages secure the tax base, which helps pay for the expensive public goods that further reduce inequality and attract high-roading firms. With more abundant public goods and better job access, central city residents look less "different," further promoting their employability. With greater regional power over what employers want—skilled labor, infrastructure, technical assistance, and credit—the ability of regions to enact and discipline free-riders and defectors from common regional norms (e.g., on fair housing and hiring, land use, tax equity– and tax base–sharing) rises.

These all seem like straightforward and politically attractive "wins" for American democracy. They simply await some leadership in their forceful articulation. When we will get it, and from whom, is a question more and more Americans are asking.

NOTES

This chapter draws on a number of previous publications, including some that were jointly authored. See Katz, "Beyond City Limits" and "Enough of the Small Stuff: Towards a New Urban Agenda," *Brookings Review* (summer 2000): 4–9; Daniel D. Luria and Rogers, *Metro Futures: Economic Solutions for Cities and Their Suburbs* (Boston: Beacon Press, 1999); and Rogers, Myron Orfield, and David Wood, *Milwaukee Metropolitics: A Regional Agenda for High-Road Growth* (Madison: Center on Wisconsin Strategy, 2000).

1. Paul A. Jargowsky, *Poverty and Place: Ghettos, Barrios, and the American City* (New York: Russell Sage Foundation, 1997).

2. Allen J. Scott, "Global City Regions: Economic Planning and Policy Dilemmas in a Neoliberal World," in *Urban-Suburban Interdependencies*, eds. Rosalind Greenstein and Wim Wiewel (Cambridge, Mass.: Lincoln Institute of Land Policy, 2000), 123–124.

3. The calculation comes from a study of fifty-nine metropolitan areas. See H. V. Savitch, David Collins, Daniel Sanders, and John P. Markham, "Ties That Bind: Central Cities, Suburbs, and the New Metropolitan Region," *Economic Development Quarterly* 7 (November 1993): 341–357. The study notes that the share of sub-

urban income associated with central-city density and income increased substantially over the 1979–1987 period, suggesting tighter linkage. See as well Richard Voith, "City and Suburban Growth: Substitutes or Complements?," *Business Review* (September–October 1992): 31. Voith found that in the northeastern and midwestern states, in the previous two decades, the relationship between city and suburban population growth had turned from negative to positive. The slower population loss (or alternatively, the population gain) in cities was associated with higher suburban growth.

4. Although the internationalization of the economy is an important trend, we believe it has been exaggerated as a factor opposing the sort of reconstructive program offered below. Most U.S. manufacturers predominantly buy from and sell to other U.S. manufacturers, and the long-run trend of the U.S. economy is toward services, which are usually not traded on even a national basis, much less internationally. Even when competition is international, alternative strategies with very different social consequences are available. Choices between them can be shaped by factors clearly under popular control. Even the diminished state, as we shall see, holds many cards.

5. In *Business Week* (November 2, 1998: 22). The article reviewed the findings of a recent study by Regional Financial Associates indicating that businesses that relocated their operations from rural to urban areas experienced sharp increases in productivity.

6. Edward L. Glaeser, "Demand for Density: The Functions of the City in the 21st Century," *Brookings Review* 18(3) (summer 2000): 10–13.

8

LEAVE NO ONE BEHIND: A POLICY FRAMEWORK ON POVERTY, RACE, AND JUSTICE

Lynn A. Curtis and William E. Spriggs

It is striking how much less talk there is about the poor than there was eight years ago, when the country was economically uncertain, or in previous eras, when the country felt flush.

—*James Fallows, "The Invisible Poor"*
New York Times Magazine, March 19, 2000

This chapter presents a policy framework for the truly disadvantaged and the inner city, based on what has been learned over the past thirty years.

WHAT ARE THE FACTS?

Since the late 1960s, the African American and Latino middle classes have expanded significantly. During this period minority entrepreneurship has increased, as has the number of locally elected officials who are minorities. The last years of the twentieth century brought the greatest economic boom in American history: Driven by the economic expansion of the 1990s, minority unemployment rates are now at record lows, although they remain significantly higher than the average unemployment rate for all Americans.[1] These positive trends have been noted by many government and community leaders, and have drawn attention also from the entertainment industry and the mass media.

The big picture also reveals many negative trends, however, about which leaders, pundits, and mass media have largely kept silent. The following trends have shaped the policy proposals we offer in this chapter:

Child poverty. After nearly a decade of economic expansion, the only superpower in the world still has more than 20 percent of its children at the ages of 5 years and younger living in poverty. By comparison, the corresponding child poverty rate is about 15 percent in Canada, 12 percent in Japan, 7 percent in France, 4 percent in Belgium, and 2 percent in Finland.[2] Today, the poor in America are better off than they were in the 1980s, but the extremely poor are worse off.[3] The market has reached its limit. The median income for women is at a record high, the share of women with jobs is at a record high, teenage pregnancy rates have been driving ever lower, and welfare as we knew it is dead; yet we have one of the highest child poverty rates in the industrial world. Clearly, the improved labor market has not delivered children out of poverty.

Income inequality. Under the regime of supply-side economics that dominated the 1980s in America, the rich got richer and the poor got poorer, according to conservative author Kevin Phillips and many others. The working class also got poorer. Middle-class incomes stayed about the same, which means that the gap between the middle class and the rich increased.[4] The 1990s taught us that a tight labor market can keep inequality from growing but cannot reverse the trend. Among all industrial countries for which reliable current social data exist, the United States has the smallest middle class and the highest poverty rates (being second only to Russia).[5] The vast differences among private expenditures per child dwarf what public per-child expenditures can do to give each American child an equal chance to succeed.

Wealth inequality. The increase in wealth inequality during the 1980s was virtually unprecedented. The only comparable period in American twentieth-century history was 1922–1929, immediately preceding the Great Depression. During the 1980s, almost all of the wealth gained went to the top 20 percent of wealth holders in America. The median wealth of nonwhite American citizens actually *fell* during the 1980s. The average level of wealth among African American families today is about one-tenth that of white families. Wealth inequality is much greater in the United States than in countries traditionally thought of as riven by class divisions, such as the United Kingdom.[6]

CEO-worker inequality. In 1980, the average corporate CEO earned 42 times as much as the average worker. In 1998, the average corporate CEO earned 419 times as much as the average worker.[7] Today, the typical worker in our corporate-defined economy puts in 160 hours more each year than the typical worker of twenty years ago.[8]

Resegregation and problems in urban education. According to the Harvard School of Education, America is resegregating its neighborhoods and schools. Over two-thirds of all African American and Hispanic students in urban areas attend predominantly segregated schools.[9] Today, the number of students who are immigrants or the children of immigrant parents outnumber African American students; and the two groups are more or less segregated from one another. The high dropout rate in the Hispanic community is a nationwide crisis. Furthermore, many immigrant children arrive in their early teens, and we have not devised the resources or constructive policies to handle language proficiency issues for students in those age ranges.

Higher education spending versus prison building. Today, the states spend more on prison building than on higher education. Twenty years ago, the opposite was true.[10]

Housing versus prison building. In the 1980s, prison building became our national housing policy for the poor. We more than quadrupled the number of prison cells, and at the same time we reduced federal appropriations for housing the poor by more than 80 percent.[11]

Racialized criminal justice. After the 1980s, during which the worse racial stereotypes were rekindled—that African Americans are inferior, ill-prepared for the modern economy, and an "underclass" devoid of values—it is little wonder that American society is having difficulty perceiving and coping with a different reality. Our racialized justice system is rationalized by the belief that

African Americans have suffered a crisis in values. Racial profiling by officers, prosecutorial discretion, and the resulting high
incarceration rates for African Americans and Latinos are not
surprising. The high incarceration rates, rather than being
greeted with alarm, are generally accepted as the explanation for
why crime rates have fallen. This is just a part of a continuum of
attitudes and beliefs that also includes acceptance of disproportionately high unemployment rates for African Americans and
Latinos. A comprehensive new report funded by the U.S. Department of Justice and six leading foundations finds that Latino
and African American youth are treated more severely than
white teenagers charged with comparable crimes at every step of
the juvenile justice system. The discrimination runs the gamut
from racial profiling by police to sentencing by judges; sentences
for drug offenses involving minorities are much harsher than
sentences for the same offenses involving whites.[12]

Race and prison building. In the early 1990s, one out of every four
young African American men in the United States was in
prison, on probation, or on parole at any given moment. Today,
despite the efforts of a Presidential Commission on Race (which
had no practical outcome, in terms of policy), *one out of every
three* young African American men is in prison, on probation, or
on parole at any given moment. In big cities, the ratio is *one out
of every two.*[13] Latinos are now the fastest-growing group of in-
mates. If present trends continue, by 2020 one in four Latino
men and two in three African American men between the ages
of 18 and 34 will be in the criminal justice system.[14]

White rural economic development and prison building. Prisons are
disproportionately filled with minorities, yet prison building has
become a job-generating economic development policy for
rural white communities, which send lobbyists with six-figure
incomes to Washington to fight for still more prisons. The result
is what is now commonly referred to as the prison-industrial
complex, too much of which is privatized.[15]

Running in place. Nonetheless, we know—based on one of the most
prestigious American studies of prison building to date, by a
panel of the National Academy of Sciences—that the criminal
justice response to crime is, at best, running in place.[16] For example, in spite of recent drops in violent crime rates, crime and

the fear it generates today are roughly at the same levels they were at in the late 1960s.[17]

NEW ECONOMY, OLD ATTITUDES

The economic expansion of the 1990s overturned much of the conventional wisdom about race and poverty, and their nexus, dating from the 1980s. The retrograde policies of the 1980s masked the remarkable achievements African Americans and Hispanics made in acquiring skills. The key factor in the economic upturn of the 1990s is the closing of the human capital gap with Whites, which began in the 1970s, made possible by affirmative action, school integration, and civil rights laws that opened the doors of higher education. The recent performance of the now much blacker American labor force, with its high productivity numbers, gives little confirmation to those who persist in blaming a skills gap between African Americans and Whites for racial differences in unemployment. New data showing that training programs tend to exacerbate existing racial inequalities in the labor market give even less sustenance to those who want to ignore the racialized character of the American economy.

Policymakers must update their knowledge of the African American workforce, understand the impact of immigration in the 1980s on skill attainment for Latinos, and create a policy framework rooted in the experiences of the 1990s, if there is to be any hope of overcoming current labor-market inequalities. Rehashing the debates of the 1980s will not lead to real progress.

In order to redress persistent racial discrimination and to help immigrants integrate into the American workforce and into local communities, the makers and shapers of policy—including independent researchers and funding agencies, as well as those in government—must grapple with the interrelated but separate problems of the inner cities and the truly disadvantaged as well as with the realities of race and class. It is asking a lot—given how wrong the prevailing view of race was in the 1980s, dominated by discussions about the "underclass" and skills-driven inequality—that we reeducate ourselves at the same time as we attempt to address urban decline; yet that is what we must do.

The lesson of the 1990s is that socioeconomic equality cannot be achieved absent appropriate government regulation of the market. The decline of institutions and laws to strengthen the hand of labor in bargaining with management drove down wages in the 1980s. The trend toward wage inequality was dampened in the 1990s by government measures restoring value to the minimum wage and encouraging full employment—both of which helped restore the bargaining power of a large sector of the labor market. If skills-based explanations for rising inequality, which dominated the 1980s, were true, then the record trade deficits of the 1990s and the boom in business investment, driven largely by computer technologies, should have exacerbated skill-based wage differences, and wage inequality should have grown. It did not.

The record of the 1990s should clearly prevent anyone from viewing the problems of the African American worker as anything other than a subset of American workers' problems. The greatest problem for American workers has been stagnant wage growth. It is important to understand that explaining the lack of success of African American workers in terms of skills or of the work ethic is merely resurrecting old stereotypes and gives primacy to market forces—which we now know cannot fully explain the lack of success of American workers.

The evidence is clear, in macroeconomic terms: When this economic expansion really began benefiting workers, in January 1993, African Americans made up about 10.2 percent of America's workforce. Since then, increases in labor force participation and employment have grown faster for African Americans than for the workforce as a whole. In April 2000, when African American unemployment reached a record low, African Americans made up 11.4 percent of America's workers. In short, America's workforce has gotten blacker.

The conventional wisdom is that African Americans suffered in the labor market of the 1970s and 1980s because they were less productive. In its most extreme, this view holds that African Americans have been "structurally" unemployable—that is, they lack the skills needed to get any job. In its less extreme variant, it held that African Americans are unskilled relative to the American workforce as a whole. Thus, there has been little incentive to employ them: The inclusion of less productive workers would cause business costs to rise, because with a less productive workforce, increases in output would be harder to achieve. If African Americans were on average indeed less productive than the American workforce as a whole, then speeding up the economy to drive unemployment down would have harmed overall economic performance, and in the end, would not really have benefited anyone.

Here is what happened as America's workforce became blacker: Productivity increased by 0.8 percent in 1993 and by 2.4 percent in 1994, fell back to 1.0 percent growth in 1995, and then took off when the African American employment rate began setting new records every month. In January 1995, African Americans made up 10.5 percent of America's workforce; three years later, they were at 10.9 percent. From 1996 to 1998, productivity increased each year—by 3.3 percent, 3.1 percent, and 4.0 percent; and in 1999, it increased by another 4.0 percent. As productivity went up, the costs of doing business fell. Unit labor costs, which measure the wages and compensation needed to pay workers to produce one more unit, fell by 1.5 percent in 1995, by another 0.8 percent in 1997, and by another 1.0 percent in 1998, and then increased a small 0.6 percent in 1999.

The lesson of the 1990s boom is that strong demand for labor can democratize the labor market. The previously high unemployment rates for African Americans and for minorities in general were not brought down by some new job training program. Clearly the workers locked out of jobs in the 1980s were productive and qualified, and when given the chance, they performed well. This experience should make us all question whether the current disparity in unemployment rates would be better solved by premarket interventions such as job training or by market interventions to sustain strong demand for all workers and to make the labor market act more fairly.

A COMMONSENSE POLICY RESPONSE

Despite the recent entrance of record numbers of African Americans to the workforce, a large number of the truly disadvantaged continue to commute on a kind of underground railway between two locations— where they either are locked in the inner-city poorhouse or locked in the prison-industrial complex. The task of framing a policy response to this dilemma has been made easier by the accumulation of scientific evidence over the past thirty years—on what doesn't work, and what does. Accordingly, we propose a commonsense policy that stops spending on what doesn't work and starts replicating what does work—but on a scale equal to the dimensions of the problem.

What Doesn't Work

The market does not work as the solution. The housing market, the credit market, and the labor market all have faults that tend to accentuate existing poverty and discrimination. We therefore must have policies aimed at correcting market failures and ensuring that poverty and discrimination do not deepen. It is important not to overregulate markets, to let them work their magic. But the 1990s teach us that it is also important to constrain markets so as to provide a more equitable outcome.

Supply-side, trickle-down economics has failed, except for the rich. The supply-side enterprise zones of the 1980s did not create many jobs for inner-city youth, according to the *Economist, Business Week*, the U.S. General Accounting Office, and the Urban Institute. The supply-side Job Training Partnership Act failed for high-risk youth, according to U.S. Department of Labor evaluations, in part because it was more a "work first" than a "training first" endeavor, and because it served only a small percent of those who were eligible. The new Workforce Investment Act is doomed to repeat the same mistakes unless those who implement it take seriously the charge to give workers control over what type of training they will receive. Implementation will have to be closely monitored so that workers can avoid repeating patterns of labor-market discrimination that already limit their mobility, just as public housing must be designed so as not to replicate housing segregation.

Welfare reform, with its scientifically unsubstantiated, ideological reliance on "work first" could become a disaster when the next recession hits. Prison building has not been cost-effective, and there is little scientific evidence that it is the primary reason for recent drops in crime. Much of the available evidence on military-style boot camps for juvenile offenders, which offer minimal social support, education, and training, demonstrates their overall failure.[18]

As policies failed and disinvestment from cities proceeded through the 1980s, policy retrenchment often was camouflaged for public consumption by political spin words like *volunteerism, self-sufficiency,* and *empowerment.* Political sugar-coating with phrases like these remains in vogue today. Although the concepts behind these words may have a role to play in national policy, the words often have been used to excess, cynically, as public relations vehicles, and without an understanding of what really happens on the streets. Too often they have masked budget decisions against investment on a scale commensurate with the needs of children, youth, families, and neighborhoods of the inner city.

There continues to be a double standard when it comes to resources. We are told that corporate executives need pay that is more than 400 times that of ordinary workers, as well as highly competent support staff and the latest high-tech equipment. In the early 1990s, the Gulf War successfully was carried out with well-trained, salaried staff and cutting-edge equipment. Yet, when it comes to serving the poor and the inner city, we often are told by naysayers that such resources don't matter that much. That is not true. Scientific evidence now is available that proves what common sense suggests: Adequate, sustained funding of paid, full-time staff and the support infrastructure of an organization make a big difference—if the funding is targeted on the replication of proven programs and is well managed.[19]

We also need to expose the lack of morality and democracy in the policies of the 1980s, which linger today. Giving to the rich and taking from the poor is not just failed economics but also failed morality. So is a policy of spending more on prison building than on higher education. The "free market," "open competition" ideology of supply-siders is a purposeful lie. And a continuing child poverty rate of over 20 percent is immoral.

What Does Work?

Experience demonstrates that there are policies and programs that can and do work, and that are both moral and democratic. There has never been a better time for the nation to carry out a practical policy of replicating what does work for the truly disadvantaged. If we don't do it now, when we have a robust economy (for some), when large federal budget surpluses are projected into the future, and when we have reparations from a tobacco industry that schemed to hook teenagers, then when will we ever replicate what works, on the appropriate scale?

National policy can be based on scientifically evaluated successes that should be replicated, as much as possible, by the inner-city nonprofit organizations that have been responsible for much of what has worked; such organizations also are neighborhood centers of moral influence. This framework builds on new technical knowledge about *how* to replicate what works and about *how* to increase the nonprofit, grassroots institutional capacity that we have acquired over the past thirty years.[20] Based on what evaluations show yields the highest long-term cost-benefit ratios, top priorities on the policy agenda should be reform of the urban public education system; a full employment policy for the inner city; and complementary reforms to create more racial and criminal justice. The following sections outline steps that can be taken to address these priorities.

Fully Fund Head Start

Dramatic new biological and chemical research findings have demon-strated that the quality of attention given to children in their earliest years determines the way their brains are wired, which provides the basis for their future social, emotional, and intellectual development.[21] These findings underscore the importance of preschool. The father of the fed-eral preschool initiative Head Start, Edward Zigler, Sterling Professor of Psychology at Yale University, recently concluded:

> The biggest accomplishment of quality preschool programs is that they prepare children for school. School readiness is the first of the national ed-ucation goals and a condition seriously absent in districts serving high-risk populations. Preparing children for school entails more than preacademic and social skills. Children must be in good health and have parents who are involved in their educational progress. This is why I support the notion of universal preschool only when there is comprehensive, two-generation programming.
>
> Attention to physical and mental health, preliteracy and other cognitive-development skills, social and emotional adjustment and parental involve-ment are hallmarks of Head Start that together contribute to preparing children for school. These effects can be attained only when quality is good, however, and Head Start has had uneven quality over its thirty-five years. In the 1990s strong efforts to improve quality were undertaken. Eval-uation shows that today Head Start is the best it has ever been. Further sup-port is needed to assist those centers that are still below performance stan-dards and to secure better salaries and curriculum.
>
> Child development does not begin and end at the ages of three and four. Early Head Start is now delivering services to at-risk families and children ages zero to three. The results are not in yet, but there is reason to believe that family support and child development services provided early in life will enhance healthy growth and establish desirable patterns of parent interaction and involvement. I believe the program will merit expansion. After the preschool age, there is strong evidence that compre-hensive, two-generation programming helps children do better in later grades (which, after all, is the point of school readiness). This finding comes from the Chicago Child-Parent Centers, which use a model closely aligned to Head Start but one that lasts for two years of preschool and several years into grade school. The project is very large and evalua-tion has been going on for five years, yielding strong support for the value

of serving children for more than a year of preschool and during the critical years of transition to school.[22]

Today, only about one-third of all eligible lower-income children between the ages of 3 and 5 years are served by Head Start, and most eligible children are in Head Start for only a year. The enrollment rates for three-year-olds are especially low. We recommend full funding for all eligible poor children, following the principles set forth by Zigler.

Create a Nonprofit Corporation for Youth Investment

Naysayers assert that the effects of Head Start diminish over time. Of course they do. As Zigler's statement implies, after inner-city kids leave Head Start at the age of 5 or 6, they are back on the mean streets. Evaluations by Columbia University, the Eisenhower Foundation, and other research institutions have shown that after-school safe havens for kids at ages 6 to 16 work as logical continuations of Head Start, providing help with homework, direction by responsible adults, and safe passage through adolescence in a risky society. Some nonprofit grassroots successes—e.g., Koban, Inc., in Columbia, South Carolina, and Centro Sister Isolina Ferré in San Juan, Puerto Rico—combine paid civilian staff with police mentors, who also stabilize neighborhoods through community-based, problem-oriented policing. Concerning older children, a Brandeis University evaluation showed that the Ford Foundation's Quantum Opportunities adult mentoring program kept high-risk high schoolers out of trouble and on track to jobs and college.[23] The National Urban League's Achievement Campaign has enlisted the support of numerous community and fraternal organizations to mentor and support the achievement drive in minority students. A test of this philosophy supported with funding from Merrill Lynch provided a group of inner-city students with the social support needed to change their life paths, after which an above average percentage went on to college.

Many local nonprofit programs claim success, but the ones highlighted here can show scientific proof of success based on control group or comparison group designs. Some of the evaluated successes are secular programs, and others are outreach efforts by religious organizations. (An exclusive focus on "faith-based" programs would have meant ignoring our primary criterion for identifying a model that can be replicated to the appropriate scale.) All showed statistically significant pre- and postevaluation outcomes using valid comparison or control groups. All of the youth development successes identified here also act as centers of moral influence.

A new national nonprofit Corporation for Youth Investment should be created to assist proven nonprofit youth development organizations in replicating themselves, to supply technical assistance, and to finance replications with federal funds. The federal bureaucracy—which often has impeded youth development in the past—could thus play a minimal role.

Replicate Successful Urban Public School Reform

In the aftermath of World War II, President Eisenhower realized that a lack of transportation financing had left the United States with an inadequate road system, so he launched the federal highway infrastructure program. Similarly, we need a federal education infrastructure financing system.

We must reject local financing of education as inadequate to the task at hand. Railing against uncertified teachers in urban schools is to blame the victim instead of the system at fault. Currently, there is a nationwide shortage of certified teachers. Urban schools are hiring uncertified teachers not because of management incompetence but because in a world of local financing, someone must lose—it is just a game of musical chairs. Local financing also robs urban schools of the resources needed to make proper investments in school buildings. As a result, thirty-year-old stadiums, like the homes of the Seattle Mariners and the Minnesota Twins, are considered too old by corporate America and are demolished; but a thirty-year-old school, in most inner cities, is considered brand new, even though it could not have been designed for the Internet age. Comparisons of per-pupil expenditures must include school building depreciation. Schools built for suburban sprawl districts are new and have a great deal of depreciation expense; considering that any school building older than 30 years has completely depreciated, most inner-city schools have no depreciation expense. Relying on local financing will not replace obsolete schools or solve the national teacher shortage. States have proven that they will not address the unequal funding of schools. We cannot solve the problems of inner-city schools without first addressing these two realities as federal issues. In a global economy, we can no longer accept less from one set of schools or students than from another. In a time of a nationally mobile labor force, a youth in an inner-city school in Kansas City, Missouri is just as important to the future vitality of America's economy as a youth in Montgomery County, Maryland.

As Jonathan Kozol observed:

> [T]he children in poor rural schools in Mississippi and Ohio will continue to get education funded at less than $4,000 yearly and children in the South Bronx will get less than $7,000, while children in the richest suburbs will continue to receive up to $18,000 yearly. But they'll be told they must be held to the same standards and they'll all be judged, of course, by their performance on the same exams.[24]

Slogans, standards, and exams do not teach reading. Only well-paid and proficient teachers do, and only if they work under conditions that do not degrade their spirits and demean their students. Money, as the rich and powerful repeatedly remind us, is not "the only way" to upgrade education; but it seems to be the way that the rich have chosen for their own kids, and if it is good enough for them, why would it not be of equal benefit to the children of poor people?

We must invest our school dollars wisely. Evaluations of the School Development Plan created and replicated widely by James Comer of Yale University;[25] full-service community schools;[26] and other school reforms, documented comprehensively by Joy Dryfoos,[27] show what we need to do to improve public education:

- Reduce classroom size.
- Restructure academic programs to focus on a core of common knowledge and skills.
- Place policy for each inner-city school in the hands of a local management team, led by the principal and including teachers, parents, counselors, and other school staff.
- Dramatically increase the involvement of and assistance to inner-city parents.
- Provide focused intervention by a mental health team for children with emotional, behavioral, or academic problems.
- Create safe environments during the school day and supportive, nonprofit, safe havens after school.
- Locate nonprofit organizations in public school buildings—to provide health, family, community, cultural, and recreational initiatives and to ensure security.

An example of a public school that is implementing most of these principles is the Salome Arena Middle Academy, operated jointly by the Children's Aid Society and Community School District 6 in New York City. Located in a new building in Washington Heights, it offers students a choice of four self-contained "academies"—Business; Community Service; Expressive Arts; and Mathematics, Science, and Technology. The school opens at 7 A.M. each morning the year around, and stays open after school, into the evening. To replicate such models, we need to establish the quasi-governmental Safe Passage Commission recommended by Dryfoos.[28] It would target federal funds and matching grants to schools and nonprofit organization partners in high-poverty, inner-city neighborhoods.

We must also have realistic policies for students who have limited proficiency in English. To imagine immigrant children all arriving as babies or at early school ages is to ignore reality. We must be on guard that in pursuing accountability standards for adults who run schools, we are not setting traps for students. It is possible to grade schools and the adults who run them without using children as hostages for getting the resources and programs needed for their success. We must also give schools the flexibility to devise ways to meet the needs of our growing immigrant population. This policy discussion must be given priority in its own right.

Legislate a National, "Training First" Jobs Policy

Based on existing scientific evaluation, one of the most promising job training models for out-of-school youth and for the reform of "welfare reform" is the Argus Community in the South Bronx. Argus is based on an understanding that there can be no political quick fixes and simplistic solutions (like "work first"). Argus gives priority to development of character and a moral value system in participants; socialization and counseling in a drug- and violence-free environment; a life skills curriculum to prepare youth to be functioning adults who can handle conflicts and manage themselves well on the job; on-site education and remedial education (including general educational diploma high school courses in an alternative educational setting); job training on site and *before* job placement; placement in jobs that are in demand and offer potential upward mobility, not dead-end jobs; and follow-up to ensure better job retention.[29]

Sufficient funds must be appropriated to ensure that workers know which training programs are the best investment for them, so that armed with the independence that the present Workforce Investment Act grants them, they can freely choose programs with a model more along the lines of Argus and other training-first successes, like the STRIVE program in New York and the Job Corps nationally.[30] All of the truly disadvantaged who need training should get it.

We must also remember that job training on a large scale is especially necessary and has proven hugely effective among the disabled. Programs like the one run by the Urban League of Nebraska in Omaha give disabled workers the holistic help they need to confront their disability and gain new work skills that complement the skills they already have. Coupled with policies allowing disabled workers to keep their Medicare and Medicaid coverage, training programs like those in Omaha enable people with disabilities to remain productively in the labor market and to live more independently than they otherwise could.

We must also emphasize education policies that give the disabled full access to technologies that are important in today's workplace: Computers need to find their way to special education students, too. Local technology training centers also should be fully accessible to the visually impaired and individuals with other disabilities.

Generate 1 Million Private-Sector, Inner-City Jobs

Two million–plus new jobs are needed in order to create full employment in inner cities. Of these, 1 million private-sector jobs should be filled by inner-city residents who have had Argus, STRIVE, and Job Corps–like training.

The current welfare reform has stripped us of an income-delivery system that can counterbalance economic downturns. The emphasis on work is a good starting point for ensuring that during economic downturns, women who previously used welfare as their unemployment insurance get employment; but the creation of mechanisms for *keeping* people employed is a necessary corollary of this approach. Toward this goal, the regulations for HUD Community Development Block Grants; HUD housing grants; Commerce Department Economic Development Administration grants; Transportation Department Urban Mass Transit grants; and other federal, state, and local economic development grants need to be revised to place much greater priority than at present on the reduction of poverty and the generation of private jobs for the inner-city unemployed. A much more efficient federal interagency coordinating mechanism than now exists is needed to co-target these reformed grants toward the places of greatest need. Federal regulations should require that localities employ the truly disadvantaged in local growth industries, following the model of the Target Industries and Employment Program of the Portland (Oregon) Development Commission.[31]

The generation of matching funds from local tax bases should be encouraged. Given the loss of tax bases from the central city to the suburbs in many places, the federal government should condition grants to states and localities on local agreements to share across the entire metropolitan area (including suburbs) the value of commercial property as well as other elements of the area-wide tax base—following successful policies implemented in metropolitan areas such as Minneapolis-St. Paul.[32]

Modeled on the successes of the South Shore Bank in Chicago, which already have been replicated elsewhere, a semi-independent National Community Development Bank, removed from federal bureaucracy, needs to be capitalized as part of a comprehensive plan to generate more private jobs in the inner city. The South Shore Bank has pioneered in reinvesting the savings of inner-city residents back into their own neighborhoods—for example, providing capital to new inner-city businesses.[33] The capitalization of community development banks and businesses should be linked to tougher enforcement by HUD of the Community Reinvestment Act of 1977, which requires banks to invest in their communities. Since the Act's passage, supply-siders and well-paid lobbyists for the rich have been trying to eviscerate it.[34]

Generate 1.25 Million Public-Sector, Inner-City Jobs

Past experience suggests that given the private sector's traditional resistance to employing the truly disadvantaged, and given the failure of enterprise zones (such as South Central Los Angeles, which went into decline after the 1992 riots), the goal of creating 1 million new private-sector inner-city jobs might be too ambitious. Yet this number is only half that needed in order to attain full employment in the inner city. We estimate that at least 1.25 million public jobs will have to be generated by federal dollars. The jobs should be implemented locally by groups like the nonprofit Youth Build USA (created by Dorothy Stoneman, to teach construction to inner-city youth);[35] nonprofit community development corporations (like the New Community Corporation created after the 1967 Newark riots by Father William Linder);[36] nonprofit youth development and youth employment organizations; for-profit entities with a social conscience (like the Washington, D.C.–based Telesis Corporation);[37] and local governments.

We propose that 250,000 public urban construction and infrastructure repair jobs and 1 million public service jobs be created.

Public infrastructure investment has shaped America's present and future. Early on, public investments built canals and subsidized railroads. Government financed the first assembly lines. The interstate highway system was built in the 1950s and 1960s with federal funds. Federal investments developed the jet engine, began the exploration of space, and helped develop the computer and the Internet. Yet public infrastructure investment declined precipitously in the 1980s, as a result of supply-side economics and the associated urban disinvestment. The 1990s have not reversed this public disinvestment. In 1980, more than 4 percent of all federal outlays were for infrastructure. By 1990, that share had fallen to less than 3 percent. As of 1997, public investment in infrastructure was at 36 percent of 1970s levels, and if the current budget trajectory continues it will drop another 37 percent. The United States is the only major industrial society that is not currently renewing and expanding its public infrastructure; and nowhere are renewal and expansion more needed than in U.S. cities and inner cities.38

Similarly, there is an enormous need for public service employment. As part of the reform of "welfare reform," we need a great many qualified child care workers. With Argus, STRIVE, and Job Corps–type training programs, child care could be a major employment sector for persons coming off welfare. Drivers and support staff workers are needed to create a transportation system that will allow former welfare recipients and other unemployed people to get to jobs in the suburbs. Teachers in inner-city schools desperately need adequately trained support staff. Community-based nonprofit youth development and community development organizations need paid staff to work with supervisors. Housing shelters also are in great need of staff. There is a great demand for drug abuse counselors. Major cities no longer have enough telephone operators to answer 911 emergency calls in a timely way. Because there are so many unmet needs, it will be easy to ensure that existing employees are not displaced. In many cases, qualified existing employees should become supervisors.

Create a More Supportive Economic Policy

In support of these job investments, the nation needs a macroeconomic policy that more honestly recognizes that trickle-down economic growth does not eliminate poverty in specific locations; a fiscal policy that sepa-

complete a drug treatment plan. Drug courts in several cities have been evaluated as effective in bringing addicted offenders into treatment and avoiding the cycle of repeated incarceration.

- Replicate proven high-quality drug treatment programs in the community, closely integrated with local drug courts, to ensure a continuum of comprehensive care for addicted offenders and their families. This implies more than the mere provision of medical treatment: It includes skills training, education, and other support services, including transportation and child care. Successful community-based programs that work with families of addicted offenders, like La Bodega de la Familia in Manhattan,[46] need to be replicated to enhance families' capacity for self-sufficiency and reduce relapse and recidivism.
- Create Web sites that provide universal access to successful models of affirmative action and racial integration.
- Invest in comprehensive strategies to reintegrate offenders into the community. Replicate much more widely the self-sufficient Delancey Street model developed in San Francisco, which already has been successful in several locations around the nation.[47]

As these models are replicated, we need to respond to the failure of the so-called war on drugs[48] by revising our budget priorities. America spends 30 percent of its antidrug resources on treatment and prevention and 70 percent on law enforcement. In many European countries, the percentages are just the opposite—70 percent on prevention and treatment and 30 percent on law enforcement. In America, we need a ratio closer to that in Europe. Another example, closer to home, of alternative budget priorities is the conservative State of Arizona. Arizona held referendums in recent years on the high costs of prison building. Voters decided to begin to divert nonviolent offenders from the prison system into treatment alternatives. Under state law, treatment programs are funded for anyone who is convicted of a crime and has a substance abuse problem. Those convicted for the first or second time for possession of drugs for personal use are required to be sent to a treatment program rather than to state prison. An evaluation commissioned by the Supreme Court of the State of Arizona found recidivism rates to be low among convicts so diverted, and concluded that a considerable amount of money had been saved for the taxpayers of Arizona.[49] These results should encourage other states to follow suit.

WHAT IS THE COST OF REPLICATING WHAT WORKS TO SCALE, AND HOW CAN IT BE FINANCED?

Table 8.1 summarizes the total cost of our proposed investments in order to begin replicating what works on a scale equal to the dimensions of the problem. As much as possible, we encourage financing by the private sector and by state and local governments. Yet experience has shown these sources unwilling or unable to invest at anything close to the appropriate level. To be pragmatic, we need to recognize that only the federal government potentially has the resources to replicate successful programs to scale.

At the same time, we recommend that these public dollars be put to work as much as possible by private, nonprofit, grassroots organizations in concert with for-profits with records of inner-city success, and with local government. We need new, and much more democratic, private nonprofit delivery systems.

The official estimate of the federal government budget surplus over the next ten years is an astounding $4.2 trillion.[50] This surplus can easily accommodate the budget shown in Table 8.1. The truly disadvantaged have as much a claim on funds as do, for example, Social Security recipients. We must invest in those who are retired, disabled, or in need of survivors' benefits from the Social Security system. To be fair to children, youth, and the truly disadvantaged, we also must invest in *their* future — their development, schools, job skills, and communities. Americans do not need another world war in order to justify a GI Bill for investing on a scale that allows the nation to meet the needs of its children and youth.

Portions of the budget shown in Table 8.1 also should be financed by reduced spending on what doesn't work, as well as by reductions in affirmative action for the rich and grants for corporate welfare, which amount to more than $100 billion per year in handouts by the American taxpayer.[51]

Well-paid lobbyists will argue that the rich and corporations need government grants and subsidies in order to ensure a robust economy. Such claims are disputed by econometric forecasts made in 1997 by Richard McGahey, who was then at the Center for Community Change. McGahey analyzed the impact on the economy of one million jobs if their to-

TABLE 8.1   Summary of Federal Investments Proposed (in billion dollars)

Investment	Federal Cost Per Year
Replication of Head Start preschool for all eligible poor children	$7b
Replication of the Comer School development plan, full-service community schools, and related models of success in urban public school systems	$15b
Creation of a corporation for youth investment to replicate after-school safe-haven prevention models, Quantum Opportunities prevention models, and related successes	$1b
Reform of the Workforce Investment Act to replicate training-first models like Argus, STRIVE, and Job Corps	$4.5b
Creation of 1,000,000 private sector jobs for the inner city through better targeting of existing economic development grants on poverty and inequality reduction	$0
Creation of a national community development bank modeled after the South Shore Bank	$1b
Generation of 250,000 public construction and rehabilitation jobs for the inner city that are targeted on housing and urban infrastructure development	$5b
Generation of 1,000,000 public service jobs for the inner city that are targeted on public service employment in day care, transportation services, urban school staff support, nonprofit community organization support, and reform of "welfare reform"	$20b
Implementation of presidential commissions on affirmative action, racial bias in the criminal justice system, and concrete corporate ceilings; replication of the St. Louis and Gatreaux models of school and housing integration; creation of a Web site on successful models of affirmative action and integration; replication of successful community equity policing models, community and treatment-oriented drug courts, and Delancey Street–type offender reintegration models*	$2.5b
TOTAL	$56b

*This budget line item assumes substantial addtional resources through a shift in priorities in America's "war on drugs"—from 70% law enforcement and 30% prevention/treatment to 30% law enforcement and 70% prevention/treatment (or at least a 50/50 split).

tal cost were financed by reducing corporate welfare by an equal amount. Using FAIRMODEL, a widely regarded econometric model based on 131 equations that is continually updated and reestimated, McGahey compared the then-current five-year forecast with an alternative forecast including the aforementioned public service job program financed by corporate welfare cuts. Compared to the existing forecast, the alternative showed "a higher level of real and nominal economic growth, stable private sector employment, and a lower national unemployment rate." Real wage increases and inflation are virtually the same in both scenarios.[52] In other words, a shift in some resources from corporate welfare to public service jobs not only does not hurt the economy; it can actually help the economy.

What Is the Political Feasibility of a Policy Based on What Works?

Considerable support for the investment priorities proposed here can be found in public opinion polls taken over the past decade. National surveys conducted from 1988 to 1994 by the National Opinion Research Center at the University of Chicago show that a substantial majority of Americans wanted to see more money spent on improving the nation's educational system and on preventing crime and drug addiction.[53] In 1992, immediately after the Los Angeles riots, the *New York Times* and CBS News asked Americans in a nationwide poll: "Are we spending too much money, too little money, or about the right amount of money on problems of the big cities, on improving the conditions of Blacks, and on the poor?" Sixty percent of respondents said that too little was being spent on urban problems; 61 percent said that too little was being spent on improving the conditions of African Americans; and 64 percent said that too little was being spent on problems of the poor. The pollsters also asked: "To reduce racial tension and prevent riots, would more jobs and job training help a lot, help a little, or not make any difference?" Seventy-eight percent of respondents said that more jobs and training would help a lot.[54]

Complementary findings come from a 1996 poll of voters sponsored by the Children's Partnership, the American Academy of Pediatrics, the Coalition for America's Children, the National Association of Children's Hospitals, and the National Parent-Teacher Association. Seventy-six percent of the voters polled in that survey said that they would be more likely to vote for a candidate who supported increased spending for children's programs. Sixty-five percent favored proposals for children and families, even if this would mean slowing down deficit reduction. Sixty-four percent said that government should play a large role in solving problems facing children. Sixty-two percent said that they would oppose a balanced budget amendment if it required cuts in children's programs.[55]

In 1998, in the first national sampling of attitudes on surpluses after a federal fiscal year 1999 budget surplus was projected, a *USA Today*/ CNN/Gallup poll found that the biggest group of respondents, 43 percent, called for investment of any extra money in Social Security, Medicare, and education. (Thirty percent backed paying down the debt, and 22 percent favored tax cuts.)[56]

The Eisenhower Foundation's experience with media has reinforced the findings of these public opinion polls. In 1998 and 1999, the Foundation released thirty-year updates of the final reports of the Kerner Riot Commission and National Violence Commission of the late 1960s. The updates—which emphasized what social policies had and had not served to lessen the pressures causing social unrest—received saturation media coverage, most of which was favorable.[57] Criticisms were superficial and easily rebutted.[58] Among editorials, feature columns, and op-eds, we found a network of supportive opinion in every region of the nation, in towns both large and small.[59]

REPAIRING THE DISCONNECT

In sum, we know what works. We have the resources to finance what works, and on an appropriate scale. There is considerable public support.[60] But there is a disconnect between knowledge, resources, and public opinion on the one hand, and action by our leaders on the other. How can we repair that disconnect, that moral breach?

What can we, the people do? We can push for genuine political campaign finance reform; organize a long-term citizen advocacy campaign to communicate to the public that we do know what works; and forge a new political alliance.

Campaign Finance Reform

Money talks in our present political system, especially for those who support tax breaks for the rich, disinvestments from the inner city, and prison building for the poor. Today, the economic system runs the political system. We have a deeply compromised democracy based on the principle of one dollar, one vote, instead of one person, one vote. In many ways, clean money campaign reform, as pioneered in Maine and as advocated at the national level by Public Campaign, is the reform that makes all of the other necessary reforms possible.[61] Strictly limiting campaign contributions and expenditures and providing for a system of public financing for congressional campaigns like that available for presidential campaigns will not guarantee replication of what works to scale. But it could level the political playing field, allowing campaigns to be based more on issues than on money and to take into account the interests of the poor, the working class, and the middle class, and not just the interests of the rich and of big corporations.

Communicating What Works

We also can repair the disconnect by better communicating what works. Foundations and corporations that support the position of naysayers generously have funded communications and media operations in naysaying think tanks and related organizations over the past thirty years. The conservative think tanks have been extremely effective in communicating their ideology: There is little that works; the war on poverty is hopeless; and the country should cut taxes for the rich and build prisons and boot camps for the poor. At the same time, foundations that support replication of the kind of child, youth, family, community, and economic development policy articulated here—policy based on scientific evaluation— have tended to view communications, media policy, and advocacy for funding programs to scale as outside of their mission.[62]

In some ways, the media conspire with the naysayers. Most media in America are controlled by nine giant multinational corporations. There is unremitting pressure for profits. Most Americans prefer to get their news on local television. To maximize ratings and profits, local managers tend to follow the dictum "if it bleeds, it leads." Crime and violence on the 5 P.M., 6 P.M., 10 P.M., and 11 P.M. local television news shows are thought to be the best way to maximize ratings, profits, and the television manager's job security. The resulting high frequency of bloody and sensational stories also often targets young, minority males, who are demonized as offenders, and "welfare mothers," who are portrayed as inadequate parents. As George Gerbner, emeritus dean of the Annenberg School of Communications at the University of Pennsylvania, has observed, the result of the present violent and negative programming can be the "mean world syndrome." Day in and day out, the average, middle-class, suburban American viewer is left with the feeling that nothing works. The middle-class viewer is likely to conclude that policies like naysaying and prison building are the answer, not social programs.[63]

What can we do to reverse the mean world syndrome? Patricia McGinnis, president of the Council for Excellence in Government, funded by the Ford Foundation, talks about the need for "spreading the word about what works most effectively."[64] To spread the word about what works, we recommend conventional as well as alternative media strategies.

Conventional Media Strategies

One example of a conventional strategy are the strategic communications schools run by the Eisenhower Foundation and other groups for the executive directors of national and especially local, inner-city, non-profit organizations. Each Eisenhower Foundation school begins with strategic communications planning, covering print and electronic media. What exactly is an advocacy campaign? What is the message? Who are the messengers? How can they be linked to specific target audiences? A strategic plan must answer these questions and many more.

A television camera then is brought into the strategic communications school, operated by a wise, African American cameraman off duty from NBC. Each nonprofit participant must first sit in front of the camera and, in a minute or two, present the mission of his or her organization. Each then must undertake a friendly interview with a reporter. Next, each must undertake a hostile interview—and finally, be part of a press conference in which the trainers act as unpleasant reporters. Each round of such training is videotaped, replayed, and critiqued in front of all the other participants. It is hard and stressful work. But, not surprisingly, nonprofit organizational personnel respond well and learn quickly. Few previously had thought of communications as a key part of their mission.

We need to greatly expand such training. If a thousand nonprofit organizations could receive strategic communications training and retraining each year and if communications directors could be hired for clusters of local nonprofit groups in hundreds of cities, there could be significant impact nationally. More media-savvy nonprofit groups could be heard. They could put market pressure on local television stations that do not incorporate segments on what works and that continue "bleeds/leads" programming. They could teach private-sector leaders what works, and help elect public officials committed to what works and to campaign finance reform.

A number of local television stations have already made the changes recommended here (e.g., KVUE, in Austin, Texas).[65] Such models need to be communicated, shared, and replicated more widely around the nation.

Public service announcements on what works can be part of a conventional media strategy. However, we have seen little scientific evidence that public service announcements by national nonprofit organizations have had much impact. Instead, we would propose funding local nonprofit organizations, enabling them to create and broadcast "what works" messages tailored to specific locales and delivered by local youth. To employ the previously demonized as the messengers conveys a powerful message in and of itself. One organization that has already employed this technique is the youth media enterprise of the Dorchester Youth Collaborative in Boston, which uses such media messages as part of a more comprehensive strategy. The Collaborative's positive youth messages have been seen and heard locally in Boston and distributed nationally through Blockbuster Video. (The group is featured in a limited-distribution, Hollywood-financed, socially relevant motion picture titled *Squeeze*.[66])

Alternative Communication Strategies

Yet we are realistic about the limitations of mainstream television, radio, and newspaper media in communicating what works. That is why we recommend alternative venues—including, for example, in-person town meetings, electronic pamphleteering, and interlinked community Web sites.

Town meetings have the advantage of direct communication without the filter of media. They engage the audience—and can help attract more citizens to join a local coalition that advocates proactive policies based on what works. Local and state legislative and executive branch officials can be invited, as can candidates running for office. Local nonprofit advocacy organizations can propose more of what works, less of what doesn't—and then ask officials to go on record with their responses.

Religious services and accompanying social functions also are forms of town meetings. There is vast potential, we believe, for the clergy to communicate what works and the immorality of what doesn't work. A well-informed clergy can make powerful use from the pulpit of the policy successes and failures documented here.

As a supplement to in-person meetings, "low-tech" pamphleteering can be useful to deliver messages to people in the community—and, perhaps, to involve youth as the pamphlet distributors. When Bill Moyers resigned from commercial network television, he stated that corporate control had destroyed broadcast journalism and that one recourse was to "return to the days of the pamphleteer."[67] Low-tech advocacy venues are well known to grassroots, inner-city community organizations. However, many local inner-city nonprofit groups have lost their street organizing skills over the past thirty years. We need to revitalize advocacy and street organizing by local nonprofit groups.

More importantly, nonprofits need to become sophisticated in "high-tech" pamphleteering, using techniques like the one pioneered by the National Urban League, which used the Internet to Webcast its Annual Conference, providing video and audio feeds for all its sessions. "Any person with a phone line can become a town crier with a voice that resonates farther than it could from a soapbox," Supreme Court Justice John Paul Stevens has written in the first Supreme Court decision that dealt with the First Amendment and the Internet. Through the technologies of on-line publishing, "the same individual can become a pamphleteer," he concluded.[68]

Nationally, nonprofit organizations need to construct sophisticated, master Web sites. The sites should summarize what works and what doesn't work, based on scientific evaluation. The sites should link much of their information to local, grassroots, inner-city nonprofit groups. The local groups, and especially the inner-city youth they serve, should be taught how to access what-works information and how to use it for advocacy. Are you debating prison building on a television or radio talk show tomorrow? Log on to the master Web site tonight. For hate crime legislation, see the site maintained by the Leadership Conference on Civil Rights. Find out the facts to use against prison building. Click on to alternatives that succeed and prevent—like safe havens, Quantum Opportunities, and training-first.

Locally, a new generation of advocacy-based, community Web sites is needed. The community Web sites should be run by inner-city nonprofit groups and should directly involve youth. The local sites should link up nonprofit advocacy organizations with citizens who can help communicate what works to local public and civic leaders. The outcomes of town meetings can be summarized on such community Web sites. Plans for upcoming town meetings can be communicated. Each community Web site can continue to discuss budget priorities; organize against "bleeds/leads" television news; generate new, proactive communication strategies; and fight for campaign finance reform. We already have evidence that many people want to convene with their geographic neighbors, both on line and in person, and community-based Web sites linked to town meetings would do just that. Partial existing models include community Web sites in locations as diverse as San Francisco, California; Blacksburg, Virginia; and London, England. In London, Microsoft supplied computers, Internet access, and a way for persons in specific communities to communicate with one another on line.[69] An increasing number of sites make advocacy easy, like the "Contact Congress" sections for the National Urban League. Much more is possible, we believe, and it can reduce the "digital divide" between the haves and the have-nots—as well as advocate what works.

Forming a Strategic Political Alliance

Ultimately, the goal of campaign finance reform and communicating what works should be the creation of a new political alliance with a broad constituency. The alliance should recapture some of the national mood that existed after World War II—when Americans sought to build a more inclusive, equitable society, in which everyone had a fair chance of "making it."[70] The alliance must bring together middle-income Americans (who often need two or three jobs in the family to make ends meet); wage earners (who need to be reminded that their CEOs earn on the average 419 times as much as they do); and the poor (whose income status suffered in the 1980s and hardly improved in the 1990s). As Latinos are predicted to become the largest minority group in 2010, the alliance must facilitate new political cooperation between African Americans and Hispanics.

What are the common grounds for a new political alliance? One is resentment over an America that fails to live up to its democratic ideals. We can learn from other countries where inequality has become an issue: Large majorities already exist in five European countries and in Japan that want public policies to reduce economic inequalities in their societies.[71] American social policy advocates can learn from their counterparts in those countries. There is also some evidence that current class warfare by wealthy Americans is spurring a political response in the middle class and among the poor: Those in the upper income brackets who support only political candidates who promise to cut their taxes, and who call for Federal Reserve policies that coddle the stock and bond markets at the cost of job creation and income and home ownership opportunities for working people are creating resentment, because such policies increase socio-economic divisions among Americans. Working Americans are increasingly critical of policies that foster inequality or that give undue rewards to the rich and powerful, according to surveys by Alan Wolfe at Boston College. Excessive rewards to CEOs are perceived by many middle- and working-class people interviewed by Wolfe as disconnected from the efforts made to secure the rewards. This, suggests Wolfe, makes trickle-down policies politically vulnerable—especially given the enormous income, wage, and wealth gaps that opened up in the 1980s and widened in the 1990s.[72] Accordingly, middle-income and wage-earner families, including those with both parents working, may respond to messages like "reduce affirmative action for the rich" and "get corporations off welfare." Given the huge government grants and subsidies made to many industries, a dialogue can be generated on corporate "welfare kings."

Resentment over an unfair economic deal is not the only common ground that middle- and working-income people share with the poor. They share, as well, a vulnerability to the global technological marketplace. As Jeff Faux has observed, middle-income people, wage-earners, and the poor all need education and reeducation, job training and retraining, in order to compete.[73] New high-tech industries for which citizens can be trained and retrained include, for example, computer hardware and software, computer and Internet maintenance, computer-smart urban transit systems, electronic digital imaging, ceramics, advanced composites, sensors, photonics, artificial intelligence, robotics, computer-aided manufacturing, biotechnology, renewable energy, reduction of environmental deterioration, and research to cure serious diseases.

Can we secure a voting majority around government-facilitated education and training? The answer may be yes, based on new national surveys conducted by the Pew Research Center for People and the Press,[74] and by Albert H. Cantril and Susan Davis Cantril.[75] The Cantril surveys show that voters disagree philosophically on the role of government in the abstract but that majorities support specific, pragmatic government investments. Such investments include increased spending on Head Start, teacher subsidies, college student aid, and job training. The Cantril findings fit well into our frame of selective education, training, and criminal justice investments based on what works, along with our recommendation of economic investments based on the elimination of child poverty and the creation of full employment, especially for the hard-to-employ.

Basing our efforts on such information, we can and must work toward a national synergy whereby communicating what works encourages a new political alliance, which then creates more pressure for campaign finance reform, which then allows a fairer debate on what works, which then leads to even more effective communication and action by our reticent leaders.

The challenges within America require vision, not incrementalism and policy bites. Vision is needed from the grass roots to the White House. We need big solutions to big problems. That is what America always has been about. It is about dreaming and trying to fulfill those dreams, however long they may have been deferred.

In the words of historian James MacGregor Burns, "While centrists cautiously seek the middle way, leaders in science, technology, education, entertainment, finance and the media pursue their own transforming visions."[76] The next agenda needs a transforming vision that embraces both Franklin Roosevelt's commitment to effective government and Teddy Roosevelt's boldness in establishing limits to private greed.

NOTES

1. Lynn A. Curtis and Fred R. Harris, "The Millennium Breach" (Washington, D.C.: Milton S. Eisenhower Foundation, 1998), available on line at www.eisenhowerfoundation.org.

2. National Center for Children in Poverty—Columbia University, "Young Children in Poverty," National Center for Children in Poverty, New York, March 1998.

3. Jeff Faux, "Lifting All Boats," chapter prepared for *To Establish Justice, To Insure Domestic Tranquility: A Thirty Year Update of the National Commission on the Causes and Prevention of Violence*, Milton S. Eisenhower Foundation, Washington, D.C., 1999; Peter Edelman, "Who Is Worrying About the Children?," *Washington Post* (August 11, 1999): A18.

4. Kevin Phillips, *The Politics of Rich and Poor* (New York: Random House, 1990); Jason DeParle, "Richer Rich, Poorer Poor, and a Fatter Green Book," *New York Times* (May 26, 1991); U.S. Census, Historical Poverty Tables (Washington, D.C.: U.S. Census, 1997); Children's Defense Fund, *The State of America's Children* (Washington, D.C.: Children's Defense Fund, 1994); and Felicity Baringer, "Rich–Poor Gulf Widens Among Blacks," *New York Times* (September 25, 1992).

5. Doug Henwood, "The Nation Indicators," *Nation* (March 29, 1999): 10; Alan Wolfe, "The New Politics of Inequality," *New York Times* (September 22, 1999): A27.

6. Keith Bradsher, "A Gap in Wealth in U.S. Called Widest in West," *New York Times* (April 17, 1995): A1; Edward N. Wolff, *Top Heavy* (New York: New Press, 1995); "The Tide Is Not Lifting Everyone," *New York Times* editorial (September 30, 1997); and Glenn C. Loury, "Unequalized," *New Republic* (April 6, 1998).

7. Wolfe, "The New Politics of Inequality."

8. Ruth Conniff, "On the Road with Ralph Nader," *Nation* (July 17, 2000): 13–18.

9. Gary Orfield, "Segregated Housing and School Desegregation," in *Dismantling Desegregation: The Quiet Reversal of Brown vs. Board of Education*, by Gary Orfield, Susan E. Eaton, and the Harvard Project on School Desegregation (New York: New Press, 1996).

10. Robert Suro, "More Is Spent on New Prisons Than Colleges," *Washington Post* (February 24, 1997); Beatrix Hamburg, "President's Report," *Annual Report 1996* (New York: William T. Grant Foundation, 1997).

11. John Atlas and Peter Drier, *A National Housing Agenda for the 1990s* (Washington, D.C.: National Housing Institute, 1992); Lynn A. Curtis, *Family, Employ-*

ment and Reconstruction (Milwaukee, Wis.: Families International, 1995); and Sentencing Project, *Crime Rates and Incarceration: Are We Any Safer?* (Washington, D.C.: Sentencing Project, 1992).

12. Fox Butterfield, "Racial Disparities Seen As Pervasive in Juvenile Justice," *New York Times* (April 26, 2000): A1; Elliott Currie, *Crime and Punishment in America* (New York: Metropolitan Books, 1998); and "Crack Sentences Revisited," editorial, *Washington Post* (May 5, 1997).

13. Marc Mauer, *Race to Incarcerate* (New York: New Press, 1999); Marc Mauer, *Young Black Men and the Criminal Justice System* (Washington, D.C.: Sentencing Project, 1990); Marc Mauer, *Intended and Unintended Consequences: State Racial Disparities in Imprisonment* (Washington, D.C.: Sentencing Project, 1997); Vivien Stern, *The Future of a Sin* (Boston: Northeastern University Press, 1998); and Milton Friedman, "There's No Justice in the War on Drugs," *New York Times* (January 11, 1998).

14. Dora Nevares-Muniz, "Hispanics, Youth, the Commission and the Present," chapter prepared for *To Establish Justice.*

15. James Brooke, "Prisons: Growth Industry for Some," *New York Times* (November 2, 1997); Steven R. Donziger, *The Real War on Crime: Report of the National Criminal Justice Commission* (New York: HarperCollins, 1996).

16. Jeffrey A. Roth, "Understanding and Preventing Violence," *Research in Brief* (Washington, D.C.: National Institute of Justice, 1994); Richard A. Mendel, *Prevention or Pork? A Hard Look at Youth-Oriented Anti-Crime Programs* (Washington, D.C.: American Youth Policy Forum, 1995).

17. Faux, *To Establish Justice.*

18. Urban Institute, "Confronting the Nation's Urban Crisis: From Watts (1965) to South Central Los Angeles" (Washington, D.C.: Urban Institute, September 1992); William J. Cunningham, "Enterprise Zones," testimony before the Committee on Select Revenue Measures, Committee on Ways and Means, United States House of Representatives, July 11, 1991; Tom Furlong, "Enterprise Zone in L.A. Fraught with Problems," *Los Angeles Times* (May 19, 1992): D1; "Reinventing America," *Business Week* (January 19, 1993); "Not So EZ," *Economist* (January 28, 1989): 23; "Job Training Partnership Act: Youth Pilot Projects," *Federal Register* 59(71) (April 13, 1994); Doria L. MacKenzie and Claire Souryal, *Multiple Evaluation of Shock Incarceration* (Washington, D.C.: National Institute of Justice, 1994); *To Establish Justice.*

19. Lynn A. Curtis, "Youth Investment and Police Mentoring: Final Report," 2d ed. (Washington, D.C.: Milton S. Eisenhower Foundation, 2000), available at www.eisenhowerfoundation.org.

20. Lynn A. Curtis, "Lessons from the Street: Capacity Building and Replication" (Washington, D.C.: Milton S. Eisenhower Foundation, 2000), available at www.eisenhowerfoundation.org.

21. Lisbeth B. Schorr, "Helping Kids When It Counts," *Washington Post* (April 30, 1997): A21.

22. Personal communication from Edward Zigler to Lynn A. Curtis and Fred R. Harris, May 8, 2000.

23. *To Establish Justice*; S. Shirke et al., *The Effects of Boys' and Girls' Clubs on Alcohol and Drug Use and Related Problems in Public Housing* (New York: Co-

lumbia University, School of Social Work, 1993); Andrew Hahn, "Quantum Opportunities Program: A Brief on the QOP Pilot Program" (Waltham, Mass: Brandeis University, Heller Graduate School, Center for Human Resources, September 1995).

24. Jonathan Kozol, "Saving Public Education," *Nation* (February 17, 1997): 16.

25. James P. Comer, *Waiting for a Miracle* (New York: Dutton, 1997).

26. Robert D. Felner et al., "The Impact of School Reform for the Middle Years," *Phi Delta Kappan* (March 1997): 528–550.

27. Joy G. Dryfoos, *Safe Passage: Making It Through Adolescence in a Risky Society* (New York: Oxford University Press, 1998).

28. Ibid.

29. Curtis and Harris, "The Millennium Breach."

30. Ibid.

31. Alan Okagaki, *Developing a Public Policy Agenda on Jobs* (Washington, D.C.: Center for Community Change, 1997).

32. Curtis and Harris, "The Millennium Breach"; also see David Rusk, *Cities Without Suburbs* (Washington, D.C.: Woodrow Wilson Center Press, 1993).

33. Michael Quint, "This Bank Can Turn a Profit and Follow a Social Agenda," *New York Times* (May 24, 1992): A1.

34. Okagaki, *Developing a Public Policy Agenda on Jobs.*

35. Curtis and Harris, "The Millennium Breach."

36. Ibid.

37. Ann Mariano, "Paradise at Parkside Reclaims Its Legacy," *Washington Post* (June 29, 1991): E1; Bill Gifford, "Paradise Found," *Washington City Paper* (January 29, 1993): 20.

38. Jeff Faux, "The Economic Case for a Politics of Inclusion," paper prepared for the Eisenhower Foundation's Thirtieth Anniversary Update of the Kerner Riot Commission (Washington, D.C.: Economic Policy Institute, February 3, 1998); Jeff Faux, "You Are Not Alone," in Stanley B. Greenberg and Theda Skocpol, *The New Majority: Toward a Popular Progressive Politics* (New Haven and London: Yale University Press, 1997).

39. Faux, "The Economic Case"; Faux, "You Are Not Alone."

40. William Drayton, "Don't Fear Putting More People to Work," *Los Angeles Times* (June 30, 1999).

41. Unless otherwise cited, this section is based on Fred R. Harris and Lynn A. Curtis, eds., *Locked in the Poorhouse* (Lanham, Md.: Rowman and Littlefield, 1998); and Currie, *Crime and Punishment.* For more details on this subject, see www.eisenhowerfoundation.org.

42. "The Education of Al Gore," editorial, *Washington Times* (March 25, 2000); Nicholas D. Kristoff, "The 2000 Campaign: The Texas Governor," *New York Times* (June 19, 2000).

43. William G. Bowen and Derek Bok, *The Shape of the River* (Princeton: Princeton University Press, 1998).

44. Harris and Curtis, eds., *Locked in the Poorhouse.*

45. Faux, *To Establish Justice.*

46. Currie, *Crime and Punishment.*

47. Vince Stehle, "Vistas of Endless Possibility: Delancey Street Foundation Helps Felons and Addicts Rehabilitate Themselves into Responsible Citizens," *Chronicle of Philanthropy* (November 2, 1995): 59.

48. "The Drug War Backfires," editorial, *New York Times* (March 13, 1999); Christopher Wren, "Arizona Finds Cost Savings in Treating Drug Offenders," *New York Times* (April 21, 1999): A16.

49. Details for how the line items in Table 8.1 were calculated are found in Curtis and Harris, "The Millennium Breach." The $7 billion per year for Head Start is the estimated cost for expanding the existing Head Start program to all eligible poor children. The $15 billion per year for replication of successful public inner-city school reform initiatives is based on estimates by Joy Dryfoos that roughly 15,000 schools in the United States serve disadvantaged urban youth, children, and teenagers; that the average number of students per school is about 1,000; and that the average cost per student to implement reforms that work is about $1,000. The $1 billion per year for the Corporation for Youth Investment is a conservative estimate for funding, technically assisting and evaluating safe haven–type and Quantum Opportunities–type replications for a fraction of the children, youth, and teenagers who could benefit from them. The $4.5 billion per year for job training reform modeled after the Argus Community would allow training each year for a fraction of the two million-plus inner-city unemployed who need it. The $1 billion per year for the National Community Development Bank is expected to generate a fraction of the million new private jobs that is our goal for the inner city. The $5 billion per year for 250,000 new public sector construction and urban repair jobs each year is based on estimates in United States Conference of Mayors, "Ready to Go: New Lists of Transportation and Community Development Projects" (Washington, D.C.: United States Conference of Mayors, February 18, 1993). The $20 billion per year for 1 million public service jobs is based on a minimum wage that averages out to $20,000 per year, with benefits and administrative expenses. This is somewhat higher than the average assumed in Richard McGahey, *Estimating the Economic Impact of a Public Jobs Program* (Washington, D.C.: Center for Community Change, 1997). The $2.5 billion per year includes funding for replication of race-specific solutions, based on conservative estimates of the cost of significantly expanding proven successes such as the Gatreaux program for housing integration, along with the costs of a new on-line system to share facts on race and models of successful and racial dialogue. Most of the $2.5 billion is for replication of successful criminal justice, drug prevention, and crime prevention models, based in part on estimates calculated by Joseph A. Califano Jr. in "Crime and Punishment—and Treatment, Too," *Washington Post* (February 8, 1998): C7.

50. "Less Money Than Meets the Eye," editorial, *New York Times* (July 9, 2000): WK11.

51. Curtis and Harris, "The Millennium Breach."

52. McGahey, *Estimating the Economic Impact.*

53. William Julius Wilson, "The New Social Inequality and Affirmative Opportunity," in *The New Majority*, eds. Greenberg and Skocpol.

54. Peter Applebone, "From Riots of the '60s, A Report for a Nation With Will and Way for Healing," *New York Times* (May 8, 1992): A19; Robin Toner, "Los

Angeles Riots Are a Warning, Americans Fear," *New York Times* (June 14, 1992): E7.

55. Children's Partnership, *Next Generation Reports*, April 1997.

56. Susan Page and W. Welch, "Poll: Don't Use Surplus to Cut Taxes," *USA Today* (January 9–11, 1998): 1A.

57. For examples of how new stories were "framed" by the print media, see Michael A. Fletcher, "Kerner Prophecy on Race Relations Came True, Report Says," *Washington Post* (March 1, 1998): A14; Alissa J. Rubin, "Racial Divide Widens, Study Says," *Los Angeles Times* (March 1, 1998): A1; "Kerner Commission's Separate and Unequal Societies Exist Today: Report," *Jet* (March 23, 1998); and Domenica Marchetti, "Charities Must Work to Build on Successes in Fight Against Poverty, Report Says," *Chronicle of Philanthropy* (March 12, 1998).

58. For examples of several such rebuttals, see Elliott Currie, "Inequality and Violence in Our Cities," *Wall Street Journal* (March 23, 1998); Lynn A. Curtis, "Kerner Update Used Scientific Evidence," *Chronicle of Philanthropy* (April 9, 1998); Lynn A. Curtis, "A Long Way to Go," *Chicago Sun-Times* (April 26, 1998): 30; and Lynn A. Curtis, "Supply-Side Policies of the 1980s Opened Up a Class Breach," *Washington Times* (April 27, 1998): A18.

59. For examples of editorials and op-eds, see "New War on Poverty," *Philadelphia Inquirer* (March 8, 1998); "Progress and Need," *Christian Science Monitor* (March 5, 1998); "Kerner at 30," *Minneapolis–St. Paul Star Tribune* (March 4, 1998); "Racial Equity Continues to Elude Nation," *Milwaukee Journal Sentinel* (March 7, 1998); "The Kerner Report, 30 Years Later," *Boston Globe* (March 1, 1998); Barbara Reynolds, "Racial Divides Still Deserves Our Attention," *Detroit News and Free Press* (March 8, 1998); Gregory Stanford, "Still the Chasm: Racial Gap Remains Unbridged," *Milwaukee Journal Sentinel* (March 8, 1998); Brenda Payton, "Heed the Warnings," *Oakland Tribune* (March 5, 1998); Linda Wright Moore, "Deep Resolve Needed to Bridge the Race Abyss," *Philadelphia Daily News* (March 5, 1998); Dwight Lewis, "Nation's Strides Towards Equality Have Been Great, but Far More Is Needed on the Economic Front," *Tennessean* (March 1, 1998); Gracie Bonds Staples, "Still Separate but Unequal Societies—and School District," *Fort Worth Star Telegram* (March 1, 1998); Charlie James, "Millennium Report Shows It's Time to Close Black–White Economic Gap," *Seattle Post Intelligencer* (March 6, 1998); Elizabeth Bennett, "Read Any Good Reports Lately?," *Mishawaka Enterprise* (March 5, 1998); "Kerner Panel Decries Racism, While Industry Seeks Workers," *Waterloo Courier* (March 4, 1998).

60. On the issue of race, public support for the positions presented in this chapter is not as straightforward as it is for issues such as public education and jobs. For example, in spite of the evidence that affirmative action is alive and well for white males and has succeeded for minorities, a recent national *New York Times* poll found that 76 percent of African Americans were in favor of "special efforts to help minorities get ahead," but that only 46 percent of Whites were in favor. In addition, in spite of evidence that America's neighborhoods and schools are resegregating; that two-thirds of Hispanics and African Americans attend predominantly segregated schools in urban areas; and that there is deep and systematic racial discrimination in the criminal justice system that profits a rural, white-controlled prison-industrial

complex, the same *New York Times* poll found that 51 percent of African Americans and 58 percent of Whites believe race relations in America are "generally good" (Kevin Sack and Janet Elder, "Poll Finds Optimistic Outlook But Enduring Racial Division," *New York Times* [July 11, 2000]: A1).

61. Jill Abramson, "Money Buys a Lot More Than Access," *New York Times* (November 9, 1997): WK4; Kent Cooper, "Comments for the 30 Year Eisenhower Foundation Update of the Kerner Commission" (Washington, D.C.: Center for Responsive Politics, February 2, 1998); Ruth Marcus, "Business Donations Show Money Follows the Leaders," *Washington Post* (November 24, 1997): A4; Jamin B. Raskin, "Dollar Democracy," *Nation* (May 5, 1997): 11E; Joshua Rosenkranz, "Campaign Reform: The Hidden Killers," *Nation* (May 5, 1997): 16; Fred Wertheimer, "Unless We Can Soft Money," *Washington Post* (August 10, 1997): C7.

62. James Ridgeway, "Heritage on the Hill," *Nation* (December 22, 1997): 11.

63. George Gerbner, "Reclaiming Our Cultural Mythology," *In Context* 38 (1994): 40–42.

64. See www.eisenhowerfoundation.org.

65. Joe Holly, "Should the Coverage Fit the Crime?" *Columbia Journalism Review* (May-June 1996): 28.

66. Curtis, "Youth Investment and Police Mentoring."

67. Harris and Curtis, eds., *Locked in the Poorhouse.*

68. Joan Biskupic, "In Shaping of Internet Law, First Amendment Is Winning," *Washington Post* (September 12, 1999): A1.

69. Curtis and Harris, "The Millennium Breach"; "Online Community to Tap for Non-profits," *Non-Profits and Technology Journal* (July 1999): 1; Andrew L. Shapiro, "The Net That Binds: Using Cyberspace to Create Real Communities," *Nation* (June 21, 1999): 11–15; "A Wider Net," *Washington Post* (July 13, 1999): A18.

70. Faux, "The Economic Case"; Faux, "You Are Not Alone"; John Jeter, "Cities, Oldest Suburbs Becoming Allies," *Washington Post* (February 22, 1998): A3.

71. See Sophie Body-Gendrot's chapter in *To Establish Justice.*

72. Wolfe, "The New Politics of Inequality."

73. Faux, "You Are Not Alone."

74. Sean Wilentz, "For Voters, the '60s Never Died," *New York Times* (November 16, 1999): A31.

75. Albert H. Cantril and Susan Davis Cantril, *Reading Mixed Signals: Ambivalence in American Public Opinion About Government* (Baltimore: Johns Hopkins University Press, 1999); David Broder, "Voters of Two Minds," *Washington Post* (September 26, 1999): B7.

76. James MacGregor Burns, "Risks of the Middle," *Washington Post* (October 2, 1999): 37.

Part 3

SHAPING THE FUTURE

9

GREEN GROWTH: AGENDA FOR A JUST TRANSITION TO A SUSTAINABLE ECONOMY

Carl Pope and Robert Wages

This chapter was written as a dialogue between a prominent labor leader, Robert Wages, and a well-known environmentalist, Carl Pope. Wages is former president of the Oil Chemical and Atomic Workers and current executive vice president of PACE (Paper, Allied-Industrial, Chemical, and Energy Workers) International Union. Carl Pope is executive director of the Sierra Club. Both have long been active in promoting common ground—and solidarity—between the labor and the environmental movements. (See the biographical information at the end of the book.) In this dialogue, Robert Wages's contributions are in regular type, and Carl Pope's are in italics.—*Eds.*

Uniting Labor and Environmentalists

Robert Wages

The "Battle of Seattle" in November 1999 demonstrated the enormous potential of labor-environmental-community alliances. When our movements coalesce they unleash a critical mass of energy. For one brief but critical moment, at the meetings of the World Trade Organization, we shook the halls of globalized corporate power. In less dramatic fashion, a similar alliance defeated "fast-track" negotiating authority for trade agreements and is poised to impose labor and environmental standards on questions of trade. The promise of such alliances is so great that it conjures up the image of a new progressive movement capable of waging an ongoing battle for social justice and environmental protection.

Powerful corporate interests, shortsightedly trying to shape the new global economy around a discredited *laissez-faire* model from the 1900s, are simultaneously trying to roll back domestic labor and environmental protections by claiming that they interfere with job creation and economic development in the new global economy. Clearly, unions and green organizations around the world have emerged as the leaders of the new movement to establish rules for the rapidly globalizing, information-age economy of the twenty-first century in the same way that America's progressive movement in the early 1900s demanded a new social contract to deal with the concentrated economic power of the new industrial age. But we must go beyond rules, to fight for a new vision of "green growth" that will produce jobs compatible with the long-term survival of the earth's ecosystems. The budding alliance between unions and environmentalists will grow and attract public support if it is rooted in a new strategy to achieve sustainable economic growth based on empowering workers and investing in a new generation of environmentally friendly technologies.

We desperately need such a movement to counter the rapid growth of corporate power, and I believe we are ready for such a formation. However, getting from here to there requires that we face squarely the tensions that threaten to tear such alliances apart. Although we can be proud of our coming together in Seattle, we must also recognize that we are still divided by the "jobs versus the environment" myth (perpetuated by the enemies of labor and environmentalism). Notwithstanding the bold new labor leadership on global justice issues, we also must remember that divisions in our ranks have, at least temporarily, stymied the labor movement from adequately addressing huge issues such as climate change. The environmental and community movements also are divided, especially along race and class lines. People of color and indigenous peoples who live adjacent to toxic facilities and who form the environmental justice movement are often excluded from the national environmental and labor tables. So although many of us feel on a visceral level the promise of a massive labor, environment, and community alliance, it is not clear how that alliance will work in the future, if at all, and what impact the alliance will have on the construction of environmental policy.

Let's begin by attempting to understand our history. For the most part, we in the labor movement have failed repeatedly to admit to the enormity of the environmental problems we face. Long known as one of the most progressive unions in America, the United Auto Workers were less than enthusiastic regarding efforts to manufacture smaller, more fuel-efficient automobiles when the clean air debate was raging in the 1960s and 1970s. Some unions vigorously opposed recycling efforts due to the impact they had on glass manufacturing and the demand for glass products. A number of unions joined in coalition with chlorine manufacturers when confronted with the possibility of regulations potentially banning chlorine from the paper manufacturing process, fearing it would doom their industry to extinction. The Oil Chemical and Atomic Workers did not act aggressively, with the precautionary principle in mind, when it avoided confronting the widespread introduction of MTBE as an additive to gasoline. Clearly, when we have jobs on the line, we all too frequently belittle the science and exaggerate the potential job loss, thereby rationalizing our way through the science and the economics to meet the needs of our constituents.

Environmental groups also partake in rationalizing. They have failed repeatedly to admit that the regulations they propose will lead to job loss and job dislocation. They promote the most dire scientific predictions, but tend to drift toward the rosiest of job forecasts. And of course, the impacted industries seize upon this dynamic to divide us by underwriting and promoting junk science and instilling job fear among their employees. Is there any truth to be found?

From my years of serving workers in the country's most hazardous industries, I have reached two basic conclusions about what is true: Firstly, environmental science has been more accurate than not, and corporate junk science has been just that—junk. From asbestos to tetraethyl lead, industry claimed it was safe when it wasn't. We have been told lies about health and safety just as communities have been told lies about the environment. By now we, as labor, should know that if the impacted industry says a particular substance is safe, we should be careful. Secondly, job loss will always be less than what industry says it will be. However, real workers will still lose real jobs. Before the tetraethyl lead ban, we warned of massive layoffs. The actual number turned out to be about 5,000 workers who produced the substance. For those workers the loss was catastrophic. It does no good to tell them that new jobs may have been created for other workers with different skill sets, in different industries and in some other area of the country. You can't eat macro statistics.

If we are to have any chance of success at knitting workers, environmentalists, and the community together, labor needs to admit that most of the time the environmental community is reasonably accurate on the science. And environmentalists need to acknowledge that tackling serious environmental problems will dislocate workers. Labor can't wish away the science, and environmentalists can't wish away the pain of job loss. The jury is still out as to whether we have learned from our history or are doomed to repeat it.

For twenty years I have struggled to find a way out of our tragic pattern. I'm fairly certain we have found a path forward. We call it "Just Transition." We've been calling upon anyone who would listen that there had to be a way through the divide that both protected the environment and fully addressed the problem of worker dislocation. We've repeatedly tried to sustain dialogues with environmental groups to develop the idea and make it integral to our efforts. In the past three years, we have been developed a robust dialogue with people of color and indigenous people in the environmental justice movement[1] as well as the Canadian Communication Energy and Paper Workers (CEP). The result has been the formation of the Just Transition Alliance. Just Transition has different meanings for different Alliance partners. Our union sees it as a policy mechanism that takes what is a socially driven demand for action and translates the action into a framework of implementation, incorporating the needs of consumers, workers, and society at large (the community). Just Transition is not merely a way to protect against economic dislocation. In a larger sense, it is a manner of constructing socially responsible industrial policy. Our goal is to build a social and political movement powerful enough to require producers to make a transition from current problematic production to more responsible manufacturing practices—while producing more and better jobs and healthier communities.

Carl Pope

Our ability to forge a powerful blue-green[2] movement requires, from my perspective, the development of three capacities.

First, we need a vision of a blue-green economy in order to have a blue-green movement. If we are continually reacting to what Joseph Schumpeter called *"capitalism's destructive engine"* and trying to preserve bits and pieces of what we value from the onslaught of the market, we can't come together, since whatever platform we select to stand upon will be dismantled from beneath us.

Instead, we need to recognize that markets are very good at doing certain things, and centralized bureaucracies can impose rules but are rarely nimble. The challenge for everyone is simply: How can our society do those things that markets don't do well but that are important to our happiness, dignity, and survival as human beings?

Second, as Bob says, we need to be honest about our failings and to recognize that issues of class, culture, and ethnicity divide both our society and the emerging global economy, to which this country is ever more intensely connected. And most critically, we must understand that no one has ever done what we are trying to do.

That simple statement—that we are pioneers—seems trivial, and is often tossed around, but it has important consequences. If we are pioneers, there are no maps. If we are pioneers, we are going to get lost. The test of successful pioneers is not that they don't make mistakes and get lost; it is that they keep going, learning from their mistakes, and if one route up the mountain is blocked by a cliff, they try another route.

Third, time scales matter. For example, in any two-year time horizon, the public policy priorities of the United Auto Workers and the Sierra Club with regard to government regulation of fuel efficiency in autos will be in conflict. In any ten-year time horizon they merge; and in a twenty-year scale we are each other's essential allies.

Imagine that when the Japanese auto invasion began, the UAW and the Sierra Club had succeeded in working together to put in place a web of governmental regulations, incentives, and disincentives that sped up the American auto industry's adoption of new technologies to improve the emissions, safety, and fuel-efficiency of American cars. Imagine also that we grounded these new technologies in the communities that were already committed to making cars.

The result would have been cars that were cleaner, more fuel-efficient, and safer—all high Sierra Club priorities. But the other result would have been an American auto industry that was more nimble, more customer responsive. We might have had an industry that produced higher-quality vehicles sooner, one that would have been far more effective at fighting off the invasion of imports—preserving union jobs and union communities for the UAW (and, by the by, reducing our trade deficit, creating export markets, and maintaining American leadership in our signature technology—

achievements that would have produced enormous gains for the American economy and America's leadership in the world).

All this could have happened, if we had created the vision of this new auto industry and a new relationship with government that would birth it—if we had jointly possessed the courage to run some risks and make some mistakes, even knowing that some of the incentives or regulations we put in place might have unanticipated, perverse effects—and if we had been looking far enough ahead.

We didn't, of course, and the results are written on the landscape. Too many Americans drive either imports or non-union plant transplants. And those who drive American trucks or sport utility vehicles drive on techno- logically outmoded chassis from old plants, risk the lives of their families and anyone they encounter in an accident, and pour enormous quantities of greenhouse pollutants into the atmosphere.

So I would argue that in addition to the kind of honesty Bob talks about, we need an amalgam of vision, courage, and a commitment to the long haul—because only that combination can balance out the ferocious single- and present-mindedness of the market.

TOUGH QUESTIONS: JOBS AND THE ENVIRONMENT

Robert Wages

Let's talk about chlorine, which is produced and used by thousands of paper and chemical companies represented by my union, PACE.

An explosion of chorine-based chemical use in the past five decades has left questions about the manufacture and disposal of these chemicals. Of particular concern is the use of vinyl chloride as a staple in plastics manufacturing. The expanded use of chlorinated compounds is a serious matter. The scientific data continue to mount that will compel interna- tional action on handling and disposal of chlorinated compounds. In Eu- rope, a huge debate is already raging over the question of continued production of polyvinyl chloride. Its introduction and use in the manu- facture of pipe and other construction grade material creates problems for the future disposal of such materials, in light of dioxin's afterlife.

Dioxin, we know, does not naturally degrade and is bioaccumulative; thus there can be no assumed safe level. You don't have to be a scientist to understand the logic that a bioaccumulative toxin will continue to persist in the environment and will ultimately reach unsafe levels. That it persists through the food chain should be enough to concern us all.

Dioxin is a naturally occurring result of many different combustion processes and is particularly pernicious as waste in the decomposition of plastics. The disposal of plastics has raised particular concerns and has spawned an effort in the health care industry to eliminate the use of disposable plastic medical supplies such as tubing, bags, and syringes.[3] This effort has led a number of health care providers to renounce the use of these disposable supplies; and the trend is growing. The upside to this initiative is the increased use of more durable medical supplies that tend to be more labor intensive, if not in their manufacture, at least in their maintenance.

International treaties are being considered that will have a profound impact on the future of chlorine and related compounds. The United Nations Environmental Program (UNEP) is moving forward with treaty discussions on persistent organic pollutants (POPs). The POPs treaty will focus on the eleven or so dangerous chemicals, with the goal of eliminating their use and production.

Given the magnitude of this problem, I have repeatedly told our workers that if it's poison, we shouldn't make it. But we also should not lose our jobs. I am reasonably certain that chlorine is such a poison and should be removed from production, but I will not advocate that position unless I can provide for the livelihoods of the workers dependent on it. No labor leader can advocate the economic destruction of those they serve.

Clearly, workers who produce chlorine-based products need the support of an environmental movement that is willing to go beyond the simple, outright banning of these ubiquitous and dangerous chemicals. If such a ban is in the national (or international) interest, the workers who produce the stuff—and the communities where it is made—should be seen as making a heroic sacrifice for the health of the planet. The environmental movement itself should be the chief advocate of a comprehensive "conversion program"—by national legislation or international treaty, or both—that would compensate those workers and communities for their sacrifice, and would invest in creating new jobs in alternative, clean industries.

Carl Pope

Tony Mazzocchi, who worked with Bob Wages when Bob was the President of the Oil Chemical and Atomic Workers (now a part of PACE), was a mentor for many in both the labor and the environmental movements. He taught me a very powerful lesson. "Follow the jobs," he said. "Most often, pollution results from the desire of management to eliminate work, particularly skilled work. Skilled work protects the environment—but it weakens the power of management in the workplace."

Tony's favorite example was oil refineries. They are dirty. They are dangerous. And to some extent they are intrinsically dirty and dangerous because in them a toxic material, petroleum, is being put under tremendous pressure, heated up, and broken apart into fractions that are often far more toxic and dangerous.

But petroleum refineries are far more toxic and dangerous than they need to be because oil companies want to reduce the number of workers, reduce the skill level of those workers, and reduce the dependence of the plant on having those workers present. (If a refinery can run without its workers, it can run during a strike.)

A refinery is a maze of pipes, tanks, valves, drains, flanges, flues, flares, gauges, seals, and gaskets. If every one of those rather ordinary pieces of equipment is carefully and regularly maintained and monitored, the refinery will operate largely as the closed system it was designed to be. A closed system, even one full of toxic chemicals, doesn't kill workers and doesn't pollute neighborhoods. But gaskets age, valves develop leaks, pipes and flanges crack, gauges freeze, seals corrode, drains clog, and flues become caked with soot. The best way to ensure that these problems are caught and corrected before they can trigger toxic releases from the closed systems is to monitor them constantly, maintain them consistently, and replace them when necessary, before there is trouble. These are all very labor-intensive activities. Paying for those workers cuts into refinery profits—and perhaps more important, a commitment to maintenance means a refinery must shut down in a strike—the last thing an oil company will tolerate.

It is not inevitable that an oil refinery must produce pollution—or create the occupational and safety risks that kill and injure so many workers. Pollution results from decisions that are designed, quite consciously, to destroy jobs and job security, and to undermine worker power in the workplace.

Whereas oil workers have often worked with environmentalists (the Sierra Club's first joint activity with labor was to support a Shell Refinery strike over occupational safety and health issues in 1973), the relationship between environmentalists and woodworkers has been much more bitter. Repeatedly over the past thirty years the desire of mill workers and timber workers to keep their mills operating at full capacity has clashed with the desire of environmentalists to protect wilderness areas, critical watersheds, wildlife habitat, and ancient forests from the chain saw.

There is a conflict here. Real jobs are lost when major areas are set aside and protected from logging.

But more fundamentally, if timber companies had hired more workers, the conflict with environmentalists would be greatly eased. One major source of environmental destruction associated with logging is roads. Roads often produce the bulk of the erosion, fishery loss, and water quality degradation associated with logging. Timber companies could, and should, maintain roads while they are using them, and close roads when they are finished with them. But maintaining and closing roads takes labor—mainly heavy equipment operators, so it's skilled labor, and mostly union labor. Companies don't want to pay those workers; so logging roads are rarely closed and are poorly maintained. (The U.S. Forest Service alone estimates that it has a backlog of 360,000 miles of logging roads that should be retired or repaired.)

Another source of unnecessary destruction from logging is the reliance on excessively large clear-cuts. This is a relatively recent phenomenon, and the best companies don't do it. But a clear-cut—in which virtually all of the trees are stripped from the land—has one big advantage over a selective cut, in which large trees are taken out one by one but the forest cover remains intact: Clear-cutting can be done with relatively few workers operating heavy equipment, instead of the much larger number of more skilled workers needed to select and take out individual trees one by one.

But clear-cuts often don't regenerate, because the sites become excessively hot and dry out. They open up the forest to invasive species and brush. Like roads, they dramatically increase erosion and loss of forest soils. So once again, the pursuit of a less labor-intensive industrial model directly leads us to a more environmentally destructive industry.

The examples of this equation—pollution being used as a substitute for labor—are endless. Farm workers are often sprayed with pesticides, both in the fields and at home—because aerial spraying of pesticides takes fewer workers than spraying by hand or using other techniques. Strip-mining and mountaintop removal replaced deep mining of coal because it minimized labor—particularly independent union labor. Instead of hiring skilled glaziers to properly insulate and seal commercial buildings, developers simply use oversized furnace and air conditioning systems to replace heated or cooled air that leaks from the building.

Underlying this industrial practice of substituting pollution for workers are a series of perverse regulatory and tax incentives that exacerbate the *problem. The tax code, for example, levies a very heavy tax on the first $72,000 of a worker's salary, which goes to Social Security.*

This is, in effect, a big tax on hiring labor, and it hits skilled union labor—which is almost entirely compensated with salaries—the hardest. On the other hand, if labor can be replaced by natural resources—say, oil or iron ore—various tax breaks are available; and if a machine will do the job, the company gets an investment tax credit.

It is not easy to figure out how to get at the intense desire of employers to carry out their work with as little labor as possible, even at the cost of greater pollution. The kinds of environmental benefits that result from right-sizing the workforce, which in polluting industries almost always means increasing the size of that workforce, are not easy to monitor and enforce at a smokestack or an effluent pipe. The kinds of soft regulations that would force a timber company to properly maintain and close its roads and replant after harvest are exactly the kind of detailed "command-and-control" standards that have fallen out of favor in the face of intense industry resistance and public relations efforts. And because workers tend to communicate far more regularly with their companies than they do with environmentalists, they may be easily alarmed with threats of environmentally caused job losses when there actually are no such threats. I know of one timber community in northern California that in the mid-1990s went into virtual mourning for the loss of jobs in the woods and the mill. The town was festooned with yellow ribbons and posters proclaiming "Plant a Sierra Club member, not a tree"—but the local mill was operating three shifts a day and shipping more product than at any time in its history. Mechanization, not logging restrictions, had cost workers their jobs; yet even faced with the knowledge that the mill was operating at full capacity, workers still felt threatened by far-off environmentalists rather than by nearby neighbors who ran the mill.

LABOR, ENVIRONMENTALISTS, AND CLIMATE CHANGE

ROBERT WAGES

Climate change is another area where environmental science is becoming increasingly compelling. As the use of fossil fuel increases worldwide, there is the continued escalation of carbon dioxide emissions. These emissions, it is argued, have the effect of depleting the protective ozone layer of the earth's atmosphere. Dire forecasts of flooding, famine, drought, and disease have generated a call to action.

One response to the mounting scientific evidence that a global warming is taking place is the Kyoto Protocol. Kyoto has been widely supported in the environmental community, though many argue it is not nearly enough. The Kyoto agreement calls for reduction of carbon emissions to previously established levels within certain time frames, but does not provide a mechanism for how the protocol will be applied throughout the world. It has been widely denounced in the labor community as an ineffective attempt to rein in the problem of greenhouse gas emissions because it exempts the developing world—in particular, China and India.

It is argued that this deficiency makes Kyoto fatally flawed. The argument, at its core, is that only the industrialized world would have to meet the Kyoto reduction targets. Without the imposition of emissions reduction targets on developing countries, worldwide greenhouse gas emissions will continue to increase. Even if coal production and coal burning are eliminated in the United States, China alone will displace that production and then some. The exponential growth predicted for the developing world compels a worldwide solution, it is alleged, and Kyoto will simply destroy American jobs, without any assurance of an effective solution. The question is: What have we accomplished?

Assuming you accept there is a scientific basis proving the global warming phenomenon is real (and the overwhelming weight of authority affirms that it is), the answer is self-evident: We must assume responsibility for reducing carbon emissions. The argument suggesting that inaction on the part of the industrialized world is justified because the developing economies do not face the same constraints is faulty. Although it is entirely appropriate to demand action by developing economies, it is unfair and unrealistic to demand that they follow the same standards, on the same timelines, as industrialized economies.

Even industry is beginning to turn away from junk science. BP/Amoco and Royal Dutch Shell are making major investments in clean energy technologies including hydrogen, thermal, and wind. Texaco, along with Ford and GM, recently announced its withdrawal from the anti-Kyoto Global Climate Change Coalition on the grounds of "corporate responsibility," although it still questions the basic effectiveness of Kyoto. These developments lead me to conclude that vast capital interests are making constructive plans for the future. Although we do not know the details of those plans, we can be certain that the industry's future development will take place on its terms to the maximum extent possible and will not incorporate worker and community needs.

It is imperative that workers and communities also plan for the future, at the same time recognizing that some level of pain will be associated with the introduction of future environmental policies. Inevitably, social decisions will be made, and just as inevitably, workers and communities will be the last consideration despite what will no doubt be, by that time, a moral imperative.

CLIMATE CHANGE AND THE PROBLEM OF MACROECONOMICS

Carl Pope

Sorting out these options and dealing with this web of relations is, indeed, complex. But complexity is not the greatest barrier. The currently entrenched orthodoxy that refuses to look at options or conduct analysis at this level is a higher hurdle by far. Macroeconomics has virtually hijacked the policy dialogue, with its claim that market mechanisms and price signals are, a priori, the most efficient way to let the economy evolve. If it can be demonstrated that raising prices on fossil fuels as a means of reducing greenhouse pollution will hit the economy hard, it is simply assumed that any other strategy will hit it harder.

Since Just Transition strategies invariably require looking at microeconomic relationships, the current orthodoxy invariably rejects them as making an already economically unattractive endeavor impossibly expensive. Fortunately, the macroeconomic orthodoxy is wrong. Unfortunately, it is very difficult to get a hearing for this point of view in the United States today.

To understand why the macroeconomic orthodoxy is wrong, we need to understand that it is based on the principle that all economic decisions are made by profit-maximizing, entirely rational decisionmakers with equal access to perfect information. On this premise, increasing the price of carbon emissions is indeed the most efficient way to reduce the amount of carbon emitted.

But although markets are often more efficient than other mechanisms, they are not perfect, and in the consumer marketplace, where much carbon is emitted as we hop into our Jeep Grand Cherokees to get a bottle of milk, real consumers make a mockery of the rational, profit-maximizing, perfect information model.

Indeed, even the stock market, in which the profit-maximizing part of the model does apply, is widely recognized as having enormous irrational components—hence the volatility that has characterized the new century. Herd behavior, not changing economic fundamentals, has been driving the NASDAQ up and down on an almost daily basis.

But consumer markets for fossil fuels are even less "rational." In fact, an entire raft of research indicates that when people go to buy a car, they are highly sensitive to its front-end sticker price and much less motivated by its lifetime operating costs. Consumers won't spend $500 more to buy a car or an SUV equipped with fuel efficiency technology, even if this will save them $200 a year over the life of the auto—which in rational terms would be a very good investment.

But if government levied a "gas guzzler" tax, or provided a "gas sipper" rebate of $500, on vehicles based on their fuel consumption, consumers would flock to the more efficient models.

Markets do react. Price does matter. But not in the simple way that macroeconomists assume. Just Transition strategies require going beyond this oversimplified view of the world.

What might a Just Transition strategy look like in the auto industry?

It's important to understand that making cars more fuel-efficient won't reduce the number of cars consumers buy, nor the number of auto workers needed to make them. Indeed, to the extent that greater fuel efficiency requires more carefully engineered vehicles and more rapid introduction of new technologies, the number of workers employed to make cars will likely increase as we reduce the amount of carbon pollution each car puts out.

But the United Auto Workers has resisted increasing the Corporate Average Fuel Economy (CAFE) standard for good reasons. Since the arrival of large numbers of imported cars into the United States in the 1970s, American manufacturers' share of the market for small and medium-sized cars has steadily shrunk. The 50 percent of the American auto market represented by cars is now overwhelmingly either imported or built in transplanted Japanese or European auto assembly lines in states such as South Carolina and Tennessee, where the UAW has been unable to organize thus far.

Unionized auto workers, overwhelmingly, make trucks, light trucks, and sport utility vehicles. Detroit still dominates this end of the market, in part because these vehicles are still subject to import tariffs, and in part because the Japanese and European domestic markets for large vehicles are small.

The UAW's concern is that increasing fuel efficiency requirements will shift auto preferences away from Detroit's SUV and light truck unionized segment of the market, back to smaller cars and station wagons made in nonunionized plants. Jobs might not be lost, but unionized jobs could be.

In the long run, however, the UAW's current strategy of resisting the transition to more efficient vehicles is risky. At the moment Detroit has a huge profit margin on SUVs, because there is little competition from the Japanese and Europeans, and because the current models are built on old truck assembly lines that auto makers amortized years ago.

But there are no barriers to Toyota's or BMW's getting into the SUV business, a sector that represents half of the U.S. market—the most profitable half. They can and are learning how to design and make these vehicles—but since they do not have old, amortized truck assembly lines on which to build them, they are using new technology and new designs, and building better and more fuel-efficient SUVs.

Although Americans are likely to be driving a large number of trucks and SUVs twenty years from now, they are very unlikely to be driving today's primitive models, with their clumsy handling, high gas consumption, and tendency to overturn. Instead, they are almost certain to be buying vehicles that get far better gas mileage, handle better, and are safer than Detroit's current line of dinosaurs. (Steve Yokich, International President of the UAW, once commented to me that it's not auto workers who like SUVs. Serious car guys find them primitive.)

If the Big Three continue to resist investing in new technology, as they did in the 1970s, they—and the UAW—will find that the share of American vehicles built in unionized auto plants in Michigan, Wisconsin, Ohio, and Illinois will continue to decline. The Big Three, of course, will still have their global factories and business to generate profits—but the UAW and its workers will be left behind, as will the states that currently depend on the industry.

(In fairness to the current generation of automotive leaders, executives like William Clay Ford are sounding much more like technological innovators than their predecessors of the 1970s. Ford, for example, has promised a hybrid-powered SUV by 2003 that will get 40 miles per gallon of gasoline.)

So what might a Just Transition look like for the auto industry? Simply raising CAFE standards, although that is technically feasible, could easily *shift market share from American companies to their European and Japanese competitors.*

But suppose that in addition to raising CAFE standards the government levied a "gas guzzler" tax on the most inefficient vehicles and eliminated the current tax advantages for customers who buy the "behemoth" SUVs—those weighing more than 7,500 pounds.

This part of the package ensures that customers would have financial incentives to buy models with better fuel economy [efficiency], so auto companies could immediately begin installing such features as lean-burning and hybrid engines, advanced transmission designs, sleek aerodynamic designs, and high-strength, lightweight materials in their current models, generating more jobs on each assembly line.

Most of the proceeds from this tax could be deposited in a trust fund, which would be available to provide investment tax credits for auto companies that invested in new, fuel-efficient assembly lines. This would ensure that the auto industry as a whole would not be hurt by higher taxes, since the proceeds would be recycled into the industry and would actually reduce the cost of obtaining new capital for new assembly lines. (One disadvantage American manufacturers face is that interest costs are higher in the United States than in Japan, so it has always been more expensive for U.S. companies to install new equipment than for the Japanese. These tax credits would compensate for this long-standing contributing factor to Detroit's sluggishness.)

The tax credits could be limited to facilities built as replacements in the same community. This would guarantee that the new assembly lines would be built in the communities currently dependent on the auto industry, and that the more rapid turnover of manufacturing capital would not become an incentive to flee overseas or to union-hostile states in the south.

Lastly, a small portion of the tax proceeds could be used to pay early retirement benefits and other forms of worker adjustment and compensation to the relatively small number of older workers who would lose their jobs because the specific technology that employed them would not be utilized in the newer, more efficient vehicles, as lighter materials, for example, replace steel.

This kind of Just Transition strategy relies on the power and flexibility of the marketplace to reduce carbon pollution and preserves unionized auto jobs. Each auto company decides what technologies and marketing strategies it wants to use to respond to these new price signals and investment opportunities. Each company designs its own cars. The only government requirement is that fuel efficiency be improved overall; so this is a performance-based approach. If a company chooses not to comply, its vehicles will be burdened with the gas guzzler tax and the company itself with fines for failing to meet the CAFE standard. But if the company responds, it gets the capital it needs to make better cars, trucks, or SUVs.

This proposal, however, involves government intervention to shape the market toward the goals of economic security, community preservation, and environmental protection. In doing so, it flies squarely in the face of the current macroeconomic paradigm, which allows only one goal—efficient use of capital—but it also exposes the hollowness of that paradigm.

The "managed marketplace" would be just as efficient as the allegedly "free" one it replaces. The difference is solely that in the managed marketplace, the auto industry is not allowed to benefit from the free destruction of the global atmosphere or the artificial subsidy of antiunion legislation in Mexico or South Carolina. It is the initial ownership rights that have been managed differently in the Just Transition model: Workers and communities, as well as the environment, are treated as legitimate holders of rights, instead of all ownership rights being vested in corporate shareholders and management.

It is not accidental that macroeconomists always set to the side of their models what they call "the initial ownership question." Markets are efficient and even fair, if they are truly complete, and if you assign ownership rights properly in the first place. But the question of who owns what in the first place is ultimately a political decision, and one to which there is no economically "efficient" answer. The American auto, oil, coal, and utility industries act as if they "owned" the sky—as though a century of emitting greenhouse pollutants meant that the right to emit such pollutants had somehow become a piece of property. The idea that they should be awarded "free" and marketable property rights at their present levels of emission is implicitly based on this claim.

They simultaneously act as if a century of supporting the industries that emit carbon had created no rights for communities, and that a lifetime of doing often hard, dangerous, and dirty work in those industries had created no rights for workers.

The Just Transition model challenges this lopsided set of assumptions; and the greatest potential of a blue-green movement is that it can offer a different set of assumptions, which can lead us to an economy that com-

bines the economic dynamism of the market with a sustainable future for the environment, for communities, and for working families.

A Strategy for a Just Transition to a Sustainable Economy

Robert Wages

A policy of Just Transition must depend on answers to the following questions: How can we move from one production mode to another and in so doing protect the interests of the producing entity, the community affected, and the workers involved in the production? This necessarily entails a discussion of the following points:

- new "production methods";
- capital deployment for new production methods;
- cleanup of existing production facilities;
- retrofitting of equipment;
- workers' transition from one production process to another;
- transition in communities that are production-dependent (when workers are transferred to production in other communities);
- development of tax policies to produce income streams for the Just Transition and to provide income streams for the environmental cleanup required.

Future policy discussion must evolve from an analysis of new production options. For instance, if we are serious about reducing carbon emissions, what are the "clean fuel" technologies that are available? If eliminating the use of fossil fuels is the ultimate goal for a safe future, what are the replacement options to coal and oil? If we believe that solar, wind, and hydrogen energy options are suitable replacements, how will we move from our reliance on fossil fuel production to these alternatives? In assessing the feasibility of the process, what is the transition plan for workers employed within the fossil fuel industrial cycle, if the new industrial plan calls for the use of solar, wind, and hydrogen energy? How will incentives for industry be created? How will workers be trained? How will we create a "soft landing" for the specific industries affected and the workers and communities affected by a shift in industrial production? How will all this be funded? From an institutional perspective, how will unions representing thousands of workers in industrial production processes be assured of their continued existence as representatives of industrial workers?

Using the reduction of carbon emissions and chlorine as starting points, the Just Transition discussion raises myriad questions that demand answers in order to navigate the jobs versus environment discussion. It is not that these issues cannot be successfully addressed; there simply has been no effort to have a concrete discussion.

Meanwhile, despite the current boom, workers with decent-paying jobs are living through wave after wave of job insecurity with no end in sight. There are two major sources. The first is a result of the power of corporations to control the rules of the global economic game so that they are free to move, merge, downsize, automate, and subcontract at will, anywhere, anytime, without having to consider the consequences of their actions on workers, communities, or even countries. As a result, the decent-paying jobs in the most prosperous corporations are disappearing—or being replaced by low-paying jobs. There is a downward global pressure on wages and benefits. Today, the fastest-growing occupation in the United States is that of cashiers, with an average yearly pay of $12,000. There seems to be no end in sight to this instability.

The second cause of instability comes from the environmental damage that directly results from unfettered corporate control of all aspects of production. A good portion of what is produced, and how it is produced, is proving to be unsustainable. Although we might disagree about the severity, the underlying science, or the uncertainty of environmental claims, there is no doubt that the natural ecosystem is in serious trouble and that major changes will be required in order to prevent its eventual destruction. What this inevitably means is that more instability is ahead of us. The combination of corporate job destruction and the need for environmental sustainability guarantees an acceleration of job instability for years to come.

Just Transition is a concept designed to deal with this rising instability and insecurity on all fronts. It focuses on government policies—e.g., trade or environmental regulations. Normally such policies are instituted with little or no regard for their impact on workers or communities. Those workers and their communities would become a central feature in a Just Transition policy. Together with industry, workers and communities would gain access to a special transition fund that allows a fair and equitable adjustment to more sustainable production.

JUST TRANSITION AND THE GOLDEN STRAITJACKET

Carl Pope

One of the challenges faced by advocates of a Just Transition—or of a sustainable economy—is the argument that there is only one way to run an economy in today's world. That way has been summed up by New York Times *columnist Thomas Friedman, in his book* The Lexus and the Olive Tree, *as the "Golden Straitjacket"—a regime of reliance on the private sector, low rates of inflation, smaller government, balanced budgets, low tariffs, deregulated capital markets, and the elimination of government corruption, subsidies, and economic intervention. Along with a host of other advocates of this model, Friedman argues that even if we think there is a better way, global capital markets won't let us use it without extracting an excessive economic price.*

Friedman says the Golden Straitjacket produces a faster rate of economic growth, but it also reduces political options, and clearly weights the economic scales in favor of the young, the educated, and the well positioned. It yields greater inequality, less security, and less stability. Friedman—in his book, if not always in his newspaper columns—concedes that this model can produce terrible consequences, because people need dignity, security, and stability. He also acknowledges that it can devastate the natural ecosystems on which people and other species depend.

Since the essence of the Golden Straitjacket is to move fast and to reduce the role of politics in favor of the role of markets, Friedman's analysis makes a Just Transition seem like unrealizable fantasy. And certainly the inability of nominally sympathetic politicians such as Bill Clinton and Al Gore to go beyond platitudes and hold the Lords of Trade accountable either in NAFTA or in the WTO suggests that it is not going to be easy to follow this path.

Yet there is a surprising amount of room for hope, and not just because of the new energies on display in Seattle. A system characterized by fast-moving capital streams is in some ways more susceptible to being redirected than one that is more sluggish. Take a garden hose; turn the water on just a little. Try to use your finger to direct the flow in one direction or the other—it just flows around you. Now turn the faucet all the way on—put your finger in the same place—presto, you can turn it into a spray, or a fine jet directed to the left or the right. A fast-moving stream is easier to direct because smaller differences in pressure produce greater differences in direction.

I'm not suggesting that we can somehow bring back 1950s-style corporate stability, much less centrally planned economies—that's not what I understand Just Transition to be about. I am suggesting that environmentalists and labor together can apply enough pressure to the fast-moving streams of twenty-first-century capitalism to shape it beyond our wildest dreams, as long as we understand that its speed is our ally.

The current set of rules for either the U.S. economy or the emerging global trading economy are not preordained results of technological possibilities. The WTO is not a force of nature, like a hurricane. (Hurricanes do not require 6,000 pages of legalese to strip your roof off and have rarely been seen to gather in five-star hotels for more than a few hours.) No, the present rules of the game are only one of various possible sets of rules for dealing with a world in which communications are fast, transportation is cheap, and technology is rapidly evolving.

This world, which I do think is a given, is utterly compatible with the concepts of a Just Transition—it is the old politics, not the new technologies, that makes our jobs harder.

When the Sierra Club was deciding whether or not to oppose NAFTA, one of our big concerns was getting the U.S.-Mexican border zone, the world's longest toxic waste dump, cleaned up.

The border is as toxic as it is for three reasons: No money has been invested here in the provision of clean water, sewage treatment, and other infrastructure that makes clean industrial development possible. There are no governmental institutions on the Mexican border to build and maintain such infrastructure. And the absence of such governmental institutions draws the dirtiest and most irresponsible segments of industry like yellow jackets to a ham sandwich.

We calculated how much money would be needed to clean up the mess. It was a lot—$20 billion—but not a lot compared to the tariff reductions that were a throwaway part of NAFTA. So we suggested to the U.S. Trade Representative that we should slow down—slightly—the tariff reductions on goods produced in the maquiladora zone, in order to create a pool of $20 billion to fund the cleanup. We also proposed that as part of NAFTA the United States and Mexico should create a series of binational infrastructure authorities, authorized to build sewers and water systems, to clean up toxic waste dumps, and to enforce environmental laws along both sides of the border.

These proposals, needless to say, never made it into the agreement the U.S. administration negotiated. My suspicion is that a reluctance to levy "maquiladora crossing fees" to generate the money was less of an obstacle than the reluctance of the Mexican government at the time to create genuinely independent local governing authorities outside of its political control.

Serious guarantees of workers' rights never made it into the treaty for similar reasons. On a fact-finding trip to Tijuana five years after NAFTA passed, a group of labor leaders, House Leader Dick Gephardt, and I were told by maquiladora managers that being able to pay their workers higher wages would increase the profitability of their plants, because skilled workers could be retained—but Mexican government policy did not allow them to compete by offering higher wages.

What is important about our attempts to modify NAFTA is not the idea itself—although it would almost certainly have made an enormous difference in border pollution, which the North American Development Bank has been utterly unable to do. What is important is that a NAFTA with a temporary maquiladora crossing fee and a series of border infrastructure authorities would have accomplished all of the economic benefits of a NAFTA without the drawbacks. Economic integration could still proceed, Mexico could still open up its economy to competition—everything good that allegedly results from NAFTA would still happen. In addition, the border would be cleaned up. It was the old politics of the PRI regime in Mexico, not the new dynamics of the global economy, that got in the way. Even if border infrastructure authorities had been a necessary part of the price for NAFTA, along with Minority Leader Dick Gephardt's proposal that Mexico could have NAFTA if it allowed workers to organize and wages to rise along with productivity, NAFTA could still have passed.

PRINCIPLES FOR A JUST TRANSITION

Robert Wages

A working group of trade unionists[4] has developed a statement of principles for the concept of Just Transition. Following is a summary of those principles.

> A *national commitment.* Just Transition requires an overarching national commitment to a just society and full-employment economy that provides family-supporting jobs to American workers now and in the future. It fundamentally recognizes that workers and their families together make up the communities that are the foundation of our nation. For an economy to be sustainable,

workers must be organized into unions, and communities must provide citizens with quality jobs, housing, health care, education, transportation, public services, leisure activities, and a healthy environment.

Making workers whole. If policies designed to protect the public good dislocate working people, then it is the obligation of public policy to make workers whole. We need to set a very high standard for compensating workers and communities for dislocations caused in order to protect the public good. "Making whole" means maintaining full income and benefits for as long as it takes to get comparable work.

Broad eligibility. There must be a presumption that all dislocated workers in specific industries and regions affected by public policies are eligible for targeted transition assistance. Workers in many industrial sectors and regions are often threatened by multiple factors operating at the same time, often mutually reinforcing and not always easily distinguishable from one another. Public policies frequently exacerbate the impacts and hardships of dislocations due to technological and market forces. In these circumstances, Just Transition should apply to all affected workers regardless of the cause.

Fairness. The real costs of public policies that protect the public good must not be shouldered disproportionately by any one group of people. We recognize that the public as a whole may benefit from policies that protect the environment. For example, although all of us gained from the ban on tetraethyl lead in gasoline, the thousands of workers who consequently lost their jobs shouldered the real cost of that transition. Such an outcome violates a sense of fairness. In addition, these workers represent a significant resource lost to the economy if we do not reemploy their skills and experience.

Labor's role and workers' rights. Workers and their representatives must be fully involved in the design, planning, and implementation of Just Transition policies and programs from the national to the plant levels. Just Transition must also maintain and strengthen the right of workers to form unions and collectively to bargain throughout a transition process. Workers' involvement and labor rights are intrinsically linked. Unions fear that the dislocations will thin their ranks, making it more difficult to protect remaining members and to protect and improve the living and working standards for unorganized workers in existing and new industries. Union membership should be integral to all Just Transition programs.

Comparable work. Just Transition must help working people subject to economic dislocations find comparable productive work. Most workers who become dislocated want to continue working. If their jobs are eliminated due to public policy shifts, their income and benefits must be maintained for as long as it takes them to find productive alternative work. Workers must be provided sufficient forms and levels of assistance to help them find and qualify for new family-wage jobs. Dislocated workers should be given preference to receive training and be hired for the new jobs created by emerging industries within an affected region. For those who want to immediately take available jobs, even at lower wages, Just Transition must provide a wage subsidy to make them whole. However, we cannot let corporate America provide the only definition of productive work. A broad range of work opportunities become possible if we as laborers develop our own definition of what is productive.

Full social accounting. Just Transition must be based on a full accounting of the social impacts of change. Companies tend to measure costs in ways that fail to account for the full impact of their decisions on workers and the environment; but government must ensure that accounting for potential impacts of policies carried out in the public interest wholly captures the effects on workers and their communities, as well as the costs of making them whole.

Full funding. Just Transition requires a separate, dedicated, reliable, and sufficient national source of funds. To prevent the financial starvation of Just Transition, a sufficiently large, dedicated fund is needed to protect dislocated workers affected by public policies. Ultimately, all domestic economic dislocations (such as those caused by environmental regulations, utility deregulation, trade agreements, and military base closures) should be covered by these funds.

Advance planning. Just Transition requires advance planning to ensure that adequate worker assistance mechanisms are in place before the hardships of dislocation are felt. Advance warning and preparation cuts down the hardship and costs of transition after dislocation occurs. As former International Association of Machinists president William Winpinsinger said regarding defense conversion, "When the gun is at your head, it's already too late." It is necessary to establish an early-warning notification process for workers, unions, and service providers, to assure them sufficient time to plan and implement transition mechanisms prior to the dislocation.

Protections for older workers. Special attention must be paid to the needs of older, high-seniority workers during Just Transition. High-seniority workers, especially those over 50 years old, are likely to have the hardest time with transition. Many may not be able to find alternative work or participate in redefined work/school options. Those workers should be given first choice at whatever options are available, including full income and benefits until retirement, and guaranteed pension and health care benefits after retirement.

Making communities whole. Financial and technical assistance and other policies will be needed to make communities whole. In several parts of the country, especially rural areas, public policies have devastated communities and even entire regions. Even if workers are made whole, many may be unable to stay in their communities and to support the local economy. At a minimum, an impacted community should receive funds that compensate it, dollar for dollar, for any loss of tax revenues, in order to maintain the economic health of the community. Just Transition aims to sustain economic development in such areas, leading to a full economic recovery.

The foregoing principles provide a framework for how the public and policymakers can think about Just Transition as it applies to workers and communities. Clearly, the concept needs more input from low-income people of color and indigenous people so that they can become full partners in any and all transition processes. Just Transition must also support industry's transition to sustainable production. And, there are a host of open questions about how to get from where we are with current energy options and manufacturing methods to where we would ideally like to be.

Seattle represented an important watershed because workers, environmentalists, consumers, and other progressives successfully joined together to block another round of global trade talks that would have inevitably sacrificed jobs, world environmental standards, and minimum labor standards in order to open markets for transitional capital. This coalition did more than make a statement. It put the governing institutions of the global economy on notice that the workers and citizens of the planet demand the right to shape the rules—and that we intend to balance the rights of commerce with the values of democracy, environmental and economic sustainability, and inalienable human and labor rights.

To realize the full potential of the coalition that briefly shook the world, a major effort must be made to bridge the divides that separate environmentalists, labor, and other important groups in civil society. Just as importantly, we must construct a vision of a healthy, sustainable economy in which cleaning up and protecting the environment and investing in new, nonpolluting technologies produce good jobs and vibrant communities. It will take debate and conflict to accomplish this new vision; it will also take the combined forces of all those on the planet who care about good jobs, a healthy environment, and labor and human rights.

NOTES

1. I want to particularly thank the leadership of the Southwest Network for Economic and Environmental Justice, the Asian Pacific Environmental Network and the Indigenous Environmental Network for putting so much time and energy into the Just Transition Alliance. We on the labor side have learned a great deal from your passionate commitment to justice.

2. We use "green" as shorthand for the environmental movement, and "blue" to represent labor. We are fully aware that traditional "blue-collar" jobs represent but one portion of the occupations of working people (both unionized and nonunionized). In today's economy, workers may be "pink collar," white collar, and many other colors. Shorthand is just that.

3. Health Care Without Harm is a coalition that speaks specifically to the proliferation of plastics in the health care industry and the hazards of disposal.

4. Special thanks to Les Leopold, Will Paul, Mike Buckner, Ken Zinn, Ron Blum, Ande Abbott, Bill Cunningham, Bill Banig, Keith Romig, Ed Wytkind, Bill Klinefelter, Mike Wright, Joel Yudken, and Jane Perkins for their contribution to this work.

10

SKY TRUST: HOW TO FIGHT GLOBAL WARMING AND PAY DIVIDENDS TO ALL AMERICANS

Peter Barnes and Rafe Pomerance

In June 2000, while many parts of America were experiencing their highest recorded temperatures, a committee of experts working for the U.S. government issued a peer-reviewed assessment of the likely impacts of climate change. If nothing is done to reduce greenhouse gas emissions, the scientists said, average temperatures in the United States will rise by between five and ten degrees Fahrenheit over the next hundred years—exceeding the projected global increase.

This warming is "very likely" to produce more storms, droughts, heat waves, flash floods, and fires, the scientists noted. Cold weather recreation such as skiing will be reduced, and air conditioning usage will rise. Forests will undergo dramatic changes, including loss of sugar maples in the northeast. In the western states, reduction in the snow pack will decrease the amount of water dams can store, compounding current stresses on water supplies. In the southeast, a rise in sea level will cause loss of beaches and wetlands and put coastal communities at greater risk of storm surges.

The report capped a decade of worldwide soul-searching about the atmosphere. The Industrial Revolution has produced great economic progress, but at the same time, it has changed forever the relationship between humanity and nature. For millennia humans have adapted to changes in the external environment; now we're causing them. Unless we curb our voracious appetite for fossil fuels, forest products, fish, and other gifts of nature, we'll alter the basic conditions that have sustained life on earth for the past three billion years.

But how, precisely, *do* we curb our individual and collective appetites, especially for carbon-based energy sources that are causing the atmosphere to warm? That's the question politicians have been loath to confront, for it seems to threaten the American way of life. Yet there is an almost painless way to tackle the problem, a way that turns the reduction of our consumption of nature into a new source of wealth. By capturing this wealth and distributing it equitably, we can ease the transition to a low-carbon economy. This wealth—potentially, a trillion-dollar windfall—is called *atmospheric scarcity rent*.

What on earth—or above it—is atmospheric scarcity rent? Scarcity rent is what the owners of goods that are in high demand collect from other people *just because of scarcity*. The *Mona Lisa*, for example, has a high scarcity rent because there is big demand for it and only one original. In general, the scarcer (relative to demand) things like buildable land, Mark McGwire home-run balls, and New York taxi medallions are, the higher their scarcity rents.

Atmospheric scarcity rent is a new phenomenon that reflects the scarcity of important services the sky provides to human users. For example, the sky "carries" electromagnetic waves that are indispensable to broadcasters and telecommunications companies. These waves are scarce because there are a limited number of usable frequencies that don't interfere with each other. When Congress in 1997 gave broadcasters—at no charge—a large chunk of the electromagnetic spectrum to use for digital broadcasting, opponents like Senator John McCain called it a $70 billion giveaway.

The specific form of atmospheric scarcity that concerns us here is that which results from the limited capacity of the atmosphere to absorb carbon dioxide. Our demand for sky-borne carbon storage is, of course, the flip side of our demand for fossil fuels—the more we burn the latter, the more we require the former. Up till now, we've paid handsomely for oil, but nothing for air to hold its combusted wastes. That disparity is about to end.

In the new era of scarce sky, there will, of necessity, be an *economy* of sky. Property rights will be established; prices will be charged; and money will change hands—lots of money. The battle that's looming is over who'll get that pie in the sky. As MIT economist A. Denny Eller-man has noted: "[The scarcity of sky] raises fundamental issues of equity and the definition of rights, which are preeminently of the political realm. In fact, there will likely be agreement on the creation of the scarcity only as there is agreement on the allocation of the rents thereby created."[1]

Our proposition is that the scarcity rent should go to all of us equally — one citizen, one share. We've launched a campaign to reduce U.S. carbon emissions and share the scarcity rent through a Sky Trust. The rest of this chapter explains our rationale, and how a Sky Trust would work.

A primary function of government is to define and enforce rules of property. But there are a number of valuable assets — the sky among them — for which there aren't yet clear property rules. The atmosphere and its limited absorptive capacities are just *out there*, waiting to be taken. Consequently, the sky has been subject to what biologist Garrett Hardin called *the tragedy of the commons*.

In his famous 1968 essay, Hardin wrote: "The rational herdsman concludes that the only sensible course for him to pursue is to add another animal to his herd. And another. . . . But this is the conclusion reached by each and every rational herdsman sharing a commons. Therein is the tragedy." The tragedy of the commons occurs also in environmental pollution; here, though, it is not a question of taking something out of the commons but of putting something in. The rational polluter finds that its share of the cost of the wastes it discharges into the commons is less than the cost of purifying its wastes before releasing them. Since this is true for everyone, we are locked into a system of "fouling our own nest."[2]

Hardin believed, erroneously, that this tragedy resulted from common ownership. He thought there was no way to fix it, short of full-scale privatization or coercive government action. What he didn't foresee was the invention of "cap-and-trade" systems.

Cap-and-trade systems begin with a cap: a total amount of permissible pollution. The cap translates the natural scarcity of waste storage capacity into information that markets can respond to. Typically, the cap is lower every year, so pollution can be gradually phased down.

The next step in a cap-and-trade system is the creation and assignment of property rights — the right to emit a certain amount of waste (for example, a ton of carbon) into a commonly owned sink (such as America's share of the atmosphere) within a given time period. These rights are created and assigned by government. The sum of all of them is equal to

or below the cap. They're a bit like leased parking spaces in a large public garage. Whoever rents the spaces can use them, trade them, or sell
them; but once the garage is full, that's it.

Cap-and-trade systems were a brilliant invention. They enable market
economies to prevent nest-fouling, and allow businesses to figure out the
cheapest method. If a business can reduce its pollution for less than the
cost of an emission permit, that's what it will do. If it can't, it will buy a
permit from another company that can. The result is that pollution is reduced at the lowest cost to society.

The first major cap-and-trade system applied on a national scale was
designed to curb sulfur emissions, a cause of acid rain. Because coal
comes with a fair amount of sulfur in it—and because sulfur dioxide in
the air turns to sulfuric acid—smoke from power plants in the Midwest
produces acid rain in New England and New York. Sulfur emissions can
be reduced in a number of ways: Energy efficiency can be increased,
low-sulfur coal can be burned, coal can be chemically cleansed before
burning, scrubbers can remove sulfur-dioxide while it's in the smoke-
stacks, and utilities can switch to gas-fired plants. All of these measures,
however, cost money. And as long as the price of emitting sulfur is zero,
there's no reason for a utility to spend that money.

In 1990, Congress passed and President George Bush signed a law requiring that within the next twenty years U.S. sulfur emissions be cut by
50 percent. To get below this cap, the law gave coal-burning utilities a
gradually declining number of sulfur emission permits to use, sell, or
trade. A secondary market soon developed for these permits, and as this
chapter is written, they're selling for about $150 a ton—a price set purely
by supply and demand.

Nowadays, a coal-burning utility has several options. If it can reduce
sulfur emissions for less than $150 a ton, it can do so and sell its permits
at that price, making a small profit, or it can save its permits for future
years. If it can't cut emissions for less than $150 a ton, it can buy permits
from another company, from a broker, or from the Chicago Board of
Exchange.

The cap-and-trade system has been highly successful in reducing sulfur emissions. This has persuaded some policymakers that a similar system should be used to reduce carbon emissions—a view we share.
However, there are two important questions that cap-and-trade systems
raise but don't, by themselves, answer: (1) Should the initial emission
rights be given away free to existing polluters, or sold to bidders in a

competitive auction? (2) If the rights *are* sold rather than given away, to whom should the revenue go? To put it more succinctly, who should own the sky?

In considering these questions, it's important to distinguish between *use* of the sky and *beneficial ownership* of it. In a cap-and-trade system, the right to *use* the sky—that is, to emit gases into it—is linked to ownership of emission permits that can be freely bought and sold. The right to the *economic benefit* from the sky—that is, to receive the income derived from the sky—is something else. Henceforth, it's this right we'll be talking about.

In pondering the question of who is, or should be, the beneficial owner of America's chunk of sky, a good place to start is with Roman law, whence our system of property law derives. Roman law distinguished between four types of property:

- *Res privatae*, private things—things in the possession of an individual or corporation;
- *Res publicae*, public things—things owned and set aside for public use by the government, such as public buildings, highways, and navigable waterways;
- *Res communes*, common things—things accessible to all that can't be exclusively possessed by an individual or government; and
- *Res nullius*, unowned things that have no property rights attached until they're taken into possession and become *res privatae* or *res publicae*.

The category that concerns us here is *res communes*, things common to all. In this category, the Romans included air, sea, shore, navigable rivers, and wild animals. There's thus a very old and clear distinction between common property and state property, and the sky is decidedly a piece of common property. Like Roman law, English law distinguishes between state property and common property. England also added the institution of land owned in common by villagers. Such common lands could be used for growing crops, grazing animals, and collecting wood, so they were more than wild nature—they were a source of sustenance and income. They were distinct from the common areas owned by the king in that they were not open to all people. They were a community asset, accessible only to members of the village.

In the New World, many early settlements also had common lands (the Boston Commons was once a shared sheep pasture). Further, the old distinction between *res communes* and *res publicae* was kept alive in a judicial concept known as the Public Trust Doctrine. This doctrine says that although legal title to rivers and shorelines might reside in the state, the state merely holds them "in trust" for the people, who are their beneficial owners. A few state constitutions say this explicitly: That of Hawaii declares, "All public natural resources are held in trust by the State for the benefit of the People."

The U.S. Supreme Court has upheld the Public Trust Doctrine on numerous occasions. As University of Texas law professor Gerald Torres has explained: "The beneficial interest in any *res communes* is held by the people in common. The state does not own a river or the sky like it owns the furniture in the state house. The power of the government to divest the people of their common interest is limited. Even where such a divestiture is justified, the proceeds of that transaction belong to the people."[3]

Practically speaking, there are three possible beneficial owners of America's chunk of the sky: private corporations, the federal government, and citizens through a trust. Corporate ownership isn't as farfetched as it might seem. U.S. history has been marked by numerous giveaways of common assets to private corporations, from the land grants to railroads in the nineteenth century to the recent gift of spectrum to broadcasters. The amount of scarcity rent that has since flowed to these fortunate corporations was (and still is) enormous. There seems little reason to add atmospheric scarcity rent to this total.

The argument for federal ownership of carbon absorption capacity is stronger than the case for corporate ownership. Presumably, the federal government represents the public interest, and therefore its ownership of the sky would, ipso facto, serve the public interest. This presumption, however, is arguable. If we look at the historical record, it's not at all clear that the federal government has managed common assets in the public interest. Quite to the contrary, it has all too often disposed of valuable common assets (land, minerals, timber, water, and spectrum) at prices far below market value.

The reason for such poor stewardship isn't hard to uncover. Like any political body, the federal government is subject to pressure from private interests that stand to gain from use of common assets. Though in theory the federal government defends the interests of all citizens, and of future as well as present generations, in practice it accommodates private interests who want favors *now*.

Even if the government *did* receive fair market value for carbon storage capacity, that would solve only half the problem. Although the right amount of scarcity rent would go *into* the U.S. Treasury, there'd be no assurance that it would come *out*—or if it did come out, who would get it. The odds that it would be equitably distributed are not high. After all, the state has its favored constituents, and these days they tend not to be poor. It's possible, of course, that a progressive allocation of federally collected atmospheric scarcity rent *could* be achieved through congressional appropriations and/or tax cuts. The question for progressives is primarily one of strategy. Winning a onetime battle over property rights—where the issue is "one person, one share"—is one thing; winning repeated and obscure battles over the tax code and annual appropriations is quite another. We believe the wisest course is to fight and win that onetime battle, and to establish a fair distribution of atmospheric scarcity rent for decades to come.

What, then, is the third alternative? In 1998, the Corporation for Enterprise Development proposed creation of a U.S. Sky Trust that would capture atmospheric scarcity rent on behalf of all citizens equally.[4] One of the present authors, Peter Barnes, was the architect of that proposal. Independently, in 1999, four economists at Resources for the Future—Raymond Kopp, Richard Morgenstern, William Pizer, and Michael Toman—proposed a plan to reduce U.S. carbon emissions gradually and to use the scarcity rent to alleviate economic impacts.[5] Rafe Pomerance is a leading advocate of this plan.

Both proposals rely on capping and then selling, rather than giving away, permits to bring carbon into the U.S. economy. Fossil fuel companies at the top of the carbon chain—that is, at the mine mouth, wellhead, or port of entry—would be required to own a permit for each ton of carbon they introduce. In the first year, there would be a ceiling on the price of carbon permits of $25 a ton (roughly 6 cents per gallon of gas), with the ceiling then rising at a set rate for five years. Seventy-five percent of the revenue would be paid in equal dividends to all citizens; and 25 percent would go into a Transition Fund, which would assist workers and communities adversely affected by reduced carbon use. The Transition Fund's share would decrease by 2.5 percent per year for ten years, at which point all revenue would be paid out in individual dividends.

How much is the revenue—that is, the scarcity rent—likely to be? In the early years, when the price of carbon is capped, revenue from carbon permit sales will be in the range of $35 billion a year. Later, the numbers will get bigger.

Of course, the prices of fossil fuels will rise once markets reflect the true scarcity of sky. Most households will pay more for gasoline and other products that embody burnable carbon—a fact that naturally causes fear among politicians. But the antidote to higher prices is dividends paid out of scarcity rent—a predictable income stream that will offset the losses due to higher prices.

Keep in mind this fact: If carbon emissions are limited, we as consumers will pay higher prices *whether or not there's a Sky Trust.* These higher prices will result from scarcity—that is, from demand exceeding supply—not from the cost of carbon permits. The sale of carbon permits merely *captures* the scarcity rent; it doesn't *create* it. Without permits and dividends, prices will *still* rise, and most Americans will lose buying power. With permits and dividends, a majority of Americans would recover what they pay in higher prices, and even come out ahead.

In this sense, a Sky Trust is a scarcity rent recycling machine. The formula driving the machine is this: *From* all according to their use of the sky, *to* all according to their equal ownership of the sky. Those who burn more carbon pay more than those who burn less. If you drive a bigger car, you pay for a bigger carbon parking space. Yet, as equal beneficial owners, all receive an equal share of the scarcity rent. Thus, you'll come out ahead if you burn less carbon, but lose money if you don't. Money will flow from overusers of the sky to underusers. This isn't only fair; it's precisely the incentive we need in order to crank down pollution.

As it turns out, this shift of money from high to low carbon users also favors families with lower incomes. That's because poor families tend not to drive big cars, occupy big homes, or fly around the world in jets. A study by economist Marc Breslow confirms this. Using Census Bureau and other government figures, Breslow found that if U.S. households were ranked by income, the bottom 60 percent would, on average, gain money with a Sky Trust, and the top 40 percent would lose.[6]

A Sky Trust would be a civic institution embodying our common ownership of a shared inheritance. It can be compared to the Alaska Permanent Fund, which distributes dividends from Alaska's oil properties on the basis of one citizen, one share. In 1999, that dividend was $1,770 per Alaskan.

What Alaska did with its oil, we think the United States should do with our share of the global atmosphere. Here is our pitch to Congress: Establish the Sky Trust soon. Grant it property rights to the sky. It will cost you nothing. It will generate dividends for all your constituents, yet take not a penny out of the federal budget. It will help families and children, yet require no new taxes. It will impose no new regulations on business, yet open many business opportunities. It won't bloat the federal bureaucracy. Most importantly, it will help protect our air and stabilize our climate.

Politically, the Sky Trust would have broad appeal. Conservatives can appreciate it because it's market-based and pro-family, and gives money to people rather than to the government. Liberals will like it because it benefits low- and middle-income households and protects the environment. Moreover, the Sky Trust has nothing to do with the Kyoto Protocol, which many Republicans oppose. Rather, the Sky Trust is inspired by the 1992 Framework Convention on Climate Change (the Rio Treaty), which former President George Bush signed and Congress ratified unanimously. The Framework Convention commits the United States to reducing its carbon emissions to the 1990 level, the same initial target called for by the Sky Trust. The Kyoto Protocol, in contrast, sets a binding emissions limit of 7 percent *below* the 1990 level.

We propose that Sky Trust be set up with a five-year trial period. During these first five years, the price of carbon would be capped. This cap would start at the equivalent of 6 cents per gallon of gas, an amount that is barely noticeable. It then would rise at a single digit rate for four more years—all the while paying dividends. In addition, billions of dollars would flow into a transition fund that would help coal miners, farmers, and others. After five years, if voters aren't happy with the Sky Trust, Congress can fix it or let it lapse.

Though the Sky Trust won't make anyone a millionaire, it has long-term implications for wealth and income distribution. It builds new "pipes" in the economy through which more money, in the future, may flow. When Ida May Fuller received the first Social Security check in 1940, it was for $22.50; now the average monthly benefit exceeds $800. As the twenty-first century progresses, other gifts of nature besides the sky will become scarce. The Sky Trust would establish the principle that the scarcity rent from these commonly inherited assets belongs to all of us. Perhaps a portfolio of dividend-paying trusts might one day be a birthright of Americans, extending the notion of one "person, one vote" to "one person, one *share*."

Viewed in this way, the establishment of a U.S. Sky Trust would be a historic achievement, comparable to the Homestead Act of 1862, the Federal Reserve Act of 1913, and the Social Security Act of 1935. Like the Homestead Act, the Sky Trust would create a new class of property owners—in effect, every citizen would have an equity stake in the sky. Beyond this, the Sky Trust would manage the carbon flow through our economy, much as the Fed manages the money flow. And it would define a new formula for moving money within our economy: *From* all according to their use of a commons, *to* all according to their equal ownership.

The importance of this new formula can't be overstated. It differs significantly from two other formulas we've grown familiar with: public assistance and Social Security. The underlying formula for public assistance is *from* all according to their tax liability, *to* all according to their need. The underlying formula for Social Security is *from* all according to their wages, *to* all according to their disability and longevity. Both these formulas, though broadly accepted, are not without controversy. What's more, they've gone about as far as they can go—public assistance, because Americans don't like taxing Peter to pay Paul; and Social Security, because payroll taxes can't get much higher. The new Sky Trust formula, in contrast, has room to grow. It channels money from overusers of nature to underusers. And as nature gets scarcer, more money can flow this way.

Moreover, it's hard to argue *against* the Sky Trust's formula. That consumers should pay for what they use is one of the oldest principles of markets; here it's simply extended to an asset that, foolishly, had previously been priced at zero. Similarly, that dividends should flow to property owners is a sacred tenet of capitalism; the only novel notion here is that of equal and universal ownership of a shared inheritance.

But how else could ownership of the sky be divided? You can argue that human-made assets should be unequally distributed in order to encourage individual effort. But how can you argue that sky ownership should be unequally divided? After all, no person lifted a finger to create it. The atmosphere is a purely inherited asset, and not from anyone's parents but from the common creation.

A U.S. Sky Trust, in sum, would marry the cap-and-trade system for rationing a scarce natural asset with a trust for preserving common ownership. It would thereby remedy not only the ecological tragedy of the commons but also the oft-forgotten loss of the commons by the commoners—a loss that typically occurs when a commons becomes commercially valuable. That, ultimately, is the elegance of the Sky Trust. It's equitable, ecological, *and* market-based. It's politician-friendly *and* customer-friendly. If there's any other system that can better help us adapt to the scarcity of sky, we have yet to see it.

There are, of course, people who say that *any* policy that limits carbon burning will cause great harm to the American economy. Our gross domestic product (GDP) will shrink, consumers will be poorer, and hundreds of thousands of workers will lose jobs. "All pain, no gain" was for a time the mantra of these Cassandras—most of who worked in one way or another for the fossil fuel industry.

We don't argue that there'll be *no* pain. Change *always* causes pain. It's always hard to adapt to the new, and often harder to let go of the old. Whenever a new industry emerges, or an old one dies, some people gain and others lose. By the same token, the warming of the earth's atmosphere will surely cause pain. At the extreme, it will cause a large number of people to lose their homes, health, and livelihoods. At a minimum, it will cause a smaller number of people to lose jobs and money. The politics of climate change is thus, to a great degree, the politics of pain management. The Sky Trust doesn't deny this. On the contrary, it consciously seeks to *minimize* the pain from climate change and to distribute it as equitably as possible.

Over the long run, the key to minimizing pain is to minimize the geophysical effects of climate change—rising sea levels, death of ecosystems, more intense floods and droughts, and the spread of tropical diseases to now-temperate zones. That can be accomplished by cutting carbon burning as quickly as possible. The short-run task is different: It is to lessen the *economic* pain of reduced carbon burning. The Sky Trust performs this task well in three respects.

First, it relies on gradualism. Given time and forewarning, the U.S. economy is amazingly resilient. What caused gas lines in the 1970s was a large *sudden* leap in fossil fuel prices; the five-year phase-in of the Sky Trust is designed to avert a repeat of this. During the phase-in period, carbon emission prices would start low and rise gradually. Everyone would know in advance what prices were coming. Investments in conservation and in new technologies could be planned accordingly.

The Sky Trust's second pain-reducing tool is its use of scarcity rent to pay dividends. Absent some way to offset higher carbon prices, all Americans will lose buying power. With dividends, most Americans' buying power is protected. In fact, for a majority of Americans, it's *more* than protected—they come out ahead even without taking steps to conserve.

By conserving they can gain even more. And most of those who don't gain or don't conserve will be able to afford the loss.

The Sky Trust's third pain reducer is its Transition Fund, which will provide special assistance to those most directly affected by reduced carbon burning. To the extent that anyone can be fairly compensated for losing their livelihood, the Transition Fund can do it. A rough estimate is that it will have $8 billion a year to spend for ten years. Some of that money would go to laid-off workers, some to low-income consumers, some to hard-hit industries and communities. These choices would be made by state and local governments. The point is that thanks to the capture of atmospheric scarcity rent, there will be enough money to make these pain reductions possible.

And what about the American economy as a whole? A number of recent econometric studies suggest that the Sky Trust will cause virtually no macroeconomic harm. Some of the studies predict a small, brief slowing in GDP growth due to higher carbon prices. None predicts a large or a long slowing. Some even predict a *positive* impact as higher carbon prices spur innovation and new investment.[7] This means, at a minimum, that we're not facing an economic disaster. Even in the worst-case scenarios, GDP *doesn't fall*—it simply grows a little more slowly than it would with lower carbon prices. In other words, there'll be more jobs and more wealth no matter what happens to carbon prices—the only question is how much more.

Just as Americans adapted to the scarcity of land, so we will adapt to the scarcity of sky. In the economy of the twenty-first century, there will be less carbon burning and more E-mailing, less movement of bulky things and more movement of bits and bytes. There will be growth of a different color, but growth nonetheless. And the Sky Trust will spur it.

NOTES

This chapter is based on a book by Peter Barnes entitled *Who Owns The Sky? Our Common Assets and the Future of Capitalism*, forthcoming in spring 2001.

1. A. Denny Ellerman, "Obstacles To Global CO_2 Trading: A Familiar Problem," Massachusetts Institute of Technology, Joint Program on the Science and Policy of Global Change, report no. 42 (November 1998). Available at www.mit.edu/globalchange/www/rpt42.html.

2. Garrett Hardin, "The Tragedy of the Commons," *Science* 162 (1968): 1243–1248. Available at www.dieoff.org/page95.htm.

3. Memorandum prepared for the Corporation for Enterprise Development, August 1999.

4. Peter Barnes, "1997 Entrepreneurial Economy Review" (Corporation for Enterprise Development, Washington, D.C., 1998): 22–27.

5. Raymond Kopp, Richard Morgenstern, William Pizer, and Michael Toman, "A Proposal for Credible Early Action in U.S. Climate Policy," a Resources for the Future policy paper (February 1999), available at www.weathervane.rff.org/features/feature060.html.

6. Marc Breslow and Peter Barnes, "Pie in the Sky," paper presented to the Natural Assets Workshop in Santa Fe, New Mexico, January 21, 2000.

7. See, for example, Energy Information Administration, "Analysis of the Impacts of an Early Start for Compliance with the Kyoto Protocol" (July 1999), available at www.eia.doe.gov/oiaf/kyoto/cost.html; John P. Weyant and Jennifer N. Hill, "Introduction and Overview," and Christopher MacCracken, James A. Edmonds, Son H. Kim, and Ronald D. Sands, "The Economics of the Kyoto Protocol," *Energy Journal, Special Issue: The Costs of the Kyoto Protocol: A Multi-Model Evaluation* (1999); Christopher Probyn and Will Goetz, "Macroeconomic Impacts of Greenhouse Gas Control Policies," paper presented at the Climate Change Analysis Workshop "The Post-Kyoto Climate: Impacts on the U.S. Economy," in Washington, D.C., June 6, 1996; Robert Repetto and Duncan Austin, "The Costs of Climate Protection: A Guide for the Perplexed," World Resources Institute, Washington, D.C., 1997; and Interlaboratory Working Group on Energy-Efficient and Low-Carbon Technologies, "Scenarios of U.S. Carbon Reductions: Potential Impacts of Energy-Efficient and Low Carbon Technologies by 2010 and Beyond," Oak Ridge National Laboratory, Lawrence Berkeley National Laboratory, Pacific Northwest National Laboratory, National Renewable Energy Laboratory, and Argonne National Laboratory, September 1997.

Part 4

EMPOWERING PEOPLE
IN POLITICS

which frequently violates the letter of the law and invariably violates its spirit.[2] The difference shows up most dramatically in the high rate of unionization (37.3 percent) among public workers, whose supervisors rarely fight hard against organizing efforts, compared to the low rate (9.4 percent) among private sector workers. Unions win about 85 percent of representation elections among public employees, but only slightly more than half of private sector elections. Even after a union wins an election, private sector employers often successfully resist negotiating a contract—as much as half of the time, according to one survey.[3] The law has become, in many cases, a tool that employers use to undermine unionization as well as collective actions (e.g., strikes) that give workers power in collective bargaining. The effect of labor law and its current enforcement is to discourage unionization and collective bargaining—the obverse of what is supposed to be the national policy.

UNIONS MATTER

Americans are more prosperous now, and many work in different ways than people did in the 1930s, even discounting hype about a new economy. But the reasons for workers to organize remain just as valid as in the New Deal era. In the wake of nearly three decades of growing inequality, which was only slightly slowed by a record boom during the 1990s, it is absurd to think that issues of social and economic class have disappeared. What *has* nearly disappeared is vigorous public discussion of the issues, in part because of the weakness of the labor movement. There is still a huge imbalance of power between employers and individual employees, despite the increased number of legal protections for particular groups (such as the protection of Blacks and minorities against racial discrimination) and despite increased workplace standards; and that inequality contributes to broader economic inequality and social instability. Also, government protections—such as guarantees of workplace safety or a minimum wage—are more effective if workers are organized and are able both to enforce rights on the front line and to adapt flexibly to differing situations by negotiating with management. Finally, it is clear that democracy is far richer and more meaningful if extended from the ballot box to the workplace. Industrial democracy would guarantee that the hours at work and the long reach of the job into personal life (through such influences as wages, health insurance, pensions, and allocation of people's time) are not governed by an authoritarian regime, where the only way of expressing discontent is to risk one's livelihood and quit.

The decline of unionization has serious consequences for society beyond the minutiae of contract negotiations and grievance procedures. Union weakness has contributed in part to the dramatic rise in inequality of both income and wealth. And it has hastened the decay of civic life, not only because fewer workers take part in unions but also because fewer unions are available to nurture leaders for other social organizations, such as neighborhood groups, grassroots political party operations, and civil rights movements. Weaker unions also translate into declining political participation. Union members are more likely to be registered and to vote than are nonunionized workers. Also, when unions and other worker organizations are thriving, political debate is more likely to focus on broad issues of economic well-being that might inspire many nonvoters to believe that politics and government might make a difference in their lives. If workers can freely organize at work on the basis of common economic interests—just as they might organize in the community to protect the environment, provide activities for kids, or improve education—then political democracy is likely to be strengthened.

The future of unions is not simply a question of abiding by national laws and international treaties or judging the economic and political value of unions to society. Despite popular descriptions of the United States as a consumer society, work remains central to virtually everyone's life—a source not only of consumer income but also of satisfaction, identity, and community standing (with rewards of different jobs varying greatly in all these dimensions). But in the midst of this liberal democracy, work life remains semifeudal, with many contemporary legal notions stemming quite directly from common-law rules governing masters and servants. Furthermore, unlike other marketplace exchanges, there is an element of force lurking behind the exchange of wages for work, since workers depend on their employers for their livelihood. Also, the immense power of corporations in public life and their importance as the realm within which people spend much of their lives make it even more important that fundamental political rights to organize and speak be protected at work.

The right of workers to organize and act collectively should be considered as fundamental a human right as the right to vote, freedom of speech, or freedom from discrimination. If working people are to enjoy their full dignity and potential as human beings, they must be able to freely associate with others who share common interests, to express themselves in meaningful ways about central issues in their lives, and to exercise collectively a socioeconomic power that can in some fashion counter the massive economic power of giant multinational corporations.

Freedom of association is as fundamental to democracy as is freedom of speech. If it is denied at work, where it is critical not only for the lives of individual working people but also for the overall direction of the economy, then democracy is greatly compromised. Workers should be able to freely form organizations at work, just as they would freely join churches, parent-teacher associations, fraternal clubs, or political parties—without interference by their employers. Indeed, employers are now prohibited from trying to influence their employees' choice of elected officials at work, and they are prohibited from interfering in union members' election of officers; but they are still permitted to fight vigorously, sometimes even viciously, against workers deciding whether to have an organization that advocates their interests.

THE ASSAULT ON WORKERS' RIGHTS

Despite the strong claim for workers' rights as human rights, changes in the law, politics, and economy have weakened workers' ability to exercise these rights. Equally important, there has been a long-standing, deep-seated refusal to change notions of the rights of private property to accommodate workers' fundamental rights. As legal scholar James Atleson has argued,[4] almost from its inception the National Labor Relations Act suffered erosion in the courts, as judges repeatedly decided that common-law notions of the right of private property took precedence over the clear, if inadequate, protection of workers' rights. Owners' rights to run their business without interruption almost always trumped workers' rights to a voice on the job, despite the legal mandate to maintain some balance. With very few exceptions, such as some increased protection of union democracy and extension of the law to cover more categories of workers, every major legislative revision of core U.S. labor law in the past sixty-five years tipped the balance of power toward employers. This shift in power was compounded by changes in management style (from grudging acceptance of unions to aggressive union avoidance); politics (the triumph of a more combatively antiunion conservatism in the 1980s); and culture (including the idolization of the free market, a declining sense of solidarity among working people, and the diminished identification of unions with broader social justice causes). As the right to organize and bargain has shriveled both in law and in practice, there has been a growth in some other employee protections. There are more laws proscribing discrimination against workers on the basis of race, gender, age, disability, sexual preference, and other grounds, for example; but at the same time it has become easier and less costly for employers to discriminate against workers for acting collectively or forming a union (and such discrimination makes the other rights less reliable and enforceable).

Work today also takes place in an economic and a legal environment that is quite different from that of the 1930s. Corporations and markets are more global, increasing competitive trade pressures on workers but more importantly making capital more mobile. Manufacturing workers have experienced the greatest pressure and relative loss of jobs to the triple whammy of imports, capital flight, and new technological advances; but globalization also directly and indirectly affects large swaths of the service sector.

Instead of corporations pursuing integration of people and activities within one firm—the dominant trend of the previous hundred years—there has been a move in recent decades toward a disintegration of the corporation, with dominant businesses sitting atop a network of contractors and subcontractors and often linked at the top in strategic alliances. The power of the largest corporations has not diminished, but the way it is exercised has changed. Globalization, waves of mergers and hostile takeovers, and the growing power of financial markets have encouraged executives to focus on short-term profits and shareholder returns, often at the expense of the average employee.

Workers—despite the human relations exercise of calling even the lowliest clerk an "associate"—are seen more often as costs rather than assets, and virtually never as people with fundamental human rights within the corporation and workplace. A core of workers and managers may be relatively privileged, but there are strong tendencies both to minimize the responsibility of management and the firm to workers and to transfer the risks from fluctuations of business fortune to workers and away from managers and the business. Now nearly 30 percent of the workforce consists of some type of "contingent" worker—temp, permatemp, lease, contract, subcontract, part-time, or independent contractors, for example.[5] The result is an understatement of the number of people who are highly dependent on a core business for their livelihood but

Democrats in control of both Congress and the presidency, failed in 1978—the era before Reagan, when Democrats were in general more responsive to unions than they have been over the past two decades. For more than a quarter century, labor leaders grew weary calling for labor law reform. (Sometimes, unfortunately, unions used the growing legal and employer obstacles as an excuse for not working harder and adapting to become more effective.) In Clinton's first term, former labor secretary John T. Dunlop chaired a commission that compiled a compelling indictment of the failures of labor law. But it offered a mixed-bag compromise proposal that pleased neither labor nor management. Businesses were quite content with most of the current ineffectual law (except that they wanted greater freedom to establish committees that unions rightly disparaged as a reversion to the old, discredited company unions). Even a modest effort to limit employers' use of permanent replacements during strikes—a practice prohibited in most industrial democracies other than the United States—was blocked by a Senate filibuster in 1994.

It is not surprising, then, that hope for strengthening the nation's labor laws any time soon had faded even in union circles. As the year 2000 elections were unfolding and most of the labor movement had committed itself early on to support Al Gore, there was almost no talk of pushing dramatic new labor law legislation even if he won. Labor unions, however, haven't forgotten the issue. Indeed, in the late 1990s the AFL-CIO launched a new public education campaign about the right to a "voice at work." Gore had already been better educated by unions than are most politicians about violations of labor law, through exposure to workers who had been fired, harassed, and frustrated as they tried to organize. Increasingly, unions—often through local counterparts of the AFL-CIO, called "central labor councils"—have demanded that in return for a union endorsement, politicians pledge not only to protect workers' right to unionize in the legislature or executive office but also to show up at rallies and picket lines to support workers who are trying to organize.

Yet even under the best of circumstances—which in their viewpoint would include a Democratic sweep of Congress and the presidency—unions do not expect much progress on basic workers' rights and are not prepared to make many demands, either for major or minor changes. The problem is not simply rock-hard Republican opposition and likely Senate filibusters but also weakness of support for basic labor rights among many Democrats. There is little political space for fashioning compromises: Unions are less interested in pushing for them, and employers and their allies offer massive opposition to even modest demands for reform. If it's going to take a major battle and all the organizational resources that implies for even a tiny step forward—so the argument goes among many strategists—why not wait until a meaningful transformation can be achieved?

THE REFORM AGENDA

Because the failure of existing policies has been evident for so long, it is not hard to put together an outline for a revised labor law. The proposals of the AFL-CIO to the Dunlop Commission in 1994 remain a good framework. They recommended broadening coverage—in particular, ending the exclusion of "independent contractors" and many "supervisors" from coverage—and expanding the notion that workers may effectively have more than one employer, such as a garment worker in a contract shop that is effectively dominated by a manufacturer or large retailer. The AFL-CIO also recommended changing the process by which a union becomes recognized as workers' representative, by permitting the National Labor Relations Board (NLRB) to conduct card checks to verify support from a majority but also by changing representation campaigns. If unions choose to call for an election, the law should dramatically shorten the waiting period before the election; give union representatives more access to workers; remove special legal protection for employer interference; eliminate federal subsidies for antiunion campaigns; establish stronger penalties for employer violations of labor law; improve enforcement; and authorize arbitration of first contract disputes that are not resolved within a reasonable period. In a break with tradition, the AFL-CIO also proposed making it possible for workers who do not constitute a majority at their workplace to form a minority union and get official recognition.

To bolster workers as they bargain with their bosses, the AFL-CIO proposed making it easier for unions to insist on combining units under one employer or employers within an industry for more centralized bargaining. The federation proposed expanding the issues on which employers are required to bargain in good faith and the information they must provide union negotiators. Arguing that businesses are increasingly "part of an interdependent, interrelated set of creditors, suppliers, contractors and the like," the AFL-CIO argued for repealing the 1947 Taft-Hartley formation about the firm freely, discuss what will be in the best interest for the future of the firm and its employees, and solicit ideas from employees on how to motivate them to do their very best work. There will be disagreements: That's why there is bargaining. But if employers establish a basis for trust, then workers and unions are not so foolish that they will destroy their own jobs. Workers strike and engage in comprehensive pressure campaigns only as a last resort or because of deep-seated, unresolved grievances, not because they like industrial warfare. Indeed, if partnership is the goal, as most executives profess, then it requires some rough parity between the partners, which the proposed changes would restore.

But if unions are going to gain the power to represent more workers more forcefully in the name of workers' rights and industrial democracy, then both the law and the unions themselves will have to make a stronger commitment to internal union democracy. Even under current conditions, unions are among the most democratic institutions in which most people participate. There has also been progress—from both external pressure and internal reforms—in making leaders more accountable in some unions. But many union leaders still distrust internal democracy. Even those who are not simply trying to defend their own power may argue that too much democracy undermines the effectiveness of the union as an organization engaged in defending itself and its constituents against relentless onslaught. Moreover, they argue that employers typically use calls for union democracy as a club to attack unions, like the so-called "paycheck protection" proposals, which would have crippled union political activity. But if unions are granted more power under the rationale of workers' rights and the extension of democracy, then union legitimacy will depend upon internal democracy. Unions can best counter employer rhetoric about union democracy by boldly developing their own internal strategy to strengthen democracy. When organizers recruit new members, they tell them—correctly—that a union is not something alien. They are the union and they will make the decisions. That promise must be rigorously fulfilled. It would best be realized by the labor movement taking the initiative itself to nurture democracy as a part of building the long-term campaign for redefining American labor law. But despite the problems raised by government regulation of the internal life of a free association of citizens (similar to issues raised by government regulation of political parties), such regulation is also a legitimate part of any significant legislative reform.

The goal of these reforms is to enable workers to play a much greater role in governing their own lives, especially the economic activities that are so fundamental to all civic life and politics. The question might be raised about whether unions are the right institution. Of course, nothing prohibits workers from joining in professional associations or other groups that can advance workers' interests; and professional groups can—as happened with the National Education Association—evolve into collective bargaining institutions. Reform could also make it possible for groups of workers who don't constitute a workplace majority to bargain collectively with their employers, and even for more than one organization of workers to exist in the same workplace—a practice common in Europe but a departure from the standard in the United States of granting exclusive representation to the union that wins a majority.

Some academics, despairing of the declining representation of workers through unions, or admiring western European institutions for the co-determination of workplaces by workers and employers, have argued for an American version of the European works councils. Yet it is unlikely that U.S. employers will readily agree to mandated works councils unless the councils are weak and meaningless, or unless the employers are forced to do so by a far stronger labor movement. Indeed, in Europe works councils largely developed in the context of a strong labor movement, and they function best when unions play a vigorous role in them.

There is one area, however, in which an experiment along these lines could prove productive: For some years, unions have supported mandating joint employer-employee safety committees in all workplaces above some minimum size. If workers decided who would represent them, and if these committees actually had power to enforce Occupational Safety and Health Administration regulations, then they could be a significant step toward giving workers more power on the job. But even this is no substitute for the core right of workers to freely associate with coworkers.

A CAMPAIGN FOR WORKERS' RIGHTS

Any significant reform will require a long and multifaceted campaign, building the case with the public, increasing and mobilizing labor's strength, and laying the groundwork with initiatives on many fronts. It seems likely that no major legislative victory will occur until massive social and political upheaval forces the issue onto the agenda. It is only through the exercise of social power, which public policy now limits, that a movement will be able to win the legal changes that protect workers' rights and power. If legislative victories are won, it will be in large part because unions have already mobilized social power on their own, and the law will both ratify that social power and make it possible to consolidate and extend it.

There are five arenas in which unions and their allies can make progress as part of the long march to meaningful labor law reform: changing the labor movement itself; creating a more supportive, broad framework of public policies; expanding the social wage; creatively using federal executive and budgetary authority; and undertaking initiatives at the state and local levels.

Obviously the changes now underway in labor unions are crucial: more organizing, more member mobilization, more innovative tactics, more coordination, more global solidarity. Though still a fledgling enterprise, unions are doing more to educate the public about the harshness of employer opposition tactics, though unions too rarely manage to make managerial tactics such as the commonplace firing of a union supporter during an organizing campaign into high-profile causes-célèbres.

The election of John Sweeney's team to leadership of the AFL-CIO in 1995 both reflected changes underway in some unions and provided a catalyst for accelerating change. But the campaign to build a stronger labor movement, including greater legal protection for workers' rights, ultimately relies on transformation of individual unions, right down to the local unions where workers can be mobilized. For many years, most unions have devoted minimal resources—less than 5 percent of their budgets—to new organizing; and many have conducted organizing campaigns in clunky, outdated, and ineffective ways. Despite the odds, some unions showed that they could win when they put effort into organizing and mobilized both their existing members and the workers who were trying to form a union in dynamic campaigns. Increasingly, unions have also worked outside the framework of the law, organizing without formal elections under NLRB supervision. In such cases, unions apply whatever pressures they can to persuade employers to recognize them. Indeed, even though union organizing has increased in recent years—mainly in a few unions, like the Service Employees, Hotel and Restaurant Employees, UNITE (garment and textiles), AFSCME (public employees), Communications Workers, Steelworkers, and Carpenters—the number of NLRB elections declined in 1999. According to calculations by the Labor Research Association, the NLRB election process reflected only

26 percent of the new members organized. Some were governed by other laws—state public employee statutes or the Railway Labor Act—but a growing number were organized through "card-checks" by employers. Increasingly, unions have tried to use their political clout and bargaining power to persuade partially unionized employers to remain neutral in organizing drives and to recognize the union through a card-check. These actions are harbingers of changes that unions would like to see enshrined in law.

Unions have found new ways to get around the legal and corporate restraints on their power to represent workers. Although the law makes it difficult, unions increasingly treat the drive for union recognition and a first contract as a single, continuous campaign, not the two-stage process outlined under the NLRA. Likewise, despite the difficulty in striking and the limits on what the law deemed "secondary" solidarity actions, unions have won difficult battles by building coalitions, mobilizing international support, attacking the financial underpinnings of corporations, exploiting corporate political and regulatory vulnerabilities, and using a wide range of pressure tactics on the job (such as having workers do only what supervisors specifically tell them to do). A few unions, notably the Steelworkers, have decided not to let difficult strikes peter out into ignominious defeat but rather to continue to escalate tactics as time goes on. Most of these new strategies require the active involvement of members, which creates more accountability of union staff and officials and may help democratize many unions.

Too few unions have committed significant resources to organizing; but even the initial efforts—limited in part by the lack of enough experienced organizers—have helped to stem the decline. Recruiting new members and expanding the labor movement, as the AFL-CIO has emphasized, is the key to any resurgence, not only because labor needs an expanded base of support but also because successful organizing is likely to require both the mobilization of existing members and an infusion of new energy and ideas. New recruitment will also heighten public awareness of freedom of association at work as a basic human right, and because of the limitations of the law and the antagonism of corporations, may provoke a crisis that will create an opportunity for far-reaching legal reforms.

Unions have just begun to tap potential in two areas. First, they are beginning to demand that government officials, especially those elected with labor backing, take a public role in supporting union organizing efforts and criticizing labor law violators. This is part of making the labor movement itself more of a permanent force for direct action. Since Sweeney was elected president of the AFL-CIO, union strategists have emphasized building a political apparatus of rank-and-file workers that continues after election day to work on educating working people and their families about key issues rather than simply making election endorsements or simply pouring money into party and campaign coffers. But theory and practice frequently diverge, and much labor political work still follows old patterns that subordinate labor unions' key interests and their ability to inspire their members to the election of a supposed friend.

Unions have made dramatic steps toward wider alliances with other social movements and citizen groups, but there is untapped potential for a broader-based labor movement in the millions of workers who once were union members but are no longer—because of layoffs, changed jobs, or other reasons—and the millions who would like to be in a union but aren't, possibly because an attempted representation election fell short of a majority. It is understandable that unions, which are not devoting enough resources to conventional organizing, might downplay organizing these more peripheral workers, especially since associate member programs oriented around credit cards or other benefits have not proven very useful. But unions are missing opportunities for building a broader social movement by not keeping track of these largely sympathetic nonmembers and not trying to communicate with them.

Union activities—whether organizing, bargaining, or doing political work—take place within a larger policy framework that can deeply influence union success and the exercise of workers' rights. There are at least three fronts where unions and their allies can work more aggressively to make the context for their work more favorable: Federal Reserve Bank policy, global economic agreements, and immigrant rights. With the Fed's actions now being the main lever of macroeconomic policy, and given the widespread deference accorded the bank's governors by even most Democrats, it has become even more important to build a higher-profile movement critical of Fed priorities, especially its commitment to fighting tomorrow's possible inflation by increasing unemployment today. Few factors make a greater difference in workers' bargaining power or hope for social and political change than the level of unemployment.

Second, the movement challenging corporate globalization has become crucial, not only because it gives a high profile to the issue of workers' rights but also because it has created a diverse coalition critical of corporate power. Although it focused initially on abuses of workers' rights overseas, the critique can be turned on the United States as well, as the Human Rights Watch recently did, citing the United States for failure in laws and enforcement to comply with international standards. Indeed, the United States has one of the worst records of any country in ratifying even the core conventions of the International Labor Organization, despite professed U.S. support for stronger linkage between trade and those core rights. Winning ratification of more core standards would not make a substantial, immediate difference to American workers, but it would give renewed credibility, at home and overseas, to the obligation of governments to protect those rights. Similarly, unions and their allies need to continue to insist on enforceable labor rights provisions as part of any global economics and trade agreements. These provisions should be tied to an alternative model of development for poor countries that does not rely on suppressing workers and wages in export industries.

The labor movement's participation in protests for developing-country debt relief and against World Bank and International Monetary Fund policies is important not only for humanitarian reasons but for the protection of workers' rights, even in the United States. Austerity policies of the international financial institutions and heavy debt burdens have led to legal and economic policies that undermine labor rights and organizations in developing countries, intensifying the threats of imports or capital flight on U.S. workers who want to unionize and improve their conditions. Individual unions, as well as the AFL-CIO, have also given greater emphasis to global solidarity with other unions in battles with individual companies and in challenging corporate priorities for the global economy. The domestic and global struggles go hand in hand: Without greater constraints on multinational corporations and enforcement of workers' rights, competitive pressures will drag workers downward in both advanced and developing countries. Indeed, more low-wage workers in Asia than workers in the United States will probably lose their jobs or find their wages depressed in the short run by China's entry into the World Trade Organization. But without a strong domestic movement for labor rights within the United States and every other country, there is little likelihood of any global governmental commitment to real enforcement of workers' rights.

Third, in early 2000, the AFL-CIO reversed policies on immigration, arguing for a new amnesty program for undocumented immigrants, elimination of sanctions against employers who hire illegal immigrants, and "full workplace rights" for all immigrant workers. The experience of some of the most aggressive organizing unions, such as the Hotel and Restaurant workers (HERE) and Service Employees International Union (SEIU), had demonstrated that immigrant workers—whatever their legal status—not only need unions but are ready to organize. Immigration laws were used to intimidate and discourage them from defending their rights or joining a union, not to penalize employers who exploited them. In California, in particular, immigration rights, union organizing, and a new, progressive, grassroots politics have been fused into the closest approximation yet of the new civil rights movement that labor needs to mount. The Justice for Janitors campaigns, organizing among hotel workers, construction workers, and farm workers, and various state and federal legislative races, all give signs of this movement's potential.

Taken together, campaigns for a more worker-friendly Federal Reserve, workers' rights on a global scale, and immigrant workers' rights in the United States would increase the chances of unions' organizing and bargaining successfully. But workers' rights and union power do not rely solely on collective bargaining. Legislative regulation of the workplace can also strengthen the organization of workers. One of the goals of organized labor has always been to "take wages out of competition"—that is, to encourage business to compete on efficiency or quality rather than for cheaper labor. The minimum wage, which is still far below its historic high from the late 1960s in real purchasing power, is the classic effort to maintain a legislative floor beneath workers' wages. In recent years—mainly at the local level—there has been a revival of the demand for a "living wage." In the decades after the Civil War, workers' organizations in the United States often called for abolition of "wage slavery" and for the establishment of a workers' cooperative commonwealth. By the late nineteenth century, however, union leaders were willing to accept wage labor if it paid enough for workers to attain an acceptable standard of living. Cultural expectations, not the marketplace, were thus the yardstick, and the labor movement asserted that all workers had a right to what now might be called a middle-class style of life. Over the years, this came to include adequate wages and a range of employer-provided benefits and government programs that provided a supplementary social wage, such as unemployment compensation, Social Security, Earned Income Tax Credit, Medicare/Medicaid, food stamps, and welfare programs.

Beyond raising the minimum wage so that it is pegged at half the median wage, the major task now is structuring a social wage that has universal appeal and benefits like those provided by Social Security but that also redistributes income progressively and broadly. For example, the Paper, Allied, and Chemical Employees Union has for several years promoted the idea of a "just transition" for workers displaced by environmental regulations or other policy measures that may impose short-term heavy costs on a few workers for widespread social gain. But the "just transition" model, itself inspired by the GI Bill after World War II, could be universalized into a more aggressive governmental effort to provide income support, education, and ultimately, new jobs for all who need them. It is a step beyond the idea of a "living wage" for those who are working to a guaranteed job or living income for everyone willing to participate in training and education programs. Workers at a wide range of skill levels would benefit from such a comprehensive, active labor market policy, but it would likely be of most help to the most vulnerable. By combining education with income support for displaced or unemployed workers until they are able to find work, such a policy would not only protect workers from poverty but also give them the opportunity continually to upgrade their skills. If such a program were integrated into existing colleges and vocational schools, there would be less stigma for displaced workers and more political support for the program. When the next business downturn coincides with the new limits on welfare, the need for this type of government intervention in the labor market will become more apparent.

For both organized and nonunion workers, almost regardless of income levels, the highest priority for an expanded social wage is creating a universal health care system—ideally, a progressively financed system with a single public insurer, like Medicare. Taking medical costs out of the employer system now is as important as taking wages out of competition. The employer-financed benefit system simply feeds into cost-shifting games that boost overall health care costs and that leave more and more workers without insurance and adequate care. Employer-financed health care is also an incentive for many businesses to fight unionization and shift more workers into contingent job categories.

Winning universal health insurance, or even a comprehensive active labor market policy, would require a popular crusade on the scale of the new movement for civil rights at work. But these efforts are ultimately complementary, both in the political coalitions built and in the resultant improvements in workers' lives. Although powerful insurance companies are the main obstacle, the movement for single-payer health insurance also has been hampered by continuing division within the labor movement, which can agree only on the principle of universal coverage.

WHAT A FRIENDLY ADMINISTRATION MIGHT DO

Even if the chances for major labor legislation are slim in the near future, the federal government, especially under a sympathetic executive, can still advance workers' rights through executive action and the power of the purse. Some administrative actions do not require congressional approval, and a president friendly to labor could probably win some budget battles more easily than major policy reforms.

First, and most obviously, the administration could greatly increase the budgets for the National Labor Relations Board, the Occupational Safety and Health Administration, the Department of Labor's Wage and Hour Division, and other enforcement agencies, most of which suffered cutbacks under Republican congressional leadership. They may talk tough about law and order, but when it comes to the workplace, they have tried to fire or at least disarm the sheriff. Despite some progress, there are still intolerable delays in conducting elections or resolving complaints at the NLRB, frequently because of inadequate staffing. In 1998, the Department of Labor found that six out of ten garment workers in Los Angeles were not paid in compliance with the Fair Labor Standards Act, and in 1996, the Department found the same level of violations of minimum-wage and overtime laws in the nursing home industry. With the current number of OSHA inspectors, the average business might be inspected once every sixty years.[8]

Yet even a doubling or a tripling of budgets—an unlikely reversal of the downward trend—would not adequately enforce existing laws. There is another option for improving enforcement, which unfortunately would require legislation, but which would have special appeal because it would save taxpayers money. Now unions can—and do—reduce violations of laws on workplace standards when they are present; but there are several legal barriers—mainly developed through the NLRB and federal court cases—that make it difficult for unions to help unorganized workers enforce labor standards. If unions were permitted to bring class-action lawsuits against major employers who consistently violate wage and hour laws or occupational safety standards, or if unions could file private lawsuits against employers for violation of the National Labor Relations Act, employers would take their legal obligations much more seriously.

Second, the federal government could insist that federal money not be used by any recipient to oppose unionization of workers; or preferably, that any business or organization that receives federal funds agree to remain neutral if its employees are contemplating forming a union. Employers, from hospitals to defense contractors, have for years used public money to fight unionization. One of the most egregious cases involved a six-year fight by Avondale Industries, a large New Orleans shipyard heavily dependent on federal contracts, to resist a vote by its 5,000 members to unionize. Avondale, which was found guilty of more than 100 labor law violations in combating the union, charged the government—and was reimbursed—for more than 15,000 hours of time employees spent as captive audiences in company meetings, listening to antiunion pitches. Several federal laws, including the Workforce Investment Act, the Head Start Programs Act, the National Community Service Act, and Medicare, already prohibit employers from using public money to fight unions (and several state statutes do the same). At the initiative of Vice President Al Gore, the Clinton administration proposed Responsible Contractor and Cost Principle Reforms for federal procurement that would have broadened this prohibition to include all federal contractors.[9]

Employers, however, can and do get around such prohibitions. When union organizers in Ohio protested that Head Start centers were conducting expensive antiunion campaigns, for example, the centers simply said they were using sources of funds other than federal money to combat unions, and the Department of Health and Human Services accepted their defense. The only really effective remedy to such action is to require all recipients of public money to remain neutral about unions. (The California legislature passed such a law in 1999, but Democratic Governor Gray Davis vetoed it.) There is no reason why public money should be used to support enterprises that interfere with the clear albeit frequently violated national policy in favor of collective bargaining, let alone used directly or indirectly for overt antiunion campaigns. Employers who want to harangue their workers against unions can do so at their own expense.

The federal government also could use its influence through procurement and reimbursement to help enforce existing laws. For example, the federal government, which bought more than $165 billion in goods and services in 1997, clearly could refuse contracts to labor law violators under the Federal Acquisition Regulations requiring that the government deal only with "responsible contractors," who among other attributes "have a satisfactory record of integrity and business ethics" and the workforce capability to fulfill the contract. But the federal government has not done so. The General Accounting Office, in two separate reports, stated that many contractors had violated labor laws. In 1993, the GAO reported, eighty firms that had violated the National Labor Relations Act—some of them chronic violators—had received 13 percent of all federal contracts. Contractors with a history of violating OSHA regulations received 22 percent of all federal contracts in 1994.[10] The AFL-CIO independently found extensive evidence of major manufacturers, food processors, hoteliers, health care providers, and other businesses with gross labor law violations that had been awarded major government contracts.[11] The Gore initiative was an attempt to "clarify" the responsible contractor provision in ways that would redress labor law violations; but as the AFL-CIO argues, the initiative breaks no new ground. It does not permanently debar these businesses from federal contracts but gives them the opportunity to reverse their lawbreaking and become eligible again for contracts. One might, in contrast, plausibly argue that any employer effort to interfere with workers' freedom to form a union evidences poor business ethics, even if the form of interference is not illegal. In addition to the passage of the proposed reforms, we would advocate that every cabinet appointee make clear to contract officers that they are expected to pay close attention to the protection of workers' rights.

STATE AND LOCAL INITIATIVES

Faced with unfavorable terrain in Washington, worker advocates have in recent years turned much of their attention to state and local governments, hoping to win breakthroughs there that could provide models for other jurisdictions, eventually including the federal government. However, apart from the usual business argument that any effort to raise local standards will lead to the flight of businesses and loss of jobs, decentralized initiatives on labor rights face a distinct problem: In many areas the federal government expressly preempts authority to regulate labor-management relations.

There are ways to circumvent this barrier to some extent. Some unions are taking advantage of conservative rhetoric about federalism and decentralization to argue that Congress should pass laws enabling states to establish their own single-payer health systems or to adopt card-check recognition or other reforms that accept federal labor law as a minimum but strengthen workers' rights within the state. In many cities around the country, Jobs With Justice, an organization of local community-labor coalitions, has established nongovernmental workers' rights boards that call attention to employer labor law violations and also offer a mechanism to validate majorities of workers who have signed union cards and demanded recognition by their employer. It is conceivable that local governments could also establish such boards, though the role played by local boards might be more that of bully pulpit than of legal enforcer.

Local and state governments also can use their power of the purse to protect workers' rights and promote unionization. A "living wage" movement has formed around the principle that public money should not be used to create jobs that leave workers in poverty. By mid-2000 the living wage movement, which started in Baltimore in 1994, had won legislation in forty-one local government bodies that set a wage for city contract employees at the poverty level or above—typically, between $8 and $12 an hour—with provision in some cases for health insurance as well. As the movement develops, it is linking up with a parallel effort in many areas to demand public accountability from businesses that receive economic development aid and tax breaks. Some unions—especially the Hotel Employees and Restaurant Employees—have worked with living wage campaigns and other local allies to protect workers' rights on new projects such as convention centers, stadiums, and hotels that are built with public subsidies or on public lands. Some local ordinances they have won give preference to contractors who are likely to ensure labor peace (which is often interpreted as neutrality toward unions); others require recipients of public aid to recognize unions when a majority of workers have signed union cards. In yet other instances, local laws require that businesses at public facilities (e.g., airports) retain employees for some minimum period in order to prevent churning of contractors and employees as a way of avoiding unionization or a negotiated contract. Although much of the legislation relating to a living wage and other workers' rights affects only a few private contractors to city or county governments, these laws establish the principle that businesses benefiting in any way from public money must respect workers' rights. In that regard, the laws open new options for local initiatives to help workers organize.

Although the federal government ultimately must address many of the problems of contingent workers, there are currently a number of state and local initiatives—some enacted, others still only proposals—that could enhance workers' rights. At a minimum, states can conduct official studies of the contingent workforce, as have Rhode Island and North Carolina. Legislation proposed in several states would take steps either to equalize pay and benefits between standard and nonstandard workers or to prevent discrimination in the provision of benefits to contingent workers. States also can regulate temporary employment or day labor agencies and prevent employers from misclassifying workers as independent contractors in order to avoid providing benefits such as unemployment or worker compensation. California and New York have passed laws establishing the responsibility of garment manufacturers and retailers for labor violations by sweatshop contractors—a first step in removing the insulation from responsibility so common in contemporary employment relations.

There is still a need to win state legislation guaranteeing collective bargaining rights for many public employees, especially in eleven states with no bargaining rights for public workers. There are also other legislative possibilities at the state and local level that have barely been tapped. For example, state governments could pass laws, as Montana has done, stating that employees can be fired only with just cause. Now virtually all workers in the United States can be fired "at will" by their employers, without any justification. Also, states and cities can adopt, as a growing number have, prohibitions on purchases of goods or services from sweatshops. Although the Supreme Court overturned a Massachusetts law prohibiting state purchases from companies doing business in Burma, a notorious violator of human rights, selective purchasing laws in general have not been invalidated. Third, public pension funds have begun to adopt "responsible contractor policies" that effectively discourage the use of low-wage, nonunion building service contractors in office or other buildings owned by the funds.

There is intrinsic value in these and other state and local initiatives for the workers affected. Equally important, such initiatives will help build a movement encompassing organized and unorganized workers, unions and community groups, to make workers' rights a central public issue. The more pressure politicians feel to take action on these issues, the more likely it is that they will address such issues in their campaigns and their political agendas. The more workers hear about their rights on the job, the more they will assert and demand those rights. As state and local efforts succeed, the pressure for federal action is also likely to increase. Combined with campaigns on globalization, Federal Reserve Board policies, immigration, social wages, and federal spending, a new workers' civil rights movement could build public and political support for a broad reaffirmation of democratic principles at work.

FROM PIPE DREAM TO CRUSADE

Could that result in a victory for substantial labor law reform? It's hard to find too much optimism even among the ranks of the energetic activists in the labor movement. "I regard legislative change as a pipe dream," said a strategist for one of the nation's most militant and innovative unions. "This movement arose by its own devices and will survive by its own devices." Yet the campaign is worth the effort, whatever the legislative outcome, because in its own right, it will build workers' power to defend themselves on the job.

The fight over workers' rights is not a conventional legislative battle; it is not a contest where grassroots agitation is needed to supplement the usual congressional testimony and lobbying. This fight poses issues as fundamental as those raised by the civil rights movement; and it will take a movement of the same dimensions to win it. Indeed, given the demographics of the most exploited workers — disproportionately African Americans and recent immigrants, predominantly from Latin America and Asia — the struggle for workers' rights is in part a direct continuation of the civil rights movement. Changes in work have also spurred new interest among highly skilled workers such as doctors, nurses, aerospace engineers, software designers, and university professors (especially adjunct and graduate teaching staff) in forming unions.

A movement for civil rights at work could embrace the vast majority of working people who already say they want more of a voice at work and could draw support from a new coalition of labor unions and religious groups, intellectuals, community organizations, environmentalists, immigrant and traditional civil rights organizations, and women's groups. The "Seattle coalition" against corporate globalization, though likely to be troubled by tactical differences, shares a core commitment to promoting workers' rights globally, which can be focused on the United States as well as on China. Indeed, as the conflict over control of the global economy unfolds, labor rights will clearly be at center stage. Yet the key to any new labor rights movement will be the mobilization of workers themselves, pressing the limits of the law, challenging corporate abuses, and disrupting business as usual. Without the emergence of a social crisis on many fronts, there is little likelihood that a movement for workplace democracy and workers' rights will break the stranglehold of corporations over both political parties and force the elite to respond to popular demands.

Any new workers' civil rights movement needs to pursue these varied efforts, from the local to the global, not as unrelated reform band-aids for various ills but as part of a campaign that asserts both the human rights of workers to organize and act together on the job and the necessity of democracy in the workplace. Viewed in that way, each small victory—a responsible contractor requirement, the regulation of a temporary employment agency, protection of a harassed immigrant worker trying to join a union—becomes a step toward securing, whether in law or in fact, a victory in the emerging global crusade for economic democracy and workers' rights.

NOTES

1. Richard B. Freeman and Joel Rogers, *What Workers Want* (Ithaca and London: ILR Press/Cornell University Press; New York: Russell Sage Foundation, 1999).

2. Kate L. Bronfenbrenner, "Employer Behavior in Certification Elections and First-Contract Campaigns: Implications for Labor Law Reform," in *Restoring the Promise of American Labor Law*, eds. Sheldon Friedman, Richard W. Hurd, Rudolph A. Oswald, and Ronald L. Seeber (Ithaca, N.Y.: ILR Press, 1994).

3. Gordon R. Pavy, "Winning NLRB Elections," in *Restoring the Promise of American Labor Law*, eds. Friedman et al.

4. James Atleson, *Values and Assumptions in American Labor Law* (Amherst: University of Massachusettes Press, 1983).

5. Ken Hudson, "No Shortage of 'Nonstandard' Jobs," briefing paper, Economic Policy Institute, Washington, D.C., 1999.

6. David M. Gordon, *Fat and Mean: The Corporate Squeeze of Working Americans and the Myth of Managerial "Downsizing"* (New York: Free Press, 1996).

7. Clyde Summers, "The First Fifty Years: Questioning the Unquestioned in Collective Labor Law," *Catholic University Law Review* 791(47) (spring 1998).

8. Craig Becker and Jonathan P. Hiatt, "Employment Law As Labor Law," as delivered Dec. 10, 1999, to a conference of The Labor Law Group in Scottsdale, Arizona.

9. Jonathan P. Hiatt, Lynn Rhinehart, Catherine Trafton, and Gerard Waites, "Comments of the American Federation of Labor–Congress of Industrial Organizations (AFL-CIO) in Support of Proposed Responsible Contractor and Cost Principle Reforms (FAR Case 99–010)," unpublished paper.

10. GAO (U.S. General Accounting Office), "Worker Protection: Federal Contractors and Violation of Labor Law," October 1995; and "Occupational Safety and Health: Violations of Safety and Health Regulations by Federal Contractors," August 1996.

11. Hiatt et al., "Comments of the American Federation of Labor–Congress of Industrial Organizations."

12

DEMOCRACY THAT WORKS: CLEAN MONEY CAMPAIGN REFORM

Ellen S. Miller and Micah L. Sifry

Money has always played a prominent role in American politics. Reasonable people may disagree over whether its influence is greater or less than in the past; but today, thanks to laws requiring extensive disclosure of campaign contributions, it is clear that money, not votes, is the primary currency of democracy. Well before the public casts its ballots, wealthy campaign contributors vote with their money, determining which candidates will have the resources to run serious campaigns and effectively disenfranchising the vast majority of citizens. Under the current system of privately financed elections, nearly all candidates for office (except the richest ones) are dependent on this funding. Even the best-intentioned representatives feel the pressure of the money chase. As a result, moneyed interests subtly shape public policy and set limits on political debate.

Thus the problem of money's role in politics has become a central concern for progressives, reformers, and democrats of all stripes. Historically, reformers focused first on fulfilling the nation's promise of political equality: struggling for the right to vote for women and for Blacks, and fighting for meaningful enforcement of that right through the civil rights movement and efforts to broaden voter registration, such as the motor-voter bill. But now that most everyone can vote, the question people are beginning to ask is, Why doesn't it make much difference? And the answer many are giving is: Because money determines who can run, and what they will or will not do once elected. Which is why some veteran voting rights activists say that getting private money out of public elections is the unfinished business of the voting rights movement.

Politics in America has always been a contest between organized people and organized money. Even as they focused on extending the right to vote, progressive reformers also have long tried to restrain the power of concentrated money. The first federal law banning direct corporate contributions to candidates was passed in 1907. Campaign finance reform is but one piece of a larger, ongoing struggle to make democracy real, which has been waged since the country's birth. But two factors make campaign finance reform a particularly high priority today. First, the rising costs of campaigns—driven by the increasingly sophisticated technology of voter manipulation (direct mail, broadcast advertising, polling, and the like) and by the arms-race mentality of most candidates—is causing more people to realize that they are being priced out of participating more effectively than if they faced a poll tax. Second, the growing awareness of how special interest money buys special influence and distorts the democratic process is leading many to support campaign finance reform in order to make other reforms more possible.

WHO GIVES WHAT

According to a 1996 report by the Center for Responsive Politics titled "The Big Picture," which covered the last presidential election, "The single most important source of campaign dollars for Senate candidates, presidential candidates and the political parties are individuals who can afford to write checks for $200, $500, $1,000 or more."[1] (In House races, political action committee [PAC] money is somewhat more significant than individual donations.) Not only are the people giving this money a numerically tiny group—just one-quarter of 1 percent of the population—they are incredibly unrepresentative of average Americans in background and outlook:

- Ninety-five percent of the big money contributors to the 1996 congressional campaigns were White, according to a recent academic survey supported by the Joyce Foundation.[2] Less than 1 percent identified themselves as persons of color. In contrast,

African Americans, Hispanics, Asians, and Native Americans make up close to 20 percent of the U.S. population.

- Eighty percent of the big donors were men, whereas women make up 51 percent of the U.S. population.
- Nearly half the donors were over the age of 60 years; but just 13 percent of the American public are 65 or older.
- Eighty-one percent of the donor class of 1996 had annual incomes of over $100,000, and 20 percent actually topped $500,000. In comparison, according to the IRS, in 1997 (the most recent year for which data are available) only 6 percent of taxpayers filing returns declared income over $100,000. Just 1 percent declared income over $200,000.
- More than half of the donors in the Joyce survey said they support cutting taxes even if that means reducing public services. (Only one-third of the public agrees with that proposition.) By a two-to-one margin, the donor class opposes cutting defense spending and supports free trade "even if jobs are lost." Pluralities reject national health insurance and disagree with spending more to reduce poverty. Only on the social issues of permitting abortion and allowing homosexuals to teach in public schools do donors as a group support positions similar to or more liberal than those supported by the general public.

In 1998, successful Senate candidates spent an average of $5.2 million on their campaigns, compared to $2.8 million spent on average by losing Senate candidates, according to the Center for Responsive Politics.[3] That year, successful House candidates spent an average of $650,000—triple the $210,000 spent by the average losing House candidate. Ninety-eight percent of all incumbents in the House were reelected. This does not mean that money alone buys elections; in many House races incumbents were reelected to safe seats that even a well-financed challenger would have had difficulty winning, given the realities of partisan gerrymandering. But money buys candidates their viability. It wards off potential challengers, particularly within the incumbent's own party. It suppresses the voices of financially weak candidates and constituencies. Money is often decisive, and it is perceived as such by incumbents and challengers alike.

The impact on governance is enormous. Those incumbents who worry about their reelection or political advancement naturally tend to the concerns of deep-pocketed donors, especially when the issues at stake are far from public consciousness. One can document a host of special favors sought by and granted to wealthy interests in recent years: business lobbyists delaying an increase in the minimum wage and tying it to exorbitant tax breaks for the wealthy; pharmaceutical manufacturers blocking efforts to reduce the prices of prescription drugs; bankers picking taxpayers' pockets to protect the cozy profits they make on student loans; credit card agencies skewing the bankruptcy code to make it harder for people to escape crippling debts; alcohol producers rallying to block tougher drunk-driving standards; health insurers and health maintenance organizations (HMOs) watering down attempts to regulate the managed care industry; polluters delaying the implementation of tougher air-quality standards and softening the White House's position on global warming; big airlines shifting ticket taxes onto the backs of frequent travelers and smaller airlines; and meat and poultry packers blocking proposals to strengthen food safety enforcement. The list goes on and on. In every case we find the narrow interests of organized money swinging the vote against the broader public interest.

No other single factor explains as well the upward redistribution of wealth engineered by both parties in the past twenty years. For example, almost one-third of the tax cut called for by the 1997 budget agreement went to the richest 1 percent of Americans—from whose ranks, according to the Joyce survey, come nearly 50 percent of big campaign contributors.[4] That bill also included a lucrative gift to a horde of corporations opposed to paying any taxes at all, at a cost of between $20 to $60 billion to the treasury over the next ten years. The chief beneficiaries of this elimination of the alternative corporate minimum tax had given candidates for Congress more than $13 million from 1995 through 1997.[5] When Congress finally voted to increase the minimum wage in 1996, it included in the bill a provision for $20 billion in tax breaks to an array of wealthy corporations.[6] (All of these handouts to corporations inevitably trickle up to the wallets of their shareholders, who are disproportionately of the upper class.) A follow-on proposal to increase the minimum wage by another dollar an hour was saddled with some $75 billion in tax sweeteners, most of them aimed at wealthy individuals.[7] When the president signed the IRS reform bill into law, he embraced a provision further cutting the tax rate on capital gains. More than three-quarters of this subsidy will go to the wealthiest 5 percent of taxpayers, from whose ranks come almost 80 percent of big campaign contributors.[8]

In the 1997–1998 election cycle, corporations, groups, and individuals representing business interests gave eleven times as much in campaign contributions as did labor interests. The finance, insurance, and real estate industries gave more than $150 million. Federal campaign contributions from heavy industries with the greatest interest in blocking and rolling back environmental regulations—oil and gas, mining, electric utilities, and automobiles—totaled $48.2 million, compared to just $814,712 from environmental groups. From 1997 to the present, the National Rifle Association and its allies have outspent handgun control advocates by almost twenty-three to one.[9] Of all of the special interest money given to congressional candidates, almost none represented the millions of Americans who are poor, or parents of public school children, or victimized by toxic dumping or agrochemical contamination, or who are small bank depositors, or people dependent on public libraries, transportation, hospitals, or housing.

"When powerful interests shower Washington with millions in campaign contributions, they often get what they want. But it's ordinary citizens and firms that pay the price—and most of them never see it coming." *Mother Jones? The Nation?* Actually, that quote comes from the editors of *TIME* magazine, which early in the presidential election year 2000 published a special issue[10] entitled *Money and Politics: Who Gets Hurt?* An article headlined "How the Little Guy Gets Crunched" summed up nicely what happens to those of us who don't contribute to political campaigns:

> You pick up a disproportionate share of America's tax bill. You pay higher prices for a broad range of products, from peanuts to prescription drugs. You pay taxes that others in a similar situation have been excused from paying. You are compelled to abide by laws while others are granted immunity from them. You must pay debts that you incur while others do not. You are barred from writing off on your tax return some of the money spent on necessities while others deduct the cost of their entertainment. You must run your business by one set of rules while the government creates another set for your competitors.

TIME also pointed out many of the special privileges that fall to the fortunate few who can afford to pay to play:

> If they make a bad business decision, the government bails them out. If they want to hire workers at below-market wage rates, the government pro-

vides the means to do so. If they want more time to pay their debts, the government gives them an extension. If they want immunity from certain laws, the government gives it. If they want to ignore rules their competitors must comply with, the government gives its approval. If they want to kill legislation that is intended for the public, it gets killed.

TIME magazine's conclusion: Our unjust system of public elections funded by wealthy, private interests gives us "government for the few at the expense of the many."

Of course, other factors influence policymaking in Washington (and in the statehouses). Special interests spend a huge amount lobbying the federal government—more than $1 billion each year. And Congress and the White House do occasionally pay some heed to the voters, particularly when an issue—such as tobacco or health care—is given wide coverage by the media. But here, too, wealthy interests have learned the value of expensive broadcast advertising and Astro Turf campaigns, and they have often managed to smother or stalemate seemingly powerful popular impulses for action.

THE SOLUTION

As the problem of money in politics has worsened and our knowledge of it has deepened, a growing network of activists and organizers have coalesced around a far-reaching solution that aims at the heart of the issue: candidates' dependence on private money to finance their campaigns. Obviously, not all people have the same amount of money. As long as money is a critical ingredient in elections, people with more money or access to wealth will have a distinct advantage and people with less will have a distinct disadvantage. And those who are thus handicapped include the vast majority of Americans.

Public financing of campaigns has long been the preferred solution of reformers, but for a long time many doubted that it could ever become law. Some still do. However, since the breakthrough victory by reformers in Maine in a 1996 ballot referendum (which was approved by a margin of 12 percent) and the concurrent creation of Public Campaign, a nonpartisan, nonprofit organization based in Washington, D.C., momentum has been building behind full public financing. Under Clean Money campaign reform, also known as Clean Elections, candidates who voluntarily agree to limit their spending and to reject campaign contributions from private sources can qualify for grants of full public financing for their campaigns. Primaries are covered as well as general elections, opening up the possibility for real competition within the parties, which is critical if we are to reduce the dominance of money in elections. Additional funds are also made available, up to a predetermined limit, if a Clean Money candidate is outspent by a privately financed opponent.

Because the system is voluntary, the Clean Money approach is in full accord with the Supreme Court's landmark *Buckley v. Valeo*[11] ruling, which struck down any mandatory limits on individuals' spending on their own campaigns as a violation of free speech. The *Buckley* court did explicitly approve of public financing systems that condition participation on voluntary acceptance of spending limits. So far, all legal challenges to Maine's pathbreaking experiment have been rebuffed in the courts, with the most recent victory having been scored at the federal Court of Appeals level in February 1999. (The opponents of Maine's Clean Election system declined to appeal that ruling to the U.S. Supreme Court.) But the fact that the system is voluntary shouldn't mean that few people would enlist. It is likely that many—if not all—candidates will opt for an approach that frees them from the fund-raising treadmill and offers them a competitive (though not unlimited) level of financing, free of special interest ties.

As of this writing, three more states have joined Maine in enacting a Clean Money–style system for their own elections: Vermont's legislature passed a bill covering statewide elections in 1997, and voters in Arizona and Massachusetts supported Clean Elections initiatives in 1998 (by 51–49 and 67–33 percent, respectively). The states of Missouri and Oregon also had strong campaigns under way to pass similar initiatives on the November 2000 ballot.

Although these efforts show a promising future for Clean Money reform in states where direct initiatives are possible, the Vermont victory shows that legislative campaigns also can also be won. In spring 2000, both houses of Connecticut's legislature enacted a Clean Money system for gubernatorial elections, only to see it vetoed by the state's Republican governor. That same spring, advocates succeeded in moving a Clean Money bill through the New Hampshire state senate and came close to winning in the assembly as well. A Clean Money "Impartial Justice" bill for the financing of judicial elections was approved by the Wisconsin state senate. In New Mexico both chambers of the legislature passed different versions of a bill to put a Clean Money amendment to the state constitution on the ballot, though the session expired before the two bills could be reconciled. More than 2,000 elected officials nationwide have endorsed this approach. One thousand have done so in North Carolina alone, including the state treasurer, 150 county commissioners, 500 town council members, and more than 200 mayors. Activists in all of these states are optimistic about how far they have already moved this issue in their legislatures, and they expect to deliver more Clean Money successes in the next few years.

Aiding in these efforts is the fact that Clean Money is no longer an abstraction. After surviving court challenges from right-to-life groups and the local chapter of the ACLU, the Clean Elections system is in full bloom in Maine. A total of 121 candidates for the state legislature qualified to run with Clean Elections financing in the 2000 election—nearly one-third of the total. Thirty-two percent of candidates who chose the Clean Election option were incumbents. Sixty-three percent of the Clean Election candidates were Democrats; 34 percent, Republicans; and 3 percent, Green Independents. A diverse array of new candidates came forward as a result of the new system—local civic activists, small-business owners, teachers, social service providers, and environmentalists. Many said that they would never have run if they had had to raise money the old-fashioned way. Many longtime incumbents voiced relief that they would no longer be seen as beholden to private donors, and relished the new opportunity they had to focus on their constituents and their concerns.[12]

The Clean Money system in Vermont also took effect for the 2000 elections, with several gubernatorial candidates—the incumbent Democratic governor, Howard Dean; a Republican, William Meub; and a Progressive, Anthony Pollina—seeking to qualify for full public financing for the election as this chapter was being written. Unlike Maine's, Vermont's system only covers statewide offices, with the expectation that state legislative offices will be phased in after legislators have a chance to study the statewide system. Arizona's Clean Election Act went into effect for 2000 as well; but a legal fight on a technical issue not pertaining to the public financing aspect of the law delayed the law's implementation, and therefore most incumbent state legislative candidates were unable to run under the new system. Still, as of late June, at least fifty-four candidates—one third of the total running—had announced that they were seeking to qualify for Clean Election funding. The Massachusetts state law, covering statewide and state legislative candidates, will go into effect for the 2002 elections.

According to a national survey of 800 likely voters conducted in late March 2000 by the Mellman Group, the Clean Money model enjoys robust support. "Now I'm going to read you a description of a specific proposal that some people say will change the way federal election campaigns are financed," the pollsters told respondents. "Under this proposal, candidates would no longer raise money from private sources. Instead, each candidate would receive a set amount of money from a publicly financed election fund. Spending by candidates would be limited to the amount they received from the fund." By a margin of 68 to 19 percent, voters supported the idea.[13]

Majority support for Clean Money crosses party lines: Democrats (76 percent in favor–15 percent opposed) and independents (71–14 percent) are most supportive; but Republicans also favor it by more than a two-to-one margin (59–27 percent). Even self-identified "conservative Republicans" favor it by almost twenty points (51–32 percent). Even after hearing all the arguments that opponents have made against Clean Money—that it is "welfare for politicians," that it will lead to higher taxes and cuts in more important social programs, that it will give money to fringe candidates, and that special interests will find ways around it— public support remained at the two-thirds level. Why? Because most people agreed with the counterarguments: that this is an important first step toward restoring democracy; that candidates should be chosen on the basis of their ideas, not their bank accounts; and that this proposal will level the playing field so good people with good ideas can get elected, even if they don't have connections to the rich and powerful.

A DIFFERENT APPROACH

As we look toward the future and envision how this reform will fare at the federal level—where Senators Paul Wellstone (D.–Minn.) and John Kerry (D.–Mass.) and Representative John Tierney (D.–Mass.) have introduced Senate and House versions of Clean Money legislation—it is important to understand what is different about the Clean Money approach to organizing and public education. To build the kind of coalitions and staying power we believe it will take to win, the issue must be framed around questions of power and equality, not just ethics in government. Instead of focusing on channeling private money's role in elections and punishing people who break such regulations, real reform must be seen as making it possible for candidates without access to wealth to run competitive campaigns for office. This means empowering average people in politics and making it possible for anyone who has grassroots support to have a chance at winning public office.

Talk about power and equality rather than rules and ethics naturally leads to the formation of reform coalitions that, although they include the traditional "good-government" groups and constituencies, are much broader and more populist in tone and style. Although groups like Common Cause and the League of Women Voters have been central to local Clean Money coalitions, many organizations that view the current system as unjust and unfair to their constituents, ranging from environmental and tenants' organizations to seniors and religious groupings, have also been key players. Local labor unions are often central partners; the national AFL-CIO endorsed the principles of Clean Money Campaign Reform in 1997.

In May 2000 the AFL-CIO executive council strengthened its stand, calling for a comprehensive, seven-part approach that included public financing of primary and general campaigns for Congress and the White House and limits on individual and PAC contributions solely to enable candidates to qualify for public funds. Leaders in the business community also have been prominent in state efforts, ranging from leading real estate developers in New York City to top executives in Massachusetts, Maine, and Washington state. Many issue constituencies, such as the environmental community, have joined in; and the approach is making inroads also among inner-city religious organizations and immigrant groups.

Grassroots organizations like Clean Money reform because it empowers anyone who can mobilize a large base of support behind a candidate, regardless of whether that candidate has access to money. Elected officials find it attractive—or at least some of them do—because it liberates them from the fund-raising rat race and the perception of conflict of interest that permeates the existing system. Public interest groups favor it because they see the potential of electing candidates not beholden to powerful special interests. Unions are coming on board because they understand that they can't compete in the money game and want to take a proactive approach to the issue. Some business leaders have begun to back reform because they are tired of participating in the campaign finance race and worry about its effects on public trust.

Of course, making democracy more people-centered than money-centered carries the possibility that others with a different definition of the public interest and real grassroots support, such as populist right-wingers and religious fundamentalists, will take advantage of the opportunity to fully finance their candidacies free of special interest influence. But this is what democracy is all about. Progressives should have the courage of their convictions and faith in the good sense of the American people, who, after all, favor many proposals for social and governmental action that are now blocked by the power of moneyed special interests.

Imagine the opportunities, once a Clean Money system is created for federal elections: Environmentalists in big states could put up their own leaders for Senate; defenders of beleaguered social programs could rally behind viable congressional candidates who aren't beholden to Wall Street. A tenant of a public housing project backed by ACORN could mount a serious run for Congress. The AFL-CIO could pull a presidential candidate from its own ranks. And all of these candidates would have enough funding to reach the voters in a serious way. Finally, we would have real choices on election day. The question is how to get from here to there.

What We've Learned So Far

There are five key components, we believe, to winning this fight: focusing on the problem of money in politics; rallying around a real solution; organizing to build broad coalitions and to energize grassroots activists; framing the message so as to win support from the general public; and gathering the resources to fight the antireform opposition head-to-head. All of these elements came together in the successful ballot fight in Maine; and although there is no one-size-fits-all formula for political action, the Maine experience offers a useful guide to activists in general.

First comes the need to concentrate public attention on the role of money in politics and on all of the problems it creates. Pioneering work in this sphere was begun by the Center for Responsive Politics in the mid-1980s (led by Ellen Miller). In the early 1990s, activists connected with the regional organizations Northeast Action, Western States Center, and Democracy South started producing and disseminating similar research on the role of moneyed interests in state politics. A prerequisite for such efforts is full disclosure of campaign contributions and spending; in many states, this is the first reform needed before any larger effort can get off the ground. Once such information is available, it is relatively easy to discover which industries and lobbies dominate the financing of campaigns, what sorts of special favors they have sought and gotten, how much it costs to run a successful campaign, and so on.

This groundbreaking research changed the way people think about campaign finance. Before the Center began analyzing and coding contributions from individuals by their industrial connections, most people thought the central problem was money from PACs. The media mainly wanted to focus on specific cases of political quid pro quo, even though it is hard to find a "smoking gun" showing exactly what an industry lobbyist sought from a congressional candidate or representative (or vice versa). The Center's research and the parallel work of state analysts changed the thrust of such inquiry.

Analysts discovered that more money was flowing from individual donors with clear connections to industry than from PACs, and that much of this interested money was concentrated on the legislative committees overseeing particular industries. That is to say, most money from the finance sector flows to banking/financial committee members, regardless of party; most agribusiness money goes to agricultural committee members, and so on. In comparing the ratios of actual giving by business interests versus labor interests, resource users versus environmentalists, and other, similar categories, many in the labor and environmental community began to see and to understand the need for campaign finance reform.

This new research also demonstrated clearly that the problem was not just a federal one. State-level projects discovered that the cost of campaigns for state legislative and statewide offices was exploding, in some cases at an even faster rate than for federal campaigns. Here, too, more money was coming from individual, interested donors than from PACs, and much of this money was targeted at key committees and legislative leaders. Analysts carefully documented the many key aspects of this problem: (a) campaigns that cost too much; (b) special interests that were buying special influence; (c) politicians who were stuck in a money chase that forced them to spend more time in fund-raising than in communicating with their constituents about substantive issues; and (d) good people deciding not to run because they could not raise the funds needed to be viable candidates.

In the late 1980s, a loose-knit group of veteran activists with years of experience in the peace, civil rights, and environmental movements—known as the Working Group on Electoral Democracy—spent several years studying the problem of money in politics. At the end of this period of study, they devised the Clean Money/Clean Elections solution. Only by creating an alternative way of financing campaigns, they reasoned, would it be possible to limit campaign spending, dampen special-interest influence, end the money chase, and make it possible for good people to run without being beholden to wealthy donors. Conversely, they saw that as long as campaigns remained privately financed—no matter what limits or other formulas (e.g., partial subsidies) one might use to level the playing field—nonwealthy candidates and voters would be at a distinct disadvantage.

But coming up with a solution on paper and bringing together the forces necessary to turn it into a reality are two different things. In Maine, the Dirigo Alliance, with the help of organizers from Northeast Action, spent four years painstakingly building a broad coalition of labor and business leaders, good government groups, environmentalists, seniors, religious groups, and current and former elected officials. By the time Maine Voters for Clean Elections rolled out 1,100 volunteers to collect 65,000 signatures in one day in November 1995—enough to qualify their initiative for the next year's ballot—it was a robust force in state politics. (Even the local chapter of the Christian Coalition was involved in some of the early coalition discussions. Although it later declined to support the final version of the initiative, that early participation apparently helped convince its leaders to stay neutral on the question rather than oppose it.) The importance of this base-building and coalition-forming work cannot be underestimated.

The next step is to frame the message in a winning way. Rather than focusing on the *mechanism* of the solution, public financing—a technical fix that tends to remind listeners of all the mind-numbing jargon around the campaign finance issue—it makes more sense to emphasize the problem and its solution. On its own, public financing does not command majority support in surveys. Only when it is tied to spending limits and the idea of candidates rejecting private financing does the concept receive robust levels of support. Thus, reformers learned to talk first about what their proposal would do rather than about how it worked, and to do so in the context of the problem. The phrases *clean money* and *clean elections* were invented by Northeast Action's organizers, responding to their early interactions with voters in Maine who said that these phrases described most clearly and simply what the campaign finance issue was all about. Reformers in other states have drawn on these lessons and applied their own insights, talking about "fair elections" and "political accountability" as well. The wisdom of this approach has been confirmed by several in-depth polls and by focus group research.

One significant and welcome result is that it has been somewhat harder for the defenders of the status quo to mobilize public opinion on their side. After all, who wants to support a system that most of the public views as "dirty"? In Maine, there was little organized opposition to the Clean Election initiative. In Massachusetts and Arizona the opposition, centered around the lobby shops that profited from the system in place, got a late start and found that reform advocates had adroitly painted them into a corner.

Another important ingredient to winning is making sure that the reform being proposed genuinely excites grassroots activists. For a long time, reformers have sought a victory in Congress based on an inside-the-beltway strategy of incremental improvements and legislative maneuvering and compromise. This is the essence of the McCain-Feingold bill, which has been whittled down over successive Congresses from a broad piece of legislation to a narrow ban on soft money. Initially, the bill would have given congressional candidates certain public resources (discounted advertising on television and radio) in exchange for their abiding by spending limits. In the face of opposition, those provisions were dropped, leaving a bill that mainly addressed soft money and electioneering "issue ads." Finally, in an effort to draw a few Republican votes, the Senate version of the bill was whittled down to a bare-bones prohibition against soft money. And yet McCain-Feingold was still blocked by Republican filibusters in the Senate, with few signs of any grassroots demand for its passage. When it comes to the campaign finance issue, the more comprehensive the solution, the greater the public support. Partial measures and complicated compromises generally do not have much grassroots pull.

All of these ingredients—problem, solution, coalition-building and message work, plus a serious emphasis on fund-raising—have come together in each of the Clean Money victories of the past four years. In Massachusetts, seven years of research, legislative drafting, coalition-building, and grassroots organizing culminated in a smashing election day triumph of 67 percent versus 33 percent. To the west, Arizonans for Clean Elections, formed just two years prior, was able to claim a 51 percent–49 percent win, despite the state's archconservative political climate.

The Massachusetts success demonstrated clearly that both ordinary citizens and civic elites could be activated to support a comprehensive reform of campaign financing. Six thousand volunteers contributed their time or small donations to the campaign. From the twelve members of the Massachusetts congressional delegation to the inner-city ministers, from Boston Brahmin civic stalwarts to the state's top labor leaders, the range of prominent public endorsers of the reform was phenomenal.

In Arizona, initial polling numbers showed voter support for the basic Clean Money concept equal to that in more liberal Massachusetts, a result due in part to years of well-publicized scandals in state government. Unlike their Bay State colleagues, however, the Arizona Clean Money campaigners had to battle an entire political establishment that was opposed to substantive change. Despite stern opposition from most political columnists, newspaper editorial boards, and a number of the state's leading elected officials, state reformers still emerged victorious.

GOING ON THE OFFENSIVE

Public Campaign was founded at the beginning of 1997 to nurture and expand these state-level campaigns with the goal of ultimately winning fundamental reform of the financing of federal elections. We have learned a lot from our engagement in the fight so far. First, it makes sense for reformers to go on the offensive. By reframing the debate and forcing opponents to defend a system that the public believes is amoral and corruptive, we can change the dynamic of the campaign finance issue. Activists can mobilize a broader base than just the good-government constituency and can build strong coalitions on the ground. But such efforts cannot be rushed. Even when we do our homework, victory is not always easy.

In Connecticut, for example, reformers led by the Connecticut Citizen Action Group, Democracy Works, and the local chapter of Common Cause successfully turned public outrage at a fund-raising scandal (involving a former state treasurer who was caught soliciting bribes in return for investing state pension funds and giving kickbacks to people who contributed to his campaign) into support for the passage of a far-reaching measure. But that was not enough to sway the state's conservative governor. And in Massachusetts, even the resounding two-to-one victory of the 1998 Clean Elections initiative has not deterred the Democratic leaders of the state legislature from trying to tamper with the law's implementation. Only vigilant and concerted efforts by Mass Voters for Clean Elections have prevented the powers that be from undermining the law, which is due to take effect in 2002.

And although 121 candidates have come forward to qualify for Clean Elections funding in Maine, this achievement would not have occurred without extensive legal work assisting the state in defending the law from court challenges, and ongoing efforts by the Maine Citizen Leadership Fund to educate candidates—incumbents and challengers alike—about how to run under the new law. The early reports from Maine suggest that the law is working well and candidates are enjoying the liberating effect of not having to spend any time raising private funds. The law has also led to a greater number of contested primaries than in 1998. But it will probably take several election cycles before its full effects on the political process in Maine are apparent.

Of course, we expect the success of Clean Money in the states to have a huge impact on all sorts of interested constituencies and national organizations that are, understandably, focusing their energies on other day-to-day priorities. Many of these groups have been in a defensive mode since the early 1980s, trying to preserve the last scraps of the safety net or to hold the tide against the radical dismantling of government. Most of them know that money plays a big role in shaping these fights, but they are so hard-pressed to hold the line that it is difficult to get them involved in a proactive reform effort.

Still, steady progress is being made. Since Public Campaign's inception, national organizations including the AFL-CIO, the ACLU, the Sierra Club, INFACT, Center for Policy Alternatives, USAction, the National Voting Rights Institute, and the Alliance for Democracy have all made full public financing a priority in their own work, as have several religious groups, including the Religious Action Center of Reform Judaism, Church Women United, and the Unitarian-Universalists. Many of these groups joined in Public Campaign's "Elected Leadership Project" last year, which resulted in more than 2,000 endorsements of the principles of Clean Money reform by elected officials at all levels around the country. The 1998 report "The Color of Money," which detailed how people of color are affected by the realities of campaign finance, opened a new front in the fight.[14] It was followed by a landmark conference at Howard University organized by the National Voting Rights Institute and the Howard University Law School, which gave birth to the Fannie Lou Hamer Project, a coalition of organizers dedicated to completing the work of the voting rights movement by achieving meaningful campaign finance reform.

As private money in elections continues to spiral out of control, new participants will be drawn into this cause. In the 1996 presidential campaign, campaign finance reform was not even an issue. In 2000, thanks to the efforts of John McCain and to a lesser degree Bill Bradley, it was a major factor in the primaries, with Republican voters assigning it a higher priority than abortion and education. Meanwhile, the arms-race mentality that leads many politicians to ever greater efforts to raise cash was generating more scandals, and these were leading to more public outrage and greater demand for change. This happened in Connecticut, as noted above, and in North Carolina, where the press reported that seats in government agencies were for sale to top campaign contributors. Now that more state-level campaign finance data are being computerized and analyzed by the National Institute on Money in State Politics, the ugly truths about private money's role at that level will become more accessible.

The biggest lesson in this fight is that there are no shortcuts. Changing how power works in America so that average people have more of a voice is no small task. If it were easy, it would already have been accomplished. In that light, there are a number of lessons to be heeded and steps that must be taken in the next few years as we build toward an ultimate victory at the federal level.

First, reformers have to treat this as a moral issue and a take-back-democracy fight, not a technocratic issue to be left to experts and insiders. We are not going to win sweeping changes in how campaigns are financed without mobilizing the broad public against the status quo, in the same way that the civil rights movement mobilized public opinion against segregation. This requires defining a clear and simple goal—creating an alternative way of financing elections so that ordinary, non-wealthy people can get elected and politicians will no longer be dependent on wealthy special interests—and keeping our eyes on that prize. Partial measures, like a soft-money ban, are helpful first steps toward that goal and can provide galvanizing victories to reformers. But banning soft money alone will not solve the problems of money in politics; making this the sole rallying cry of the campaign finance community would be like Rosa Parks saying that it would be all right with her if she could just sit in the middle of the bus. Nor should we accept trade-offs that compromise the central principle of empowering average people in politics.

Thus, it makes no sense for reformers to dabble with proposals that would close the soft-money loophole while opening wider the hard-money spigot, as has been proposed by some who want to triple the individual contribution limit from $1,000 to $3,000. At present, just one-quarter of 1 percent of the voting population gives more than $200 to a federal candidate or party committee. Only about 170,000 people give $1,000 or more. The financing of politics is out of reach for all but the very few in our society who can afford to pay to play. As journalist Bill Moyers said in a speech to the Center for Voter Education in Raleigh, North Carolina, increasing the individual contribution limit "would be like allowing the front-running racer to take steroids while hobbling those bringing up the rear." Polls show that the public's top priority for campaign finance reform is to limit the influence of wealthy special interests, not to increase it. When asked specifically about their attitudes toward raising the current limits on campaign contributions, voters are strongly opposed. Fewer than one in ten voters (9 percent) support raising the limit to $3,000, according to the March 2000 Mellman poll cited earlier. Over half (51 percent) want to keep the current limit, and almost a third (30 percent) favor reducing the limit to $500.

This also means more aggressively challenging the defenders of the status quo. A good example of this occurred when activists led by the New Hampshire Citizens Alliance "crashed" a Concord news conference that had been called by a group of conservative Beltway organizations in September 1999. The conservatives, led by Grover Norquist of Americans for Tax Reform, were there to denounce the McCain-Feingold bill and the bill's lead sponsor, Senator McCain, who was then languishing in the single digits in the state polls. Wearing buttons reading "79%"—the percentage of New Hampshirites favoring campaign finance reform, according to a recent poll—the activists overwhelmed the Washington lobbyists and effectively showed how out of touch these insiders were with their own base on this issue.

Second, reformers shouldn't be fooled by their press clips or lists of endorsers or even by their victories. Achieving a democracy where average people have as much chance to win office as the rich will be a struggle at every stage. A comparison here with the nationwide movement to ease voter registration laws, which reached its height with the passage of the motor-voter bill in 1993, is instructive. Like the Clean Money fight, the voter registration movement, centered around the organization Human Serve (founded by Frances Fox Piven and Richard Cloward), began with a focus on state-level victories. Starting in the early 1980s, several sympathetic state governors including those of Ohio, New York, and Texas issued executive orders mandating expanded voter registration efforts in state agencies (e.g., motor vehicle registration and social service offices).

A number of other state legislatures also passed similar laws. Then several national organizations, notably the League of Women Voters, the ACLU, the NAACP and the NAACP Legal Defense Fund, and Rock the Vote, made it a legislative priority. The bill narrowly passed in Congress, only to be vetoed by President Bush. Later, following President Clinton's election, the National Voter Registration Act became law.

But although most state motor vehicle agencies have complied with the law, making it significantly easier for anyone with a driver's license to register to vote, implementation by social service agencies has been spotty at best. Piven and Cloward's vision of tens of millions of poor people entering the active electorate has not come to pass, though the voter rolls have grown since the law's passage. One problem has been tremendous bureaucratic resistance from rank-and-file agency workers—many of whom are overworked and underpaid. None of the institutional players who might have put more muscle behind implementing the law to its fullest—the public employees' unions and the state Democratic parties, in particular—have pushed to change this reality.

The lesson for the Clean Money movement is that it is not enough to prevail in a legislative battle; you must also have the power to win the war of implementation. Entrenched interests will oppose change at every stage, and other influential actors will be happy to offer symbolic victories without real content. Thus, there is no substitute for building real and sustainable grassroots capacity at the state and local levels. Like easier voter registration laws, Clean Money is just a tool. Tools can do nothing by themselves; they need gardeners to pick them up. Of course, we think Clean Money systems will make the gardeners' work easier and more fruitful. But still, the ultimate effect of having these new tools will come only if people decide to use them.

Third, the growing movement needs to devise more intermediate steps around which people from across the country can unite. Although winning and implementing Clean Money at the state level remain the core building blocks at this stage of the struggle, there are other tactics to try that would further build the movement's visibility and capacity. The right fights can make you stronger, heightening attention to the problem, drawing in new allies, and honing public understanding of the issue. And smaller victories demonstrate power. This might involve targeting a particularly large donor and calling for a boycott of its products—"Don't Buy X Until They Stop Buying Politicians." Or it might involve coordinated efforts around the country focused on a particular issue, such as the role of pharmaceutical company campaign contributions in keeping prescription drugs too expensive for most Americans. Another idea is to organize among political donors who are disgusted with the process. Though Clean Money activists are already linked in a daily way through the Internet and E-mail—www.publicampaign.org is a gateway to the movement—they have only begun to scratch the surface of the possibilities for organizing through this new medium.

Direct action aimed at exposing the day-to-day money chase, whether through street demonstrations and theater or through nonviolent civil disobedience, is another route to explore. Starting in fall 1999, the Alliance for Democracy, a progressive, populist group with chapters around the country, began a series of rallies in Washington, D.C. that culminated with activists demonstrating inside the Capitol Rotunda and getting arrested while trying to read statements indicting Congress for "crimes against democracy." In conjunction with Earth Day 2000, more than thirty people were arrested, including Doris Haddock (the ninety-year-old woman known as "Granny D," who walked across the country for campaign finance reform); writer Bill McKibben; and the leaders of several major environmental organizations, including the Rainforest Action Network and Ozone Action. These actions have gained ever greater amounts of public support and media attention. Civil disobedience was also pivotal in defending the Clean Elections Act in Massachusetts. Historically, no great movement for social change has ever succeeded without some pressure in the streets, where people put their bodies on the line to block or at least dramatize an injustice.

Fourth, Clean Money has to become an electoral issue. Republican Senator Mitch McConnell likes to say that where a politician stands on campaign finance reform has never made the difference in any election. After Senator John McCain's surprisingly strong showing in the 2000 primaries, this claim has less credibility. Until McCain dropped out of the race, close to 10 percent of Republican primary voters cited campaign finance reform as the single most important issue affecting their vote, according to the Voter News Service exit polls. Upwards of three-quarters of them voted for McCain—a voting bloc larger than the pro-life vote. The issue outranked abortion and education in its importance among Republican primary voters and was among the top four or five issues cited by them overall. McCain's ability to draw votes from across the political spectrum was another indication that the public is ready to support a bold challenge to the campaign finance status quo—or at least to use a politician's position on campaign reform as a prism through which to judge his character.

The Mellman Group's March 2000 poll also found that opposition to campaign finance reform could cost a member of Congress on election day. By a margin greater than two to one, voters said that they are likely to vote against a candidate who opposes Clean Money–style campaign reform. Indeed, a third of voters said they would be less likely to vote for a candidate who is of the same party and agrees with them on most issues but opposes this proposal. A third of the electorate may be willing to strike out against congressional representatives with whom they share other fundamental political positions, if the reps desert the banner of real reform.

This proposition has yet to be tested in the field—but it will be in the coming years, as Clean Money activists in the states start focusing more attention on their federal representatives. Organizers are beginning the process of identifying swing districts where resources should be targeted and where members of Congress may be susceptible to grassroots pressure around the issue of sweeping campaign reforms. Ideally, any effort to target individual members would be linked to pressing more of them to sign on to federal Clean Money legislation.

Fifth, reformers need to keep activating the activists, as there are many connections still to be made. When the leaders of several environmental groups in Connecticut stood on the Capitol steps in Hartford on Earth Day 2000 and described the just-passed Citizens Elections reform bill as the most important piece of *environmental* legislation passed that year, the moment represented the best kind of coalition work seen yet by the campaign finance reform movement. Faced with barrages of concentrated cash, environmentalists have not given up the battle to translate public opinion into better public policy on the environment; but many also have become committed supporters of far-reaching campaign finance reform. In 1999, the Sierra Club national board voted to endorse the principles of the Clean Money model—namely, full public financing for candidates who abide by spending limits. "The main reason many politicians side with the polluters is their never-ending need for campaign cash," said Sierra Club President Chuck McGrady. "Public campaign financing will eliminate the influence of donors who want to weaken environmental laws, and it will shift power back to voters and volunteers." Now the Sierra Club is working with Public Campaign to engage a broader array of environmental groups in the campaign reform cause.

It takes time to build committed partnerships. In just over three years, campaign reform advocates have made similar headway within the religious community, with labor, and with seniors' organizations. But much more can be done, starting with additional research connecting more issues to the need for Clean Money–style reform. For example, although the "Color of Money" report was effective in documenting the extent to which communities of color are shortchanged by the present campaign finance system, more work needs to be done relating this fact to specific issues like public school funding versus prison construction; nutrition and local health services; and the linkage between the difficulties minority candidates have in raising sufficient funds from private sources and their underrepresentation in government.

In general, we have to keep working to connect this issue to concrete, day-to-day concerns, and reach ordinary people with that message. Public Campaign's E-mail bulletin, "OUCH!—How Money in Politics Hurts You," regularly goes out to thousands of activists and journalists, with timely analyses of current legislation and political issues.[15] Both John McCain and Bill Bradley showed that the public can be rallied to the cause of campaign finance reform when it is directly connected to issues such as health care, taxes, education, and military reform. Activists in Iowa and New Hampshire took this approach further than ever before with last year's presidential primary, producing several newsmaking reports on key issues such as prescription drugs and Social Security, and culminating with a twelve-page voter guide entitled "They Give—Guess Who Pays?" that was distributed to over 250,000 New Hampshire voters. Senator Russ Feingold has begun a similar service by his "Reading of the Bankroll" during Senate debates on major pieces of legislation—making public the names of the largest contributors with an interest at stake. But much more can still be done to spread this message further.

Sixth, we need to keep working to convince more people that the Clean Money solution is viable. In this fight, hope is our biggest ally and cynicism our biggest enemy. The more people feel that nothing can be done and that big money will always rule, the harder it is to convince all the audiences that matter—activists, organizers, elected officials, elites, the media, and funders—that change is coming and is worth supporting. This is why the implementation of Clean Money reform in state government is so important. As Walter Karp wrote in his book, *Indispensable Enemies:*

There is in this Republic one great wellspring animating citizens to act in their own behalf: their own understanding that by means of politics and government what is wrong can be righted and what is ill can be cured. In a word, political hope.

The very opposite condition, the condition safest for party power, is public apathy, gratitude for small favors and a deep general sense of the futility of politics. Yet there is nothing natural about political apathy, futility and mean gratitude. What lies behind them is not "human nature" but the citizens' belief that politics and government can do little to better the conditions of life; the belief that they are ruled not by the men whom they have entrusted with their power but by circumstances and historical "forces," by anything and everything that is out of human control; the belief that public abuses and inequities are somehow inevitable and must be endured because they cannot be cured.

The condition of public apathy and futility, however, is swiftly undone by reform and even by the convincing promise of reform. Every beneficial law reminds the citizenry anew that the government—which is their government—can help them remove evils and better the conditions of life. Every law that remedies an abuse reminds the citizenry that other abuses can be remedied as well. Every beneficial law rips the cover of inevitability from public inequities and rouses the people from apathy. Reform in America does not bring passive contentment to the citizenry. It inspires active hope.[16]

The earliest indications from Maine's first election under the Clean Elections law do inspire hope. Far more candidates than expected stepped forward to seek Clean Elections financing, and all but one succeeded in qualifying for funding. Their comments about the process (House candidates had to collect fifty five-dollar contributions and signatures; Senate candidates had to collect 150) tell us we are on the right track:

- "Without Clean Elections I couldn't even think about running for office. I just couldn't afford it," said Shlomit Auciello (Democrat, challenger), self-employed artisan.
- "The main reason I did it was that this is what people want. I thought about what would happen if someone—either a person or some outfit—gave me $250, then told me how I ought to

vote. I figured I'd have to take into account my own conscience, how people in the district feel, and this donor. At least now I've eliminated one of them."—Chester Chapman (Republican, challenger), owner of a small machine shop

- "Even people who didn't know me believed so strongly in Maine Clean Elections that they wanted to help. I had to ask people to stop sending in the checks!"—Linda Clark Howard (Democrat, challenger), retired schoolteacher and community volunteer
- "I spent a lot of 'kitchen table' time explaining the system to people. Once they knew what it was, they really liked it. They like that it means no soft money and no PAC money will be used. I want to work for the people of Maine and I don't want to be beholden to anyone else."—Glenn Cummings (Democrat, challenger), director of an education nonprofit
- "It will definitely change some things. For one thing, I'll have about half the amount of money I raised last time, but much more time to talk with people, which is a good thing."— Gabrielle Carbonneau (Republican, incumbent), registered nurse
- "We have an obligation to put into practice the system that was approved by voters in 1996. Maine is in the lead in this area. It will only work if it is used, and it is important for incumbents to embrace it. Also, the Clean Election Act is making it easier to recruit candidates to run for office."—Rick Bennett (Republican, incumbent), Assistant Senate Minority Leader and a candidate for reelection

Over the next few years, the movement for comprehensive campaign finance reform will expand along all of these fronts. But no one is under any illusion that a Clean Money, full public financing system can be won for *federal* elections in the current political context. And the voter registration battle shows the danger of "winning" merely by passing legislation, without the ability to ensure a law's implementation and enforcement. Thus it is far better to keep building the base and finding ways to unite activists across the states than it is to stake all on a premature move to the level of the U.S. Congress. Even a Democratic takeover of Congress is not a guarantee of victory—recall how the Democrats failed to pass even a modest reform bill when they controlled the House and the presidency in 1993–1994. Only a strong, broadly based, grassroots movement will be able to keep the pressure on and ensure that Congress does the right thing.

In this vein, having a committed president, ready to elevate attention to this issue, will obviously also be critical in the end. The president can do much to advance the cause even before we get to that point. He can go out of his way to link the issue to the bread-and-butter concerns of the American people, so that it becomes harder for wealthy special interests to continue purchasing special legislative favors through their campaign contributions. He can appoint a high-level "democracy advocate" or citizens' commission empowered to push for greater attention to reviving citizen engagement in politics. And he can "walk the walk" by embracing the Clean Money initiatives that are under way in the states, helping make sure that they are fully implemented, and holding them up as models for reforming congressional and presidential elections.

Winning Clean Money campaign reform at the federal level will be a huge victory that will transform the calculus of politics. And yet, we must conclude by pointing out that this reform is not a panacea. Concentrations of money and economic power will still influence politics through lobbying, independent expenditures, think tanks, and the like. Other reforms will be needed before anyone can claim that we have a democracy that works. Equal access to the media, same-day voter registration, fair ballot access for third-party and independent candidates, and some form of proportional representation or instant-runoff voting will still be needed to fully open the system. But even without those reforms, Clean Money will make dramatic changes in how candidates run for office and who gets elected. It will enhance the influence of grassroots organizations on politics and reduce incumbents' susceptibility to pressure from powerful donors, thus making other much-needed policy changes more likely. This is clearly the gateway reform.

NOTES

1. Center for Responsive Politics, "The Big Picture: The Money Behind the 1996 Elections."

2. John Green, Paul Herrnson, Lynda Powell, and Clyde Wilcox, "Individual Congressional Campaign Contributors: Wealthy, Conservative, and Reform-Minded," a survey funded by the Joyce Foundation of Chicago and conducted by researchers at Georgetown University, the University of Akron, the University of

Maryland, and the University of Rochester (1998), available on line at www.opense-crets.org/pubs/donors/donors.htm.

3. Center for Responsive Politics, "The Big Picture: The Money Behind the 1998 Elections."

4. Citizens for Tax Justice, "Tax Plan Violates President's Principles," news release (July 31, 1997), available on line at www.ctj.org/html/final.htm.

5. Citizen Action report cited in Cecil Connolly, "Tilting the Balanced Budget: Six Industries That Gave a Total $35 Million Each Benefited From Package, Group Reports," *Washington Post* (August 22, 1997).

6. Eric Pianin, "How Business Found Benefits in Wage Bill," *Washington Post* (February 11, 1997).

7. Citizens for Tax Justice, "Senate GOP Minimum Wage Hike Provides $75 Billion in Upper-Income Tax Breaks," news release (November 8, 1999), available on line at www.ctj.org/html/mwsen.htm.

8. Citizens for Tax Justice, "Brief Description of and Comments on the 1997 Tax Act," news release (August 1997), available on line at www.ctj.org/html/desc97.htm.

9. Center for Responsive Politics, "The Big Picture," 1998.

10. *TIME Special Issue, Money and Politics: Who Gets Hurt?* (February 7, 2000).

11. Supreme Court, *Buckley v. Valeo*, 424 U.S. 1 (1976).

12. Public Campaign, "Clean Money in Action" (June 14, 2000), available on line at www.publicampaign.org/articles/br_maine6_14.html.

13. Memo from the Mellman Group, available on line at www.publicampaign.org/articles/4–3report/report4_3_00.html.

14. The full report is available on line at www.publicampaign.org/ColorOf-Money/index.html.

15. To subscribe to OUCH! free of charge, send a one-line E-mail message reading "subscribe ouch" to majordomo@linuxcare.com.

16. Walter Karp, "Indispensable Enemies: The Politics of Misrule in America," *Harper's Magazine* (October 1993).

13

A MOVEMENT FOR ECONOMIC SECURITY IN AN AGE OF CHANGE

Roger Hickey

In June 2000, Republican presidential candidate George W. Bush proclaimed his support for privatizing part of the Social Security system. Bush said he would divert a portion of payroll taxes to pay for private stock market accounts, a plan likely to require slashing guaranteed benefits by over 50 percent for future retirees.[1] Some political observers expressed surprise that Bush would dare to tamper with Social Security, often called the "third rail" of American politics because "if you touch it, you die. But candidate Bush's decision to make Social Security privatization a centerpiece of his run for the presidency is only the latest milestone in a long campaign, financed by Wall Street and other financial interests, to convince Americans that the entire social insurance system is financially unstable and that Social Security, Medicare—even health coverage for the uninsured—can best be accomplished through market mechanisms.

The pervasive impact (inside the Washington beltway) of this conservative worldview, which has already won over most leaders of the Republican party as well as many "New Democrats," can be explained partially by the influence of political contributions from Wall Street brokerage houses, health maintenance organizations (HMOs), insurance companies, and other special interests. These political contributors stand to benefit from a national policy that would shift trillions of dollars of Social Security taxes to private accounts, turn Medicare into a voucher system dominated by HMOs, and provide health coverage through "medical savings accounts." But in recent years, an increasing number of financial and corporate interests have gone beyond giving money to politicians in order to achieve specific policy changes. Through their support for conservative think tanks and public policy propaganda organizations, they have underwritten an even more ambitious effort to change the context of American politics: a long-term campaign to undermine the public's faith in government's ability to do anything well, especially when it comes to improving economic opportunities, and to conjure up a future in which we are all on our own—to make it or to fail in the marketplace.

This bold new political crusade might well succeed if the majority of Americans fit the demographic profile most often celebrated these days by the media: the dot.com millionaire. However, most Americans live from paycheck to paycheck. Most of us have family responsibilities that consume virtually all of our income—from raising children to caring for aging parents, from paying on a mortgage to trying to save for retirement or college tuition. And although most of us believe in the American dream, we have just lived through decades of real declines in wages and family incomes, during which only those families with more than one breadwinner were able to maintain their incomes. For a long time, the question most Americans asked of their government representatives was, Will you make life *worse* for my family? But in recent years, they have begun to demand action on a more activist agenda that could actually make life better. A new majority coalition is emerging that rejects the conservative, antigovernment ideology and instead supports bold, pragmatic initiatives that can help provide economic security in an age of change.

In an important new book, *America's Forgotten Majority: Why the White Working Class Still Matters,*[2] Ruy Teixeira and Joel Rogers examine the lives and voting habits of the majority of white Americans who don't have a college degree. They remind us that this vast lower-middle class, which even today represents 55 percent of the electorate, at one time joined with African Americans and others to form the backbone of support for the New Deal and for the Democratic Party's post–World War II activist economic program. This program included the GI bill; public investments in roads and housing loans that created the suburbs;

and the universal, single-payer health insurance program for all Americans over age 65, known as Medicare.

The tragedy of American politics from the 1960s onward is the way in which opportunistic politicians, from George Wallace to Richard Nixon to Ronald Reagan, managed to use issues such as busing, welfare, and affirmative action—as well as the pitched battles over Vietnam and cultural change—as political wedges to split large portions of the white working class away from their natural home in the Democratic Party. But equally tragic has been the failure of Democratic Party leaders to offer an activist government solution to the economic dislocations experienced by all working Americans. Teixeira and Rogers argue that a new, progressive economic agenda that offers hope, opportunity, and economic security to hard-pressed working families could unite the forgotten majority with African Americans, Hispanics, and other Americans struggling to attain or retain middle-class economic status. The result could be a majority for change that would transform American politics. It's been a long time coming.

From the mid-1970s to the early 1990s, Americans were buffeted by economic dislocations that left the vast majority running upward on a downward wage escalator, struggling just to stay even. From 1973 until 1998, the hourly wage of a typical worker in production and nonsupervisory jobs—essentially, the non-college-educated worker—declined by 6 percent.[3] Looking back on this period, experts now generally agree that this unprecedented wage and income reversal—and the resulting polarization of wealth and income—was the result of economic shocks and bad macroeconomic policies, the destruction of good manufacturing jobs (by technological change, import competition, and U.S. corporations shifting production abroad), and the weakening of labor unions' ability to bargain for higher wages. Whatever the cause, in the 1970s and 1980s many workers looked to their traditional allies in the Democratic Party and discovered they were not offering much help for struggling families. Reagan and the Republicans likewise offered no activist government solutions. They promised tax cuts, which mainly helped the rich, and they promoted "traditional values." Many working Americans—especially those who didn't identify with the civil rights gains of the 1960s and 1970s—decided to vote for a tax cut and more than a decade of conservative rule.

Bill Clinton won the presidency in 1992, with a campaign that pledged to put people first. He promised to help those Americans who "work hard and play by the rules" and still find themselves slipping backward. His agenda included expanding domestic investment for education, fighting child poverty, rebuilding public infrastructure, and establishing a new system of lifelong job training. Perhaps most importantly, he promised universal health insurance. Eight years later, Clinton's record was mixed. His failure to get his health care plan through Congress, and his unwillingness to sell his economic program as the progressive tax-the-rich plan that it actually was, led directly to the devastating loss of the Democratic Congressional majority in 1994 and to an aggressively conservative new Congress led by Newt Gingrich. Clinton also quickly discovered that keeping the economy growing had a price: Federal Reserve Board chair Alan Greenspan was willing to lower interest rates, but only if Clinton gave up his public investment agenda and focused exclusively on deficit reduction. In recent years, economic growth has finally turned wages upward again even for the forgotten majority and for the poor. Ironically, although the growing economy is expected to produce enormous federal surpluses—estimated at $1.87 trillion (just counting the non–Social Security surplus) over the next decade—the federal government has become wedded to the conservative fiscal goal of eliminating the entire national debt by 2012. This Calvin Coolidge–style economic plan will leave little money for innovative ideas to help working Americans who are still recovering from long decades of declining wages and stagnant incomes.

After Democrats lost control of Congress in the 1994 elections, Bill Clinton benefited politically from the extremism of the new ultraconservative Republican Congressional majority led by Newt Gingrich. The great majority of Americans, who want to see education funding increased, were appalled when Gingrich tried to abolish the Department of Education. Most voters of all economic and age groups also reacted negatively to his attempts to radically gut environmental protection laws. And the number of Americans who strongly support Medicare and Medicaid turned out to be far larger than the small group of ideologues who wanted to drastically cut those programs or replace them with so-called market alternatives. By standing up in defense of these popular government programs (in a battle that the conservative New Democrats advised him not to fight), Clinton not only won support as the populist champion of the people; he also demonstrated the limits of conservative, antigovernment extremism.

More sophisticated conservatives, such as George W. Bush, learned from this experience. The newly retooled "compassionate conservative" campaign to roll back government marketed a much slicker and somewhat more moderate-sounding package—with churches and charities expected to take up the slack. But voters have been showing signs that they want practical help, not antigovernment ideology and a small tax cut. They are increasingly putting the politicians on notice that they need and expect the active assistance of government in the struggle to meet family responsibilities and achieve a little economic security. And the politicians, of whatever party, will have to respond.

For example, in the same speech in which George W. Bush called for Social Security privatization, he also endorsed turning Medicare into a voucher system. His argument—supported by many conservatives but disputed by other experts—was that the Medicare system was financially overextended and that a voucher system would cut expenditures. At exactly the same time, Bush and his party were vying with the Democrats to add a prescription drug benefit to Medicare. The fact that the Republican version of this new entitlement would cost an estimated $40 billion over five years[4] did not even give them pause. The polls show that millions of retirees are financially strapped because they must pay too much for drugs, and the politicians, liberal and conservative, are scrambling to appear to give the voters what they want.

The Next Agenda makes the case that a new era of government activism may be building, driven by citizens and voters who are experiencing economic pressures. As the authors explain, relief for working families will require that the public sector create new protections, public investments, social insurance, and opportunity-fostering institutions that an individual or a family simply cannot manage on their own. Ironically, many of the economic insecurities driving this new wave of activism are the direct result of the triumph of the conservative worldview in the Reagan, Bush, and Clinton years.

It is impossible to deny that the world is becoming more economically integrated. But the uniquely conservative and free market model that has dominated U.S. politics in the past several decades has meant that Americans have been exposed to the destructive forces of globalization in a way that citizens of other industrialized economies—in Europe and Japan—have not. Americans have lived through the period when other nations, such as Japan, seemed to "eat our lunch" in one industrial sector after another, causing huge dislocations. Then U.S. corporations learned to get "lean, mean, and competitive," moving production offshore, downsizing, and outsourcing. The result has been continuing economic upheaval on a large scale: the loss of good jobs, a war on unions' ability to enforce wage increases (or organize new workplaces), and a rising level of insecurity as jobs shifted to the new (generally, nonunionized) service sector and the volatile new information sector. Some have reaped large rewards from the change. Consumers have enjoyed a flood of less expensive goods. But most workers have ended up working longer hours, with less security—even in a time of low unemployment.

Advocates of aggressive global integration sometimes acknowledge that their version of extreme capital mobility has its domestic and international costs—in lost jobs, declining wages, economically devastated communities, and eroded environmental standards. Occasionally they even make the case, if only as an afterthought, that the U.S. government should invest in "adjustment policies" to retrain workers, rebuild affected communities, and create new economic opportunities so that the "benefits" of global trading regimes may be shared by the immediate losers as well as by the obvious winners. As *New York Times* columnist and author Thomas Friedman wrote, "I believe you dare not be a globalizer in this world, . . . an advocate of free trade and integration, without also being a social democrat, ready to spend what it takes to bring the have-nots, know-nots and left-behinds along—otherwise they will eventually shut the doors on you."[5] One might well doubt the sincerity of this posture, and at the same time challenge the globalizers to put their money where their op eds are. But it is also possible to be in favor of trade between nations, while opposing trade deals and international organizations that protect only commercial rights and that ignore the need to guarantee minimal labor and environmental standards. As described by Robert Borosage and William Greider in Chapter 2, critics of globalization are forming international alliances to demand new rules—and new governing institutions—for the global economy. As they demonstrated in Seattle, trade unionists, environmentalists, advocates for the poor, and community leaders are learning to use the power they have to "shut the doors" in order to demand real, legislated commitments from the globalizers.

JOBS FOR ALL AND INVESTMENT IN THE FUTURE

Former Labor Secretary Robert Reich argues that the moral core of American capitalism can be summarized in the following three principles:

1. Any adult needing to work full-time deserves a full-time job.
2. That job should pay enough to lift that person and his or her family out of poverty.
3. People should have the opportunity to move beyond this bare minimum by making full use of their talents and abilities.[6]

We don't have to take a poll to know that most Americans would agree with these simple principles. In a rapidly changing economy, they can be the basis for a national consensus about an important mission of government: helping all citizens achieve economic security.

The full-employment economy Americans have enjoyed over the past several years has reminded us once again how virtually everything in society works better when everyone has an opportunity to work. A booming economy has reversed the long-term decline in wages for middle-income and low-income workers, bidding wages up at the same time as it has expanded economic output and has given employers incentives to invest in improving productivity (both of which hold down prices). In April 2000, unemployment reached a low of 3.9 percent, well below the 6 percent level most mainstream economists had predicted would trigger inflation—and prices remained stable. The experience of recent years not only demonstrates the benefits of full employment; it should bring home once again the enormous waste—in destroyed human opportunities, in rising crime rates, in lost economic output—that will come with the next significant rise in unemployment, whether it is caused by tight monetary policies of the Federal Reserve Board or by government's excessive focus on paying down the federal debt.

Having tasted the benefits of full employment once again, working Americans are likely to demand prompt government action—from lower interest rates to public spending on jobs-creating projects—to counteract any new indications that the economy might move into recession. Once again, after the long conservative period of laissez-faire economic policy, the public is likely to expect government to take action to sustain economic growth when a downturn looms.

But what are the longer-term actions that government can take to continue to sustain robust, noninflationary growth based on increasing productivity? Conservatives have a simple solution: reduce taxes, cut back government, and get out of the way of the private sector, and the economy will boom. A new book entitled *Growing Prosperity*, by Barry Bluestone and the late Bennett Harrison,[7] gives a more complicated but more commonsense answer. Bluestone and Harrison assert that the technologies and scientific breakthroughs responsible for the productivity growth of today's information-driven, new economy are the results of smart public investments—in computer and space technologies, education, and public infrastructure—supported by a government preoccupied with beating the Soviets in the arms race and in space exploration in the 1950s, 1960s, and 1970s. Just as the Eisenhower administration's public spending on the interstate highway system made commerce more efficient, public investment in the new global highway of the Internet, made possible by the defense department's pioneering investments, has become the driver of economic growth in today's private sector.

Even the Democratic administration under Bill Clinton seemed to have forgotten that history. With the annual deficit wiped out and the booming economy producing record surpluses, both Clinton and Gore were fixated on using most of those surpluses to eliminate the entire federal debt! As my colleague Robert Borosage noted, "It is as if a prosperous couple decide to devote their rising incomes to paying off the mortgage on the house, even though they don't have adequate health insurance, are raising one child in poverty, couldn't afford to send another to college, haven't repaired leaks in the basement and have retired parents who can't afford the drugs they need."[8] If policymakers want to ensure good jobs and opportunities for the next generation of Americans, they are going to have to turn away from a budgetary policy that is more conservative than Herbert Hoover's. Some investments in the future are even worth going into debt for, just as a family with a mortgage might take out an education loan to make sure that their kids have the skills to achieve a better life.

As Jeff Faux wrote in Chapter 1, the political debate must be refocused on America's future. What kinds of public investments should be made now, to ensure that the full-employment economy the United States enjoys today is not a brief moment followed by declining growth and shrinking job opportunities? Polls show that even upper-middle-class Americans experiencing the greatest financial benefits from the current boom reject the conservative option of cutting taxes and favor a strategy of public investments—especially in education, health research, and other areas likely to enhance continued growth.

Any attempt to describe an investment agenda for a more prosperous future must also grapple with the thorny problems involved in protecting the environment and controlling global warming. As Robert Wages and

Carl Pope assert in Chapter 9, if a certain kind of industrial process or chemical must be banned or reduced for the sake of the planet, then a Just Transition policy is needed to compensate the workers and communities involved. As Peter Barnes and Rafe Pomerance explain in Chapter 10, the cost of raising energy prices to reduce global warming can be recaptured and given back to families in a way that is progressive, stimulates the economy, and pays for an adjustment fund. The transition to a nontoxic, renewable, and sustainable economy will require planning, incentives, and new investments in a new generation of clean industries in the United States and around the globe. The good news is that these new investments will stimulate a new generation of sustainable growth and good jobs as well.

JOBS THAT PAY ENOUGH TO LIFT A FAMILY OUT OF POVERTY— AND OPPORTUNITIES TO MOVE BEYOND A BARE MINIMUM

The vast majority of working Americans are struggling to get by from paycheck to paycheck. Many go without health insurance. Working mothers struggle to find and afford good child care for their kids. In the past, those who earned just a little too much to qualify for "poor people's programs" resented what they saw as subsidized or free benefits enjoyed by those on welfare. Welfare reform hasn't solved any of the problems of the poor or the working middle class; but it has, in some ways, put everyone in the same boat. The new requirement that all able-bodied citizens must work has transformed those previously seen as the undeserving poor to the deserving poor, because they are working or looking for work. It makes sense to help those who find a job, by providing the supports necessary to help them keep it and at the same time making sure the job pays enough to keep a family out of poverty. It also makes sense to provide these supports for everyone who needs them.

There is a growing possibility of forging a broadly based political alliance to demand public programs that help all working Americans— even if they help those in poverty the most. Examples of such programs are a universal guarantee of health care for all who need it, and child care for mothers going off welfare, as well as for dual-earner, middle-class couples struggling to maintain family income. As Heidi Hartmann argues in Chapter 5, the United States could even decide, as have some European countries, to support all mothers (or fathers) who need time off from work in order to raise their children.

Universalizing programs like health care and child care might create a greater demand for limited services; but it is equally likely that making these services respectable entitlements would result in improved quality standards and increased funding. The immediate instinct of reformers thus far has been to try to cover the poorest of the poor, or to provide for "kids first." But as Theda Skocpol argues in Chapter 3 of this book, and in her new book *The Missing Middle*,[9] a patchwork quilt of health insurance programs in which children are treated under one program, the elderly under another, and working adults in yet another (if they are covered by any program at all) can be confusing and intimidating for families, and might also undercut broad political support for the goal of reliable coverage for all. While working to improve the immediate conditions of children and the very poor, policymakers and advocates have an opportunity to build support also for universal programs that establish a reliable and politically popular floor below which no one will be allowed to fall.

As Reich says, most Americans would agree with the moral principle that those who work full-time should not only have the respect of their fellow citizens but also should be able to escape poverty. Welfare reform throws a spotlight on how few jobs in the American economy actually pay enough to keep a worker (or a family) out of poverty.

There was a time, back in the 1960s, when a person working full-time at the federal minimum wage was able to earn enough to keep a family with two children above the federal poverty line. Over the past thirty years, the minimum wage hasn't kept up with inflation, although in the past decade the new Earned Income Tax Credit (EITC) has generally made up the difference for those families who know how to apply for it. The EITC is an effective program; but as economist Jared Bernstein points out, it has shifted the responsibility for making jobs pay an above-poverty wage from employers to taxpayers. The minimum wage should be increased and indexed to inflation—this is a proposition that polls show is surprisingly popular, even among those who are not directly affected by minimum wage policy.

As a matter of justice, the minimum wage makes common sense. So does the idea that women should be paid as much as men working in the same jobs or comparable jobs. Powerful coalitions are building around the country to enforce this simple idea. As Heidi Hartmann points out in Chapter 5, if men and women were paid equally, more than 50 percent of low-income U.S. households would rise above the poverty level. Public policy—prodded by citizen action—ought to focus both on creating good new jobs and upgrading existing jobs so that they pay a wage that can keep individuals and families out of poverty.

There was a time when automobile assembly jobs brought a low wage, before it dawned on Henry Ford that paying his workers decently meant they would be able to afford to buy his cars. Later, Walter Reuther and the United Auto Workers (UAW) fought the auto companies (including Ford) to form a union that would guarantee good wages, benefits, and working conditions. A union can make the difference between a poverty-level job and a middle-class job; and in some areas of today's economy, a revitalized labor movement is getting back to organizing, winning victories that will eventually transform bad jobs—for example, in the growing service sector—into good jobs with decent incomes, benefits, and respect.

As David Moberg elaborates in Chapter 11, the rights of Americans to join and be represented by a union are violated daily in this country by employers and by the authorities who should be enforcing existing laws. If the majority of Americans believe that a full-time job should pay more than the poverty-level wage, then the combination of wage and benefit and labor laws should raise standards and empower workers trying to exercise their constitutional rights to be represented by a union.

Since the antigovernment conservative movement is also strongly antiunion, it is going to take a political movement of powerful proportions to improve the nation's labor laws. But just as the movement for civil rights couldn't change the law until it reminded the nation of the injustice of segregation through sit-ins and street demonstrations, so too the organizing drives of the labor movement can inspire support from the general public—reminding everyone of the justice of a basic demand for a decent wage—and winning victories for workers. The new AFL-CIO, under the leadership of President John Sweeney, has placed top priority on expanding union organizing in all areas of the economy. And the recent successes of the Service Employees International Union's drive to unionize janitors in Los Angeles and elsewhere can serve as an inspiring model for mobilizing workers in a way that wins the support of the wider community for labor rights and economic justice.

As Moberg describes, the growing movement for a "living wage" has pushed for new local laws around the country establishing the idea that public money—and public subsidy of private companies—should not be used to create jobs that leave workers in poverty. The importance of these dynamic new living-wage movements far exceeds the actual impact of their specific ordinances. The movement represents a way for activist citizens to use the power of government to declare publicly the principle that all workers should be paid a living wage—and that all workers should have the right to join together in a union.

REJECTING THE ATTACK ON GOVERNMENT, AND EXPANDING SOCIAL INSURANCE

The idea of social insurance, represented in the United States by Social Security and Medicare, is that there are certain basic human needs—such as health care, retirement security, or insurance against disability—that are so essential to everyone that the government should create a common risk pool to provide a reliable basic entitlement for all. By anybody's calculation, Social Security and Medicare have been an enormous success. Before they were established, seniors were America's most impoverished group. Today, although nobody gets rich on Social Security, it has virtually wiped out poverty among the elderly, providing at least 50 percent of retirement income for at least two-thirds of all seniors. And its benefits, unlike those of most private retirement plans, are indexed to protect against inflation.

Social Security also insures individuals against loss of income due to disability and pays benefits to families whose principal breadwinner dies. These additional social insurance features make Social Security much more than a retirement system. And Medicare, an incredibly effective single-payer health plan for everyone over age 65, ensures that all seniors have access to doctors and hospitals, no matter what their income.

If your goal is to weaken the public's faith in government programs in general, it makes sense to try to undermine and then dismantle Social Security and Medicare. For the past decade and longer, the financial industry and other powerful interests have mounted a lavishly funded public propaganda campaign with the aim of partially privatizing Social Security by diverting a portion (usually 2 percent or more) of payroll taxes to pay for private accounts that would be invested by individuals in stocks or bonds. Since Social Security is a pay-as-you-go system in which today's taxes pay for today's retirees, diverting a portion of taxes creates a shortfall—unless the benefits going to current recipients are reduced. Even conservative privatizers are not that crazy. Virtually every plan they have ever proposed promises to make sure those now retired (and people about to retire) get their full benefits. To make up for the decades-long period when the new system would be paying full benefits to retirees (until they die off) while also building up the private accounts, most privatization plans would dramatically cut guaranteed benefits for future retirees—today's young and middle-aged workers.

How do you convince young workers to give up their guaranteed benefits? One way is to convince them that Social Security is already bankrupt and that they will never see their benefits anyway. And so, for years, American workers have been exposed to a chorus of Cassandras led by Wall Street broker Peter Peterson and assorted propagandists from the right wing Heritage Foundation and the libertarian Cato Institute. Their arguments are now mind-numbingly familiar. They start by claiming that the huge baby boom generation will bankrupt the system (ignoring the fact that Congress raised payroll taxes in 1983, which means that the boomers are paying extra to build up a surplus that will pay for their own retirement). They then sound the alarm about the Social Security trustees' projection that without adjustments, the system might be able to pay only 75 percent of benefits after the year 2037. So eager are the privatizers to predict this shortfall, that they rarely if ever note that the trustees' projection is based on an economic growth rate of only 1.7 percent per year. If the economy continues to grow at a more robust rate, the future shortfall is greatly reduced or eliminated.

The goal of the privatizers is to convince Americans to take a big portion of their Social Security benefit (which is now fully indexed to rise with inflation and guaranteed for life) and trade it for an investment in the stock market, which might go up or down. That is why they go on and on about the great returns to be expected in the market. You should always beware when someone swears that you will make money, but won't back up those claims with a guarantee. Economists Dean Baker and Mark Weisbrot[10] have noted that the typical privatizer's predictions about great future stock market performance are premised on a future economic growth rate much greater than the 1.7 percent growth on which privatizers base their scary stories about Social Security running into a serious shortfall. But they can't have it both ways. If the stock market is going to continue to boom, then the economy will be growing fast enough to keep Social Security healthy indefinitely.

In the 2000 election debates, Al Gore countered George W. Bush's privatization scheme with a proposal that would give all Americans an opportunity to save for retirement (with a government match for low-

and middle-income families) via a new supplemental retirement savings account. Gore told voters that under his plan full Social Security benefits would be maintained and that he would not raid Social Security taxes to pay for it. This modified version of Clinton's Universal Savings Accounts would be financed instead from the federal budget surplus. Politically, Gore's proposal was effective, since it offered people additional savings opportunities without dismantling Social Security's core benefits.

Bush was ahead in the polls before he laid out his plan for privatizing Social Security. Gore, backed by a powerful grassroots movement, repeatedly reminded voters of the value of the basic social insurance principles behind Social Security, and explained how Bush's plan to divert a portion of Social Security taxes to fund private accounts would undermine economic security for most Americans. As the 2000 campaign season heated up, local citizens' coalitions—led by labor, women's groups, seniors, and civil rights groups—made the Bush privatization plan a defining issue in campaigns for congressional seats. Candidates who refused to sign a Pledge to Protect Social Security and Medicare[11] were confronted at every campaign stop by angry citizens opposed to Bush-style privatization.

As noted earlier, it is a strange conservative crusade against social insurance that tries to dismantle Social Security and cut and voucherize Medicare at the same time as it tries to expand Medicare (to the tune of $40 billion over five years) in order to add a prescription drug entitlement. The Democrats, of course, correctly charged that the conservative Republican plan, put forward just as the Democrats were getting some traction on the issue, would subsidize private insurance companies to provide this benefit, and that the plan was an unworkable public relations ploy. Republican members of Congress, most of whom embrace conservative principles (i.e., the free-market, antigovernment jihad), must have believed they had no choice but to come forward with a plan full of subsidies and public spending in order to compete for the support of the voters.

Several years ago, when conservatives were happy to let the free market provide prescription drugs for seniors, a small group of progressive activists and experts began to talk publicly about the reality most elderly people were already dealing with. Modern medicine increasingly works its wonders through prescription drugs, and the prices charged by pharmaceutical companies in the United States are among the highest in the world. So a number of citizens' groups (e.g., local affiliates of USAction and the National Council of Senior Citizens) started conducting and publicizing regional drug price studies. Soon they were taking seniors on bus trips to Canada and Mexico, where they could buy drugs at lower prices. When progressive politicians, such as Chicago's Congresswoman Jan Schakowsky and Michigan senatorial candidate Debbie Stabenow, started going along on those trips—or organizing highly publicized trips of their own—the pages of the Congressional Record started filling up with speeches on the need for a Medicare drug benefit. And soon the national media started covering the issue too. This is an issue born of real-world need combined with effective citizen action.

Americans are having serious problems with all aspects of health care, not just with prescription drugs. In Chapter 4, Theodore Marmor and Jonathan Oberlander recount the reasons why health care is back on the national agenda: The ranks of the uninsured have continued to grow (44.3 million in 1998, an increase of 1 million in only one year);[12] health care inflation continues to rise; and the level of dissatisfaction (on the part of patients and physicians) with the quality of medicine as practiced and controlled by HMOs and insurance companies is reaching the point of national rebellion, forcing the idea of a Health Care Bill of Rights—including the right to sue HMOs—into the first tier of hot political issues. The founders of Social Security and Medicare always saw a national system of health insurance as the next major step in the building of a social insurance system in America. For years, doctors joined with insurance companies and other interests in opposing what they called "socialized medicine"; but the experience of having their medical judgment repeatedly overruled by a clerk on the phone from the HMO headquarters has brought most doctors over to the side of patients and consumers.

An important turning point in the 2000 elections occurred at the Democratic convention, when Gore reintroduced himself to the American public as a populist crusader, willing to fight "for the people, not the powerful." Political pundits are still expressing surprise at the way Gore set up the issues for the fall campaign, stealing Ralph Nader's thunder on HMO reform, standing up to the big pharmaceutical companies on prices and Medicare prescription drug benefits, rejecting Wall Street's plans for Social Security privatization, and pledging to prevent big oil from plundering the environment. Gore was attempting to win over potential Nader voters, but more importantly he was presenting himself as a fighter on "kitchen table" economic issues important to key Democratic supporters: labor, women, seniors, and minorities. The fact that these issues play well with low- and middle-income "swing voters" means that Gore could at the same time consolidate his base and reach out to people who don't identify with either political party because for many years they haven't seen the system helping them or their families. Now that the elections are over, the job of a new progressive movement is to force the politicians to deliver on their promises to working families.

In today's economy the private market is clearly not doing a good job at providing decent, affordable health care. The private market also is not providing nearly enough high-quality child care, or enough jobs that pay a living wage, or a private pension system workers can count on, or good job training for people starting to work or for those who have lost their jobs. If the free market could do a good job by itself in providing these things, they would not be the problems that they are for families of all income levels. And in many ways, the globalized free market, unrestrained by national or international rules, is helping undermine jobs, the rights of labor, the nation's social insurance system, and its ability to protect the natural environment. In these and many other areas of life, Americans are starting to realize that progress will require an active government role, not an antigovernment crusade. And today activist groups are working hard, with some success, to put these issues on the political agenda.

THE OUTLINES OF THE NEXT AGENDA FOR ECONOMIC SECURITY

Is it possible to put together a political program that average middle-class and low-income Americans would see as making a real difference in their lives? We believe the ideas presented in this book can provide a start, although they are not comprehensive and the details are open to debate; these are basic propositions, backed by moral values. If it is true that many Americans today are looking to build a stronger nation and seeking greater security for their families, then a straightforward agenda like the following could mobilize a new majority.

> *Take special interest money out of democracy.* The new progressive movement must be premised on a populist pledge to clean up America's politics. Americans are sickened by the spectacle of corporations and the wealthy buying elections and bribing government officials. If we as citizens want a public sector that

fights for working families, then we must break the special interests' stranglehold on politics.

*The United States should be a force for global justice and sustainabil-
ity.* Just as the Progressive movement of the previous century reformed American capitalism, a new worldwide movement is
growing to demand new rules for the global economy. Americans must make their government an international force for
higher standards in employment, environmental protection, labor and human rights, and sustainable economic development—so that the global economy benefits the many, and not
simply the few.

*Everyone should be able to get a job that provides a decent income
and benefits.* Americans should work to ensure that everyone
able to work can get a job, and that every full-time job pays at
least enough to keep a family out of poverty. Public policy
should expand opportunity and close the growing wage and income gaps in the United States.

*Equality for all, and action to redress injustice, should guide eco-
nomic policy.* Past discrimination has robbed generations of
women, African Americans, and other minorities. Americans
should require wage equity by law and take affirmative steps to
assure jobs, education, and economic opportunities to low-
income victims of past injustice.

Workers have a right to a voice at work. The U.S. government should
encourage unionization in order to raise wages and foster
democracy. It should be illegal for employers, the state, or anyone else to prevent workers from exercising their constitutional
rights. America needs a citizens' movement to support organizing by pressuring corporations and by passing stronger labor
laws.

All Americans should have guaranteed health care coverage. Decent,
reliable health care—and health insurance—should be available to all Americans. The federal government should move toward universal coverage through incremental but substantial
steps that will quickly lead to a guarantee of coverage for all.

*We should support families and provide quality, affordable child care
for all.* U.S. economic policies (and now welfare policies) have
led to more and more parents working, whether they want to or
not. America has a huge child care shortage. We should create a

national system to assure quality child care for every child and every family that needs it. Federal and state governments should build comprehensive support systems for families of all kinds, starting with paid family leave.

All Americans should have adequate income and security in retirement. Social Security should be preserved and strengthened as the most reliable element of our retirement system. We must defeat those who would undermine Social Security's guaranteed and inflation-indexed benefit or harm social insurance for survivors and the disabled. We should improve Social Security benefits for women. And we should do more to require corporations to provide good pensions to their employees, and to make it easier for people to save for retirement.

Everyone should be entitled to a good education. Education should be our top priority. We must assure adequate and equal funding for public schools, and the federal government should play a much larger role. Teachers should be paid more, and both teachers and students should be held to higher standards. We must attack child poverty and rebuild poor communities to ensure every child a decent chance. And college should be affordable to all.

Job training and retraining should be available to all. In today's economy, training and retraining are essential. Every young person starting out in the job market, and everyone leaving welfare, should have access to good job training. And those who have lost their jobs, for whatever reason, should be able to learn new skills in order to get a good new job.

Revival of urban areas must be a goal for federal, state, and local governments. The economic and social health of American cities is crucial to the health of the entire country. A metropolitan economic strategy uniting cities and inner suburbs should be encouraged in order to foster high-wage, "high-road" economic development.

Global warming must be controlled via a Just Transition strategy that protects workers and communities and that invests in a new generation of green growth. The United States should be a leader in forging an international strategy on global warming, investing in the green technologies crucial to markets of the future. We should capture and pay back to citizens the costs of higher energy prices through a "sky trust" system of pollution auctions, using some of the revenue to assure the successful transition of affected workers and communities.

Americans should make the social investments needed for a healthy economy and for future growth. Citizens should demand investments in the essential services our economy needs today and in the new technologies, education systems, infrastructures, and workforces that are essential to future economic growth, jobs, and productivity. The private sector can't do it all, and wise action by the public sector will require a national debate about the kind of future Americans want to build. If we conduct this debate, the democratic system will be invigorated, a good balance between development and the environment will be struck, our children will have a better future, and the private sector will flourish in a sustainable economy.

A POLITICAL MOVEMENT FOR SECURITY IN AN AGE OF CHANGE

This book is part of a very ambitious project: Its authors' goals go beyond making a small impact at the margins of policy debates in Washington. It is not enough to stave off or even defeat the corporate antigovernment crusade. We want to help build a citizens' movement rooted in democratic activism and united around an agenda for greater economic security and opportunity for all.

The propositions outlined here and in the preceding chapters represent our attempt to articulate a bold program, simply but with moral force, that might make our fellow citizens want to be part of such a movement. As an organizing document, this agenda is in need of debate, rewriting, and testing in the real world. But work on the project it outlines is also important, because real political change is unlikely to happen unless we combine the power of ideas with the power of political activism.

Progressive political activism is alive and well in the United States. Every city and town has a rich culture of community-based organizations, some working for economic development and neighborhood improvement, some working to defend and advance the rights of minorities or women, and some attacking a multiplicity of economic and social problems through involvement in local and statewide politics. These local activist groups are often tied together by state-level and regional think tanks, lobbying coalitions, and progressive strategy groups. Many are linked in national networks by the labor movement; civil rights organizations, such as the NAACP, the Urban League, or NOW; or citizen action networks, such as USAction. Increasingly, the Internet has empowered these organizing networks, linking like-minded activists and allowing them to share information almost instantaneously.

As rooted as they are in local issues, these groups are often galvanized to work together by some impending threat or national opportunity. Over the past several decades, new models of effective political action have emerged from an ongoing dialogue between grassroots organizing groups and national campaigns. Based on these new models, a new progressive force has been evolving. Here are some examples:

- An organized citizens' campaign convinced Clinton and Gore to oppose Social Security privatization. For more than a year, Clinton's New Democrat friends had been urging him to embrace privatization as part of his Third Way philosophy. The Campaign for America's Future mobilized a powerful coalition of leaders of groups representing the base of the Democratic Party—organized labor, civil rights groups, women's organizations, disability activists, seniors, and young people. We coordinated academic analysis of the various privatization plans, forging working relationships with progressive think tanks—the Center on Budget and Policy Priorities, the Economic Policy Institute, and the Century Foundation, among others—and with individual scholars. We prepared and distributed educational materials. We tapped the organizing power of the Internet via a Web site and an innovative E-mail listserver communications system. The AFL-CIO organized community summits on Social Security in cities and towns around the country, in which local leaders of coalition educated their grassroots memberships—and communicated with the press and with their members of Congress. Local and statewide citizen coalitions to save Social Security worked the issue, especially in key primary election states such as New Hampshire. In December 1998, activists held a huge press conference in Washington, where leaders such as Jesse Jackson, the AFL-CIO's John Sweeney, and

NOW's Patricia Ireland joined with experts to send President Clinton the message: Don't privatize Social Security. Subsequently, during his State of the Union speech in January 1999, Clinton declared his opposition to privatizing Social Security. It took all that work just to prevent a Democratic president from doing the wrong thing! But the effort resulted in a real victory. Along the way, Vice President Gore and his staff learned something about defending Social Security. And perhaps most importantly, a national network of like-minded activists learned to work together to change the minds of the president of the United States and of his designated successor on an issue that all parties cared about passionately.

- The prescription drug issue—and the patients' bill of rights— were put on the national political agenda by a similar coalition, involving many of the same players. They have forced politicians of both parties to scramble to find a politically popular position that at least appears to address those issues. After the election, these networks, combining national organizations, local community groups, think tanks, and policy groups, will build on their election-year organizing to defend the social insurance system and to fight for further progress toward universal health care.

- The Invest in America coalition has been working more than a year to unite national and local groups to fight for expanded public investment, and to challenge the notion, strongly promoted by Gore, that the great bulk of the federal surplus should be used to pay off the national debt as quickly as possible. This investment coalition holds great potential for leading a nationwide debate on investment priorities in the post-deficit, post–Cold War era.

- The Seattle Coalition, which rocked the WTO and other global institutions, is evolving into a multifaceted movement to make the United States a force for global justice, uniting labor and environmentalists (Teamsters and turtles) with church people working to cancel Third World debt, farmers fighting for sustainable agriculture, and students following the link between sweatshops abroad and the policies of U.S. corporations.

No single organization or coalition encompasses all of the progressive activity now under way. But as the authors of this book emphasize in every chapter, the goals of that activity are as closely linked as are the causes of the problems Americans confront as citizens. Many systemic problems, such as the influence of money in politics, thwart individual efforts for change and demand that citizen-activists develop a common strategy. And a victory on just one issue—or even breakthrough visibility, like that achieved in Seattle—helps advance the common cause. We hope *The Next Agenda* will help promote widespread discussion of ideas and strategy among the large number of overlapping networks of activist citizens.

It is time for the progressive movement to become a more visible and more self-conscious force in national politics. For many decades, the political left in America has carefully worked for change, issue by issue. Certainly it has had some successes—most notably, in the passage of civil rights and women's rights legislation and in environmental regulation and cleanup. But even these examples remind us that major progress in a democracy is most often won through mass movements— the civil rights movement, the women's movement, the environmental movement—that make large and visible moral claims on society and that organize all parts of society in order to build a consensus for change.

When the "Seattle coalition" shook the world for a few days in 1999, it wasn't just their dramatic civil disobedience that caught the attention of the media and the public; it was also the new alliance we represented. Suddenly, tree-hugging environmentalists were joining with unionized hardhats—and with Third World human rights and development advocates—in a force that challenged the legitimacy of powerful global institutions and simultaneously counterposed an alternative vision of the global economy. This was clearly a force to be reckoned with.

The conservative movement of the 1980s was certainly not cautious about its goals. Reagan didn't offer Americans tax reform; he conjured up a vision of a "shining city on a hill," and transformed a ragtag army of conservatives into a force capable of rallying a majority of voters. Today even conservative Democrats claim to be after a larger vision of a new economy. Progressives need to come together around a bold set of ideas that are as big as Americans' vision of their country and its potential.

The Next Agenda was published just as a new president and a new Congress were inaugurated. But no matter who is in the White House and which party controls Congress in the coming years, a strategy of progressive coalition-building makes sense. Even under a Democratic president, activists learned that they had to join together in order to counter policy that would take the country in the wrong direction. But although a defensive strategy is important, it is not enough. Progressives must also work together to carry a bold alternative vision to their fellow citizens.

The lesson of the Clinton presidency is that unless progressives organize independently, they will have no leverage and no power. If we become fragmented, with each group tending only to its own favorite causes, we will have no more influence on fundamental battles over the direction of the nation than do isolated advocates or dissenters. If progressives can do no more than generate ideological background noise, they will be ignored, and others will capture the political agenda. We must try to forge a common strategy around a larger vision of political and economic change.

If progressives want to frame the political debate of the next four years—and the next twenty years—we must take our agenda for change to the American people. We are living in an age of disturbing and sometimes threatening changes but also a time of great possibilities. Most Americans have come to the conclusion that the antigovernment crusade waged by ideologues will not benefit them or their families. They are hungry for leadership that will tell the truth about the corporate interests that now run the U.S. government, and they will support a crusade to clean out the corridors of power. What they want is someone with a plan to harness the incredible productivity of the U.S. economy in order to build a stronger society and a more just and equitable nation. And growing numbers are starting to conclude that politics as usual won't get them what they want. So now is the time to get to work on the next agenda. It's time to build a political force that will fight to produce greater security and opportunity for America's working families—and for global justice and environmental sustainability for the world.

NOTES

1. Henry J. Aaron, Alan S. Blinder, Alicia H. Munnell, and Peter R. Orszag, "A New Analysis of Governor Bush's Individual Account Proposal: Implications for Retirement Benefits," Institute for America's Future report 10/16/00, available online at www.ourfuture.org/SSAnalysis.asp.

2. Ruy Teixeira and Joel Rogers, *America's Forgotten Majority: Why the White Working Class Still Matters* (New York: Basic Books, 2000).

3. Lawrence Mishel, Jared Bernstein, and John Schmitt, *The State of Working America: 1998–99* (Armonk, N.Y.: M.E. Sharpe; Washington, D.C.: Economic Policy Institute, 1999).

4. Joanne Kenen, "House Panel Passes Medicare Drug Bill," *Reuters*; *Los Angeles Times* (June 22, 2000).

5. Thomas Friedman, "Winners, Don't Take All," *New York Times* (May 19, 2000).

6. Robert B. Reich, "Working Principles: From Ending Welfare to Rewarding Work," *American Prospect* (June 19–July 3, 2000).

7. Barry Bluestone and Bennett Harrison, *Growing Prosperity: The Battle for Growth with Equity in the 21st Century*, a Century Foundation Book (New York: Houghton Mifflin, 2000).

8. Robert L. Borosage, "Prosperity Knocks," *Los Angeles Times* (February 7, 2000): A17.

9. Theda Skocpol, *The Missing Middle: Working Families and the Future of American Social Policy* (New York: W. W. Norton, 2000).

10. Dean Baker and Mark Weisbrot, *Social Security: The Phony Crisis* (Chicago: University of Chicago Press, 1999).

11. For more information on the pledge campaign, go to www.signthepledge.org. The pledge reads: "I pledge that I will defend and strengthen Social Security and Medicare for the 21st Century. I will oppose privatizing Social Security. This means I will oppose replacing Social Security's guaranteed benefits with private investment accounts. I will oppose diverting Social Security tax revenues to fund private accounts. And I will oppose efforts to reduce Social Security retirement, survivor and disability benefits, cut annual cost-of-living adjustments, or increase the retirement age; I will support measures to lower poverty rates among elderly women by increasing and improving their Social Security benefits; I will oppose all efforts to turn Medicare into a privatized voucher system or to force beneficiaries into managed care plans (HMOs). I will also support using budget surpluses to strengthen Medicare and Social Security. I will also support providing prescription drug benefits to all Americans covered by Medicare."

12. Jennifer A. Campbell, *Health Insurance Coverage 1998* (Washington D.C.: U.S. Census Bureau, 1999).

Contributors

Peter Barnes is an entrepreneur and writer who has started and run several successful businesses (including, most recently, Working Assets Long Distance) and has published numerous articles and books. His latest book, *Who Owns the Sky? Our Common Assets and the Future of Capitalism*, is due from press in spring 2001.

Robert L. Borosage is codirector of the Campaign for America's Future. Previously he founded and directed the Campaign for New Priorities, a nonprofit organization calling for reinvestment in America in the post–Cold War era. He writes widely on economic and national security issues for publications including the *New York Times*, the *Washington Post*, the *Los Angeles Times*, and the *Nation*, and is a frequent commentator on television and radio news shows. He has served as an issues adviser in a number of electoral campaigns, including those of progressive U.S. senators Carol Moseley-Braun, Barbara Boxer, and Paul Wellstone. In 1988, he was senior issues adviser with the presidential campaign of the Rev. Jesse L. Jackson. Borosage is a graduate of Yale Law School and holds a Master's Degree in International Relations from George Washington University.

Lynn A. Curtis was a Ph.D. candidate at the University of Pennsylvania when he was chosen to work on the President's National Commission on the Causes and Prevention of Violence, in 1969. Thirty years after that historic effort, he is now president of the Milton S. Eisenhower Foundation—the "keeper of the flame" for the work begun by the Kerner Commission in 1968. He is a former urban policy adviser to the U.S. Secretary of Housing and Urban Development, former director of President Carter's Urban and Regional Policy Group, and author or editor of nine books. His most recent book, coedited with Fred R. Harris, is entitled *Locked in the Poorhouse: Cities, Race, and Poverty in the United States*.

Jeff Faux is president of the Economic Policy Institute (EPI), a Washington, D.C. think tank that analyzes economic issues from the perspective of working Americans. He has written, lectured, and consulted widely on the political implications of economic trends. His most recent book is *The Party's Not Over: A New Vision for the Democrats* (Basic Books, 1996). Faux has practiced economic policy with the U.S. Department of State as well as the Departments of Commerce and of Labor and the U.S. Office of Economic Opportunity. He has held local political office in Maine; has been a manager in the finance industry; has run a small business; and has been active in numerous citizen and community organizations and in several trade unions.

Stanley B. Greenberg founded and now heads Greenberg Research, a survey firm that conducts social research on strategic issues for organizations and corporations. He served as polling adviser to President Bill Clinton and his 1992 electoral campaign as well as to Prime Minister Tony Blair, Prime Minister Ehud Barak, President Nelson Mandela, and President Thabo Mbeki. He also has advised a broad range of U.S. congressional campaigns and was pollster for the Democratic National Committee. Greenberg is the author or editor of many books on social and political change, including *Middle Class Dreams* (1995) and *The New Majority: Toward a Popular Progressive Politics*, the latter coedited with Theda Skocpol (1999). Greenberg founded his research firm in 1980, after a decade of teaching at Yale University. He was educated at Miami University and at Harvard University, where he received his Ph.D.

William Greider, national affairs correspondent for the *Nation* magazine, has been a reporter for more than thirty-five years for newspapers, magazines, and television. Greider was previously national affairs editor at *Rolling Stone* magazine. He is a former assistant managing editor at the *Washington Post*, where he worked as a national correspondent, editor, and columnist. He is the author of the national bestsellers *One World, Ready or Not: The Manic Logic of Global Capitalism; Secrets of the Temple: How the Federal Reserve Runs the Country;* and *Who Will Tell The People*. Greider also has served as a correspondent for six *Frontline* documentaries broadcast on PBS, including *Return to Beirut*, which won an Emmy in 1985. Greider graduated from Princeton University and currently lives in Washington, D.C.

Heidi Hartmann is director of the Washington-based Institute for Women's Policy Research (IWPR), which she founded in 1987 to inform and stimulate debate on issues of critical importance to women. At IWPR she has coauthored several reports, including: *The Impact of Social Security Reform on Women; Unnecessary Losses: Costs to Americans of the Lack of Family and Medical Leave; Women's Access to Health Insurance;* and *Combining Work and Welfare: An Antipoverty Strategy*. Hartmann has delivered congressional testimony and is frequently interviewed by television, radio, and print journalists. She also currently chairs the National Council of Women's Organizations' Task Force on Women and Social Security, and co-chairs the Economists' Policy Group on Women's Issues.

Roger Hickey is codirector of the Campaign for America's Future, and director of the New Century Alliance for Social Security and Medicare. He is also one of the founders of the Economic Policy Institute, where he served as vice president and director of communications. In the early 1970s Hickey helped start the Public Media Center, a public interest advertising agency in San Francisco that continues to produce advocacy campaigns for labor and environmental groups and for citizens' organizations. During the Carter administration, he was codirector of the COIN Campaign, a consumer-labor coalition that tried to convince President Carter to deal directly with the economic problems of inflation, high interest rates, and unemployment. A graduate of the University of Virginia, Hickey began his career in the 1960s as an organizer for the Virginia Students' Civil Rights Committee and the Southern Students' Organizing Committee.

Bruce Katz is director of the Brookings Institution's Center on Urban and Metropolitan Policy, and a senior fellow in its Economic Studies Program. He is former chief of staff, staff director, and senior counsel of the U.S. Department of Housing and Urban Development. He is the author of *Beyond City Limits: The Case for Metropolitan Solutions to Urban Problems;* "Moving Beyond Sprawl: Toward a Broader Metropolitan Agenda," with Amy Liu (*Brookings Review*, Spring 2000); and "Divided We Sprawl," with Jennifer Bradley (*Atlantic Monthly*, November 1999). His current projects include *Reflections on Regionalism; Metropolitan Case Studies;* and *The State of Welfare Caseloads in America's Cities: 2000.* Katz has received degrees from Brown University and Yale Law School.

Theodore R. Marmor has been on the faculty at Yale University since 1979, and is now professor of public policy and management at the Yale School of Management; professor of political science; and (since 1993) director of the Robert Wood Johnson Foundation's postdoctoral program in health policy. He has authored or coauthored eleven books and has published more than one hundred articles in a wide range of scholarly journals. He is a frequent op-ed contributor to the *Wall Street Journal, New York Times, Washington Post, Los Angeles Times,* and *Boston Globe.* His most recent book is the second edition of *The Politics of Medicare* (2000); the first edition of this book became a classic and launched his career in Medicare policy. His other recently published books include *Understanding Health Care Reform* (1994); *Why Some People are Healthy and Others Are Not* (1994); and *America's Misunderstood Welfare State* (Basic Books, 1992), coauthored with Yale colleagues Jerry Mashaw and Philip Harvey.

Ellen S. Miller is president of Public Campaign, an advocacy organization dedicated to encouraging campaign finance reform through a grassroots strategy. Prior to founding Public Campaign in 1997, she served for twelve years as executive director of the nation's premiere money-in-politics research organization, the Center for Responsive Politics. Miller also worked for the Center for Responsive Law and the Center for Auto Safety and spent six years in two senior congressional staff positions. She is a regular commentator in the media on campaign finance reform and government ethics. She also serves on the boards of the American Prospect, Earth Action, Center for Responsive Politics, and the Family Foundation. She is a 1968 graduate of Cedar Crest College and undertook graduate work at George Washington University.

David Moberg is a senior editor at *In These Times* and a fellow of the Nation Institute. Trained as an anthropologist at the University of Chicago, he wrote his doctoral dissertation on class and culture among auto workers. He has written widely about issues of work and the labor movement for a variety of publications, including the *Nation, American Prospect,* Salon.com, *Boston Globe, Working USA, L.A. Weekly, Newsday, Dissent,* and the *New York Times,* and contributed to two recently published volumes, *Which Direction for Organized Labor?* (1999), and *Not Your Father's Union Movement: Inside the AFL-CIO* (1998). He is currently writing a book about labor and the global economy.

Jonathan Oberlander is assistant professor of social medicine at the University of North Carolina–Chapel Hill, where he teaches health policy in the School of Medicine and the Department of Political Science. He was previously a Robert Wood Johnson fellow at the University of California–Berkeley and as a research fellow at the Brookings Institution. Oberlander has written extensively on Medicare policy,

American health politics, and health care reform. He is currently working on a book project for the Century Foundation that critiques market-based Medicare reform proposals.

Rafe Pomerance is the chairman of Sky Trust, an organization committed to establishing a domestic emissions trading program to control carbon emissions in the United States. From 1993 to 1999, Pomerance was deputy assistant secretary for environment and development at the Department of State, where he was involved in the development of U.S. positions and strategy on a range of international environmental issues including climate change, ozone depletion, biodiversity, and forests. Prior to joining the Department of State, Pomerance spent two decades working for environmental nonprofits, including the World Resources Institute (where he was senior associate) and Friends of the Earth (president). Pomerance has served as chairman of the board at the League of Conservation Voters and American Rivers and coordinator of the National Clean Air Coalition.

Carl Pope is executive director of the Sierra Club, America's oldest and largest grassroots environmental advocacy organization. He has worked with the environmental community for thirty years as a lobbyist, community organizer, writer, and analyst, and since 1992 has served as executive director of the Sierra Club. He coauthored California's Prop 65, the Safe Drinking Water and Toxic Enforcement Act. He has written widely for magazines in the environmental field and is the author of *Sahib: An American Misadventure in India* and coauthor of *Hazardous Waste in America*.

Joel Rogers is the John D. MacArthur Professor of Law, Political Science, and Sociology at the University of Wisconsin–Madison. He is also founder, director, and project incubator at the Center on Wisconsin Strategy (COWS)—a research and policy institute dedicated to promoting high-road economic development. Rogers has written widely on American politics and public policy, on political theory, and on U.S. and comparative industrial relations. His most recent books are *America's Forgotten Majority: Why the White Working Class Still Matters* (Basic Books, 2000), *What Workers Want* (1999), and *Metro Futures: Economic Solutions for the Cities and Their Suburbs* (1999). A contributing editor to the *Nation* and *Boston Review* and a longtime social and political activist, Rogers was identified by *Newsweek* as one of the 100 Americans most likely to affect U.S. politics and culture in the twenty-first century.

Richard Rothstein is research associate at the Washington, D.C.–based Economic Policy Institute, adjunct professor of public policy at Occidental College in Los Angeles, and senior correspondent for the *American Prospect* magazine. He also writes a biweekly column on education for the *New York Times*. Rothstein's recent publications include *Can Public Schools Learn from Private Schools?* (coauthored with Martin Carnoy and Luis Benveniste; 1999), *The Way We Were? Myths and Realities of America's Student Achievement* (1998) and *Where's the Money Going? Changes in the Level and Composition of Education Spending* (1995 and 1997). He is also coauthor, with James W. Guthrie, of "Enabling Adequacy to Achieve Reality," in the 1999 *National Academy of Sciences* volume titled "Equity and Adequacy in Education Finance."

Micah L. Sifry is Public Campaign's senior analyst. He has authored articles on campaign finance reform for the *Washington Post*, the *American Prospect*, the *Nation*, *Tikkun* magazine, Salon.com, and numerous regional newspapers. He is also an independent project fellow of the Open Society Institute, under whose auspices he is completing a book on the prospects of America's leading third parties. He is a graduate of Princeton University and has a master's degree from New York University.

Theda Skocpol is Victor S. Thomas Professor of Government and Sociology, and director of the Center for American Political Studies at Harvard University. Her recent books include *Civic Engagement in American Democracy* (coedited with Morris P. Fiorina; 1999); *The New Majority: Toward a Popular Progressive Politics* (coedited with Stanley B. Greenberg; 1998); *Boomerang: Health Reform and the Turn Against Government* (1997); and *Protecting Soldiers and Mothers: the Political Origins of Social Policy in the United States* (1992), which won five major scholarly awards. Her contribution to this book is adapted from her most recent book, *The Missing Middle: Working Families and the Future of American Social Policy* (2000).

William E. Spriggs is director of research and public policy at the National Urban League. He has served as senior adviser to the associate deputy administrator for government contracting and business development, at the Small Business Administration (SBA). He was an economist and special adviser in the office of the undersecretary for economic affairs at the U.S. Department of Commerce. He has also been a senior economist for the Democratic staff of the Joint Economic Committee of the U.S. Congress, and led the staff of the National Commission for Employment Policy during the Clinton administration. Currently, he is president of the National Economics Association, serves on *Black Enterprise* magazine's board of economists, and is a member of the National Academy of Social Insurance.

Robert Wages is executive vice president of the Paper, Allied-Industrial, Chemical and Energy Workers Union (PACE). PACE is a product of the 1999 merger of the United Paperworkers International Union (UPIU) and the Oil, Chemical and Atomic Workers International Union (OCAW) and represents more than 300,000 workers engaged in a wide variety of industrial activities. Wages served as president of OCAW from 1991 to 1999 and has been a longtime advocate of expanding the dialogue between trade unionists and the environmental community. Wages, who received his law degree from the University of Missouri–Kansas City, has held leadership positions within the OCAW since 1983 and is responsible for bargaining policy in the oil, chemical, and atomic sectors of the union as well as for international affairs and organizing.

Index